THE THREAD
OF IDENTITY

EXPLORED THROUGH THE
600 YEAR STORY OF THE RAM FAMILY

THE THREAD OF IDENTITY

EXPLORED THROUGH THE
600 YEAR STORY OF THE RAM FAMILY

RONALD RAM

AMBERLEY

'Whose child are you?' he said. Whose child is he?
The present is linked with the past, the future with both.
There's no getting away from that.'

John Galsworthy, *To Let.*

For my grandchildren

Ellie, Olive and Henry.

First published 2010

Amberley Publishing Plc
Cirencester Road, Chalford,
Stroud, Gloucestershire, GL6 8PE

www.amberley-books.com

ISBN 978 1 84868 264 1

British Library Cataloguing in Publication Data.
A catalogue record for this book is available from the British Library.

Typesetting and Origination by FONTHILLDESIGN.
Printed in Great Britain.

CONTENTS

PREFACE

People are bothered today about the lack of quality in community life. But whilst there is much talk of 'building community' in what has become a highly centralised society, achieving it in practice is far more difficult. How can we find a greater sense of identity and meaning in individual and community life, along with a more highly developed awareness of what 'belonging' means?

My own ideas have evolved over time, influenced significantly by three interlocking strands of experience. The first is my family story which provides an enormous body of information around which to reflect, particularly the part of it centred on the village of Great Waltham in Essex. I believe the story of my family can help us resolve the community related issues we face today. There is then my own experience of working with small groups over the last fifteen years. The third strand is provided by the Group Analytic Society with its work on small group therapy and emphasis on the role of large groups. I see this book as a way of sharing my personal concern and knowledge about community.

The concept of 'Thread' used in the book is important for it is a way of tying all the strands of experience together. It conveys three important insights about identity; as a 'telephone cable' which contains many different wires, or aspects, bound together; as a 'rope' by which people are enabled to hold on to and make sense of life; and thirdly as the way in which identity is passed from generation to generation in the form of cultural heritage. *The Thread* is made up of all the influences which affect people's attitudes and behaviour and establishes their belonging – some are ethical in nature but most are concerned with practical living from day to day.

My own thinking, set out through the book, is that what I call 'mutuality' is the bedrock of strong community. But we have to be clear what this means. The story at the heart of the book tells us we cannot create the sort of community we long for by Act of Parliament. It tells us real community has to be grounded in mutual respect, where people give and take around issues of deep concern to all involved. We cannot go back into the past, but we can look back to situations where a sense of community existed, like the Essex villages and towns where my family lived for six hundred years, and try to build into our present life the strengths they had.

The story of the Ram family and issues about identity are interwoven in five parts. Part 1 discusses the problems we have today about values and meaning together with what might be done about them, including how the Ram family story and other knowledge available about ordinary people can help. Part 2 explores in more depth the concepts of identity, taking account of self meaning, the impact of the local community and family, biological inheritance and the role of values. Part 3 is the Ram story, split into four sections: where the family lived and its structure; about the farming members of the family from 1327 onwards; then about those who became professionals and entrepreneurs; and finally how more prosperous and poorer family members alike lived a life without land from 1800 to 1900, which is as far as the story is recounted. Part 4 uses the Ram story to build up a picture of identity. Finally, in part 5 what has gone before is related to the modern world of Britain in practical terms.

Ronald Ram
Wrestlingworth,
November 2009

NOTE ABOUT GENEALOGICAL CHARTS

The basic start point for creating a family tree for the Ram family is 1566, the year when registration of baptisms, marriages and deaths began at Great Waltham in Essex where the family was then based. However it is possible to get a little further back because a number of them made wills earlier in that century, the first of which is dated 1530. Family information for the period between 1327 and the middle of the sixteenth century cannot be connected up so is shown as a list in Appendix 1.

Between the fourteenth century and 1900 around 700 individuals belonged to the family, a number which is impossible to include in a chart that could go in this book. So, the family tree has been split into nineteen segments that fit into the text at appropriate points. These still do not offer a complete picture of the family because for presentation purposes some individuals, mentioned and not mentioned in the book, have had to be left out. However, Appendix 1 contains a detailed family descent in tabular form.

In the middle of the sixteenth century there appear to have been three nuclear Ram families, living in or close to Great Waltham. Although it is not possible to document the precise relationships of the heads of the three families they must have been siblings, nephews, or cousins. These three families establish the original branches, two of which continue over the whole period of the book, whilst one dies out.

Each branch – those parts of the family which have a discreet identity – has been given a letter code. Within these the sequential position of each chart is indicated in its title box by a page reference to those which precede and follow it. If it is the last chart in a series this is shown by the word 'Finish'. This helps to preserve a sense of overall connectedness and makes it possible to put together in the mind's eye what the whole chart would look like. The branch codings and the number of charts there are in each is as follows.
Branch A (2 charts) starting with Robert Ram (d.1576).
Branch B (6 charts) starting with Thomas Ram (d. 1556).
Branch C (11 charts) starting with John Ram (d. 1568).

On several occasion individuals with the same forename form chains so that it is difficult to tell one person from another. When this happens they are numbered sequentially in both the text and the charts.

LIST OF FIGURES, CHARTS, AND TABLES

Tables

ACKNOWLEDGEMENTS AND CREDITS

This book has taken nearly ten years to research and write. During that time many people have contributed, and thanks are due to them all. But some groups and individuals have made special inputs, sometimes probably in unrealised ways.

For nearly ten years I have been a regular member of the group of local history writers run by Dr Jane Pearson of Essex University, who is wonderfully able to keep our enthusiasms going. Everyone is researching and writing about local history. We meet bi-monthly and share with each other issues being worked on. Another group that has provided considerable stimulus for thinking through issues about individual and group identity is the Institute of Group Analysis where I completed the Advanced General Course in group work between 2000 and 2001. I then participated in one of its 'large groups' for another two or three years. The Seminar and Group leader, Radha Bhat was particularly influential. Over the last fifteen years I have been in contact with many small local groups through my work with the Churches Commission on Mission and then the Association of Building Bridges Churches. Much has been learned about the functioning of such groups by observing how they work, through the discussions I have had with them, and working colleagues. In particular the Revd. Donald Elliott during the years 1995-2000, then Secretary of the Churches Commission on Mission, and the committee of the Association of Building Bridges Churches since 2000, have helped to pull many puzzling threads together.

Much help and encouragement has been received from individuals. Four in particular I would like to mention are the people who have read the whole text through and given me feedback about it. Jeanne Hinton contributed at an early stage. Then I had some help from The Literary Consultancy, in the persons of Rebecca Swift and one of its readers, Alan Wilkinson. My wife, Gillian, has read and commented on much of the text, often as I have been preparing it. The last person to read through the text was Alan Crosby, the editor of *The Local Historian*, the Journal of the British Association of Local History. Together they have helped me to put the book into its present shape, although of course this is entirely my responsibility. Alan Crosby has also helped over several years through the discussions I had with him around turning chapter XIII into an article for publication in *The Local Historian*.

In addition I want to thank Ron Pickford for the considerable help he has given me in preparing the figures.

The other sources of help have of course been record offices, libraries and museums, where staff have been longsuffering and unfailingly helpful, all of which are mentioned in the select bibliography. However the Essex Record Office at Chelmsford and its Colchester branch before it was closed, deserve special mention. I have worked with the staff there over nearly the whole period taken to research and write the book.

It is of course necessary to accept responsibility for errors, which I have tried to keep to a minimum, but I am sure there will be some because of the integrated nature of the text and the many individuals referred to.

Credits.
Some of the figures contain items from public collections. In each case, listed below, this is done by courtesy of the organisation concerned. Detailed references are included in the end notes.

From the British Library Board for figure 4, Essex manorial rental, 1328, and figure 11, Photograph of Stephen Adye Ram.

From the Essex Record Office for figure 5, Title page of the survey of Great Waltham, 1563, figure 6, the Great Waltham survey committee, 1805, and figure 9, plan of the Colchester house of John Ram 5C.

From The College of Arms for figure 7, Francis Ram's coat of arms.

From Cambridge University Press for figure 8, The Royal Manor and Liberty of Havering atte Bower.

MONEY CONVERSIONS

In any book of this type the issue of comparing financial values over time arises. When Robert Ram died in 1576 he gave most of his daughters and their children 5/- each. When his son Richard died in 1611 he left £10 'to the poor people of Much Waltham'. In 1788 Nicholas Ram left his daughter Jane £1600. Rents were paid and pieces of property bought and sold. All these events happen in the book over a very long timescale. What can be done to convey how such values change over time?

There is a web site founded by Professor L H Officer of the University of Illinois at Chicago and Professor S H Williamson of the University of Miami called Measuringworth.com which you can use to get quite sophisticated comparisons of worth. But judging how monetary values of all sorts have changed over time is very complex, in which shifts of social attitudes play a subtle part.

I have chosen to take two very simple comparators which provide a rough but fairly easily understood yardstick. One is the wages paid to farm labourers between 1600 to 1620. In *The Agrarian History of England and Wales*, vol. iv, chapter ix, agricultural prices, farm profits and rents, p. 653, Peter Bowden sets out what farm labourers earned at that time – an annual maximum of £10 and 8/- based on 10d a day. Allowing for some non working time it seems unlikely that agricultural earnings were much above £9 a year. The other comparator is what equivalent people earned around 1807, very roughly around £26 a year. This has been obtained from W A Armstrong, *Wages and Incomes*, chapter 7 in G E Mingay, *The Agrarian History of England and Wales*, vol. 6, 1989, p. 704.

The way wages of farm labourers were compiled could be quite complicated. Moreover wage levels varied in different areas of the country. But the overall differences were within very narrow margins, so the sums quoted above show roughly what a farm labourer lived on for a year and can be used for wider comparison making.

PART 1

THEMES AND INSPIRATIONS

SECTION 1   THEMES

I
Main Themes

The problems we have about identity today

One of the characteristics of life today is the enormous emphasis on change, which leads us to underestimate the importance of continuities in life. We have almost reached the point where we think things are not normal unless they are changing. Government appears to think it is not effective unless it is continually introducing new legislation. The focus on change is reinforced by newspapers, television, and radio, known collectively as the 'media' which infiltrates daily life almost non-stop. The media exaggerates the extent of change and over emphasises its own role. What it forgets is that underneath all this frenetic superficial activity ordinary people have their own concerns, rhythms, and code of values which have a separate existence. One of the reasons for the widespread cynicism that exists about institutional life is the contrast between the earthy values of ordinary life and the hollowness of much of the emphasis on change. History teaches that the deepest things in life do not change significantly and then only slowly, and this is borne out in the history of the Ram family.

Whatever our personal outlook on life, it is important to have some concept of meaning or our lives are empty. Today we are heavily influenced by individualistic values which have grown increasingly pervasive since the Enlightenment. These generate a self centred focus to our vision of identity and push socially inclusive broad based values to the margins. The overall result is a decline in mutual respect. Although there is an increasing understanding of this, accompanied by a drift to appreciating the importance of inclusive values it is very gradual, hesitant, and confused. In recent years inclusivity has, in certain respects, become fashionable, resulting in pressure for everything to be done in 'transparent' ways and individual rights to be respected at all costs, but individualism still reigns.

A recent book by Richard Sennett called *'Respect'* exposes the brittleness of our contemporary society and asks some important philosophical and social questions.[1] His book is ostensibly about how the modern state provides those in need with welfare services. But it is really a critique of how difficult we find it to achieve any sense of mutuality today. This is a big problem which we do not fully appreciate, and our modern society may be making things worse. The story of the Ram family shows strongly that there is probably less mutuality today than there was in Great Waltham, home of the Ram family for hundreds of years, in times gone by. The same would be true for places like it. The bureaucratic aspects of the indirect and impersonal delivery of all kinds of benefits which typifies current practice spawns lack of respect among the more marginal people. Even when effort is made to make services responsive to claimants government initiatives are framed entirely within the bureaucratic system, and so have all of its characteristics. They are invariably large scale and devoid of the personal touch.[2]

Sennett sees mutual respect as being very important in creating a more open world but is unclear how it can be done. He asks how can self worth be nurtured in what is an unequal world? He is clear that formal equality can never be a substitute for real mutual respect, which he believes can only flourish in a society where there is both personalised dependence and interdependence among the population at large. But in the kind of world Sennett describes as typical of today it is difficult to see how mutuality can thrive, and this is a real conundrum for our society. At the end of the book he writes, 'In society, and particularly in the welfare state, the nub of the problem we face is how the strong can practice respect toward those destined to remain weak'.[3] Of course the issues he discusses do not relate just to the ways our society deals with the weak and people who claim welfare benefits. In reality the same problems run right through our society. Sennett's book could have been called *Identity* and he raises issues very like those associated with this book.

What has gone wrong?
Whilst there is disquiet about the state of our society there is little clarity concerning underlying causes. There is certainly a vague feeling that community is breaking down under various pressures, which leads to indiscriminate focusing on dealing with headline grabbing issues and problem areas. People worry about the levels of crime, the high incidence of marriage breakdown, the increasing number of people who are living alone, and the decline of family life. In recent years a lot of these feelings, particularly among politicians and in the media have come to be discussed under the heading of 'respect' – or the lack of it. Why is there a lack of respect and what is the cause of the 'brittleness' we see around us?

The crux of Richard Sennett's argument is that real respect is grounded in mutuality, which can only flourish in genuinely sharing contexts. Our society is in fact far from being mutual. This lack is one of the major causes of our problems. We mostly relate to identity in terms of top down stereotypes, which govern much of the thinking of politicians, managers, administrators, political thinkers, and historians. Many intellectual expressions of identity are much more simplistic than we realise and some of our accepted wisdom about identity is a distortion of the truth. It is, moreover, possible that these stereotypes are more deeply embedded now than in the past, due to the decline in the role and importance of free standing local communities.

In this hierarchical model little account is taken of how ordinary people see identity and how individual identity is formed and played out in the context of family, peer group, and local community. Individual people are thought of almost exclusively in passive terms. Their view of identity is pressed to the margins. There is also a deep dichotomy in society which exacerbates lack of understanding about true mutuality. Whilst nearly all our social contexts are governed by hierarchical attitudes that are far from mutual, we are also highly conscious of individual rights. We have no way of bringing these two perspectives together, and the resulting tension creates much distrust, particularly of institutions of all kinds.

Without doubt the increasing lack of agreed holistic values to live by is a major source of our difficulties. There are all sorts of tension conflicts here. The most important may well be that between the pressure for individual freedom and the desire for stronger community. The simple truth is that the two things, in their extremes, are incompatible. Strengthening community will necessitate limiting individual freedom and restraining the blame culture. It will also involve rediscovering the importance of social values that emphasise responsibility for others, which is easier said than done. Such a transformation cannot be achieved simply by legislation and dictat. A moral sea change has to happen right across society in which there is a shift in accepted values by common consent. Although these kinds of developments have occurred in the past, and the Evangelical Revival of the nineteenth century is perhaps the most recent example, there is little sign of anything like that happening now.

What can we do?
The main plea of this book is that we think in a much more holistic way about identity. The book will show through the story of the Ram family and its contexts how much more complex identity is than the simplistic stereotypes we think in. It will also show that there was almost certainly more mutuality in self contained local communities than there is today. We need to break away from the top down mindset and apply a broader understanding of identity in the way we run things. However, in our anxiety about our current problems we need to be conscious of the danger of making mountains out of molehills. Are the tensions about identity any worse today than they have always been?

They must always have existed between individuals, groups and the wider society and have had to be managed throughout human history.

Even so serious issues clearly require attention. One of the questions for which answers are required is what sort of communal situations help people to share. If our large scale centralised bureaucracy has an overweening tendency to weaken our ability to do this how can we make things better? A more basic issue concerns the extent that our sense of real community might have been materially diminished because everything has become so big and depersonalised. If this is the case mutuality can only be restored if the kind of centralised society we now have is changed. And it is at this point that we can usefully look at what society was like in the village community of Great Waltham in medieval and early modern times. Mutuality has to grow out of the basic fabric of society, and cannot be created by government legislation. So we may well have to take more seriously than we do the part values contribute as Richard Sennett perceives. He believes moral values have an important part to play because they anchor people in self respect and provide the means of operating a successful system of mutual exchange.[4] A coherent body of values is the key that enables us to both belong to, and be capable of being independent from, the communities to which we belong.

One thing is certain – we cannot put the clock back. We cannot return in a wistful romantic way to a past society. My purpose here is not to suggest this. But if we want to do something creative about our current difficulties we have to recognise there needs to be some change in the way we organise our society. It has to be a way which allows the individual and small group some room and real ownership of our society, and this is where we can learn from the society of the past.

II
Linked sub themes

Telling the Ram story

As well as being a tool for exploring identity the history of the Ram family is significant in its own right. This is so for several reasons. Its story is very long for a non elite family – long enough to trace how accommodation has been made with major cultural and economic changes over many hundreds of years. In part this involved adjusting to given developments, but at certain, and important, points it required seizing opportunities and creating initiatives. Such turning points provide examples of how change occurred generally, not just in the Ram family. Because the story of the Ram family as told is linked to the contexts in which it lived, worked, and socialised, much is revealed in it about the general society of which it was a part. Because the family has always been mainly a middling one its story can contribute to better understanding about this social group, which is complex and important and still relatively poorly understood. The middling sort is short on documentation, especially over as long a time span that the Ram story provides because, by and large, people belonging to it do not leave written accounts of themselves.

The Ram story can help many people to know more about their own families. Although the direct line of descent is not traceable very far back in a lot of families, often because the male line breaks down, there is nonetheless a line of descent of some kind for everyone. It continues back through children, siblings and cousins into the dim past. Might many untraceable family stories be rather like that of the Rams, and might writing about the Rams provide help, with imagination, to illuminate them?

We can learn also from this long family story salutatory lessons about the nature of humanity. In it people are allowed first and foremost to speak for themselves through what I have found out about them and their contexts. Only then are theoretical constructs taken into account. This approach allows the emergence of a refreshing perspective on the nature of human reality. As I have come gradually to know the Ram characters across the years and have woven them as individuals into a tapestry narrative two striking impressions have developed. One is that individual people have the same basic characteristics now as they had in early modern times, and presumably if knowledge allowed, in even earlier periods. John Ram (d. 1588), farmer in Great Waltham, is just as knowable as my great grandfather, Charles Harry Ram (b. 1843), gardener of London. Secondly life, as lived by the majority of people, changes only slowly across the generations and probably almost imperceptibly. There are only three points throughout the entire family history when significant change happened in one or two generations. These conclusions may appear obvious and of little consequence, yet they are often overlooked and are in fact deeply informative about the way we live.

Exploring and writing about the lives of ordinary people

The importance of ordinary people was more or less unrecognised in the past, although in the last fifty years or so there have been significant changes in approach among historians. Before then historical research was focused on events of national importance and the socially elite. Perhaps the first influential attempt to write social history as we now understand it was by G M Trevelyan in 1944.[5] Yet without overall awareness of people's existence and contribution to society, including the non-elite in their local contexts, there can be no real realisation of what identity means. Writing about ordinary people can help to show that the traditional hierarchical way of looking at society and identity is not the only way, which is in isolation an incomplete perspective.

Whilst the development of historical writing in the last fifty years has enriched what is known about the lives of ordinary people considerably, the great growth of family genealogy in recent years has potential to expand historical knowledge in ways previously unimagined. In a way this book is an example of what is possible and should be an encouragement to many people interested in their family histories. Moreover it shows them how they might document what they find out, and set it in an enriching wider context.

This book is perhaps original in writing about ordinary people in a way which draws on several disciplines outside historical studies. One of them, sociology, is now used by historians, but others like psychology, heredity and genetics are usually not. The latter two are very new. Interleaving them all opens up new perspectives on the study of ordinary people.

SECTION 2
INSPIRATIONS BEHIND THE BOOK

III
My interest in identity

I have always been concerned about people, being fascinated by what makes them 'tick'. Around 700 people are contained in the Ram family record between John le Ram (mid 14C) of Great Waltham and those alive now, nearly seven hundred years later. The factual story of these people forms a main part of this book. But having a genealogical chart of all of them in front of you prompts broader questions about the nature of humanity itself. If I could meet John le Ram who contributed to the lay subsidy of 1327, what would we have to say to each other? Would people and the nature of the world have changed so much in the time that separates us that communication would be impossible? If we could understand each other what is it in the human psyche that makes this possible? In the seven hundred years since 1327 have some things changed whilst others have stayed the same? Questions like these lead me directly to ponder the meaning and formation of broader identity.

I suppose this basic interest has led me to choose academic studies that are people oriented. I started with history and have always retained a love of that subject, then turned to theology and the applied disciplines of sociology, and more latterly psychology and psychiatry. The spur to take up the applied disciplines has always come via practical involvements. Over the last fifteen years I have worked a great deal with enabling small groups, which led me to enquire more generally about the dynamics involved in the functioning of such groups. I eventually found answers to my queries through the Group Analytic Society and the writings of S H Foulkes, who was initially a Freudian psychiatrist and then developed the concept of group therapy in England after the Second World War.[6]

I also believe process, how things happen, is important in understanding how community works, something which leads me to be interested in identity because it is essentially a process concerned with social formation. What are the building blocks of identity and how are they knit together? I believe understanding and applying process in human affairs is much neglected, with the result that the development of ideas about social practice and policy making are more shallowly rooted than they need be.

The last source of my concern about identity is a desire to explore the origin and role of values. This has sprung from my Christian convictions, although clearly the role of values is broader than religious belief.

What is the value of raising the questions and issues posed here? I believe it is important that they are discussed today because they can contribute to the better understanding of our contemporary world. Attitudes about identity are in flux and ideas are often confused and disconnected. Exploring identity through the Ram story could be a way of prompting a more holistic understanding about identity, but how? *The New Oxford Dictionary of English* defines identity in the following ways; 'The fact of being what a person or thing is' and 'The characteristics determining who or what a person or thing is'.[7] These definitions are expressed in individual and impersonal terms, but the Ram story is about a social entity not just a body of individuals. It inevitably leads to a more broad based understanding of identity. The dictionary definitions say nothing about the 'characteristics' that make up identity, which the analytic framework of *The Thread* sets out to explore and establish.

IV

Finding out about the Ram family

A Scrap of Paper

Until 2000 I knew no more about my family story than is set out on the scrap of paper shown in Figure 1. Then, almost on the spur of the moment, having some spare time in the autumn of that year, I decided to look more closely into what more could be found out. It is rather daunting to start any project from virtually nothing, partly because it is very unclear how to make progress, or even whether any progress is possible. How one thing led to another, and how in just over a year a body of information going back to the early 1300s was put together, which included a detailed family tree from the time parish registers started, is told here.

The start point was the scrappy piece of paper which had lain semi-forgotten in a folder with other family papers for over twenty years. The William Henry referred to in it, also called Charles in some other information, was later found to be Charles Harry. My father thought this person was a butcher or farmer from Ipswich who had a large number of children, several brothers, one of whom was called Benjamin, and had been twice married. Much of this intelligence was later found to be quite accurate.[8] My father also passed on some other background information that was later authenticated. He said there had been contact with some richer relatives in Ipswich that did not work out very well, and Maldon, in Essex, was somewhere his father had been taken as a boy on several occasions to visit some aunts. Altogether there were only three leads. One was the outline family structure on the piece of paper, the second was two place names and some associations with them, and the third was about family occupations. This was not much to go on.

The most sensible way to start seemed to be to search for records in the national register of births and deaths which begins in 1837, so the Family Records Centre, now closed, was visited and searches made for Rams born soon after that date who had Charles and Henry as Christian names.[9] It did not take long to find a birth registration that looked right, and this turned out to be my great grandfather, Charles Harry, who was born in 1843 at

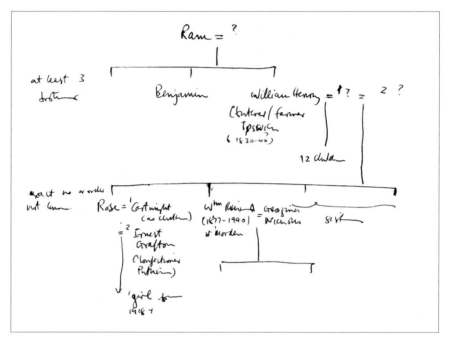

Figure 1. A scrap of paper.

Steeple in the registration district of Maldon, Essex.[10] His father is listed as Benjamin, an agriculturalist, which showed the farming link had some substance. The connection between me and Charles Harry is confirmed by the baptismal record of a son named William Richard (1877-1940) who was my grandfather.[11] So the link with Maldon emerged straight away! An examination was then made of the Steeple registers in the Essex Record Office at Chelmsford and the baptismal registrations of Charles Harry and several of his brothers and sisters were found.[12] But then the search got stuck. Looking further back into the Steeple registers produced a blank. What else could be done? This could easily have been the end of the matter.

But the situation was redeemed by a chance conversation one day at the Essex Record Office with another family researcher. The lady concerned was, amazingly to me, trying to identify all her relatives, which required extremely tenacious searching. She said that sometimes people had their children baptised in neighbouring parishes to the one where they lived, and it might be worthwhile widening the search. Her advice led to looking at the registers of Purleigh, a village nearby Steeple. This was a completely random choice, but the link that was missing turned up quite quickly. Charles Harry's father Benjamin (1814-1864), was baptised in Purleigh, the son of John (1768-1835) and Abigail Ram.[13] The relationship of John with Benjamin was confirmed by examining the will of John Ram.[14] This chance development was extremely exciting. Although persistent searching would probably have worked in the end the rapidity with which it happened seemed to be remarkable. The odds involved are perhaps not as exceptional as you might think. A man called D S Boutflower discovered a long association of his family with Apperley in the Lake District by an even greater chance happening. He was reading through some papers at a place many miles from Apperley, and which had nothing to do with his family, when he came across a reference that directed him to Apperley as the place where his family came from.[15]

Another chance happening around this time opened up the connection with Ipswich. My efforts to find the best software for plotting the family tree led me to visit a helpful supplier who operated from a farm near Sudbury in Suffolk. In discussion with her it turned out she had a strong interest in Suffolk local history. She had co-ordinated the making of an index of the Suffolk entries in the 1851 census and had copies available, so we looked up Ram and there were five entries in Ipswich, clearly a married couple with three children.[16] There was James (1793-1870) aged 58, Elizabeth (1801-abt. 1881) aged 50, Mary (1837-1864) aged 14, Willett (1839-1921) aged 12, and Edward (b. 1843) aged 8. The children had all been born in Ipswich but the father originated from a place called Berechurch and his wife from Woolwich. Who were these people and were they relations? The software supplier then looked at some burial records she had for Ipswich and this time four entries were turned up which were especially intriguing. One of them was a Benjamin Ram who died at Ipswich in 1864 and another was Mary Ann Ram (1816-1859) who also died in Ipswich.[17] On checking Charles Harry's birth certificate it became clear that his mother was called Mary Ann, so there was clearly a direct link with Ipswich through my great great grandfather.

It was the uncovering of this information about members of the family in Ipswich that finally hooked me into going on with the search. There was a strong urge to find out more, and gradually all the questions that arose from the visit to the Sudbury farm were answered. How this happened is told later.

The core of what was found out
There must be, and have been, many family stories like that of the Rams that have gone undocumented. In a recent book Chris Pomery writes, 'Only a very few complete surname genealogies have so far been reconstructed in a way that reveals the full complexity of the economic development and social fortune of all their members'.[18] Now this has not been done literally for all of the family, but it has been for the vast majority of the principal male members, and a good picture has been obtained of the economic and social development of the family since the early fourteenth century.

The first documented reference to the family is in 1327 at Great Waltham, a village near Chelmsford, the county town of Essex.[19] In medieval times its senior members were mostly farmers of moderate status. Many of them called themselves yeomen in the sixteenth and seventeenth centuries, but they were not as a whole among the largest landholders. And yet the majority of male members in practically every generation had some land or property.

A continuous line of farmers extended in and around Great Waltham from at least 1327 until the 1880s. Some of them became large tenant farmers in the period 1750 to 1850. Then this branch met difficulties, probably economic in nature. Most of its members moved to London and remained there in a diminished economic state until the book ends in 1900, at which point it had thirty five members, including wives. I am a member of this branch of the family.

In the sixteenth century further branches were founded by two brothers, William and Francis. The younger of them, Francis (abt. 1536-1617), became agent for Sir Anthony Cooke's estates in Essex and elsewhere, Deputy Steward of Havering in Essex, Clerk to the Essex Justices, and a Justice of the Peace. He lived in Hornchurch, Essex. One of his children was a London lawyer and others were farmers and London goldsmiths. This branch died out in the early eighteenth century.

The other brother, William (abt. 1532-1602) was an attorney who became Deputy Town Clerk of Colchester in the last quarter of the sixteenth century. He was also interested in botany and wrote a book on herbal remedies, called *Ram's Little Dodean,* which was published in 1606.[20] He was part of the friendship circle of John Gerard the famous botanist. As time went by William's family developed into a line of Church of England clergy, Colchester merchants, farmers and rentiers. In the eighteenth century some of them were among the most prosperous inhabitants, and they became connected by marriage to important Colchester families.

But in the early nineteenth century this line nearly died out, at which point a handful of survivors moved to London. Some of them became engineers and clerks. But one, James Ram, became a London barrister specialising in conveyancing, and a major writer on the law in the first half of the nineteenth century. His book, *The Science of Legal Judgement* provided the first major rationalisation of case law application and is still in use today, especially in America.[21] This is the James who lived in Ipswich at the time of the 1851 census. Later in the nineteenth century James Ram's family lived in London, Suffolk, Norfolk, Lincolnshire, and Cambridgeshire. Most of his sons were solicitors or Church of England clerics. An elder son married Susan Scott (b. 1844), a niece of Gilbert Scott the famous architect. A younger son joined a solicitor's firm in Halesworth in the early 1870s, which still has the name of, *Cross, Ram, and Co* across its office window. A grandson became Prebendary of York Minister.

The nineteenth century brought an end to any connection with the land and farming for all the family which became absorbed into an urban environment, mainly in London. For some the break happened gradually without loss of status, but for my immediate family it must have been traumatic and painful.

At the end of the book in appendix I there is a detailed family time line to help get an overall understanding of family members and how they related to one another.

Possible wider connections and origins.

The main story of the Ram family as told here is fully documented from original and published sources, and whilst there may be a few gaps there are no fantasies. It is told in Part 3. However, some unproven and speculative connections have come to light during background reading, and whilst they do not add much to the real story they are fun to pursue. There might even be an element of truth in them.

The first one concerns the period before any real records are available, and amounts to no more than circumstantial conjecture. One of the minor accompaniers of William the Conqueror was a man called Roger de Ramis, who was granted lands in Kent and Essex. In *Domesday People* K S B Keates-Rohan says he was a Norman from Rames, Seine-Maritime, near Le Havre, or Saint-Romain-de-Colbasc – near Gommerville, Seine. He was a Domesday Tenant in Chief.[22] It is not known definitely if he was a baron as there is no evidence of a baronial fee being paid.[23] In the Domesday Book he is described as Roger de Raimes and the *Victoria County History* allocates eleven manors to him in Essex which are scattered about in three hundreds. Three of them were in the Hundred of Hinkford: Raines {Rayne], Greys, and Sibel Headingham, although they were not the most wealthy ones. Altogether the eleven manors were worth just under £37 at the time of the Domesday Survey. He was succeeded at an unknown date by a son William, who by 1130 was followed in turn by his sons Roger II and Robert. In the years which followed the Domesday Survey the de Ramis lands passed through many family members and the last Essex reference to them is around 1235.[24]

It is not beyond the realms of possibility that the John le Ram who held land at Great Waltham in 1327 was connected in some way with this family. The Lay subsidy of that year shows three payers in Essex with the name of

Ram, who all lived within ten miles of each other and Rayne, within the little geographical triangle identified in Figure 2.[25] It is also interesting that the largest concentration of people with the name Ram outside East Anglia is in Kent, where Roger de Raimes was allocated other manors.

Another possible connection concerns a much better documented Anglo-Irish family with the same name which first appeared in Berkshire during the sixteenth century. A good part of a book written by two of my family, called *The Ram Family*,[26] contains a history of the Irish Rams even though the authors admit they could find no proof of relationship. My researches have not found a link either, but because the name is so rare there may be one. If there is a connection it must date from a time before the registration of births, marriages and deaths began. The Irish family first appears in known records through Thomas Ram (1564-1634) who was born in Windsor, went to school at Eton, and then to Kings College Cambridge where he was a fellow for a while after graduating. In 1599 he went to Ireland with the Earl of Essex as a chaplain, and settled there. He had rapid preferment within the Church and in 1605 became Bishop of Ferns and Leighlin. He appears to have been a conscientious bishop. He also acquired an estate at Gorey, called Ramsfort, presumably as part of the English Elizabethan settlements in Ireland. This estate remained in the hands of the family until modern times.[27] From the seventeenth century onwards some members of this family came back to live in England, especially in the nineteenth century. The 1881 census shows there were eighteen of them, living mainly in London. Through their Irish connections they married into the Irish nobility, and were always on a higher social plane than the family that is the subject of this book. In the nineteenth century many of the men who lived in England were Church of England clergy.

The third possible link has come to light though a chance reference I made to a detailed study of the blood royal. According to this both the Irish Rams and the Adyes, one of whom married into the Colchester Rams, are very distantly related by marriage to Mary Tudor, daughter of Henry VII. The line of descent, running upwards is shown in the notes.[28] It does not include the English Rams, but the mutual connectedness it reveals between Admiral Montague Stopford (1798-1864) and both the Adye and Irish Ram family is of some interest. One of Admiral Stopford's younger sisters, Lady Jane Stopford (1805-1873) married Revd Abel John Ram, of Clonattin, a member of the Irish Ram family, and a daughter, Mary Cordelia Stopford, married General Sir John Millar Adye. He was a cousin by marriage of Elizabeth Jane Adye, who married the younger James Ram of Colchester. Although these links are somewhat tenuous, and the individuals concerned may not have been in close contact, they probably knew, or knew of, each other, since they were all more or less contemporaries. This was particularly true of James Ram's wife Elizabeth Jane Adye and Lady Jane Stopford (b. 1805) and could have stimulated mutual interest. It seems difficult to believe that the two Ram lines were unaware of each other in the nineteenth century. Did sharing such an uncommon name lead to some speculation about inter-relatedness, or even some contact?

An unfinished story

In many ways the 1901 census marks the point that divides history from contemporary life because it is the last point at which information is widely available from published records. My energies have so far gone into looking into the history of the family before that date. Some details about immediate family members for later times are available, but bringing the story right up to date will involve making personal contacts and will not further the purpose of this book significantly. But bringing the story up to date may be completed at some point in the future. Making contact with other family members who are alive today will be helped by having the family history to show them. It is likely that some of the family are still about in London and the home counties, but probably not very many. There are certainly none left in Great Waltham or Colchester. It is possible that my immediate family contains all that remains in the male line. If other family members are still alive how will they respond to personal enquiries about their history over the past two or three generations?

PART 2

UNPACKING IDENTITY

SECTION 1   WHAT IS IDENTITY?

V
Ideas about identity

The complexity of identity
The start point in this book for exploring identity is the Ram family set in its immediate contexts. This results in an emphasis being put on viewing identity from a perspective which looks outwards from that family. It facilitates exploration in some detail of how individuals' identities are formed, within the individual person and in group associations. Moreover, the long period covered by the Ram story makes it possible to view how identity changed over time, and also which aspects do not change much or at all. The exploration of identity that is made will raise questions concerning assumptions we make about our own identity, for example in what ways our society is different from that of the past, which should help us to understand ourselves better.

Identity is difficult to understand. There is no doubt a physiological aspect but other factors like genetic makeup and environmental influences are equally important. In the Introduction of his book on the middling sort H R French reviews a range of definitions about identity that have been used by historians, political thinkers and social scientists.[1] One interesting issue he addresses is the extent that attributes about identity are real or simply perceived structures. Is class for example real to people in the different class categories or is it something observers have created to explain social groups and their relationships in a patterned way? These questions seem to make identity even more difficult to understand. But he goes on to quote one recent model of social group difference that might help to bring some order to this scene. It was originated by Richard Jenkins and called a 'unified model' of identity formation. His model is mentioned here because it has some similarity with the approach used in this book.[2] Jenkins integrates three levels of identity – the societal (formation of collective impersonal identities), the social (direct inter-relations between individuals), and the individual. At each group level there exists identity as experienced and understood within particular groups of people and as they are seen from the outside. In Jenkins' thinking all the levels of the model and the two kinds of perception about them occur concurrently and have no sequential relationship with each other.[3]

The information on which this book is based also lends itself to the identification of three levels of identity, or categories as they will be called. At the broadest level identity encompasses the structural framework of society. This is the most common way in which identity is thought about. But identity can also be categorised in two other ways, not so commonly emphasised: the formation of individuals within groups and communities, and the internally formed personality of each individual. In this framework the structural framework forms a wider background which affects individuals in a very general way, whilst the other two are focused in immediate experience.

There is, however, more to identity than establishing levels or categories and their interaction. For example perceptions of it can change according to the perspective adopted.[4] When this is based in a small group context understandings are not the same as when the viewer is concerned with identifying broad structural patterns in society. This means identity has chameleon like qualities. There are also several sources of identity. Some of its aspects have social origins, through contact with customs and people, some seem to come from individual self made perceptions, whilst others are inherited. To add to the complexity different aspects fulfil different functions. A proportion of them are concerned with dealing with practical day to day matters, like getting on with people, whilst others are more obviously spiritual and value based, like reflecting on the meaning of life. The distinction between the two is important because there does seem to be a real difference between them. The application of day to day aspects of identity change and develop in the relatively short term, under influences like economic change, whilst values which deal with the way we relate to people have a more permanent quality about them. Finally the complexity of identity is shown further by the tendency for tension to exist between the different aspects, for example as between individual rights and interests and corporate dominance and between worldliness and morality.

In the rest of this chapter identity is now explored in relation to four of the most important areas of life – development of self meaning, impact of the community, impact of the family, biological inheritance, and the role of values. Examples are provided from the Ram family.

Development of self meaning
Without awareness of one's own existence there can be no recognition of identity. The question 'who am I?' is at the heart of every individual's personal growth. Developing an identity is partly a matter of adapting to the practicalities of life, and also of searching for deeper meaning.

The relative richness of individual identity is shaped by the degree that people are free to make choices. Life chance itself was and is a hit or miss matter. For example, some people are naturally more healthy than others, some are cleverer than others, and some are wealthier than others. For family identity to be sustained over a long period healthy males have to be produced and the Ram family by its longevity shows it had this capacity. It has also exhibited an ability, at least among many of the principal members of each generation, to retain a middling status. Although relative standing in this social group has varied, with some of the family being wealthy and others quite poor, it seems always to have been their natural home. Is it sheer chance that riches or fame have eluded the family or has it been held to the middling status by something in its genes?

Apart from a fortunate marriage the only way male members of the Ram family could, and can now, boost significantly the degree of choice open to them, is through higher educational achievement. For one reason or another a good education did not come easily to people of the middling sort in the past, and most members of the family were probably not able to read or write until the middle of the eighteenth century. On only five occasions in the history of the family have individual males enhanced their life choice significantly enough to establish new life directions, and on four of them education clearly played an important part. In the sixteenth century William Ram and his brother Francis became lawyers, and another brother Christopher (d. 1572) became a clergyman. William went to University at Cambridge but left before taking a degree. Quite a lot later, in the late eighteenth century, James Ram, a descendent of William went to Cambridge University and became an important member of the legal profession. In the fifth big jump in life choice education was perhaps not so important. This happened when William Ram (aft. 1654-1732), a great great grandson of the lawyer William, became a farmer near Colchester in the second half of the seventeenth century and did much to restore the fortunes of this branch of the family. There is no indication that he was better educated than his peers.

These, and other lesser, jumps in life choice in the family often enhanced the availability of choice for several generations. This happened in all the instances just described with one exception, and that was Christopher. The family of Francis Ram lived as wealthy people for several further generations until they died out. That of William Ram the lawyer retained its professional status for two generations through children and grandchildren becoming Anglican clergymen, before it fell on harder times. Then William, the farmer, was succeeded by two generations of wealthy merchants, farmers and rentiers in Colchester, and James Ram spawned an upper middle class family that lasted at least three generations. In this pattern there is a clear tendency for fortunes to wane gradually in succeeding generations after the appearance of an able person. The same feature happened on a more limited scale in the farming part of the family based on Great Waltham.

The picture just presented shows that availability of choice in the Ram family waxed and waned, and we delude ourselves if we believe choice is always widening. The Ram story also shows it is simplistic to think of the present day world offering lots of choice, whilst that of the past offered very little. Although there is more choice today for more people about things like education, geographical mobility, and greater purchasing power, there are other areas of life where choice has probably diminished. In previous times, as will be seen, there were real choices to be made by the middling sort in running business affairs and small self contained local communities.[5] But a much smaller portion of the community at large is now self employed and self contained local communities have disappeared. The result has been a real diminution in the number of people who participate in making significant life choices outside family and private life. Is this change in the pattern of choice really an improvement?

It has just been hinted that the type of work people have has an important bearing on the formation of self. Many of the earlier male Rams had little real choice but to be farmers if they wanted to retain their traditional status, but there was plenty of choice within that occupation. One of the things we tend to overlook is the extent that people like the Ram farmers, even if they operated on quite a small scale, were entrepreneurs. Even subsistence farmers had to organise their own farming, decide what crops to plant, what animals to keep, what other activities to engage in on the side to earn extra income, deal with related problems, and at the end of the day maintain their families. If they did not do this successfully crisis came to them one way or another. The larger yeoman farmers were running real businesses. So, in Great Waltham in the sixteenth century practically everyone who was not a landless labourer, and it is likely that at least sixty percent of the men in the village had some land, was an entrepreneur in a way unknown today by the majority of people, who mostly work as employees. Whilst some employee jobs are extremely fulfilling many are routine and humdrum. Perhaps people in the past had more challenge in their lives, especially if they lived in the relative stable environment of a self contained farming community. It is arguable that the formation many people experienced in the past, although rougher and less sophisticated that that of today, generated a greater degree of self reliance. In the process they would have become rounded human beings. We sometimes forget how recently modern ways of formation, by formal education and training, have appeared – perhaps 200 years ago for the better off middling sort, and around 150 for the rest.

There is yet another way of looking at self meaning – as something private, either within the individual person or as shared among the group to which an individual directly belongs. The desire for, and expression of, privacy is a very important aspect of identity. Because it boosts the desire for independence and can lead to the questioning of power structures, institutions seek to limit and control it. The Church has supported the practice of baptism and Christian marriage in modern times as a way of controlling faith beliefs and moral practices, and government keeps records of people for a variety of reasons which also supports control of the population. Today in certain respects this desire of power holders to control the lives of individual people seems to be growing, partly because ways of collecting and analysing data are becoming ever easier and more sophisticated. There is also however a strong desire in our contemporary society for individual freedom, and institutions of all kinds are treated with suspicion by many people. Is this tension at least partly responsible for the desire of modern institutions to secure more control? People have perhaps always sought to escape from power holders. And in fact humanity, either as individuals or in groups of some kind, has an identity of its own regardless of institutions. Private identity has a long history, even in traditional and totalitarian society, although some writers see increased desire for privacy as a feature of the modern world and claim it did not exist in medieval times.[6] However long it has existed it is certainly true that as far back as can be documented people in authority have sought to suppress private identity, and that historians have probably underestimated the strength of the desire among individual people to enhance their privacy as a force in shaping historical events.

Impact of the local community

Social identity is formed within the large group, that is the social group in which people are brought up and live their daily lives. It includes both family and peer group. In today's world it can be quite specialised, for example a particular work group, but in earlier times it would have often been the whole village community in which people lived. The large group is influenced by background cultural features dominant at a particular time. How this happens will be discussed later.[7] Overall the influence of the large group is local in character and this helps to shape formation in a particular way. It gives identity a strong local focus. The influence of the family in the large group supports the idea that people find real identity in situations that are local and personal.

The Great Waltham of early modern times, and perhaps today, could be called a large group. Such a group is sufficiently confident to run its affairs in its own way. It does not require an enormous imaginative leap to see local communities like Great Waltham as an important source of individualism, desire for freedom, resistance to oppression and defence of democratic institutions. Is it entirely a chance happening that many of the early settlers in New England came from villages in Essex and Suffolk, which may well have been communities with a social structure much like that of Great Waltham? F M Stenton supports the idea that such village communities existed quite widely, but there is no understanding of exactly how widely. If there was a significant presence of them in England they are almost certainly an important source of what Alan Macfarlane calls the 'English Spirit', which he sees as unique in world culture.[8]

How was, and is, group identity formed? In *The Origins of English Individualism* Alan Macfarlane, mainly in the context of how Britain spawned the first industrial revolution, makes the case that the 'English Spirit' had its source in the considerable degree of individualism and free initiative to be found in England far back into the middle ages. He sees these qualities being a by-product of the free exchange of land and contracts which began very early, long before it happened in other parts of Europe. It was a major reason for the breakdown of a hierarchical peasant society, and the establishment of a modern kind of economy. He reckons that by the thirteenth century over half adult males in England owned no land.[9] He believes this development was in full swing by the sixteenth century, when the Ram family story becomes clearly defined. Although in detailed ways the findings of this study do not always fit with those of Alan Macfarlane there is a high degree of symmetry at the level of broad outline – that there was in England a great degree of independence of spirit. The major difference is that he sees this spirit being expressed through the enterprise of individual people, whilst this study emphasises how it was this together with the formation of local community. A recent book by Dan Jones has affirmed the importance of the community based element. In 1381 England was shaken by a revolt against contemporary misgovernment and extortionate pole taxes, known as the 'Peasants' Revolt'. This started in Essex at Brentwood at a gathering of people from surrounding villages. Within days the unrest spread rapidly in a well organised way to include many Essex, Kent, Suffolk and Norfolk towns and villages including Great Waltham. The people meeting at Brentwood swore oaths to work together to achieve one aim – 'to destroy divers lieges of the lord king and to have no law in England except only those they themselves moved to be ordained'.[10] This meeting and its outcomes showed two things clearly. There was a well organised and lively community framework among the villages of Essex and that these communities were politically aware and assertive, if perhaps rather naive. In the end the revolt collapsed into a shambles but underneath there was a framework of local community which when pressed was capable of considerable self assertion. Almost certainly it was based on the regular experience of local life and its organisation.

Impact of the family
A big issue in assessing the formation of identity is the extent of family influence. The family has a long standing and complex history. The range

of family types that have existed, and still do, is reviewed at some length by Rosemary O'Day.[11] Each type develops as a convenient way of coping with the needs and challenges of everyday life in a particular social and economic environment. This in itself demonstrates the importance of the family in individual formation.

In all the contexts involved – in rural, semi-urban and urban situations – and for the whole period covered by this book, the linear nuclear family is a key feature of life for the Ram family and all the other families they came into contact with. It provided a main part of the framework around which life was lived for the vast majority of people. This type of family structure has applied in England from the earliest times. One of the important findings here is the evidence provided for the way in which the functioning framework of the Ram family clearly remained basically the same, even though it adapted to meet changing social and economic patterns. The story of the Ram family illustrates several ways in which family life contributes to the formation of identity: through inheritance practice, the role of women, through family and inter-family networking, and the passing on of genetic inheritance.

Inheritance practice among middling families helped to generate an understanding of identity in which sharing is important. It is abundantly clear that from time immemorial inheritances among farming members of the Ram family were designed to share heritable resources, particularly land, as equally as possible among sons if there were any. The aim was to give all of them a reasonable start in their own adult lives. Sometimes, if this was not possible or the fairest practice, the land was sold and the proceeds divided among the heirs. Cash and goods were also shared and daughters were included in these disposals as well as sons. The sharing was not done on an entirely equal basis, but in a way which took account of needs. This practice was typical of the middling sort and contrasted with customs followed by the gentry and aristocracy, in which all or most of the land went to the heir, ideally the eldest or most senior living son. Members of the Ram family who went to live in urban settings, or who moved away from farming followed the same practices as their forebears even though the immediacy of the need to pass land to the next generation ceased. Traditional inheritance practice remained as a shell – even when only small pieces of land, houses, or cash were involved. In Tudor and early Stuart times where land was not the major heritable item it was common for heads of families to establish a trust for the benefit of all family members. Francis Ram of Hornchurch, who owned some land but was not dependent upon it for his living, did this. Such practice grew up partly to guard against state sequestration of inheritances given to minors, and to deal with frequent and early and untimely death. It also echoed the custom of the agrarian middling sort of sharing heritable resources equally. It was quite common for family members to be left sums of money on condition that they contribute to the upbringing of younger siblings, or support mothers in old age. This was not simply a way of passing on wealth from one generation to the next but more of a mechanism that helped to sustain family loyalty and identity. It is almost impossible to tell how far loyalty in the younger members of the family stemmed from economic necessity or love of parents, but parents were certainly constrained to do the best they could for their children. It has to be remembered that both donors and receivers in inheritance situations were bound up in a social and economic system in which there was no state provision for people, other than the poor law. In this circumstance old and young in families were very dependent on each other.

Women played an important, if sometimes amorphous, role in formation within family life, partly because until very modern times, they were unable, except as widows or unmarried women, to make legal contracts. This means they are almost entirely absent from the formal records of a family like the Rams. But it is self evident that mothers have always had an important role in the early formation of children, and the influence of women through motherhood was reinforced because of the learning environment it provided, certainly in earlier times. There were normally many more children in a household than now and the nurturing nature of the family continued for much longer as a result. Women also played wider development roles besides those directly connected with motherhood, and glimpses of these are visible from time to time, often in wills or legal agreements which affected them. They began to leave property in their own right, particularly in London urban settings, as early as Tudor and early Stuart times, and there are several examples in the Ram family of how they played an independent role in supporting the bringing up of younger children or grandchildren. They usually did this as widows.[12] There are examples in the Ram family of early deaths among heads of households which thrust upon widows the task of teaching younger sons the skills of farming and of keeping the farm going until they could cope with the responsibility themselves. Although this did not happen frequently examples are to be found throughout the Ram story.[13]

The Ram family has always contributed to the formation and maintenance of identity through its fostering of networks of various kinds, within the family and with other families. This is one of the most interesting things that has come to light from all the information collected about the Ram family. These networks certainly occurred from early modern times onwards.[14] Similar circles clearly existed among more elite families whose history is documented, and examination of the pictures that hang in stately homes often reveals their existence. A powerful example is the extended family picture of the Walpole family in North Norfolk.[15] But many Quaker and other middling families exhibit the same features in the eighteenth and nineteenth centuries, so it was definitely not particular to the Ram family.[16] Indeed the way the Ram family was linked so widely with others suggests such practice was widespread among the middling sort.

As time went by the immediacy of the family frameworks among the Ram family gradually weakened as it dispersed geographically, between Central Essex, Colchester, Suffolk, Cambridgeshire and London. But the family did not break up as a result of such movements.[17] How did family life survive and how was its role in formation changed? There was quite a lot of visiting backwards and forwards, between those who remained at root locations and people who moved elsewhere. Many of the children of Francis Ram who moved to London in late Elizabethan times visited Hornchurch and some of them were buried there, especially their young children who went back home when sick. Hornchurch was probably a place of respite from the illness and sickness so prevalent in London, especially at times of epidemic. The Purleigh Rams in the nineteenth century kept in visiting contact with younger members of the family who moved to London. Siblings and aunts visited nephews and nieces and brothers and sisters. Sometimes these types of contact were extended to include cousins. No doubt the part played in formation by the extended and dispersed family was diluted, with each immediate linear nuclear family having to exist on its own resources in a way that had not been the case in earlier times, but contact and support among family members clearly continued and survived.

The function of networks in developing identity, within the family and with others, are very complex. They were and are particular forms of the large group. Most of them probably originated around economic and marriage interests. The seeking and giving of patronage associated with early modern times involved pursuing job and marriage possibilities in ways we find difficult to understand today. The formal systems that now surround job applications and appointments simply did not exist until relatively recently, and since people as a whole lived more locally than we do now, the development of close inter-family networks was very natural and sensible. Economic partnerships forged in one generation could be extended into succeeding ones and grow to include marriage alliances as well. This clearly happened in the networks of Francis Ram and his immediate family around Havering and London, the connections of Robert Ram (d. 1576) in sixteenth century Great Waltham and neighbouring villages, as well as on an elaborate scale in eighteenth century Colchester. Such alliances brought mutual benefit in good times and support in dealing with difficulties, but it would be a mistake to view them as just being about jobs and marriage. In the days before any social security services the family and extended networks with other families provided means of defence against early and untimely deaths and support in old age, particularly for widows. In a number of them there were signs they included genuine friendship and common cultural interests.

The part values and heredity play in the formation of identity requires some mention in the immediate context of the family, even though they are dealt with more specifically further on. It cannot be disputed that the family makes a unique contribution in genetic terms, for biological inheritance occurs through the family. And it now seems certain that this influences a wider range of characteristics, including the values, or code of behaviour by which people live, than was once thought. A more difficult issue is the influence of the family in social enculturation, and there is considerable debate about this. It will shortly be seen how a famous study of social influence, the Minnesota Twins study, limits family influence in favour of that of peers and the wider community. Other views suggest there was and perhaps is little reality in family life beyond the immediate organic group.[18] But on the other hand Rosemary O'Day gives more place to kinship influences.

Where does the truth lie? The community of Great Waltham in medieval and early modern times was more or less self sufficient and many people lived out their lives there. In such circumstances the nuclear family functioned rather differently to the way it does now when families are much more geographically dispersed. In 1610 at least nine inter-related nuclear families belonging to the Ram family lived in Great Waltham. What was the mix of family and peer influences on their social enculturation? How did they get on with each other? Did such proximity lead to economic co-operation? Did it, as seems likely, enhance influence in village life? Was the influence of peers more or less strong than in the looser sort of society we have today? How was the family network affected by the fact that many families had a presence in several villages in the local area? The answers to most of these questions can only be guessed at for there is not enough hard information to know what happened. In all these matters the family must have exerted influence on the enculturation of infants and more generally in competition with peer groups. But it is far from clear what the balance was and if it has changed over the centuries. Some psychologists tend to play down the influence of the family and use the findings of the Minnesota twins study to support their view. On the other hand greatly increased knowledge about the action of genes in inheritance may lead to some downgrading of the influence of social factors. It is possible the role of the family is more important than is sometimes thought. Respondents to a recent survey on rural life, based on the 2001 census, suggest significant numbers of people look to friends and family as sources of their values and not modern opinion makers.[19]

Rosemary O'Day sums up her arguments about the family in the following way. '… the family was no less important or independent than class, nationality, gender, education, age or any other variables commonly employed in historical explanation in informing the values, beliefs and behaviour of people in times past and present'.[20] She believes family has a force and significance of its own, which is often ignored by opinion makers and commentators on social matters. It is independent of, and can be in conflict with, forces of social control. The family's true importance is not as a reflector of contemporary society and economy, but as '… an agent in society, in some senses more potent than class or gender or education. It can convey existing values and behaviours; it can transform; it can enable members to select from the menu before it, whether in terms of career, life partner, moral standards, social conscience or religious belief'.[21]

Ideas about how identity is formed

Through most of the twentieth century in America the dominant view about the formation of individual identity was that the general environment, and particularly peer influences, was its only source. But this position was never wholly accepted in Europe where there has always been a greater willingness to allow that other factors play a part. A study of enormous importance in influencing contemporary understanding about human formation is the Minnesota Twins study by Thomas Bouchard which questioned the overarching importance of environment. William Wright's book *Born That Way. Genes, Behaviour, Personality* is a fascinating account of that study and its impact.[22]

The Minnesota studies were received more favourably than earlier studies of twins because other influences were lessening the impact of environment on psychological theory. One in particular was the realisation by specialists in the field that brothers and sisters who shared 50 per cent of their genes were often quite different even though they were brought up in the same environment, and two explanations emerged. One was behavioural in emphasis and suggested that in reality siblings had non shared environments, i.e., each child in a family had a slightly different early upbringing and their peer culture was different. This idea was boosted by studies which showed that non-shared environment had a much bigger impact than shared, and that the latter had a negligible impact. The other explanation that also became accepted was that individuals shape their environment around the genetic features of their inheritance. Individuals' hobbies, their marriage patterns, and occupation could be seen as an extension of their genetic makeup.

The Minnesota studies were developed over a number of years and culminated in a major publication in 1986. By that date 44 sets of separated twins were involved. Also included were 331 reared together twins – 217 identical and 114 fraternal. The study identified and examined eleven personality traits, together with a number of physical characteristics – 28 altogether. The genetic importance found for each was expressed as a percentage called a 'figure of hereditability', a term that related to the group population, not individuals within it. The traits which showed the strongest hereditary content were traditionalism, or willingness to yield to authority, (.6) and social potency – assertiveness, drive for leadership, and taste for attention (.61). Social closeness – need for social intimacy and loving relationships – had a low heritability correlation (.33), which means environment is relatively more influential in that area. Most of the other traits scored at intermediary levels. Five scored a correlation with heritability of between .5 and .6 – stress reaction, absorption, alienation, well being, and harm avoidance. Three were between .4 and .5 – aggression, achievement and control. Although the findings are only for the group of twins studied they could be expected to be not very different for the population at large.[23] Bouchard later insisted that whilst he and colleagues expected to find traits with a high degree of heritability they also expected to find traits that had no genetic component. They were astonished when they found that whilst the degree of heritability varied widely – from scores of .3 to .7 – every trait they measured showed some degree of genetic influence. Many showed a lot.[24]

In the 1986 publication the Minnesota researchers left it to the evolutionary theorists to make sense of behavioural variation, but did say a species that was genetically uniform would have created a very different society from ours, and that however human variation originated it 'is now a salient and essential feature of the human condition'. The paper's conclusion was remarkably simple; people are different, and they are different to a large degree because of genetic differences.[25] Heredity was identified as a more significant determinant of IQ than environment. (about .73). For personality the influence of heredity was somewhat less but still substantial. The study also found common family environmental influences play only a minor role in the determination of personality.[26] Although people are all different we are only so within a limited range – otherwise humanness would not mean anything.

So, it would appear some consensus has been established by these studies that both nurture and heredity play a part in forming the behavioural and value patterns of individuals, and this understanding has influenced the choice of both *Thread* yardsticks and related analysis. But William Wright writing as late as 1999 suspects old ideas live on. 'In spite of much scientific evidence to the contrary, the two fallacies – immutable genes and malleable environments – linger on'... This 'explains why so many informed people accept in principle a genes-behaviour dynamic but have yet to incorporate the new view into their cognitive data banks'.[27]

Overall, the Bouchard studies demonstrated that heredity is significant in forming human identity. One of the most remarkable of its findings was the extent to which genetic components are responsible for behavioural characteristics. Other studies made the same conclusions.[28] Some of them came to the view that children mould their own environments by means of the interaction of their social environment and their genetic makeup. Quite a lot of social psychologists came to believe that this process is much more important in child development than the environment shared with other family members. Sandra Skarr has been a major figure in this field.[29] The Minnesota study also made some surprising discoveries, and one of them concerned what makes people religious. A few behavioural traits not in the basic testing appeared to have a genetic component, and one of these was religiosity. It was found that twins might follow different faiths, but if one was religious, his or her twin more often than not was religious as well.

The findings of this book suggest that there is strong stability and continuity in human behaviour. Yet if it was acquired entirely by social means there would almost certainly be considerable change over time, so much so that humanity would change its nature. In many ways the story of the Ram family and the worlds they lived in supports Rosemary O'Day's view that the detailed expression of human behaviour changes from age to age but its essence is always the same. How does this happen? This question opens the way to consider a genetic component. None of the enquiries discussed above explained exactly how genes might play a part because they are all based on behavioural observation. The very recent studies of the human genome are beginning to go beyond this, and related ideas are now beginning to percolate outside the expert field. It is clear that the influence of genes is almost certainly wider than establishing our physical makeup. The earlier ideas of some social psychologists that genes play a part in how we behave is being confirmed. It may also be the case that genes operate in a cross influencing way between physiological and behavioural identity, which confirms Sandra Skarr's view of how children mould their own environments. This would explain how children who are born of the same parents and grow up in the same home can be so different. But although the genome studies are leading to general claims about the influence of genes, how their involvement fits together in detail and what their overall influence is remains far from clear. Some of the claims currently being made will no doubt turn out to be in error, and others may become of enormous importance. Clearly unravelling the genome and understanding how genes work can ultimately help to show how heredity plays a part in forming our identity. A very interesting recent book has tried to discuss all these issues in terms lay people can appreciate.[30]

It seems likely that identity is formed by the interplay between genes, environmental influences and our physiological makeup in which one element is not always dominant. One of the people who developed ideas about the part genes play in these interactions wrote that he came to realise '... the genome wasn't the monolithic data bank plus executive team devoted to one project – keeping oneself alive, having babies – that I had hitherto imagined it to be. Instead it was beginning to seem more a company boardroom, a theatre for a power struggle of egoists and factions'.[31] One example of what can happen is the suppression of the immune system following the death of a loved one. Normally the genes power that system but in the trauma of loss psychology takes over temporarily. This is but one example of many that could be mentioned. Developments in archaeology are also playing a part. These accept that there is a basic genetic base which is identified with our species and was acquired in our early development, almost certainly before the time when we started to leave Africa – about 60,000 years ago. This base included capacity for speech and childhood learning, and shared cultural heritage. It also included simple technical knowledge, like how to make fire and clothes, and a considerable range of social skills covering interaction within social groups. Since then, as human beings have dispersed round the globe they have developed different 'developmental trajectories' based on adaptation and learning. This is why human societies can appear so different. But they all remain within the limits set by a common genetic base. How these developments happened are part of a new academic discipline called cognitive archaeology.[32]

The unravelling of all that happens in the process of forming identity is still in its infancy. and is beyond the scope of this book, but the important thing for the immediate context is that there are clearly several factors at work and that the whole process is very complex. William Wright believes substantial tensions in understandings about the ways we obtain our identity still have to be resolved. In his view many of the brightest and best educated – the 'brain-proud' as he calls them – refuse to accept genetic involvement in formation because of fears about loss of autonomy. This group of people are most disposed to believe their thoughts come from pure reason and not from heredity. This is one of the reasons why the two fallacies – that of immutable genes and malleable environments – linger on. Anything therefore that helps to throw more light on the issues involved, like this study of the Ram family, is of potential value.

The role of values

In the framework of this book values are taken to be an important part of identity, but in a catholic way which encompasses very practical rules for daily living, as well as religious experience and spiritual beliefs. Regard for the place of 'values' is so debased today that the word 'choice', which is better understood, could be used as a substitute. Choosing between one thing and another involves values whether we like it or not, because how to do this is informed by the values we hold, or do not hold. Values are the guide we use to make choices. In chapter XXIV a chart plots how individual people might view identity looking out on the world from their own place in it, using the Rams as guinea pigs. In this perspective of identity the values that appear most important are those, and this might be expected, that directly influence day to day living in significant ways, like choice, (and factors which influence choice – life chance, wealth, influence, and power), individual beliefs and values, religious practice, family Influences, and dealings with people.

The very basic type of values deal with everyday standards of conduct – fairness, reciprocity, recognition that dealing with people honestly generally develops positive relationships, and so on. To use and apply this type of value does not require much religious understanding, although formal religion upholds them as good practice. Neither do they involve much reflection and they might even be instinctive. The contribution that these types of values make to identity formation is discussed later.[33]

The other type are focused on deeper reflection about the meaning of life, usually involve spiritual devotion and theological reflection, and enable people to come to a deeper appreciation of the importance of everyday values. They have a more specialised role and some people may be more sensitive to them than others. In 1951 a United States psychologist called Gordon Allport did research into kinds of human prejudice, throwing some light on how people approach formal religion in the process. He suggested that there are two types of religious commitment – extrinsic and intrinsic. People who have extrinsic religiosity support religious institutions for what they can get out of them or because it is the social norm, which conveys respectability or social advancement. People who have intrinsic religiosity are different. Allport thought this group sees religion as an end in itself and tends to be more deeply committed. Religion is the organising principle of their lives. Allport found that certain character traits went with these differences. Prejudice is more common among extrinsically religious people. Intrinsic religion seems to be associated with lower levels better adjustment to society and less depression. On the other hand intrinsic religion seems to be connected with higher levels of guilt, worry, and anxiety.[34] It would also seem that some people, possibly Allport's intrinsically religious, have greater spiritual sensitivity, which includes reflecting more on the meaning of life, and how they find meaning in their own lives. In our society it is difficult to estimate the proportion of people who have intrinsic or extrinsic approaches to religion. Formal church going is the main public expression of religious commitment, which involved many people up until relatively recently. But how should such attendance be interpreted in the context of the formation of identity? It certainly gives no insight as to whether people's attitude to religion is extrinsive or intrinsive.

If the arguments of Gordon Allport are accepted one way of estimating the proportions of people in each camp, is to use the Ram family as a test case. There is relatively little direct information about how members of this family viewed churchgoing and how seriously they took religious belief. The general impression that emerges from all the information about them is that they were not particularly religious but were honest and, certainly at Great Waltham, willing to contribute to community affairs and to be a 'good neighbour'. There are hardly any recorded brushes with the law. Outwardly the family's allegiance to the Church of England is remarkably solid over hundreds of years, as is shown by the fact that nearly every family member has been baptised into the Church of England since records began. Most of these were probably in the extrinsic group.

Were all the family in this group? Probably not. From early modern times onwards more personal information is known about the members of the family who probably had an intrinsive kind of religious capacity. In the sixteenth and seventeenth centuries some of them were quite radical Protestants, and it was among the descendants of this group that a high degree of religiosity has been consistently if erratically present down the centuries. In one way or another this group provides public signs of real religious commitment and shows itself to be different in a number of ways from the rest of the family. All of them belong to the same branch, being descended from John Ram (d. 1568), farmer of Great Waltham and Pleshey. His will showed him to be a fervent Protestant.[35] All eleven members of the family who became clergymen, married clergymen or married into clerical families came from this branch.

Three of John's sons can be identified with the same religious position by the profiles of their lives. Francis became Steward to Sir Anthony Cooke (d. 1576) – who organised the tutoring of the future king Edward VI. William was Deputy Town Clerk at Colchester which was hotly reformist, and the third brother, Christopher was a Church of England cleric. One of his parishes was extremely reform minded. A son of William and two of his grandsons became Church of England clergy. This nuclear family comprised the first known family members to break away from the traditional involvement in farming and achieve upward social mobility. It may well be this occurred on the back of, or in association with, their religious enthusiasm. The interaction of their religious beliefs with social advancement was possibly not apparent to the individuals involved, for there is no evidence that their commitment to radical Protestantism was simply a cynical ploy to make personal gains.

The early years of the Protestant reformation in England were ones in which being serious about religion could be personally costly as well as beneficial.[36] If anything the dilemmas grew more difficult in the seventeenth century. Robert (1564-1638), one of the sons of William of Colchester, was a graduate of Cambridge University and became a Doctor of Divinity in 1602. He was rector of Copford, just on the western edge of Colchester, and vicar of Great Birch nearby from at least 1591 until his death. It might be expected that he would show radical tendencies taking into account his family background, education, and his closeness to Colchester. But what information is known about him makes it look as though he was a trimmer of sails. This was not the case in the family as a whole for several of his daughters married clergymen who lost their livings because of their identification with either the Parliamentary or Royalist causes.[37]

The strong religiosity of this branch reappeared in the nineteenth century, when it was solidly upper middle class. Three family members became Anglican clergymen, a tradition which was continued into the twentieth century. As in the seventeenth century close religious associations were not confined to family members who took holy orders. Stephen Ram (b. 1831), a solicitor son of James Ram, married into the Scott family that included many clergy over several generations. There was also a tendency for the clergymen sons to marry into other clerical families, so quite complex networks based on holding professional posts in the Church of England were formed. Nearly all of the men from the Ram family who went into the Church were educated at Cambridge University. Such patterns was not uncommon in clerical families during this period. It is obvious that clergy were drawn into networks that encouraged further extension by marriage. But why did Stephen Ram, a solicitor, marry into such a family unless he felt at home in such circles? It is likely that he had evangelical sympathies for his wife was the daughter of Revd Thomas Scott (1807-1880), the elder brother of the architect Sir Gilbert Scott (1811-1878). Gilbert Scott's family background was very evangelical. In his book of Recollections he recalls in an amusing way life as a boy in Gawcott, Buckinghamshire, where his father was 'perpetual curate'. His family were shunned by many clergy because of their evangelical leanings.[38] At that time evangelical does not mean quite what it does today, being characterised by a desire to take Christianity and religious life seriously. Even though Gilbert Scott fails to give a clear picture of his elder brother's own religious outlook, it is reasonable to suppose their views were not diametrically opposed, as they got on well together.

It was quite common in the eighteenth and nineteenth centuries for the junior sons of gentry and aristocracy to become clergy and perhaps the extension of such traditions into upper middle class families was a copy cat phenomena.

For some of them work of this type was possibly just a professional job open to those who were disinclined, or did not have the ability, to be a lawyer. But at least one of James Ram's sons had a deeper call than that. Edward Ram was for many years incumbent of the parish of St John's Timberhill in Norwich, effectively devoting his life to the renewal of a run down church. His spiritual energy came from a deep association with the ritualist movement in the Church of England that meant much more than restoring the use of vestments, candles, and other practices then regarded as Roman Catholic. The movement was in fact underpinned by a desire to make the clergy really professional and devoted to their people, and to the mission of the Church. Edward Ram's religious life was far from extrinsic in form, but may not been of the same for his younger brother Ralph (b. 1845) or nephew Stephen (b. 1867). Ralph ran a school in Holbeach for most of his life and then held minor clerical posts in Cambridgeshire. It is unclear what motivated him. Stephen rose to some prominence in Yorkshire and eventually became a Canon and Prebendary of York Minister. He was a thoroughly professional man but as with Ralph the nature of his religiosity is unclear. Yet in this branch of the Ram family there is much evidence to suggest it had a deeper than usual interest in religion, which was possibly genetically based. Overall about half the family comes from this branch.

In writing the story of the Ram family it is hard to escape the conclusion that all kinds of values help to bind them and society as a whole together. Values are long lasting and the most basic of them are central to defining human beings as a species. If we lose our sense of values we lose our humanness. The really important understanding about values is not whether they are instinctual or socially learned, but that they play a basic part in the formation of identity. 'Trust is at the heart of practically all human relationships'. We have a fundamental biological urge to trust each other, because it is advantageous to do so. We are not so competitive as some would like to have us believe. Trust is something within our programmed being and is stimulated by a hormone, oxytocin.[39]

SECTION 2   HOW LEARNING
ABOUT ORDINARY PEOPLE HELPS

VI
Identity explored through historical writings

The development of historical studies in local history

This book is grounded in the history of people who up to very recently have not been much written about, so it is important to assess how general studies of history help, and do not help, to deepen understanding about people. Only exceptionally do the poor, the middling sort, and the not so famous, produce individuals who draw attention to themselves in the affairs of state, or get remembered and written about by people beyond their immediate circle. Unless special effort is made to find out about this huge group of people, our view of the past is based on a tiny minority of all those alive at any one time, with the result that a vast pool of contribution goes unrecorded and unacknowledged. Michael Braddick believes that what happens in the local context has always influenced and partly shaped the wider society and its institutions – perhaps a lot more than we often recognise.[40]

One way of studying the world of ordinary people is by collating basic statistical records of individuals into a corporate analysis of some kind – about for example the village, a social class, or factors to do with population growth, fertility, and family size. In the 1960s enquiry of this kind was spurred on by two developments. One was the great growth of sociology as an academic discipline, which encouraged the analysis and interpretation of the social forces at work in our society, and inevitably included ordinary people. The second was growth in the use of computers that made the handling of large amounts of statistical information much easier. New techniques in historical study were developed in an area that came to be called historical demography. This work was led by a group of social historians at Cambridge University who belonged to the Cambridge Group for the History of Population and Social Structure.[41]

There are other strands in the growth of interest in the history of non-elites. W G Hoskins raised the profile of local history after the second world war, becoming Professor of English Local History at Leicester University in 1948. At that time there was no other similar post. In 1981 David Hey edited a reissued version of *The History of Myddle* by Richard Gough.[42] Based on pen pictures of village people this was written in the early part of the eighteenth century and first published in 1834. The 1981 reissue is widely known and has further stimulated interest in local history. David Hey worked at Sheffield University for many years and became Professor of Local History there, writing a number of books about family history.[43] The other more recent factor is the growing interest people have in identifying their own family past. Such information, if analysed systematically and objectively, can produce invaluable new insights about our past.

Three contributions that stem from the Cambridge Group for the History of Population and Social Structure are particularly relevant to this book. One is by M K McIntosh, [44] another by Keith Wrightson and David Levine,[45] and a third by L R Poos.[46] The first is about Havering in the sixteenth and seventeenth centuries (a member of the Ram family was Havering's Deputy Steward from 1563 to 1604), the second about Terling in roughly the same period (Terling is an Essex village around five miles from Great Waltham), and the third concerns Great Waltham itself in the medieval period. Keith Wrightson made a later more general input on the subject in a book published in 1982 which has recently been reprinted.[47] Over the last twenty years further work has led to growing awareness that society is more complex than earlier writers thought. In 1996 writing in a book about authority in early modern England Wrightson drew the following conclusion. 'Bereft of the old secure assumptions about the stages and direction of social development, we have to think again'.[48]

It will be seen in this book that the reality of human life is not always as historians present it and that generalised understandings can be oversimplified. Findings from the story of the Ram family are used to examine a variety of historical theories. How family inheritance happened is a useful example. Ram family practice is broadly in line with historians' ideas about inheritance practice among the middling sort in England. But it will become apparent there are a surprising number of exceptions to the rule. Sometimes the eldest son in the Ram family gets most of the inheritance, and sometimes he does not. Sometimes inheritances are shared more or less equally. Sometimes the family land is sold and proceeds of sale distributed among heirs, male and female. The key lesson from this is that the Ram family practised inheritance in ways which were most appropriate to immediate circumstances and not according to a prescribed legal or customary pattern. This is true of all generations from the times wills become available – from the early sixteenth century onwards.

Another understanding gained from this study is that there can be substantial differences in inheritance practice, even in communities that are very close to each other geographically. For example, Alan Macfarlane made a very detailed study of Earls Colne, less than fifteen miles from Great Waltham, where, ...' From 1540-1750 there survive over three hundred written wills for inhabitants ... At least half of the transfers of land registered in the sixteenth and seventeenth centuries were between non kin.'[49] Now there may have been more short term commercial transfers in Earls Colne than in a very agricultural community like Great Waltham, but over the same period of time the pattern of transfers affecting the Ram family was quite different: a much higher proportion were within the family. What are the reasons for this difference? An example of how general changes in society can vary, in the way they happened and in their timing, concerns land holding practice between the sixteenth and eighteenth centuries. In broad terms farmers changed from being small scale free and copy holders to larger scale renters of land on a commercial basis. But the way this happened and its timing in Great Waltham was very different to equivalent developments in Terling, about seven miles away.

Another way this book relates to methods of studying ordinary people is the emphasis it puts on qualitative data. The quantitative, statistical, emphasis is often used because it is an easier, and perhaps safer, way to write about them. Whilst this approach is obviously of great value, it has limitations because it cannot get inside individual people. It also finds it difficult to deal with subjective material like ideas, family values, and attitudes about the world, which lie within the consciousness of individual people or small groups, particularly families. This omission means an important element in historical enquiry is missing, which has a negative impact on our overall understanding. However, in social science research qualitative techniques and methods are now much more acceptable. These have been used in this book to interpret circumstantial evidence in wills, deeds and other general documents. It is a sort of *'reading between the lines'* completed with care. The methods used in this book may provide a bridge between the quantitative analysis school and the simple story tellers.

Writing about people and families

The writing of social historians about local and family history over the past twenty years or so has helped to fill important gaps in broader historical understanding and it has raised the issue that there are significant elements in human affairs besides the political and social activities of elites. It has led to the increasing realisation that looking at the world through the experience of ordinary people introduces another way of seeing events, society, and ultimately identity.

A practical example may help to make the point clear. Francis Ram, who features in a later part of the book[50] was Steward to Anthony Cooke, a not insignificant figure in Tudor society, and in traditional terms Francis Ram owed everything to the patronage of this man who was his employer. It was through him that Francis, of quite humble yeoman origins, was introduced to wider roles in the Essex magistracy and to local government in Havering. Without the patronage of Anthony Cooke such involvements would have been unavailable to him. But a closer examination of relationships between the two men suggests patronage, and the power that is related to it, may not only be downwardly focused, as is it often presented to be. Anthony Cooke needed someone with the skills and abilities of Francis, and both men gave and received in their relationship. Life in the sixteenth century presented everyone of whatever social level with both threat and opportunity, and the same is true today. Individuals are not much concerned about overall impersonal patterns, but are definitely interested in developing their own thread of experience and personal interests.

Family stories are a good way of exploring diversity in society for they reveal the full extent of the variety and complexity of human relationships. Although M K McIntosh wrote latterly about Havering as a society her initial interest was with Anthony Cooke and his family, for in her original thesis she explains how valuable studying families can be.

> ... The justification of a biographical approach in a family study is strong. Lives viewed within the common setting of a single family are more readily understood and evaluated, for the unusual and distinguished stand out clearly against the shared background. The historian, using skill and caution, is often able to use family biographies to bridge the gaps in his sources by drawing information from other members of the family and the general context.[51]

So the family and individuals within it can be used as a way into a wider world, and as a vehicle for linking them together. McIntosh registers that the family unit is a force for stability in the rapidly changing world of Havering in the sixteenth and seventeenth centuries.[52] She believes it has both a social and an economic importance. It is the unit which inculturates children, particularly when they are very young, and for most people provides the focus for daily living.

Having stressed the importance of the family it has to be said that much of the writing about it is rather fractured. There is little agreement about how the family counts. Authors have different start points and interests, and it is still an area where insights are developing quite rapidly. Much of the earlier work of historians on the subject was focused on the rich and wealthy. H J Habakkuk was one of the first systematic writers about the family, being drawn into it by an interest in economic concerns connected with the development of large estates. In his researches he concluded that attitudes to love and marriage in the landed family became more personalised as female property grew increasingly important to landowners seeking dynastic advantage through marriage.[53] Ralph Houlbrooke wrote about the family through the eyes of diarists which created an impressionistic impact on the reader.[54] Alan Macfarlane used the full and long diary of a seventeenth century Essex clergyman as a source for analysing family life and values in more general terms.[55] The understanding which emerged is quite sympathetic to the importance of family values, but of course his evaluation is based on a single individual. Lawrence Stone covered a much longer time scale and was more analytical than either of the other two, but drew a rather unsympathetic picture of family life and did not discuss values and the part family played in their transmission.[56] He also saw a major change between the period of the sixteenth and seventeenth centuries when family life was quite open but depersonalised, and the eighteenth and nineteenth centuries when it became more closed but loving. Ralph Houlbrooke writing in 1998 does not agree with Lawrence Stone's rather dismissive view of the family, believing its influence was consistent and stable: '...there are good reasons for thinking that the character of the English family changed relatively slowly between the fifteenth and eighteenth centuries, and that the appearance of change is due far more to the evolution of the media of expression than to major shifts'.[57] There are some studies about family life and values that have a particular focus, which tend to have quite short time spans – for example *Family Fortunes* by Leonore Davidoff and Catherine Hall. This concentrates on the middle classes and the place of women in the eighteenth century.[58] In many ways it is an excellent book and nowhere is a claim made that the picture presented represents the appearance of a new social group, but the fact that the material discussed is entirely eighteenth century can easily lead to the understanding that this is the case.

More recent work gives greater prominence to the importance of family life as a specific part of social structure. Eileen Spring's study of aristocratic families is one of the latest contributions to the subject, in which there is a chapter about theories of the family. The development of thinking in this area is reviewed in which she sets out her own ideas.[59] She believes landowners were perpetually engaged in a balance between preserving the family and being fair.[60] 'The whole history of landowners' interaction with the law shows ... that they were determined to provide for their children' ... in sensible ways within the social framework they lived within.[61] Eileen Spring's contribution serves to remind us that, sometimes in the discussion of theories about family life and structure, this common sense insight gets lost. What was true of aristocratic families was almost certainly true of all land holding groups, and in the end, of the vast majority of parents of whatever background. Such approaches are certainly evidenced in the history of the Ram family.

Some later writers have gone further to lay emphasis on the importance of the family as a social force in its own right, including those not in the topmost layers of society. This represents a new understanding of the importance of the family in cultural life. About half of the first part of Keith Wrightson's book on *English Society, 1580-1680*, called *Enduring structures*, dates from the early 1980s, and is given over to various aspects of the family.[62] Rosemary O'Day has written in the middle 1990s a book almost entirely devoted to the family and family relationships. She says that until recently scholars have been afraid to study the history of personal relationships.[63] Both writers take a positive view about the role of the family.

There is still much to learn about the part played by the family in the transmission of values. In the past there was perceived to be a close inter-association between family values and religious belief, but what impact has the decline of religion had on family values and their transmission? The significance of family on values must be more profound for some people than others, and the focus of its influence changes from age to age. It may also be true that family and values are more important for the better off than the poor, since, if you have spare wealth, there is more room for things beyond mere survival. All these insights point to the importance of studying the family unit. It has been and still remains a basic building block by which society 'keeps going' and passes on its cultural heritage.

Class, the Ram family, and identity

Class is probably, apart from property, the most important marker of identity in our hierarchically minded society. But many historians are reluctant to think of class in the modern sense as existing before the nineteenth century. On top of this the notion of class itself is an ambivalent term. Ideas about class tended to originate from research into the landed elite, that is often seen as dominant in all sorts of ways. As a result there has been a tendency to see social life as a struggle or polarisation between the elite and the people, which obscures distinctive input from the middling sort. No direct challenge has ever been made to J H Hexter's ideas about the 'myth of the middle class', namely that it is inappropriate to apply nineteenth century terminology and understandings to early modern times.[64] Hexter believed that you could not apply terms retrogressively to a society that did not itself use them. He also argued that the term 'middle class' was applied too widely, to include so called gentry who were really capitalists living in the country, and entrepreneurial artisans. He urged the term 'middle class' should only be used in relation to merchants, traders and yeomen, and that such groups in pre nineteenth century times could not be automatically identified with similarly named social groups in the nineteenth century. He argued it is just not possible to 'understand Tudor people as though they were Manchester manufacturers'.[65]

Hexter's chief concern was to explain how and why the middling sort were subordinate to the landed elite. He argued that they were not a clear cut social group, because people taking up trade or other money making occupations sought to establish themselves as part of the landed elite as soon as possible. In this process the physical and intellectual capital and leadership of towns was constantly having to replenish itself. The overall result was that the landed classes retained their socially elite position. Hexter denied the gentry could be considered middle class, and emphasised their common identity with the peerage within a landed aristocracy.[66]

In all of the debate and discussion there remains the question raised by Hexter as to whether modern notions of class and class difference, largely Marxist in origin, existed in the past. Little is said in these discussions about the part of Shani d'Cruze's definition of the middling sort which sees the independent trading family as 'the foundation for social, cultural and political independence' within the economic freedom of the middling family.[67] In fact in the discussion and theorising outlined little attention has been paid to the role of individual families, other than the politically famous or the very rich.

Most subsequent empirical work on the middle classes has taken Hexter's conceptual framework for granted. One potential problem with such an approach 'is that economic transactions are being used as proxies for social values'.[68] Hexter interpreted the purchase of land by the middling sort solely as a process of registering social aspirations, but was that necessarily the case? It could have been simply a rational means of investing accrued capital. If the circulatory nature of the process is emphasised why see the landed bit of it as dominant? After all urban life was becoming the principal cultural element in society. London obviously led the way. After 1700 there was a decline in middle class investment in land as alternative possibilities increased – especially the stock market, property and government debt.

Most historians have continued to present landed people as the dominant group, although empirical work has been done in recent years to get a clearer picture of the 'middling sort' in towns. Certainly in the mid 1990s there was far less clarity about what happened in rural situations. Mildred Campbell's *The English Yeoman*, which dates back to 1960 has not been superseded. Moreover most historical research on rural issues has had an economic rather than a social focus and has taken account of regional or local communities rather than a social group across time. However, the work of Wrightson and Levine on Terling in Essex, and other places, has drawn attention to the attitudes of 'parish elites' in rural places before and during the civil war. Much of this local work does not attempt to 'speculate about national pattern or significance' and some historians of this type are not wedded to attempting any such thing. [69]

One of the possible reasons for perceived difficulties in the definition of the middling sort is that many historical studies are based on a relatively short times scale. This can generate a tendency to take a shorter view of issues than is really required. An example of this is the book by Leanore Davidoff and Catherine Hall, already referred to, on the eighteenth century middle class. Looking at the evolution of society over a longer time span can generate a greater sense of the degree to which there is continuity in economic and social developments. In his work on English individualism Alan Macfarlane raised serious doubts about the validity of several embedded concepts, including Marxist communism.[70]

One of the important insights obtained from the story of the Ram family is what it reveals about the place and identity of the 'middling sort' and the 'middle class'. Throughout its history this family has been middling in the sense that many of its senior male members were certainly not among the labouring or poor classes and were equally clearly not among the gentry, rich or aristocracy. But within that range some Rams have been of higher social status than others, and some have been quite poor. So what exactly does middling mean for the Ram family? The nineteenth century professionals were clearly middle class in the modern sense but the eighteenth century entrepreneurs in Colchester were not much different and neither were their professional forebears in the sixteenth and seventeenth centuries. It could also be argued the farming Rams show this social category to be as visible in Great Waltham in 1400 as it was in the nineteenth century. The impression gained from the Ram family story is that this social group, whether described as middling or middle class existed from at least the sixteenth century onwards. H R French in his recent book on the middling sort comes to a rather similar conclusion. 'The problem is that these developments (the idea that a distinctive middle class culture first evolved in the mid to late seventeenth century) appear less original when viewed in a longer historical perspective. In particular, historians of the late medieval period have questioned whether the formation of an urban 'middling' identity was unique to the early modern era'[71]

Possible developments in historical studies

Encouragement of a broad approach to the use of historical material is a feature of this book. It encompasses traditional study methods, but draws on others not often used by historians, and it also uses historical material as an aid in the examination of contemporary social issues. This has resulted in the gaining of some interesting and new insights about life today and in the past. Studying the Ram family through the technique of *The Thread* will show, in ways that might surprise some people, how much our life today has continuity with the past. This book without doubt encourages the idea that studies in local history are important, a view which has only gained ground in the last fifty years. Even now such work tends to be seen as a specialist niche not much related to the major areas of historical enquiry. Relating the Ram family story to its involvements in a variety of local contexts demonstrates clearly that local history is about more than simply the study of the local scene. Local history can be built into and contribute to the better understanding of the broad historical picture.

Moreover the integrated use of traditional historical studies, the social sciences, and newly emerging sciences like genetics in this book opens new possibilities for looking at and studying history. For example the approach reveals that a well developed social life does not exist only among the rich and highly bred. It is quite clear that the Ram family, and presumably many similar families, were part of social networks just as worthwhile as any experienced by elite families and individuals. This is an angle often missing from earlier historical studies, which tended to convey the notion, perhaps unintentionally, that no-one outside the topmost social layer really mattered or contributed to history. What has been found out about the Ram family is supported by even a cursory reading of the diary of Thomas Turner, a mid eighteenth century shopkeeper in Sussex who played a very active and constructive part in the running of his village community.[72]

Another important insight opened up by this book that is relevant to the development of historical studies is the encouragement given in it to take a bottom up as well as the usual top down approach to analysing events. Studying the Ram family in the way it has been opens up new angles on looking at society. Parts 4 and 5 are much concerned with discussing related issues, with chapter XXIV specially concerned to draw out how identity may seem from the perspective of individuals who are non elite, and how different the world can look from this viewpoint.

A new area of historical enquiry that is growing very rapidly today are the genealogical family studies made by individuals. Searching for ancestors is very popular, and it is supposed to be the most rapidly growing hobby, at least among older people. How far will the information obtained change people's understandings about themselves, identity and history? What people find out will almost certainly be passed on to their children, so it will have an impact on younger generations as well as those who do the searching. Yet why is there so much interest in previous generations? Is it merely the product of better education and increased leisure time among people in their fifties and sixties? Or is there a more profound reason? Is it partly something that is born of our times, in which the traditional forms of belonging appear to be increasingly lost? Are people searching for their past because finding it will help to develop a greater degree of rootedness in their own lives? Such considerations relate closely to the issue of identity and the concerns of this book.

Discoveries in genetics are beginning to have a practical impact on genealogical studies. It is now possible to make DNA tests that throw light on the geographical origins of our earliest ancestors and on the genetic relatedness we share with other humans. Because the Y chromosome is passed on from father to son in a fixed way it is of considerable use in testing male relatedness. A remarkable study which illustrates the significance of this is the short paper by Bryan Sykes and Catherine Irven, of the Institute of Molecular Medicine at Oxford University, on the Sykes family. Using genetic testing techniques they discovered to their surprise that it is highly likely the origin of the Sykes name, not uncommon in the North of England, can be attributed to a single founder.[73] It is now even possible to get your DNA tested by sending off a swab sample in the post to a professional tester and a recent book explains how DNA can influence genealogical studies at large.[74] How far DNA testing will affect the work of genealogists has yet to be seen, but it is immediately apparent it might have two impacts on the study of the Ram family. It could prove the Irish and English families are related, but it could not show exactly how. The Sykes paper also reinforces the likelihood that the Ram family, and many other small families, originate from a single person.

Three important questions can be asked about the increasing study of family history. Will all the information about unknown families that is becoming available lead to new insights and understandings about the past? Will it change our interpretation of history? And most importantly will it change our attitudes to the present? There is no doubt that the possibilities for new knowledge are considerable. One of the things that has emerged from studying the Ram family is that a surprising amount can be found out about people who are ill documented and might be thought to be undocumentable. Most of the information put together about the Ram family has been generated indirectly from sources in which they appear as minor participants or as statistics. Yet when all of the separate facts are collected together they make up a jigsaw which is surprisingly informative. It might be thought that it would be even more difficult to learn about poor people, but it may be easier to document them than the middling sort because of the comprehensive records kept by the Poor Law authorities. Many of the county record offices are keen to give support and help to studying families whilst their records are becoming increasingly accessible. The same is true of the national archives at Kew. Reading this book may in fact be an inspiration for many people to push on with studies of their own family.

VII

My family researches – a case study in unpacking identity

Challenges raised by studying the Ram family

Without a doubt a major outcome of my researches into the Ram family is the snapshot of human identity which it provides. The understanding that has come to me through studying my family is both personal and more general. On the personal level it has raised self awareness. Knowing about your family history enriches self estimation and rootedness. At a more general level appreciation of what life was like in various local communities has been greatly enlarged, which has illuminated my understanding of how they functioning in the past. A body of historical information, including insights into individual people, has been obtained which would otherwise have been completely lost. All this has happened even though I have a life long interest in studying history.

The information that has come to light about the Ram family has raised a number of questions in my mind, some of which have relevance to the nature of identity. One of the most intriguing is the length of time family folk memory lasts. Initial information, passed down to me proved to be reasonably accurate, but it did not go further back than Benjamin Ram, who was born in 1814. Since the mid nineteenth century my branch of the family has lived mainly in London, and although wider family contacts were maintained up to 1900 none now exist outside the immediate family. It is not even known if there are other family members alive. When a family is relatively scattered in large cities like London it is understandable that family contact can be lost and with it folk memory, but how long did such memories exist when generations followed one after the other in a single village for hundreds of years, as they did in Great Waltham?

My middling family has a very long history and has produced some interesting and able people. Would the same be true for nearly all families if their past could be documented? Relatively few families retain their names over long periods, partly because the male line dies out or the name is so common it is impossible to trace relatedness, but of course everyone alive today has a line of ancestors going back into the dim past. It is most likely that many families could be shown to have had interesting people at some point in time if their histories were known. If it is true that talents are spread around over time people might be more proud of their families and realise that rough and ready distinctions between those who 'count' and those who 'do not count' can distort reality.

The previous chapter has shown that attitudinal blocks to writing about ordinary people – that they are just not worthy of consideration – are a thing of the past. But the same chapter also showed that the lack of direct records makes studying ordinary people difficult. Yet that chapter also showed the task is not impossible for there are various ways of finding out about people by indirect means. In 2002 a family history was published that was based on family letters, in which the author comments at one point, about how he has used the letters to build a story. He writes that on a number of occasions the letters,

> ... say little, and I've filled in some of the gaps. It's not my usual method to fictionalise. And even here what I've set down scarcely qualifies as fiction. With fiction you can let go, constrained only by the logic of your inventions. With my mother, who isn't an invention ... there's a demand for honest reporting. Though certain to fail, I want to fail with honour. Which means honouring the truth of who she was.[75]

I have used wills, deeds and other formal documents in a rather similar way. Wills are an invaluable source of information about people, not only those written by family members but, perhaps just as importantly, ones from outside the family in which Rams are mentioned. More is written later about how wills have been used.[76]

Even if telling the story of a middling family is difficult, similar interpretation and interpolation of stories, documents, and events is required in all forms of historical study, however well documented. McIntosh in her thesis justifies the telling of family stories in the following way. '...Finally, although the biographer may have a fascinating account to present, he must be prepared to defend himself against the accusation of being a mere storyteller, recounting the interesting because he lacks the ability or sources to describe the significant.'[77] The methods used, and ideas expressed in this book cannot be statistically based, for my family chose itself and is one out of millions. But its story still contains much information, and the reader has to assess the validity of the arguments derived from that by the way the evidence is presented.

Completing a jigsaw puzzle

I have already told the story of how I got hooked into following up my early enquiries about the Ram family. It was at this point when I was widening my search that I discovered the Mormon Index. It was a major breakthrough which made it possible to avoid laborious searching through many individual parish records. This is widely available in various local centres, often libraries, and contains detailed transcriptions of the registers of baptisms, marriages and burials for many parishes up to the time when the national registers began, and sometimes beyond this point.[78] All the entries in Essex for the Ram family were photocopied from the Index at Cambridge Public Library. It was soon discovered that John Ram of Steeple (1768-1835) had been born in Great Waltham, where he had married Abigail Boltwood in 1799, and this established a link between the author's known forebears and the large numbers of Rams the Mormon Index showed had lived there from the time registers of baptisms, burials and marriages started in 1566. This made searching very much easier, and identified a focus point for the family. The Great Waltham registers in the Essex Record Office were examined to check the accuracy of the Index, and even though its reliability is sometimes doubted, very few errors were found. The Index's records for London and Suffolk have also been used.

The second invaluable source for establishing the basic genealogical picture of the family has been the census records, particularly from 1841 onwards when more detailed questions were asked and the individual returns were kept after the census was finished. Once again the Mormon sources were of great help, particularly their transcription of the 1881 census.[79] The census returns more or less took over as the basic genealogical source when the Mormon Index of individual parishes stopped.

The third basic record used has been wills. As well as their wider importance they are extremely useful for substantiating genealogical connections between succeeding generations. The earliest one from the Ram family dates from 1530. During the sixteenth century they are written in Secretary Hand which, when combined with poor writing, is very difficult to construe. But it is English and reading it gets easier with perseverance! Many family members, especially the main male figures in each generation left wills, and in one family branch there is a continuous sequence of them from 1576 until 1726. All told there are over 160 family wills, or wills that relate to family members, between 1530 and 1901.[80]

Other basic genealogical records have been obtained from *The Ram Family*, a book printed in 1940 by two family members, which contains a well researched compendium of information sources about anyone called Ram back into the middle ages. It was not found in the British Library until after quite an amount of research had already been completed, but my work was not wasted as the two accounts basically agree – which adds confidence to the correctness of overall findings. *The Ram Family* also filled in some gaps about the family tree for the part of the family which came to be based in Colchester which I was having difficulty with. The book contains a short written account of the family which does not include the Great Waltham farming branch. The authors were aware of the omission and said it was due to the lack of early baptismal and other registrations for Great Waltham.

These were in fact found at a firm of book auctioneers in London some years after the book was written and are now in the Essex Record Office.[81]

One factor that helped the research was the rarity of the family name – spelt Ram even from medieval times, but sometimes Rame, Ramm or Ramme – for there are only 732 entries in the 1881 census with that name, including spouses, of which 609, including spouses came from the Eastern counties of Essex, Suffolk, Norfolk and London, with most living in Norfolk, Essex and London. Spelling of the name had become quite standardised by 1881 – nearly all Ramm in Norfolk and mostly Ram in Essex and Suffolk. Both spellings were equally present in London. The people in my family tree account for about 90 per cent of all the Rams in the 1881 census who were born in Essex and Suffolk. The rarity of the name makes it easy to build up connections between individuals. David Hey in his book *Family Names and Family History* says many families come from a particular place or locality. He mentions the Ram surname and says its distribution pattern is consistent with a single family origin.[82]

The Mormon Index used in conjunction with family wills eased construction of the family tree considerably. Initially individual genealogical charts for each nuclear family group were prepared using the Mormon Index. These were then interconnected, just like pieces in a jig saw puzzle. The wills were a great help in making uncertain links clear. If it was not obvious how individuals or family groups fitted into the tree as a whole they were set aside, sometimes to be included later if their place became clear. In nearly all cases it was possible to fit each nuclear family group in because it filled an obvious space, made apparent by patterns in naming, age distributions, and the availability of a 'slot'. Working in this way the Ram family came to life and it only took a relatively short time to complete its genealogy back to the time when the registers started in 1566. In fact the baptism of a John Ram (1566-1612) is the first entry in the Great Waltham register![83]

The finished jigsaw

The family tree contains about 700 individuals, of whom around 430 are lineal family members. Before the registers of baptisms, marriages and burials start in the latter third of the sixteenth century it is impossible to draw up a genealogical table so all the individual references to family members have been built into a time chart for the years 1327-1567.[84] The genealogical table for the years after the mid sixteenth century is shown in sections at relevant points in the text. Appendix I presents the whole chart as a 'time line' in written form with brief notes on individual people.

There are only two important points of uncertainty about the line of descent after the start of formal registration, both of which are in the seventeenth century. One is in the Great Waltham branch and the other in the Colchester branch, although in both cases the most likely links are supported by strong circumstantial evidence. At Great Waltham the uncertainty really arises because two immediately succeeding members of the family died without making wills. They were both called Richard and were almost certainly father and son, although the son predeceased the father. In the Colchester branch a combination of family movement between Colchester and Stoke by Nayland, about five miles away, poorly preserved registers and a lack of wills is the source of the problem. Each difficulty is discussed in full at the appropriate point in the story of the family.[85]

The genealogical data on which this book is based only includes people who have clear links with the family that originated in Great Waltham, where all the earliest identified individuals belonging to it were found. This excludes one or two fairly large family groups with the name of Ram that appear in the censuses from 1871 to 1901 and lived quite near Great Waltham, for example in Waltham Cross and around Ingatestone and Fryerning. Also excluded are a number of small scattered families within a radius of twenty or thirty miles of Great Waltham that have the same name but no proven link.

Making statistical analyses

A statistical analysis of the distribution and size of the family at 25 year intervals between 1575 and 1900 is included in Appendix 2. But it is not possible to do elaborate statistical analyses on items like life span and age at death because in earlier times either date of death, and more especially date of birth, is often missing. Moreover, it is not clear how far the overall total number of 700 people, or the total recorded for any particular period, accurately includes every individual. It may well be that more men are recorded than women. The baptisms and burials of children who died as infants tended not to be registered.

One analysis that is possible is how personal names were chosen, and because the data base covers a very long time span it is possible to detect trends and patterns in the way they were given. The analysis is based on the lineal family members for whom dates of baptism are known, just over 320. Of these 160 are girls and 163 are boys. Most of this information covers the period 1550 to 1900, which is spread reasonably evenly across the centuries; 59 in the sixteenth, 98 in the seventeenth, 55 in the eighteenth, and 99 in the nineteenth.

What has been found out about Ram naming practices has been related to wider research on naming patterns contained in a recent book on the period 1550-1700.[86] The findings of this research show the most common names in all social classes for boys were John, Thomas and William. But higher up the social scale there was a greater tendency to use other names. Among the gentry George appears (1590s), Edward (1640's) and Richard (1660's).[87] For all other groups – yeoman, artisans, husbandmen, and labourers – the five most common names throughout the period from 1550 to 1700 (usually in this order) were: John, William, Thomas, Richard, and Robert.[88] There was a tendency for more 'non saint' names to be given in the higher of the five social groups, although after 1660 the proportion of Biblical names in all of them increased.[89] In the last decade of the seventeenth century 55 per cent of artisans, 59 per cent of yeomen, and 58 per cent of husbandmen had Biblical names compared with 46 per cent for gentlemen and 42 per cent for labourers.[90] There is evidence that names were clustered around three broader social groupings – the gentry, yeomen artisans and husbandmen, and labourers.[91] There was also a tendency for names that became fashionable among the gentry to filter down into other classes over time.[92] Generally, if a name was commonly used it remained so. The use of other less common names was open to substantial variation.[93] The proportion of children given traditional English names fell over the period.[94]

During the sixteenth century there was a growing trend to name children after their parent, and not godparents as had tended to be the case earlier. For boys there was a marked shift in this direction in the 1590s and for girls somewhat later, in the decade 1610 to 1619.[95] It was also more usual to name boys after fathers than girls after mothers. These trends developed earlier in the South and South East than elsewhere.[96] It was more likely that this practice would be applied to first born than later children.[97]

The allocation of names in the Ram family did not follow the general trend entirely but it was fairly close to it. If anything there was a tendency for more non Biblical names to be given than for the class the family belonged to, but that may be because they lived in the South East of the country where modernising tendencies happened earlier. In the sixteenth century 81 per cent of the names given were Biblical and in the seventeenth the proportion was 53 per cent. The most frequently used names for boys were John, Richard and Thomas (equal second), William, Francis and Robert. John was used twice as much as any other name. Only three names appear in every century – John, William and Joseph. There was in fact a tendency for names to appear in one branch and to be used quite frequently for a period after which they fell out of fashion. The existence or significance of such naming patterns is not mentioned in Scott Smith-Bannister's book. Francis was popular in the Hornchurch branch in the sixteenth and seventeenth centuries, the same was true of Benjamin in the Great Waltham branch during the eighteenth and nineteenth centuries, but the use of Thomas practically died out after the sixteenth century. Within these parameters there was a marked tendency for the name to follow down each generation through the eldest son. Sometimes a name not used for a long time reappears, and it is unclear whether this happens by chance or deliberate intention.

Scott Smith-Bannister does not say a great deal about girls, and there is no equivalent analysis to that made for boys. The Ram data shows the overall pattern of name usage is roughly the same for both girls and boys. A similar number of names are used five or more times, twelve for boys and ten for girls. The continuous use of some names with others having a time in fashion and then dying away, is also found in girl naming. Four girls' names are used in every century from the sixteenth to the nineteenth – Elizabeth is just the most popular with Mary a close follower up, whilst Jane and Sarah are less popular. Their use is not entirely even however, for Elizabeth is commoner in the seventeenth century, whilst Mary is used more later on, especially during the eighteenth century. Jane is more popular in later centuries, particularly the eighteenth, and Sarah in the seventeenth century. The other names used five or more times were fashionable at particular periods; Alice, in the nineteenth century, Ann in the seventeenth and eighteenth centuries, Bridget in the eighteenth century, and Hannah in the eighteenth and nineteenth centuries. Throughout the four centuries covered by the book there was almost as much naming of daughters after mothers as sons after fathers.

In the nineteenth century two new developments appeared in the way personal names were given to members of the family. Around mid century the practice developed at all social levels of giving children two personal names not just one, and a few in the upper middle class part of the family were given three. Another new feature was the custom of using family names as personal names, although this died out towards the end of the century. It became quite widespread in the branch which became professional upper middle class. James Ram was born in Colchester and moved first to London and then to Ipswich. He was a lawyer and an important writer about the law. Many of his sons were also lawyers, mostly solicitors, or Church of England clergymen. James married Elizabeth Jane Adye of a military family, which produced generals in three successive generations during this period.[98] She obviously held her family in high regard for many of her children and grandchildren had Adye as a second personal name. Other family names were used in the same way. One of James and Elizabeth's younger sons was called Willett, the surname of another family Elizabeth was connected with, and his eldest son was also called Willett (b. 1875). The second of James and Elizabeth's sons married Susan Scott, and several of their children were given Scott as a personal name, including a girl grand daughter as late as 1922. These developments were in keeping with general trends in naming practice during the nineteenth century.

It is difficult to discern whether naming patterns indicate awareness of family identity across the generations. One obvious aspect of naming patterns in the Ram family is how closely prevailing fashions and trends were followed. This might have happened because people felt a communal relationship with others, but it could equally have occurred because people followed general fashion. There were clearly trends for the same forename to be used in successive generations, but this may not mean children were really named like this to reinforce family identity. After all in earlier times there were very few names to choose from. On the other hand it might have happened out of regard for those who had gone before. But there are several naming patterns which potentially do reflect concern for family identity. Starting in 1725 the relatively uncommon name of Benjamin occurs eight times over the next hundred years in the farming branch of the family. It is difficult to avoid the conclusion that following the original use of the name it became a 'family' name in a way that reflects awareness of family identity. The use of Francis also occurred in a rather similar way in the branch that broke away from farming, although in a more scattered way. It first appeared in the mid sixteenth century in someone who established himself as one of the most substantial figures produced by the family, was continued in his immediate family over several generations and then reappeared in the same branch in the eighteenth century. The third usage that certainly indicated awareness of family identity was the practice of using the maternal family names of Adye and Scott as forenames in one part of the family in the nineteenth century.

Issues about men and women

Much of the book is about men, especially the principal figures in each generation, which means identity tends to be seen from a male perspective. In many ways this is inevitable because the family is mainly accessible through activities dominated by men, such as dealing with property, work and formal community involvement. The importance of men in these aspects of life has been a general feature of our society for many hundreds of years.

By and large women made an illusive and mostly undocumented contribution to family and community affairs. For instance, nothing is known about the wife of John Ram, whose three radical Protestant sons left farming in sixteenth century Great Waltham for professional careers, but she may have been as important an influence on them as her husband, and possibly more so. Even in the traditional society of Great Waltham wills show that women could be active in managing family affairs. The frequent occurrence of early and sudden death up until quite recent times required women to act with authority, often as widows. There is little evidence of similar activity by unmarried women, although they have always been able to take on roles similar to men. In the sixteenth century women who lived in the more advanced society of Hornchurch and London left property to next of kin. Christian Greene (d. 1639), a maternal grandmother of several Rams, and a widow, left property in her own right for their benefit. In Great Waltham this never happened for property, usually in the form of land, was invariable passed from one man to another. There are other signs that wives played an influential part in the detailed life of their individual families. Elizabeth Adye in the nineteenth century ensured that her family name, and a related family name Willett, was given to numbers of her children as second personal names. When women do have a recognisable role and identity, and this happens more than might be supposed, their involvements and contributions are included.

Personal stories about the family

These enrich understandings about identity and help to overcome the skewing effect of male dominance in formal areas of life. Many of them bring out the social side of family life and the active part women played in it. One example concerns William Ram (abt. 1560-1620), a member of the Colchester branch, who was an innkeeper cum yeoman in Romford for many years. He became involved during 1603 in the preparation of the will of Thomas Kempe, a Romford blacksmith. This was a plague year and rudimentary efforts were made to apply quarantine rules.

> Thomas Kempe, lying sick of the Plague in his house in the town of Romford, sent for the deponent to come unto him, who presently went near unto his house. And after his coming he, this deponent, being in the street, called to them within the house to know what the cause was wherefor he was sent for, whereupon the said Kempe, coming to his window of his chamber where he lay as it seemed, looked through a pane of glass which was taken down to let air into the room, and speaking to this deponent told him that he had sent for him to trouble him with the making of his last will and testament".

Kempe then dictated the will, Rame went home and wrote it out, came back and read it out in a loud voice –

> ... coming as near to the house as he durst. The testator approved the document. The will was signed by those witnessing it in the street. Rame delivered the said will at the door of the testator's house to one of the household.[99]

Another story example, this time about a woman, concerns Rose Ram (d.1592), who as a widow in Great Waltham was actively engaged in livestock farming! The content of her will is most unusual, interesting, and, to us, rather amusing.

> To Agnes my daughter my best black cow and one of my best couples of my ewes. To Joan my daughter my red cow and two ewe sheep and their lambs next the best, on condition that she pays John my son 5sh. May Day next. To Margery my daughter my brown bullock and couples of my ewe sheep. To my daughters Rose one ewe sheep and her lamb, and Agnes my best bed in the parlour. The residue of my goods to Thomas my son whom I ordain executor.[100]

Rose was one of the few 'farming wives' and it sounds as though her animals meant more to her than the items of furniture clothing and bedding that were listed in most women's wills of the period.

The importance of putting the family in context

It was always the intention to set the story of the Ram family in its context. This helps to understand the family better, increase knowledge about the wider world they were part of, and also sheds light on aspects of identity. It has taken nine years to research and write this book and through that period I have had conversations with a number of people which have reinforced the importance of setting a story like that of the Ram family in context. Chapter XIII was written up as an article for *The Local Historian*, the journal of the British Association for Local History, and whilst this was happening the editor talked to me several times about the importance of providing contextual background. He said he wished more people who wrote about their families would do this, and in the process enrich historical studies immensely.[101]

Contextualising the family helps to bring out two very important understandings about identity – how things changed, and also how they stay the same. For me discovering the great difference between life in medieval and early modern Great Waltham and the present day is a striking example of the former. In earlier times it was customary for people, certainly at the 'middling' levels, to take a lot of individual responsibility for themselves, their families, and their local communities. We tend to think earlier times were undemocratic and narrower than our own. But in some ways people probably had more freedom and potential to exercise responsibility over their lives and in their communities than most of us have today. In the conclusion of George Evans' book about a Suffolk village called Blaxhall he contrasts the village of the past and the village of today. The 'old' village was largely self sufficient and based on a community focused on farming. The inhabitants did not live together in chance association and were integrated by their common concerns and interests that were greater than class and status. The present day village is quite different, with far less common interest and community power. The village no longer runs itself.[102] George Evans sees the parish council as the one institution that might integrate the 'new' village. To do this '....a parish council would need to concern itself not only with its statutory powers and permissive duties, but with anything and everything that is likely to promote the welfare of the village it represents'.[103] 'In so doing it will transform itself and weld the village into something like a true community, with the full consciousness of a closely shared achievement'.[104] More will be said about these points later but the key insight is the change between the old and the new and the fact that for a real community to exist as in the past control needs to be restored to the local scene. An example of what stays the same is the continuity of family life that is discernible throughout Part 3.

Another great gain from putting the family in context is the contribution made to thinking about the 'middling sort', which by and large, the Ram family has belonged to. A fascinating picture is provided of how the family adapted to an economy in which farming became less and less dominant, whilst retaining its middling status. It reveals the characteristics and development of this social group across a very long time span, which is not extensively researched and documented. It also helps to clarify ideas about the term 'middling' in three respects. Firstly, what does middling mean? Secondly, is the modern middle class the same as the middling sort of earlier times? Thirdly, how does the notion of a middling sort affect class consciousness?

Researching the context
The task of doing this is considerable. Just for a moment think about the timescale and changes that occurred across it. Between 1300 and 1900 massive developments happened in the structure of society, politically, socially and economically, all of which impacted on the family and their local contexts. Of course, these also required researching. There are four major ones – Great Waltham, Colchester, Havering, and London, each very different from the other, and there are additionally a number of smaller rural settings. Chapter IX goes into detail about where the family lived. Dealing with all these inter-related variables has required a great deal of painstaking and original research. This is partly because very little has been written down about family members, or by them. But establishing the background context can also be difficult. For example putting together the picture of Great Waltham presented in Chapters X to XIII was very time consuming as no detailed work has been done on the village's history after medieval times. There is nothing about it in the *Victoria County History*. Four sources, additional to registrations of baptisms, marriages, and burials, have been used extensively in my contextual researches.

The most important of these has been the great volume of records, of many types, held at the Essex Record Office. For the period prior to the mid sixteenth century the official documents and village records of Great Waltham, have been examined extensively. The court rolls of Walthambury Manor have been extremely useful, which are in fact one of the best continuous series of such documents in the country. But their contribution has been patchy for several reasons – they are not equally informative for all periods, and they are sometimes not very legible. Moreover they are in Latin until the eighteenth century, except for a short period during the Commonwealth. Many people, including me, do not understand this language today, and a great deal more could have been found out about the medieval period if more transcriptions had been available. Having all of them transcribed privately would be an enormous and costly exercise. Having said this factual information can be gleaned from them relatively easily even without knowledge of Latin. One of the lucky breaks I had was that Revd Andrew Clark wrote several articles in the early twentieth century about Great Waltham based on the court rolls. There are masses of miscellaneous papers in the Essex Record Office which contain scraps of information about family members at all periods. Digging such information out requires considerable tenacity and perseverance, but sometimes unexpected things happen which bring great reward. I was once reading through a group of note books when, quite by accident, I came across an isolated paper dated 1817 which was a land agent's survey of a farm at that time run by my great great great grandfather.[105]

The second original source has been wills, which have proved a rich mine of information about property ownership, inheritance practice, social relationships, and the social status of the family. About 90 per cent of the heads of family units in the Ram family made wills which seems an extraordinarily high proportion, and the only really significant gaps are in the seventeenth century. It is particularly easy in Essex to trace inter-connections because F G Emmison collected and published in summarised form many Essex wills, some of them with support from American sources interested in Essex people who were early migrants. In these publications he made very detailed indexes which facilitate cross referencing.[106] Wills are of course legal documents and do not necessarily tell the whole truth about a person or their relational situation. But if used with care they often provide much useful information. Some wills make small gifts to a number of people who are interlinked by blood or friendship which assists establishing links between them. Sometimes separate wills each mention an individual or group of individuals and this enables useful insights about mutual relationships to be obtained. Wills also augment information partly available in other sources. Quite often added authority and authenticity is generated by the fact that they cross confirm facts and relationships documented by different people at various times and quite separately. In this way it is possible to build up quite extensive pictures of people and their relationships which otherwise would go unrecorded.

An example is a useful way of making this point more real. Nicholas Cotton (d. 1583) was an important local figure in Hornchurch in the sixteenth century. McIntosh mentions him on several occasions.[107] In his will he leaves Francis Ram and his wife small sums of money 'towards making rings to be worn in remembrance of me'. As Deputy Steward of Havering Francis Ram was bound to come into contact with Nicholas Cotton, but the will reveals that they were good friends too, because 'My loving friend' Francis Ram was made overseer of the will. Besides being an important man locally, Nicholas Cotton was probably of humble origins, and knowing that Francis was on intimate personal terms with him tells us indirectly something about the social circle of Francis. The will also reveals that Nicholas, Francis and his brother William and their wives knew each other socially, for it also mentions William Ram and Marion (d. 1602) his wife as Nicholas Cotton's 'loving friends'.[108] This information tells us something about the geographical range of the contacts for although Francis and Nicholas lived in Havering William Ram lived in Colchester. There may well also have been professional interests between the three men for all of them were working lawyers and could develop contacts that were mutually useful. The fact that the wives are mentioned suggests these relationships went beyond professional interest. So, from a few sentences in Nicholas Cotton's will we are able to glean a significant amount of information about friendships and inter-relationships of several members of the Ram family. They let us indirectly into the inner lives of people who left no direct records.

All sorts of information can be obtained indirectly from wills. For instance there is a run of nine detailed wills in the family of Robert Ram, from his own in 1576 to that of Joseph Ram (d. 1726), which includes all the main members of the family and reveals the broad fabric of social relationships and economic fortunes.[109] During the later years of the sixteenth century and through most of the seventeenth century preambles to wills often include statements about religious belief, which presumably reflects the heightened focus on religious belief during that period. Some researchers have questioned whether the views reflected in preambles are those of the writer of the will rather than the testator. This may have happened as many writers were priests when the bulk of the population was illiterate, and they continued to write wills well after the mid sixteenth century. But their involvement does not mean preambles failed to reflect testators' beliefs, especially where they were strongly held. Some preambles are so fulsome that it is difficult to believe they were not the views of the testator.[110] Marjorie McIntosh made an analysis of the types of religious preambles to Havering wills and she considered the following one to be a fairly long and Protestant offering – 'I commend my soul unto Christ Jesus, my maker and redeemer, in whom and by the merits of whose blessed passion is all my whole trust of clean remission and forgiveness of my sins'.[111] It is also possible to build up a general view of people's attitudes to religion through examining many preambles. Richard Smith in a recent study of Colchester made a detailed study of ones in the wills of office holders between 1570 and 1639 and divided them into five categories, ranging from Catholic to Calvinist. Well over half of them were firmly Protestant, with around six per cent being Calvinist.[112]

The third source has been deeds relating to property and marriage settlements, particularly from the eighteenth century onwards. These are sometimes very detailed and provide information about tenancies which covers size of holding, rent paid, and attached conditions. There are even hand written notes which augment the formal documents.

The fourth original source has been census returns. All of these from 1841, when the information contained in them became more full, have been examined with considerable care. The later ones in particular can reveal large amounts of information. The 1881 census, for example, makes it possible to find out who lived next door and in the other houses in the immediate neighbourhood.

A large number of books and published records have been used. The Essex Record Office has a good collection of university theses which relate to Essex, so they are much more accessible than would be the case if individual universities had to be visited. Reference to the books and theses consulted are made in the footnotes and a general list appears in the Bibliography.

A guide for others

This chapter has partly been included in the hope that it might inspire others to write about their own families. Quite often when I have visited county record offices, or the Family Records Centre in Bloomsbury when it existed, most of the people there have been tracing their ancestors. I sometimes wonder why they are doing this and some of them may have been inspired by television programmes. There are other reasons though because many people were visiting record offices before 'tracing your relations' was taken up by television. No doubt there are many reasons why tracing ancestors in increasingly popular. Curiosity and more leisure time when people are in their fifties and sixties may be important reasons. But there are many other things to spend leisure time on. One way of looking at this question is by asking myself, why did I do it? I have always been curious about my forebears. And for me the interest increased as I grew older. It was not simply a question of having more time available to do the searching. There is no doubt that as you get older you tend to think more about the past in your own life. I suspect that taking an interest in forebears is an extension of this development. It is probably part of becoming more mature. When you are young experience does not count for much and attention is focused on the future.

There are other questions I ask myself as I see people sitting in front of microfiche machines looking up copies of parish registers of baptisms burials and marriages. How much do they find out, and how long do they keep the interest up? Some may not find much because they get stuck, like I nearly did. Before 1837, when the national registration of births began, it is impossible to search for forebears unless a particular parish where they lived can be identified. If one is found and it is a long way from where people now live they will have to travel to view the registers, probably in the local record office, which is not possible for everyone. But if the search is successful, what do you do with the information? It can be kept in a draw and brought out occasionally to show relatives or grandchildren, or it can be researched further and flesh put on the genealogical skeleton. Then it can be written up and printed. All of this is really exciting and it is a pity more people do not do it and then present their findings to the appropriate local record office. The availability of many more family records will greatly enrich the work of social and local historians and others interested in how ordinary people have lived in the past.

SECTION 3 HOW *THE THREAD OF IDENTITY* HELPS

VIII
Explaining *The Thread*

The use of The Thread

A range of theories and ideas about identity and how it is formed have already been discussed earlier in this part of the book. The picture they present is far from clear. Later in the book the aim is to extend, reflect on and illuminate further thinking about identity, drawing on the enormous number of facts, impressions, and ideas about the Ram family collected in Part 3. *The Thread of Identity* or *'The Thread'*, for short has been created to assist this process in two ways. It is helpful as a concept because the term conveys three important insights about identity; like a telephone cable it contains many different wires, or aspects, bound together; it can also be seen as a 'rope' by which people are enabled to hold on to and make sense of life; and thirdly identity can be thought of as a thread because it is something which is passed from generation to generation in the form of cultural heritage. *The Thread* is ultimately an analytical device or tool for collating and presenting a large amount of related but so far unconnected information within a coherent framework. Through the elements built into its structure *The Thread* takes account of qualitative as well as quantitative data.

In Part 4 Identity will be explored from three perspectives. The first one is based in the search for an overall framework of society, the second outlines how identity might have appeared to individual members of the Ram family and others like them, whilst the third one explores how it might have seemed to the kind of groups they were part of. *The Thread* will be used to create two related pictures. In the first one individuals and groups are fitted into the wider framework or hierarchical structure. This picture and the model derived from it is widely used today by many social commentators, including historians, and provides the basis for nearly all our thinking about identity and how our society works. This picture is called *looking for an ordered world*. But the second one, called *looking outwards from the local community*. is most unusual. It introduces a view of identity looking out from local groups and the individuals that form them. It stands as a counterweight to the hierarchical model, which although valid because our society is without doubt shaped hierarchically, is not the only one. Only to view identity in a hierarchical way is misleading, because the exploration of identity ought to include asking a simple question – how do individual people and small groups look at reality? Do they start with the global general picture or do they look out from themselves and their local personal world?

Building The Thread's structure

It is a truism that any analytical framework needs to assist the purposes it is intended to serve, which is here to facilitate exploring and understanding the nature of human identity, individual and social. Achieving this has required drawing on three areas of enquiry outside historical studies. Two of them are effectively new disciplines.

One of them is contained within the debate there has been, and still continues, about the relative influence of inheritance and socialisation in individual and group formation. A broad outline of this debate, often called the 'nature or nurture' debate, is provided in Chapter V.[113] A sort of consensus is now emerging that both inheritance and socialisation are involved in determining human behaviour – which is perhaps an obvious common sense understanding. It requires the structure of *The Thread* to include both socially acquired and inherited elements.

The second of them concerns the part genes play in shaping human individuals, which is also outlined in Chapter V. It must be remembered that appraisal of the relative influence of environment and heredity has historically been conducted solely through external observation of people. For example in the Minnesota studies the extent that a trait was seen to be behaviourally or genetically determined was based on the degree of similarity or divergence observed in paired twin behaviour. But the unravelling of the human genome has introduced all sorts of implications which it is difficult for us to grasp at present, especially as the speed of related discoveries and ideas is so fast. Studies based on DNA sampling show how human populations have developed from the earliest times and clearly demonstrate there is transfer of a genetic element across the generations which affects behaviour directly.

So far most interest in genetic discoveries has been focused on the implications of genetic discoveries for the control of disease. But they have also been revealing how genes affect not only physical features, like the colour of hair, but also behavioural patterns, although exactly how this happens is still being unravelled.[114] Such discoveries are making it increasingly necessary to re-examine how identity is formed. A very simple example can be used to illustrate the point. It is a general characteristic of human beings that they smile when they are happy and frown when unhappy or worried. Is this sameness a sign that these phenomena are influenced more by instinct than socialisation? The unravelling of the human genome will almost certainly lead to greater importance being attached to the influence of heredity on human behaviour. It is possible now to look directly at the action of our genes on our behavioural patterns, and a new science of Evolutionary Psychology is developing which is concerned with understanding the origins of current behaviour. Its findings about the way apes lived in communal groups are particularly relevant to understanding human communities.[115] All these issues are discussed in a book by Matt Ridley called *Genome*.[116] The unravelling of the human genome will almost certainly lead to greater importance being attached to the influence of heredity on human behaviour, which is why *The Thread* takes account of genetic factors.

The third and most important influence on the structure of *The Thread* comes from psychiatry and the practice of group analytic psychotherapy, a development of one to one Freudian analysis which is applied mainly through small groups. Instead of meetings between an analyst and a single patient a small group of patients explore their problems together under the guidance of a conductor who is a trained therapist. These principles were developed by S H Foulkes from 1940 onwards in private psychiatric practice. Of greater direct interest here is that he also used the same principles in conjunction with the Maudsley Hospital to assist the more effective management of the hospital. He called this application a 'large group', which he saw as a device to facilitate self administered reflection about working processes and how to make them more mutually effective. He came to see hospitals as therapeutic large group communities. His practice was to involve everyone in them in free flowing communication which aided understanding between patients and staff, improved management and helped patient recovery. Since the early beginnings the same principles have been applied in all sorts of institutions and institutional settings.[117] S H Foulkes' large group ideas have relevance to the structure of *The Thread* because its key concepts can be applied to the study of social interaction in any large group.

Much of the subject matter of *The Thread* is connected with relating to others, often in and around groups, some small and others large. Family units are themselves social groups, and there are other kinds of groups which they interact with. In view of this the part of *The Thread* structure concerned with individual formation in groups and the role of groups is based on Group analysis principles. A special edition of *Group Analysis*, the journal of Group Analytic Psychotherapy, is particularly helpful in relating 'large group' principles to this study.[118] Its subject is '*A Group Analysis of Class, Status Groups and Inequality*', and one paper in it defines a number of factors for assessing how large human groups function.[119]

The completed structure.

The structure of *The Thread* is clearly experimental, and not supported by wide testing, which of course could be carried out by using it in other studies. It is set out in Table 1 and consists of 19 'yardsticks', or units of assessment, collated within three groups, or influences as they are called here.

Table 1. The analytical structure used in *The Thread*.

Yardsticks	Basic Definitions of the Influences	Definitions For Looking For an Ordered World	Definitions For Looking Outwards From the Local Community
1a. Economic frameworks. 1b. Demographic frameworks. 1c. Customary frameworks. 1d. Political frameworks. 1e. Legal frameworks.	Influence 1. Forces which generate change in society.	Agents of change.	Being shaped by the broader world.
2a. Freedom of choice among the middling sort. 2b. Life chance. } Arbiters 2c. Wealth. } of 2d. Influence. } choice. 2e. Power. 2f. Individual beliefs and values. 2g. Religious practice.	Influence 2. How individuals and groups consciously express themselves – their hopes, individuality and ambitions.	Individual choice in the midst of conflicting pressures.	Being shaped from within.
3a. Family influences. 3b. Citizenship. } 3c. Mirroring. } Dealing 3d. Exchange. } 3e. Interaction of mind and body. } with 3f. Management } people of diversity. } 3g. Coming together } in the group.	Influence 3. How individual and group formation occurs, either through socialisation or genetic inheritance.	Agents of individual and social cohesion.	Being shaped in and by the local community.

The yardsticks in influence 3 are based on the paper in the Group Analytic Psychotherapy journal just mentioned. The yardsticks in influences 1 and 2 have been added to these to cope with the other aspects of historical and social analysis required, and have been derived from the mass of data collected about the Ram family and its contexts. Each influence has a basic definition and two sub-definitions, one for each of the two pictures discussed earlier in this chapter – *looking for an ordered world* and *looking outwards from the local community*. The two variants are necessary because the perceived impacts of the yardsticks are different in each picture.

An explanation of the basis upon which the yardsticks have been grouped within the influences is provided at the beginning of Part 4 in chapter XIX.

PART 3

THE RAM STORY

SECTION 1   FAMILY SETTINGS

IX
The distribution and demography of the family

Of the eastern counties

Before starting to tell the family story it is important to establish an overall picture of where it lived. From at least the fourteenth century up to 1900 most of the Ram family has lived and moved around within the area shown in Figure 2, but has not been continuously present anywhere. Circumstantial evidence suggests it originated within the marked triangular area. Movement was often initiated by someone going to a particular location, usually through the acquisition of a farm or because of marriage, and once initiated a connection tended to continue for several generations, after which it died out. All the places where the family lived for a reasonably long time are marked in bold on Figure 2, which represents the family heartland. London was always the main draw away from the this area where some of them lived in the sixteenth, seventeenth, and nineteenth centuries. Descriptions of the main places where family members lived are provided at appropriate points in the story.[1]

There was a greater degree of mobility in the nineteenth century, especially in one branch which established nuclear family outposts in Halesworth in Suffolk, Norwich in Norfolk, Holbeach in Lincolnshire and in rural Cambridgeshire. They were all based on several sons of James Ram. James himself was born near Colchester but worked as a lawyer in London from 1823 to 1837, and then, from 1837 he lived in Ipswich. In 1851 he had chambers in 4, Stone Buildings, Lincoln's Inn as well as at Ipswich but from 1854 to 1870, when he died, the Law List shows him to have been exclusively in Ipswich.[2] Two of James' sons who had been born in London, James and Stephen, went to work and live in London, whilst most of those who were born after the move to Ipswich, lived in East Anglia – Willett in Halesworth, Edward in Norwich and Ralph in Holbeach and in Cambridgeshire. This distribution seems to have been wholly directed by professional opportunity.

The only place a family member is known to have lived that was remote from the area described above, was Penarth in Glamorgan. Thomas Ram (b. 1840) a son of Benjamin IV worked there as a house carpenter in 1881. At that time there was an enormous development of docks and housing, but he returned

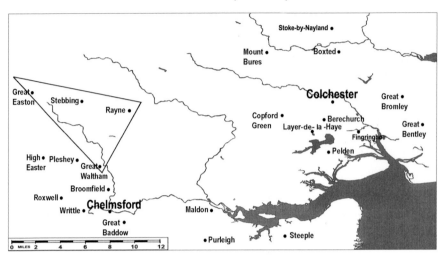

Figure 2. Ram places of residence outside London.

to London at a later date where he brought up his family. No record has been found of family members migrating abroad.

Great Waltham and Colchester have been the places with the longest continuous family associations. Connections with the first of these places had begun by the beginning of the fourteenth century and did not end until the late eighteenth and early nineteenth centuries when there was a movement away to neighbouring villages – to Roxwell, Purleigh and Steeple. Why this migration happened is not known, but it is likely to have been connected with the availability of farming opportunities. The connection with the Colchester area was continuous from the mid sixteenth century until the early nineteenth century. Some of the family lived in the town and others resided in surrounding villages whilst retaining business and social connections. At different periods three places were particularly important focus points for the Colchester branch of the family. One was Copford in the sixteenth to eighteenth centuries. Another was the area around Stoke by Nayland and Great Bromley between the seventeenth and nineteenth centuries, where a farm held by the family at Stoke by Nayland from 1622 to 1871 is still known as Rams Farm.[3] The third area is to the south of Colchester around Layer de la Hay and Berechurch, where family members lived from the late seventeenth to the early nineteenth century.

The migration to London in the nineteenth century uprooted most of the family from long established patterns of life. It almost certainly amounted to the biggest and most rapid transformation ever experienced, in which most of the family were sucked into London's web, either for a short or longer term. In 1881 41 out of 65 known family members, or 65 per cent, were there and in 1901 the proportion had risen to 72 per cent. There was considerable variation in the circumstances surrounding these moves. James Ram from Colchester, moved via his educational achievements into the upper middle classes, but for Benjamin IV's sons, from the failed farming background, there was a significant decline in status. His sons were all manual workers, and they were probably painfully aware of this downturn. It may have been made worse by the fact that the break with the past happened in a way which involved support from another branch of the family that were much wealthier and of a status way above theirs.

The detailed pattern of movements to London in the nineteenth century were so complex that further comment about them is required. Both the better off and the not so well off moved about so much that it is not possible to draw them on a map that could be got onto one page. For example James Ram (b. 1828), from the wealthier side of the family, baptised three children between 1853 and 1859 each in a different place – Charlotte in 1853 at Paddington, Jane in 1854 at Hammersmith, and Edward in 1859 at East Beckham, Kent. The last of these places was near Penge where the family settled down for a longer period. Another example from the poorer Rams is Benjamin V (b. 1839), son of Benjamin IV who went to live in Ipswich. His first five children were baptised between 1865 and 1879 in Pimlico, Acton, Little Ilford (Middlesex), New Maldon, and Barnes. Although there was a much greater degree of movement in the nineteenth century than in previous centuries, more or less all of it was within Essex, London and East Anglia, so the family remained close to its roots, even if in a looser way. In order to present some impression of where people lived Table 2 has been prepared which shows where adult males lived in 1881.

Table 2. Where adult male members of the Ram family in London lived in 1881.

Name	Where they were born	Where they lived
Relations of Benjamin Ram (d. 1864).		
William (uncle).	Great Waltham 1796.	Roxwell, near Great Waltham.
Benjamin (son).	Steeple 1839.	113, Blenheim Court, Kensington.
Thomas (son).	Steeple 1840.	Penarth, Glamorgan.
Charles Harry (son).	Steeple 1843.	2, Pump Court, St Sepulchre Parish.
Arthur (cousin).	Purleigh 1846.	36, Glenarm Road, Hackney.
Descendants of John Ram of Colchester.		
John H (grandson).	Chelsea, St Luke 1829.	10, Newland Street.
William (grandson).	Colchester 1830.	30, Brook Street, Hackney.
Arthur (gt. grandson).	St George, Middlesex 1855.	10, Newland Street.
John Henry (gt. grandson).	Pimlico 1855?	42. Marmion Rd., Battersea.
Walter (gt. grandson).	St George Middlesex 1857.	10, Newland Street.

Descendants of James Ram.		
James (son).	St Giles in the Fields 1829.	2 Waldergrave Rd, Penge.
Edward (grandson).	Hammersmith 1859.	2, Waldergrave Rd, Penge.
Stephen Adye (son).	Chelsea, St Luke 1831.	32, Oakley Sq., St Pancras.
Willett (son).	Ipswich 1839.	Soap House Hill, Halesworth.
Edward (son).	Ipswich 1843.	The Chantry Court (Theatre St). Norwich.
Ralph Adye (son).	Ipswich 1845.	Master's Lodge, H St, Holbeach.

Family demography

The Ram family has always been small and around 1800 there was a real demographic crisis. It has been possible to chart a picture of numbers and distribution of male members over time which is shown in Appendix 2. This pinpoints where individuals were born, where they lived their adult lives, and how many were alive at 25 year intervals between 1575 and 1900, by each of the main branches. Part A only includes individuals aged 21 or over but part B covers all males, grouped into under and over age 21. There is some under recording in both parts because of incompleteness of records, particularly in the earlier centuries, but the general picture is nonetheless informative.

The appendix shows clearly how movement developed outward from the original centre at Great Waltham, and then became focused on London during the nineteenth century, to be followed by some further movement out of London. Although migration in the nineteenth century was part of family life, for both the better off and poorer members, the patterns they experienced were not exactly the same. Once the farming branch moved to London, almost always with status diminished they stayed put. But quite a large proportion of the more affluent branch, usually university educated, moved back out of London in search of professional jobs, either as clergy, teachers or solicitors. This shows that the trend for professional people and graduates to migrate to jobs was certainly operating by the mid nineteenth century, and may have done so before then.

A particularly interesting feature of Appendix 2 is what it shows about patterns in the numerical size of the family. There were never more than around 20 adult males alive at any one time, and for nearly the whole period before the third quarter of the nineteenth century there were under 10. It shows just how fragile the family group is, and how easy it is for the male line to fail. The number of adult males was underpinned by a varying number of minors, in which the mean proportion of adults to minors was around 58 per cent, and at only two periods were total numbers boosted by increased numbers of young, between 1575 and 1650 and after 1800, although it was not until the second half of the nineteenth century that later growth became marked. The ups and downs of Ram family numbers mirrored general population trends quite closely. Most of the large nuclear families were produced in the sixteenth and early seventeenth centuries and from the mid eighteenth century onwards. But unlike the population at large there was no long term growth, for over the twelve or so generations between 1575 and 1900 the size of the family hardly changed. There are indications that bulges occurred in times of general prosperity, and that these sustained it for several generations. Smallness of family numbers tended to be associated with periods of general economic difficulty.

Another issue raised by Appendix 2 is the extent that branches and individual nuclear family groups became split off from others in the process of migration. The evidence indicates sub-branches of a main branch kept in contact with each other. For example when members of the Great Waltham branch moved to Purleigh and Steeple, about six miles from each other and about fifteen from Great Waltham, in the early years of the nineteenth century they kept in touch with each other. Some of the children belonging to the nuclear family who lived in Steeple were baptised in the parish church at Purleigh. In 1835 the last surviving member of the Great Waltham branch was asked to be a member of a management trust set up when one of the family members in Steeple died, so the contact between Great Waltham and Steeple continued for some time. On two occasions, first at the turn of the sixteenth and seventeenth centuries, and later in the nineteenth century, younger members of the family who moved to London seem to have lived near each other or formed social circles, sometimes around a particular London church. There was less connection between the branches, but there are some examples of inter-association. When Benjamin Ram IV, a member of the Great Waltham branch and a farmer in Steeple fell on hard times in the 1850s he went to live in Ipswich and had contact with James Ram, the surviving member of the Colchester branch who lived there. Benjamin had a daughter baptised at the church frequented by his richer relation, who would have been technically quite a distant relative. Altogether there are enough examples of continuing relationships between different groups to indicate that geographical dispersal did not lead to complete breakdown of the family as a meaningful entity.

SECTION 2   FARMING RAMS

X

Great Waltham

Great Waltham is where the documented history of the Ram family begins and one branch lived here as farmers for hundreds of years. For this reason a short pen picture about it is required as a preface to this section. The village is near the south eastern extremity of the Essex till, that is boulder clay with a chalk content that was deposited by ice during the last ice age. This is the backbone of central Essex's geology and forms its geography, which is characterised by rolling undulations through which run quite deep stream and river valleys. One of the largest rivers in the area, the River Chelmer, flows through Great Waltham. The soil is quite heavy clay and the farming has always been mixed, but with an emphasis on cereal crops.[4] In addition to farming there have been cottage industries of various kinds and when the cloth industry was significant in Essex numbers of weavers worked locally.

Today the village lies a few miles beyond the advancing sprawl of modern Chelmsford, the county town of Essex. But it is still surrounded by farms and fields. In past times the main road from Chelmsford to the north ran through the village, but it is now by-passed. Comparison between current Ordnance Survey maps and earlier plans and surveys show clearly how little the area has changed over the years. Many field boundaries even today are hundreds of years old, although there has been some enlargement by the removal of hedges. The current field pattern has a strong resemblance to that shown on a survey made of the main manor in the parish in 1645. Track and road patterns are similarly old. The other villages in the immediate neighbourhood are Pleshey and Little Waltham, both in their own parishes. Pleshey is now very small but was once a medieval castle, which, when it was in its prime dominated much of Great Waltham's agrarian life.

Because Great Waltham was the centre of the early history of the family and remained important to it up to the mid nineteenth century it is important to know something about its history. In medieval times the local community at Great Waltham gradually expanded as more of the waste was ploughed up. This process was typical of Essex, where, gradual clearing of the waste led to the formation of 'greens', areas of local pasture in a scattered pattern of settlement, that eventually developed into hamlets that came to be called End, Green, or Tye.[5]

At Great Waltham several ends grew up around the main manor in the central part of the parish because the parish is very large, and at 7,500 acres one of the largest in Essex. This development is clearly visible in Figure 3. Moving round anticlockwise from Great Waltham village there were Broad's Green and Fanner's Green, which together became known as South End, Romhey End (now Rolphey Green), North End, Fourth (now Ford) End, and Litley End. Great Waltham village sits like the hub of a wheel, but off centre and down in the south eastern corner. In between the main village and the surrounding hamlets are individual farms and their houses, many of which have very long histories.

In earlier times the central feature of the parish was Walthambury Manor, but by 1550 it had been split into seven – Walthambury, Chatham Hall, South House with Sparhawks' Fee, Langleys, Warners, Rectory, and the Hyde. Most of these appear on later maps as farms. Walthambury remained the largest by far.[6] A detailed breakdown which dates from 1563 lists the component parts of Walthambury Manor as follows. The demesne lands which comprised Manor Farm and farm steading were let to a tenant and contained, 764 acres of which 431 were arable, and 3 mills. There were three parks; Apechild of 306 acres, Littley of 21 acres and the Old Park, the size of which was not stated. There

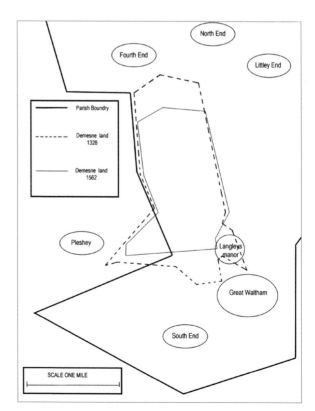

Figure 3. Diagrammatic map showing the evolution of Walthambury Manor.

were also 47 acres of wood.[7] Four major datum points are used in Figure 3 for tracking how the demesne lands became progressively smaller. The first is a survey produced by Poos for 1328, who estimated the demesne lands then amounted to 920 acres and other tenanted farmed land to 2266 acres.[8] In 1328 there must still have been a lot of waste and woodland. The second datum point is a very detailed Elizabethan survey of the whole parish in 1577. Then the traditional tenanted acreage, i.e., free and copyhold, amounted to 3092 acres. This was 800 acres larger that in 1328 and sizeable amounts of waste must have been reclaimed between the two dates to produce this result. The next datum point is a detailed survey of the demesne lands belonging to Walthambury Manor made in 1645.[9] They then amounted to 789 acres, and the shrinkage of them by about 130 acres in the northern and south eastern extremities accounts for how, at least in part, the rented acreage increased between medieval and early modern times.

The last datum point is a survey of 1805, made in anticipation of changes in the operation of the poor law. This survey was very detailed. Walthambury Manor had now become no more than a farm of 672 acres. The major landowner in the parish at that time had bought up land on a piecemeal basis during the eighteenth century which finally ended the old manor identities and functions. According to the 1805 survey the size of the parish was 6028 acres, of which 2359 were in Church and South Ends, 1932 were in Howe Street and Chatham Ends, and 1736 were in North, Ford and Rolphy Ends.[10] All these figures are probably fairly rough estimates. For instance modern sources state the parish to be significantly larger than 6000 acres, so either the boundaries of the parish have changed, or for unknown reasons a proportion of the land was left out in 1805 or the size of some holdings were understated. Nonetheless all these surveys together give a helpful picture of how Great Waltham changed over time.

Although the demesne of Walthambury Manor was a dominant presence in the village during earlier times, there were significant areas, particularly in South End, which were not part of it. These probably belonged originally to the smaller manors in the south of the parish, which lost effective administrative powers at an early date. The Ram family lands were in this area. One of the more puzzling features of Great Waltham is that the enclosed land held by small farmers existed side by side with a number of open fields that were part of the Walthambury Manor demesne. These still survived in the mid sixteenth century and constituted one of the largest open field units in Essex. References in one family will suggest parts of these fields were rented on a similar basis to other land. The northern area of the parish retained traditional land use practices the longest. An uncertain feature about the parish is the area of it that Walthambury Manor included and collected rents from. Although the sixteenth century surveys show that rents were being paid for land in all the ends it is never clear to whom.

XI
The Family Glimpsed
Through Medieval Records

Earliest references

The first known information about the Ram family in Great Waltham is to be found in two documents: the 1327 lay subsidy and an Essex manorial rental of 1328. Together they make it possible to see where the family fitted in economically and the sorts of feudal obligations that were laid upon them.[11] They also give a simple picture of the economic and social structure of local society, and provide a convenient entry into this part of the story.

Early in the fourteenth century the lay subsidy was the most usual form of royal taxation and the 1327 tax was granted to defend the kingdom from attack by the Scots. The rate was not always the same, e.g., a twentieth in 1327, whilst in 1332 it was a fifteenth on rural areas and a tenth on boroughs. Between 1307 and 1332 there were nine lay subsidies which are much more useful to historians than the later ones as they contain detailed lists of the payers in each place and the amount they paid. From 1334 a different procedure was applied, in which the tax was based on a total sum, or quota on each community, that was open to negotiation but was not to be less than the collective sum paid by individuals in 1332. This method did not produce a list of named individuals, and led to the sums collected becoming fixed, which of course meant over time the tax did not reflect the real wealth of individual communities.[12]

For the lay subsidies before 1334 two or three chief tax officers were appointed in each county or other responsible district to administer the tax. They were usually local landowners of high status. In turn they selected between four and six sub-officers in each taxation unit. These went from house to house on the appointed day valuing the relevant movable goods, recording the information, and collecting the monies due. There was some corruption in which the collectors lined their own pockets. It was because of numerous complaints in 1332 that the method of collection was changed in 1334.

The returns for each place in 1327 were simply lists of the people who paid with the amount contributed, and do not provide a complete count of all heads of families in a community, or all of the wealth of those included. The poorest people did not pay. In that year the taxable minimum was 10/- worth of goods, on which a tax of 6d was levied. In practice taxable minimums were set at higher levels than this to protect the poor, a practice which was particularly common in Essex. Certain goods were excluded in the counties, such as armour, horses and treasure, and in the towns some household goods were not taxed. In practice most household goods, food and tools were not liable, and the grain that was taxed was probably the surplus available for sale. Grain and stock were often given a conventional rather than a market valuation. The 1327 lay subsidy can provide information about some things, but not everything. In local lists it does help to identify the more prosperous individuals and their relative status in a local community. Knights and gentry often paid about 1£.

In Great Waltham 125 people contributed to the lay subsidy. At the head of the list was John de Bohun, Count of Hereford, who paid 13/6, which was rather less than many of his equivalents. The next biggest contributor paid 6/-, and then there were three who paid 5/-. After that 5 people paid between 2/- and 5/-. A much larger number of 55 paid between 1/- and 2/-. The rest, in total 60, paid less than l/-. So it seems that the pattern of contribution at Great Waltham was fairly flat, but clearly there was the one at the top, a few wealthier people and then two large groups, the largest of which was the bottom group.

Two members of the Ram family were tax payers. John le Ram paid 1sh. and 5d and was in the middle of the next but bottom group. Thomas (mid 14C), in the bottom group, paid 7½d. Both made relatively small payments but they were clearly not among the poorer members of the community. At that time the Rams in Great Waltham were most likely middling size farmers, who, like everyone else on the manor, worked within the framework of the medieval system. The lay subsidy throws light not only on the Ram status in Great Waltham but also its presence elsewhere. The other Essex references to people with the same name, almost certainly related, are two in Great Easton, and one in Stebbing. In Great Easton Alice Ram (mid 14C) paid 10¼d and William Ram (mid 14C) paid 8¼d. In Stebbing Richard Ram (mid 14C) was one of the biggest payers at 4/-. These two places are both within ten miles of Great Waltham.

What proportion of the Great Waltham population did the 125 payers make up? Most of them would have been the heads of family units, but how many more families were there who did not pay? In order to assess this it is necessary to have an idea of the parish's population at that time, which is not known accurately. Poos calculated the number of males aged 12 or over, who were connected with Walthambury Manor, to be around 220 for the period 1327-1342[13] and at least a quarter, or 55, of these would have been too young to pay tax. On this basis the 125 contributors to the tax of 1327 represented nearly three quarters of all the families, which means about a quarter of them did not pay. But this calculation may not be entirely accurate, because the degree to which Walthambury Manor boundaries coincided with those of Great Waltham parish, on which the lay subsidy was almost certainly based, is unclear. Poos says there were 300 tenants in Great Waltham in 1328, by reference to the rental for that year, but exactly how this calculation was made is not clear. [14] If it is assumed the 125 contributors in the tax return came from the whole of Great Waltham, not just Walthambury Manor, and that Poos was accurate in his assessment of the total number of tenants, then the contributors to the lay subsidy made up no more than 40 per cent of all the families, in which case many more people than a quarter did not pay.

The manorial rental is a listing of tenants on many manors in the county of Essex that was made a year later. It is a thick parchment scroll in the British Library, written on both sides, with the information about Great Waltham appearing on the last piece of parchment of the reverse side, which meant looking through the whole document to find it! Deciphering the contents of the rental is complicated by the fact that duties are not listed separately for each individual but are identified by back reference to the first person to do them. Its contents are very different to those of the lay subsidy, certainly as far as Great Waltham is concerned. For one thing only the customary tenants of Walthambury Manor are included, twenty one in all, with their size of holding, and for another the main information contained in it is about the manorial services they were responsible for providing. There is no reference to the rents they paid.

The detail about John Ram is shown in part of figure 4 and reads as follows. 'John ate Cherche; John le Ram; Andrew le Smyth; John ate Helle[?] de Lythhey[?]; Walter Lurk[?]. Each of them holds and does the same as the aforesaid R[????] ate Cromhe[?]', who 'holds one acre of land and does [???] similarly [??? section too faint to read but possibly 'as Agnes Benyt']. Everyone included is required to help with farming on the manor in various ways, like mowing or lifting the hay, but there are also additional duties which in John le Ram's case are possibly the same as those of Agnes Benyt, namely to 'carry the letters of the lord to Chelmsford or Donmawe (Dunmow) for one work or to London or Walden or otherwise at whatever distance for two works of her allocation, and shall provide [???] to help the brewing just as the aforesaid[?] Richard [???] at Cromhe[?]'. [15]

Who were the 'customary tenants'? The nature of landholding and ownership practices in the later middle ages will shortly be discussed, but there were two main differentiations: between freeholders, who held their land by written warrant but were still rent paying tenants, and customary tenants whose right was not written down. The lay subsidy does not say which of the 125 contributors were freeholders and who were customary tenants. The number

Figure 4. Essex manorial rental, 1328.

of customary tenants is quite small compared with the contributors to the lay subsidy, and only about 60 per cent of them contributed to it at all – small amounts between 21d and 6d. Such a big difference in numbers is puzzling, but there might be several reasons. People who held their land freehold were not included in the lay subsidy, some people may have died, but probably not many in the space of a year, and the rental may be incomplete.

Together the two documents provide different and complementary information about the nature of the community Great Waltham was in 1327 and 1328, and how the Ram family fitted into it. The lay subsidy contains a sort of social pecking order and a picture of how people were distributed between the levels it contained. The manorial rental says nothing about these matters but sets out the community duties that customary tenants still contributed within the medieval system, which would have applied equally to freehold tenants.

How the medieval system worked locally

We tend to have a very basic and stereotyped understanding of how things functioned in medieval times. At school most of us learned about how the medieval manor worked, about the open field system, and about lords and peasants. Such a picture distorts reality as it would have existed for the Rams, for no system works as simply as all that. The only personal records about members of the family during this period are references to them in legal and formal documents, from which it is difficult to decipher precise meaning. This can only be understood against the background of the medieval system actually worked in Great Waltham. In reality there was more flexibility and elements that we would recognise as modern than might be imagined. Although the worlds of then and now are very different they are clearly linked by the fact that people have not changed very much underneath. People lived their own individual lives then as they do now.

One quite basic reality to understand is that by the fourteenth century the open field system did not apply widely in Essex, and may never have been used in some parts. Although open fields existed, particularly in the North West of the county. There were one or two in Great Waltham, but they were a relatively fringe feature. Around 1400 in the open fields at Great Waltham, as elsewhere, the manorial tenants held a medley of strips on which to grow their grain, or to make hay in the fields kept as meadow. Most of these scattered holdings were very small, but each villager could possess several. More typically landholdings in Great Waltham, as in Essex as a whole, were in the form of small fields, or crofts, held by individual tenants, a pattern which resulted from Essex being among those areas of the country which had an evolved landscape, that is where enclosure originated very early and happened gradually over time in piecemeal ways. In some areas of Essex many of the basic field patterns are of Roman or even pre Roman origin. In early Anglo Saxon times great estates were established, but by the late Saxon period these had become broken down into smaller manors through the passage of time, and are those recorded in Domesday Book. Information from that record suggests that around 30 per cent of the land was waste, and 20 per cent woodland, so only about half of it was cultivated.[16]

In the expansion of population which followed the Norman conquest more and more of the Essex waste was ploughed up to provide the food required. During the Middle Ages population grew sufficiently in Great Waltham for each of the main hamlets, or ends, to have their own constables, and in later years there was also separate poor law provision. South End was probably the earliest area to be settled. It was the largest end and easily the most populous part of the parish. In 1577 there were fifty individual landholdings in South End, and the next largest was Litley End with 33 holdings. All the Ram family lived in South End.

Local life had a momentum of its own within the medieval manor system. Transfer of individual fields occurred between tenants and disputes about hedging and other matters concerning these fields were not uncommon.[17] The strips in the open fields were similarly transferred from one villager to another by agreement.[18] There was considerable wrangling and litigation over the terms on which strips and fields were held between tenant and lord and tenant and tenant.[19] There is not a lot of evidence about local cultivation practice but what there is suggests enclosed tenements in Essex were managed quite flexibly. '...individual tenants could vary crop rotations and convert land from arable to pastoral use and back again, especially in the fifteenth century when land use became more mixed'.[20] Poos discusses a one off example in Great Waltham of stocking and cropping practice in 1369, where a tenant had 40 acres of wheat, 38 acres of spring grain, ten quarters of seed wheat, ten quarters of seed oats, and some animals – two horses, one bull, six cows, 20 ewes and a ram – with a plough. He comments that this example is typical of general practice in this part of Essex.[21] Essex, and particularly central Essex, was a complex countryside in the later Middle Ages, which had a high density of people on the land, and was also market oriented and locally industrialised.[22]

Revd Andrew Clark studied the court rolls of Walthambury Manor around 1904 and found that a number of 'old holdings' could be identified in the mass of splitting up that was going on towards the end of the fourteenth century. These holdings were called virgates or 'yerds' or 'yards' and with such a holding came responsibility to contribute two oxen to the common plough of eight oxen. Those with a half yard contributed one ox, but Clark does not make clear whether the original virgates were in the form of a number of strips or individual fields.[23] He thought a virgate or yerd or yard was 30 acres, but there is some uncertainty about this, and it probably varied from place to place. In Great Waltham at the time of the 1577 survey a yard was definitely 50 acres. This has been established by cross comparing rents charged per acre and per yard portion in that survey.[24] Andrew Clark also made a list of such units which existed around 1400. Known virgates included: Adgore's, Alizandre's yerd, Jacob's, Palmer's yerd, Henry Walle's, and one ¾ yard was called Levegor's. There were numerous half yards: John Andrew's, Bertramme's (which seems to have originally been Bartholomew Ramme's), John Blecche's, Sawyne Blecche's, Richard Eve's, Hamund's, Horsnayll's, Sawyn Kyng's, Lefchild's half-yerd, Oldfield's, Ryches's, Shergote's in South -end, Trewe's (or Truwe's) half-yerd, and Waryne's. Equally common were quarter yards: Alice Cavell's, John Herrye's, Outgates, Walther de Oxenbregge's, Ramme's, Thomas Ramme's, Rybode's Sawkyne's, Sawyer's, and Wrongy's. The frequent occurrence of Christian names in these divisions of the yard lands suggests partition of the original copyhold between (say) two brothers.[25] The origin of these land units and related names probably went back several hundred years.

It is impossible to make sense of village community life in medieval and early modern times without some understanding of contemporary land holding and ownership practice. In the later middle ages all cultivated land was split between freehold, copyhold and demesne. The only exceptions to this pattern was land held as a Knight's Fee, which had originally supported a Knight, and therefore had military connections, but by Elizabethan times the original meaning had mostly been lost. The fee was often very little. Only two aspects of it remained of much importance – the 'relief' and the right of wardship and marriage. The relief was a fine paid on admission to lands, and was also common to freehold and copyhold types of landholding. The Knight's fee form of landholding was abolished in 1660.[26] In 1421 there were four holdings of this kind in Great Waltham. They almost certainly represent the four subordinate manors that were separated out from Walthambury Manor- Warners (Aslyn's) which comprised 1½ virgates, yerds, or yards, Langley's (Marescall's) which was half a virgate plus a mill, the Hyde of three virgates, and South House that totalled five virgates. As time went by this type of holding was hardly distinguished from freehold, which was not quite the same as we understand it. Although the holder's title was 'held freely' by written deed and inalienable, freeholders still paid rent to the Lord of the Manor and fulfilled some medieval manorial duties.

The manorial system gradually changed and modernised in the fourteenth and fifteenth centuries and as this happened villein, or non freehold, tenure gave way to copyhold. The following information is based on A W B Simpson's book on the history of land law.[27] By the late fifteenth century the crown was supporting copyhold title in common law, but it was probably not until the late sixteenth century that such recognition was fully established, when the copyholder was able to lease lands without the lord's licence. Actual practice was governed by custom in different manors. Copyholders were never subjected to a uniform system of land law, but the tendency was towards uniformity. The distinction between copyhold and freehold title became progressively lost from the sixteenth century onwards, and there was a growing tendency to call both types 'customary' holdings. The only disadvantage the copyhold might have was connected with the possible payment of a fine on death or surrender. In some places landowners increased these to the extent that traditional holders were excluded, which opened the way to leasing land and charging commercial rents. This practice was very variable.

Copyhold land was conveyed in a special way, in which land was held 'by copy of the court roll' – the copy being the holder's title deed. When a change of title occurred the copyholder surrendered his lands into the lands of his lord, who then admitted the grantee. The transaction was recorded in the manor court roll by the steward of the manor. Originally this happened in public with all the copyholders present, but such practice gradually became obsolete and was formally abolished in 1841. There was probably very little attempt by lords to refuse recognition of proposed transfers of copyhold titles, and by the eighteenth century the law courts began to allow writs to be brought to compel a lord to comply. The court roll became a sort of register to titles of copyhold land, for since all transactions were recorded upon the roll, it provided conclusive evidence of a copyholder's rights. Copyhold itself was abolished in 1925. In practice the copyholder became free of manorial interference but the legal framework was still that of the manorial system.

The medieval world was governed very locally, and the following remarks about how this happened in Great Waltham are drawn mainly from three sources; Poos, three articles which Revd Andrew Clark wrote about Great Waltham in 1904 and a more general background book called *Medieval Society and the Manor Court* .[28] Because Essex was much sub-infudated before 1300, local lords were common. Land ownership in medieval Great Waltham was dominated first by the de Mandeville family, then by the de Bohuns who held enormous estates in Essex, including Walthambury Manor and the nearby Pleshey Castle, and finally by one of Edward III's youngest sons, Thomas Woodstock, Duke of Gloucester. These families were usually non resident. By around 1400 the demesne land at Walthambury Manor was let and the manor house had fallen into decay. Eventually Walthambury Manor reverted to the crown during the fifteenth century.[29] The actual workers of the land were mainly tenants of a second rentier layer, who were also mostly non resident, or of the crown.

The frequent absence of landowners and the main sub lessors encouraged local autonomy. The only professional worker who had any influence was the owner's steward who was usually a lawyer and almost certainly non resident, so the village or 'vill' (more properly translated as town) was run mostly by the local people who were elected from those who were resident. They oversaw the regulation of the fields, collected lump sums paid to the lord and others, acted as collective tenants, e.g., in the preservation of a piece of pasture for common use, maintained law and order, and reinforced prevailing norms and values through the local manor court and its jury, which was chaired by the steward. In these processes some voices counted more than others, particularly the men who filled the positions of reeve, juror, churchwarden and constable. They were not a clique, but there was an element of oligarchy in their selection. Sons followed fathers as office holders, and the wealthier tenants tended to be prominent among the office holders. But this aspect should not be exaggerated because most of the villagers held relatively small amounts of land which encouraged the sharing out of manorial roles, and all of them had to live together. But neither should the sense of community that existed be idealised. The court rolls reveal there were conflicts about property, personal disagreements, social issues, and other matters. It is difficult for us across the passage of time to understand exactly how the village community worked. One thing is likely – that the villagers overall sought to run the village for their own benefit.[30]

The customary manor court, or court baron as it is sometimes described, dispensed a wide range of business, administrative and judicial. It met at Pleshey Castle during the high middle ages and afterwards at Walthambury Manor. It was managed by the steward of the manor. All the other officials were local residents who completed their tasks mostly on a voluntary basis. The Beadle, who had powers of distraint and collected dues and quit rents, was paid fees for these tasks but they were quite inadequate. People could get out of being beadle for a payment of 20/-. The records of the manor court at Walthambury, which begin in the second half of the thirteenth century, contain one of the best set of manorial records in the country. Such documentation in the form of parchment rolls grew rapidly more common in the fourteenth century.

All tenants were bound to attend the court personally, or had to get permission on payment of a fine to be excused. There was an obligation to serve on the jury (The homage). In the later middle ages this body always comprised twelve people, but the names of those who served on the jury at Great Waltham do not seem to have been recorded. They often had to make out of court enquires to settle matters brought to the court, and deal with administrative issues in the manor. There were also many jury sessions each year to decide claims made by tenants, and oversee the normal upholding of the court's powers, which included transfers of lands and sub leases. The jury also dealt with road maintenance. The legal jurisdiction of the court baron covered food and leather standards, but by 1400 many of the original purposes of these controls had become meaningless. They continued as a sort of tax. Great Waltham was divided into three districts and each had its set of officials, i.e., constable and two ale tasters. Each district had five 'common brewers'.

Another important representative group in the manor court was derived from the Frankpledge tie, which dated from Anglo Saxon times and knit together the bulk of the male population (the only exceptions were some freeholders and men who were servants of a great household). All males between twelve and sixty were grouped into sets of ten, with the original purpose of being corporately responsible for individual wrongs done in the group, but by late Plantagenet times the chief function was to ensure the mass of the people took an oath of allegiance to the king, which each male did when he was twelve. In each ten or 'tithing' the lord nominated a spokesman, who were collectively known as 'capitales plegii', or head men. In later years they were elected. Sometimes the court roll listed the names of the men chosen at roughly annual intervals. Poos made a detailed review of these records.[31] At Walthambury Manor there were usually about thirty head men. Their chief duty was attendance at the court and its business, and collectively they formed a jury which oversaw the maintenance of law and order. This dealt with breaches of the peace brought before it by individual head men. Most law breaking was dealt with locally and only a few serious cases were sent to the assize court. Manor court punishments were very mild compared with those handed out by the higher courts. No one was ever imprisoned.[32] Strictly speaking this aspect of the manor court, sometimes called the court leet, was quite separate from the customary manor court which dealt with administrative matters. It was really part of the hundred court but had become connected with the manor court for convenience. Poos argues that by the fourteenth century '…it had come to represent a shared financial obligation on the part of the local community toward whatever seigniorial organ possessed the right of holding the leet'.[33] In all probability the two aspects of the manor court became merged in the later middle ages.

The lay subsidy of 1523-1526

This particular lay subsidy is reckoned to be a major source of information about the distribution of wealth because of its effort to include all the taxable wealth of the country. As with the lay subsidy of 1327 individual people can be ranked in economic terms relative to others. Because of the criteria used it was virtually a poll tax on males/people over the age of sixteen. It taxed individuals in one of three ways, depending on which one would produce the greatest amount. These were land to the annual value of £1 or more, the capital value of goods above £2, excluding standing corn and clothes, and wages of more than £1 a year for those over sixteen.

This sounds a fairly simple formula, but it was complicated by the way the tax was levied. The subsidy was granted for four years, and for the first two years land was assessed at 12d in the £, and moveable goods at 12d in the £ where the value of goods was greater than £20, and at 6d in the £ between £2 and £20. Wages over £1 were to be assessed at 6d, although it was often 4d in practice. But after that only the well off were taxed and the rates of tax were different in each year. In year three only land worth more than £50 was taxed – at 12d in the £, and in year four only moveable goods worth more than £50 were taxed, at 12d in the £. The changes in levels of tax and the fact that payments were collected by locally appointed tax officers opened up the possibility of confusion and avoidance. A four year exercise of this kind in the early years of the sixteenth century must have been very difficult to organise and sustain, and in several areas of the country guidelines had to be reissued and corrected because of confusion. It is certain the tax was not applied uniformly all over the country.[34]

At Great Waltham no more than three collections appear to have been made, and in only one of them, the first one that was probably made in 1523, are the actual payments clearly relatable to the levied tax rates.[35] In their book on Terling Keith Wrightson and David Levine have applied four socio-economic categories to the returns for that village and I have attempted to relate them to the Great Waltham information.[36] The results are contained in Table 3. Although the bulk of people in both parishes fall into categories II and III, the relative weights are different. Category II is less dominant at Great Waltham.

Table 3. Lay Subsidy 1523-6. Great Waltham and Terling socio-economic analysis.

Category and tax criteria.	Social position.	Great Waltham taxpayers.		Terling taxpayers.	
		No.	%.	No.	%.
I £10-54 land or goods.	Gentry/ very large farmer.	4	3.4	9	11.8
II £2-8 land or goods.	Yeoman/big husbandman/ craftsman.	39	33.0	28	36.8
III £2 goods.	Husbandman/ craftsman.	46	39.0	18	23.7
IV Under £2 land or earnings.	Labourers/cottagers.	29	24.6	21	27.6
Totals.		118	100.0	76	99.9

There are also some problems about how well the Terling categories fit Great Waltham. Firstly, significantly more people at Great Waltham are taxed on goods of under £2, and although they have all been allocated to category III it is possible some of them should really be in IV, which would make the overall social shape of the two places more alike. Secondly, the quantity of people in category I at Great Waltham is under half the number at Terling, even though it was a considerably bigger parish, and this is surprising. It is possible these differences are due to avoidance at Great Waltham for the returns give the distinct impression that all the payments, other than the lowest are lower than they should be. This suspicion is heightened by the picture obtained from the 1577 survey which suggests that there were a number of quite wealthy families in the parish.

Notwithstanding the difficulties associated with using the lay subsidy data it confirms that the Ram family almost certainly belonged to the developing yeoman class. Their position is not unlike that revealed in the lay subsidy of 1327, and it may even have improved somewhat. In the sixteenth century the highest payer from the Ram family was Thomas Ram (early 16C), Senior who paid £5.2.6 and the lowest amount was paid by his son Thomas (early 16C) at 20sh. 6d. All of the family except Thomas Junior contributed amounts that put them in level II, defined by Wrightson and Levine as 'Yeoman/big husbandman/craftsman'.

Power and status in the community I
The fact that the medieval land owners and their principal sub tenants were mostly absentee, and that Walthambury Manor had reverted to the crown in the fifteenth century, has been discussed already. As a result no great lord dominated local life in Great Waltham, so village and parish affairs were run by the people who lived there, probably under the leadership of the middling sort,

including members of the Ram family. There was no change to this situation
in the Tudor years, for although Richard Rich a government lawyer who later
became Earl of Essex, bought Walthambury Manor around 1536 and held
his first court there in 1539, there is no evidence from parish documents that
he was active in local life. Although he lived near Great Waltham at Chatham
Hall his interests were more concerned with national affairs and the buying
up of very large amounts of land in Essex as it came onto the open market
with the closure of the monasteries.

The families that ran Great Waltham during the late medieval and early
modern period were in fact local people. The most prominent of them was
the Everarde family that had yeoman origins, and gradually became of gentry
status. Their story really belongs to a later time but like many yeoman farmers
their roots went back into the late medieval period. The Everardes probably
came to Great Waltham from Mashbury, a village about two miles from Great
Waltham in 1515, when Thomas Everarde married Joan the daughter and co-
heir of John Cornish who owned the small manor of Langleys. This was one
of the manors that became detached from Walthambury Manor during the
Middle Ages. Thomas Everarde acquired half the manor in 1515, whilst the
other half came to Richard, his son, in 1529.[37] This manor, with around thirty
acres, gave the family a small freeholding which they gradually built up to a
much larger rented holding during the sixteenth century.

It is clear from an analysis of all the names which appeared in the list of head
men for the years 1509, 1510, and 1511, just before the Everardes came, that
a group of families were important in running Great Waltham. In 1509 there
was a total of 49 head men, in 1510 there were 39 and in 1511 there were 36,
so on average there were 41. Even though some names are illegible fourteen
family names definitely appear two or more times during these three years,
which suggests they were among the more influential and weighty names in the
parish. At least seven of these fourteen families were still present in 1577 with
most of them being among the larger tenant land holders: the Sorrel family
were the second largest with 270 acres, the Barnarde family was the third
biggest with 138, and then the Childe, Ellis and Ram families had somewhat
less with 86, 67, and 53 respectively, although the Pond and Goodeve families
both had small holdings. Six family names, Pond, Ellis, Ram, Coffin, Child,
and Barnard appear for all three years from 1509-11.

This information raises an important question. What proportion of the total
population did the head men and the leading group within them make up?
Andrew Clark attempts to make an estimate of adult male population at the
turn of the fifteenth century by reference to the common fine of a penny each
that was paid to the lord at the beginning of each annual session of the manor

court. He believes this was looked upon as purchasing immunity from all petty offences committed during the past year, and that its total, usually about 11/-, represented roughly the count of adult men in the parish. On this basis the lowest number was 104 in 1397, and highest was 145 in 1401. Andrew Clark comments that these numbers are far lower than would be expected if each tything or head man really spoke for ten others as they supposedly did. It is possible the numbers of head men remained constant as overall population declined in the fourteenth century.[38] Poos' findings are that the number of tenants fell at Great Waltham during the fourteenth century, slowly at first and then to 104 in 1351, just after the Black death.[39] In a later dissertation Poos lists the tything penny data from 1265 until 1483, which more or less agrees with that presented above.[40] Two of the Great Waltham returns for the lay subsidy of 1523-26 appear to come close to including the whole adult male population with totals of 118 and 131 which are also not very far away from Andrew Clark's figures for the years around 1400 or those of Poos. So, if the average adult male population is reckoned to be 125 the forty or so 'tything' men in the period 1509-11 probably represented about 40 per cent of them, whilst the smaller group of fourteen names which appeared regularly just over 11 per cent. This suggests that over one third of the population were involved in local leadership but that a smaller proportion may have been more dominant.

An issue of importance about the tything men is how the people in this leading group came to be part of it. The surveys of Great Waltham in Tudor and Stuart times make it possible to see how land holding and participation in local affairs correlated with the earlier period.[41] Although about half of the smaller leading group were large landholders with over 100 acres, the other half held considerably less than some individuals who did not appear in the lists of leading people at all, with two of them having very small holdings. This information makes it likely that the leading group was not dominated by the most economically powerful, and challenges the idea that power and influence resided entirely within a high status group. The size of family presence may have been another factor which boosted local standing. Some large landholders who were not in the lists of tything men were the sole representatives of their family, whereas the Everardes, Barnardes and Sorrels, had seven, eleven, and seven nuclear families in the village. Some landholders were non resident, which obviously limited their influence. A factor that strengthened potential for influence was almost certainly long family residence, for most of the families who were frequently represented in the list of tything men were of this type. It was probably inevitable that long presence, combined with a fair degree of competence, helped to sustain leadership positions. This still happens today after all.

Some of the posts held by local people had considerable responsibility and influence, particularly that of Constable. Mildred Campbell says the Constable's job was an important, and onerous office. Holders were elected by the manor court in the middle ages but other arrangements had to be made when these ceased to meet. People of substance were sought, often from among yeomen, but not exclusively so.[42] Because of the demands on him, and the importance of his office in village society, each constable was probably chosen from a small group of better off tenants. He was therefore nearly always a chief pledge, or tything man.[43] Campbell also quotes John Seldon's words – 'The parish makes the Constable, and when the Constable is made, he governes the parish'.[44] The Constable was answerable to the manor court and to the magistrates. There was a lot of overlap with the church wardens. The Constable had a number of tasks, including arresting law breakers, keeping the parish clear of vagrants, searching for men wanted on bastardy orders, escorting paupers being removed, finding billets for soldiers, and conducting ballots for calling out the militia. It was an unpaid and unpopular job. Constables may often have not been hard on fellow parishioners, but they were the only means magistrates could rely on for enforcing the law in a parish.[45] John Ram(me) (late 14 C), was Constable in 1395 for South End when the post holders were elected by the court jury. It will be seen that the Ram family members were often Constables in the seventeenth century, and this probably represented the carrying on of a long standing tradition. It is highly likely that members of the family were Constable more than once during this period but the records have not survived to show this.

There is, however, some uncertainty about the sort of people who filled the Constable's post and what it entailed. The status of those selected was probably higher in the middle ages than later, because the authority of the job was gradually emasculated by the development of new administrative practice from the seventeenth century onwards. Bryan Keith-Lucas in his book on *The Unreformed Local Government System* has this to say.

> Of the (village) officers the oldest and traditionally the senior was the Constable. Dating from before the Conquest,…he had a general responsibility for the good government of the village, accountable to the chief or high constable of the hundred and bound to answer to his charge at the Sheriff's Tourn. The Constable was appointed by the Crown and was not a servant of the parish. As the court leets died out the post came to be appointed by the magistrates on the nomination of the vestry, or sometimes of the outgoing constable.[46]

A picture of the Ram family in medieval times
Between the first documented presence of the Ram family in Great Waltham in 1327 and 1328 and the lay subsidy of 1523-26 there are twenty five recorded

references to the family being in or near Great Waltham. These are listed in Table 4 and they provide no more than tantalising glimpses of the family. The number and regularity of the references makes it almost certain that it was resident in and around Great Waltham from at least 1327 onwards. Sometimes the items concerned are quite simple. In 1525 there was a grant of two acres in Thorncroft to John Ram (early 16C), but others are much more complicated and involve a number of people. A good example is one from 1511 which is recorded in the *Essex Feet of Fines* and appears in full in Table 4. A 'fine' was an amicable agreement, real or fictitious, made between parties with the consent of judges, and enrolled in the court concerned. The earliest examples date from the twelfth century. Fines probably originated in actual suits for recovering possession of lands and other heriditaments, but the practice gradually developed of devising fictional equivalents to register legal entitlement. It would appear in this case that there was a transfer of a sizeable block of land from William Odyern and his wife to the plaintiffs who were acting as a consortium. Was this a late medieval property deal, or was it a transfer between significant individuals and the bulk of the plaintiffs are simply witnesses? Whatever the case John Ramme was significant enough to be a plaintiff along with people like William Sewall, Richard Barnard and John Wyseman who were major land holders in the parish. A number of the references suggest the Ram family were prosperous enough to be actively involved in property and land dealing. Just occasionally there are personal glimpses of individual people, as when the court roll records in around 1400 that Valentine Ramme (early 15C) cut willows and maple to the value of 2d and was fined 4d.[47]

Only from the mid sixteenth century does joined up information about Ram family life become available as the result of two major developments. The registers of baptisms marriages and burials began in 1566, and from around the same time it became standard practice among senior male members of the family to leave wills.[48] The earliest known was made by Geoffrey Ram (d. 1530) who lived at High Easter, about five miles from Great Waltham, and held land there and in Great Waltham. His will presents a picture of family life in which the nuclear family group is of central importance. This feature is entirely consistent with that documented many times in the next chapter, and is present throughout the family story.

Some appraisal of the family's economic status is possible. Most of the principal family members were farmers, although how much land they had is unclear. Some of them must have held more than others and the amounts probably varied from generation to generation. According to Andrew Clark's list they held half and quarter yards, which would have placed them among the larger farmers. They held both freehold and copyhold titles. The principal family members probably held between thirty and fifty acres, assuming a 'yerd' was 50 acres. Moreover, in 1563 Sabyan Ram (mid 16C), held a freehold half yard, and in 1577 Agnes Ram (d. 1582), widow of Robert, held a half yard jointly with her son Richard (d. 1611), which placed them among what Felix Hull identifies as a high status group of copyhold and freehold tenants known as 'yardland', 'half yardland', and 'quarter yardland' tenants, who early in the middle ages were required to contribute oxen to the common plough. By the mid sixteenth century having this kind of holding had come to be a status symbol, but responsibilities were also involved. For example in Great Waltham the post of Beadle was filled from among yardland tenants.[53]

Table 4. Public events in the Ram family at Great Waltham, 1327-1529.

1327	John Ram pays lay subsidy in Great Waltham.
1327	Thomas Ram pays lay subsidy in Great Waltham.
1373	John le Ram had lands in Great Waltham.
1381	John Ram paid poll tax in Great Waltham.
1398	Grant of lands from John Ram plus others to Sir John Stonhache in Great Waltham.
Circa 1400	Existence of Bertramme's ½ yard and two ¼ yards – Ramme's and Thomas Ramme's
Circa 1400	Valentine Ramme cut willows and Maple to the value of 2d and was fined 4d.
1408	Valentine Ram, John Ramme and Thomas Ram in Great Waltham.
1413	Further grants of land involving John Ram.
1417	Demise from ...... Including John Ram of South End.
1421	Demise from John Ram senior now dead.
1422	Richard Ram of Waltham, Fuller.
1432	Richard Ram of Waltham, Fuller.
1433	John Ram a witness to a grant in Great Waltham.
1441	John Ram a witness to a grant in Great Waltham.
1442	John Ram a witness to a grant in Great Waltham.
1450	Pardon concerning Cade rebellion for people in Great Waltham. Includes John Ram and William Ram.
1457	Lease from John Hall of Pleshey, John Alfrith, Jun., and Thomas Ram of Great Waltham to William Skynner of Chelmsford, Thomas Aleyne of Pleshey and Roger Bright of the same tenement.[49]
1472	Lease from Margaret Everard, relict of John Skinner, late of Pleshey, John Alfrith, and John Clerk to John Cowper (alias Driver) of Great Waltham, John Glascok, Sen., William Ram and others of the same tenement.[50]
1473	Grant of 3 tenements in East Street Colchester – Thomas Ram one of several grantors.
1492	Thomas Ram, senior, witness to a demise in Great Waltham.
1495	Grant from William Ramme senior of Great Waltham to ....

1511	Feet of Fine No. 45. 1511 Trin and Mich. John Josselyne, esquire, John Wode, William Pavyer, William Sewall, Thomas Fydge, Ralph Josselyn, William Clerk, Thomas Skott, Richard Barnard, John Wyseman and John Ramme pl (plaintiffs). William Odyern and Isabel his wife def. (deforciant). I messuage, 160 acres of land and 6 acres of meadow in magna Waltham. Def. quitclaimed to pl. and the heirs of John Josselyn. Cons £100.[51]
1512	Thomas Ram a witness to a grant in Great Waltham.
1521	Demise from John Henkyn plus others to Geoffrey Ram (High Easter) and Robert Ram. (Great Waltham) and others of Fullers plus five crofts.
1523-1526	The Lay Subsidy. The following family members were tax payers in Great Waltham. In 1523? Thomas Ram paid £5 2.6 on goods, Thomas Ram at 'Chylldes', who from other lists in this Lay subsidy appears to be the son of the first Thomas, paid 20sh. and 6d. on goods, William Ram paid £4.2.0 on goods, John Ram paid £3.1.6 on goods and Geoffrey Ram paid the same. In 1524 Geoffrey Ram does not appear but John Ramme pays £8.1.6, presumably on goods but that is not made clear, Thomas senior pays £7.1.2, Thomas Junior pays £5.0.10 and Robert Ramme, who was not in the other list, pays £8.1.6.
1530	Feet of fine No. 16. Richard Glascok, William Pynchon, Thomas Everard, Thomas Glascok, and John Ram pl. John Sewall def. A moity of the manor of Chyknale Trenchefoyle, a moity of 200 acres of land, 20 acres of meadow, 160 acres of pasture, 20 acres of wood, and 60s rent in Chyknale Trenchefoyle, Chyknale St James, Mashhbury, magna Waltham, and Bromfield, and a moity of the of the advowson of the church of Chyknale Trenchefoyle. Def. quitclaimed to pl. and the heirs of Richard. Cons. £160.[52]
1537	William Ram of Felsted owns property at Great Waltham called Marshalls.
1541	Grant from Robert Ramme etc, of Great Waltham of Fullers plus 5 crofts to Richard Everarde.

There are only two other occupational references, one to Richard Ram (early 15C) as a fuller. By the end of the fourteenth century there were certainly two or more fulling mills in Great Waltham as they are mentioned in the manorial rolls between 1300 and 1480.[54] Fulling was part of the finishing process related to cloth making. Family members also held tenements and cottages, which usually had an amount of land with them. The other is to John Ram (early 16C) as a butcher.

In her book *'The English Yeoman under Elizabeth and the Early Stuarts'* Mildred Campbell has a section about the medieval origins of the middling social rank in rural areas. She defines the yeoman in the following terms. 'They were a substantial rural middle class whose chief concern was with the land and agricultural interests ... Whether they were upper or lower depended on the character of the place where they lived, their own relative wealth and numbers there, and the number and quality of other residents'.[55] She suggests that in arable areas they held mainly between 25 and 200 acres, and that the yeoman was clearly to be identified with larger farmers who were developing farming on a commercial basis.[56] Although the yeoman farmer flourished in Tudor and Stuart times the characteristics Mildred Campbell attributed to them were no doubt to be found in their forebears in the fifteenth and early sixteenth centuries. The bigger farmers among the Ram family would have been in this category.

Something else which emerges from the documented references in Table 5 is that family interests were not confined to Great Waltham. Other connections tended to be in nearby villages, particularly High Easter, and the Great Waltham surveys show this pattern was true of many families, particularly among those that held fair amounts of land and were long resident in the area. No doubt chance developments, like a marriage, the availability of a particularly attractive piece of land at a convenient time, or an inheritance, helped to bring such situations about, and they provided added opportunity for advancement, economically and socially. But at least one other Ram involvement was farther a field. In 1473 Thomas Ram (late 15C) was one of several persons involved in a grant concerning three tenements in East Street, Colchester. This event also shows family interests were not confined to farming.

A number of the references in Table 5 are connected with 'demises', probably the conveyance of estates on the death of individuals, and involvements as witnesses to legal documents, often property deeds. For instance in 1421 there is a reference to a 'demise from John Ram senior (early 15 C), now dead'.[57] In 1433, 1441, and 1442 John Ram (mid 15C) witnessed grants in Great Waltham.[58] Acting in this capacity has a social significance, in that it shows the people involved form part of the community who 'get asked to do things'. In other words it is a sign of trust and respect.

Another contribution made by the Ram family was as 'capitales plegii', or tything men, the function of which has already been described, although it is not clear exactly what role this group fulfilled in the early sixteenth century. It is possible that as the judicial and administrative aspects of the court gradually merged this group came to head up both aspects of manorial administration. The lists of tything men which appear at the head of Walthambury Manor court roll between 1509 and 1543 show that, with the exception of three years family members were always in the list. One of them, Thomas Ram (mid 16C), was in it every year from 1534 to 1543, as Table 5 below shows. Members of the Ram family also figured in wider political activities. In 1450 two of them received a pardon for taking part in the Cade Rebellion. Whilst Jack Cade was a central individual player it was essentially a grass roots protest about mis-government, heavy taxation, and the losing of foreign wars under Henry VI. The rebellion was centred in the South

East in Sussex and Kent but had significant support in Essex. Almost certainly the Essex contribution can be seen to be based in the longer term history of Essex participation in anti-authoritarian unrest, in which Lollardy played a part. Unlike the peasants' uprising of 1381 the Cade rebellion produced a detailed political programme or manifesto. Many of the local people who participated were pardoned, and whilst the majority of those involved from Essex were from areas close to London there was support from other more distant areas. In fact nearly half the Essex men pardoned were from two places; Maldon where there were twenty eight names and Great Waltham where there were no fewer than sixty names. The list of the pardoned gave the occupation of the people involved and roughly half were husbandmen or yeomen and a quarter were craftsmen. It is clear that in Essex the support for the Cade rebellion came from the middling sort and that in Great Waltham feeling ran high.[59] The Great Waltham contribution must say something about the social importance of the middling sort in the village and the association of the Ram family with that influence.

Table 5. Ram family who were 'capitales plegii', or tything men, between 1509 and 1543 at Great Waltham.

1509	Names unclear.		
1510	Robert Ram.		
1511	Robert Ram, jun.	Johanis Ram, jun.	John Ram, sen.
1512	John Ram.		
1513	John Ram.	Robert Ram.	
1514	Robert Ram.		
1515	Robert Ram.		
1516	John Ram.		
1517	Robert Ram.		
1518	Robert Ram.		
1519	Robert Ram.		
1520	Robert Ram.		
1521	William Ram.	John Ram.	
1522	Robert Ram.		
1523	Robert Ram.	William Ram.	John Ram.
1524	Record missing.		
1525	Robert Ram.		
1526	Robert Ram.	William Ram.	
1527	No Ram.		
1528	Robert Ram.	William Ram.	
1529	Robert Ram.	William Ram.	
1530	Robert Ram.	William Ram.	
1531	William Ram.	Robert Ram.	
1532	William Ram.	Robert Ram, jun.	

1533	No Ram.	
1534	William Ram.	Thomas Ram.
1535	Thomas Ram.	William Ram.
1536	Thomas Ram.	
1537	Thomas Ram.	
1538	Thomas Ram.	
1539	Thomas Ram.	
1540	Thomas Ram.	
1541	Thomas Ram.	
1542	Thomas Ram.	
1543	Thomas Ram.	

How did the Rams achieve their prominence in these influential groups? It did not come solely from economic importance, for although they were among the larger land holders in 1577, they were certainly not among the largest. The family's position was almost certainly assisted by their large numerical presence and long residence in Great Waltham. Only one other family that contributed to the lay subsidy in 1327 was present in the tything lists in 1509-11. It is however, possible that some families resident then were also present in 1327, because only the better off paid the subsidy of that year. Long residence was unusual because population turnover, even in medieval times was fairly rapid. Marjorie McIntosh found that at Havering over the period from 1497 to 1617 only about 25 per cent of families had been present for between four and five generations (roughly 100-125 years).[60] Mobility was more common in medieval times than we sometimes think, but family names also disappeared because they died out in the male line.

It does seem though that long residence linked with the retention of family identity was an unusual phenomenon. The longevity of the Ram family in Great Waltham probably made family members conscious and proud of their past history. It would have been something that distinguished them from others. They may have played on their history to gain advantage and influence, sometimes consciously but perhaps also unconsciously. They might have felt that certain standards were expected of them, particularly the main family members in each generation. It would also have given them confidence in a variety of ways: in the management of their affairs, in the making of marriages, in their assumption of leadership, and in self belief.

XII
Copy and Freehold Farmers, 1550-1650

The Tudor and Stuart surveys

The limited and shadowy picture of the Ram family presented in the last chapter changes quite remarkably when it comes to dealing with the second half of the sixteenth century. This is because several sources become available that can be explored in interactive ways; wills, registrations of baptisms, marriages and deaths, and especially a number of parish surveys. But assembling and presenting the information which follows has not been straightforward. The lack of general background information about Great Waltham, particularly the absence of any work on it by the Victoria County History has led to the completion of a fairly large amount of original research on the parish, albeit in a way that assists the main aims of this enquiry. No general study like those on Terling and Havering has ever been made, and the only detailed enquiry that relates to early modern times was made by Felix Hull, who had a special interest which was different from the objective here.[61] The current research has led to new understandings about the complexity of life in the local community and the sources of power, influence and status.

Five surveys were made over a relatively short timescale: in 1563, 1577, 1583, 1616, and 1622.[62] The one made in 1577 is particularly detailed, legible, complete, and well preserved, so it is the one generally used. Part of the title page of the first survey of 1563 is reproduced in Figure 5 to give a flavour of their appearance and the importance attached to them. It reveals how the survey came to be made by '... John Cross, gent, Steward to the Right Honourable Sir Richard Rich, Knight, Lord Rich Lord of the said manor and by his commandment upon a due search of the two? extent(s) of the said manor made in the second year of the reign of King Edward the Third and by the Rental and Court Roll of the said manor and also by the recognitions and oaths of' – there then follows a list of forty five individuals, many of whom were the larger and middle sized yeomen farmers who made up just under a third of the tenants. It is possible they were the tything men for that year. The presence of their names indicates the survey was made with their involvement and they may have played a part in initiating it even though the wording states

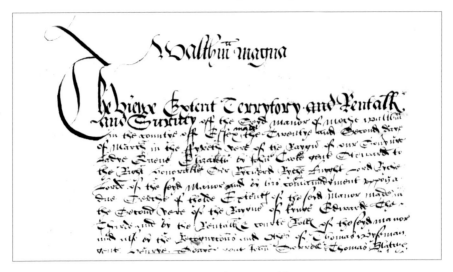

Figure 5. Title page of the 1563 survey of Great Waltham.

it was done at the order of the Lord of the Manor. It has to be said though
that it is not really clear how the Great Waltham surveys originated. For some
reason such records were very popular in Elizabethan and early Stuart times,
possibly because tenants were increasingly conscious of their proprietary rights
and had an interest in documenting them. This understanding is not without
support, and there was a general growth in the writing down of rights during
this period, often by way of surveys similar to those made at Great Waltham.[63]

The 1577 survey listed all the tenants together with the blocks of land each one
held, including their acreage. It also noted whether land was held freehold or
copyhold, the rent paid for each block, and if each tenant was resident or non
resident.[64] It was also broken down by each of the 'ends' of the parish – South,
Romhey, Fourth, North, and Litley. Freeholders amounted to 45 per cent of
all tenants and copyhold tenants accounted for the remainder, as is shown in
Table 6. Using the survey is not entirely without complication for there is some
uncertainty about how far it covers the whole parish. The rented land came to
3092 acres, and even if the demesnes of all the manors are added a significant
amount of the present parish of 7500 acres remains unaccounted for, assuming
its modern boundaries have been unchanged since ancient times.

Table 6. Total tenanted Land in each End at Great Waltham, 1577.

Parish End.	Freehold acreage.	Copyhold acreage.	Total acreage.
South.	506.5	409	915.5
Romfrey.	147.5	160	307.5
Fourth.	11	254	265

North.	179.5	323	502.5
Litley.	376.5	327	703.5
Not known.	163	235.5	398.5
Totals.	1384	1708.5	3092.5
Per cents.	45	55	

Woodland, waste, and perhaps the open fields, would have accounted for some of the difference. Another question is the lack of reference to commercial leasing. There is no mention of this at Great Waltham until the survey of Walthambury Manor that dates from 1643, so it is assumed it did not exist in the sixteenth century. Hull found that leasing was not common practice in Essex during Elizabethan times but that when such holdings did occur they were individually quite large.[65]

How much land each tenant held in total varied considerably, but nearly half of them had ten acres or more, as Table 7 shows. About a quarter of the tenants held very small amounts of land of 5 acres or less. Almost always the bulk of the land held by one person was in one or other of the Ends, although some people held small plots elsewhere. However, where several members of one family lived in the Village it was quite common for them to have the bulk of their land in different Ends. Only a quarter of personal holdings were thirty acres or more, the size that agricultural economists believe to have been the contemporary dividing line between basic subsistence farming and a more assured and potentially commercial enterprise. Below around thirty acres people had no margin of defence against poor or failed harvests and associated poverty and hunger.[66] This means the vast majority of tenants needed to combine farming with other employment, and there was considerable opportunity to do this in Essex, for example to take on work connected with the wool trade that boomed in the sixteenth century and was locally based in and around Colchester. The fact that some families had several holdings between them could have had economic significance as there may have been some pooling of resources, although the extent to which this happened is not known.

Based on the dividing line between subsistence and commercial farming mentioned above around 20 per cent of the Great Waltham tenancies were capable of producing money earning surpluses, and something like 15 per cent of them were probably significant business enterprises. Richard Everarde (mid 16C), was the largest land holder by far in the surveys. He held just over 300 acres, freehold and copyhold, whilst other members of the family held a further 130 acres. After him John Foster held 212 acres, Olive or Alice Criggs held 143, Thomas Hunt 132, Richard Barley 125, Thomas Wyseman 116, John Waltham 113, John Hankyn 81, and then there were the great majority of holdings.

Table 7. Size of tenancies at Great Waltham in 1577, by parish End.

Total size of individual holdings (acres).	End where land held.					Location of holding not known.	Total tenancies.	
	South	Romhey	Fourth	North	Litley		Number.	Percent.
100+.	2		1	1	2	1	7	5.2
50-99.	6	2	1	2		1	12	8.75
30-49.		3		2	4	1	10	7.3
10-29.	8	2	3	8	8	8	37	27.0
Less than 10.	7	6	7	4	6	7	37	27.0
Unidentified (mostly very small).	5	3	1		23	2	34	24.75
Totals.	28	16	13	17	43	20	137	100

Robert Ram who died in 1576 held about 40 acres and this placed him among the top 10 per cent, but quite a long way short of the largest. There seems little doubt that in Tudor and Stuart times Great Waltham was a parish of relatively small holdings and that nearly all of it was held either freehold or copyhold.

Table 7 does not reveal the full complexity of land holding patterns. Many people had several holdings, both freehold and copyhold, each of which was treated as a separate rented unit. It is impossible to tell from the 1577 survey how far the holdings of one person were in a single block of land and Richard Everarde can be quoted as an example which illustrates the complexity. His 303 acres was made up of thirteen separate and rented parcels which were additional to Langley's Manor of around fifty acres, which he owned.[67] Five of the holdings were freehold and eight were copyhold, and ranged in size from 3 to 46 acres. The rents for each of the 13 sites were all different, the lowest being about 2d an acre and the highest 10½d an acre. Four other family members had holdings of their own, and their total holding amounted to 434.5 acres. This was almost certainly accumulated gradually, before and after Langley's Manor was obtained. A number of other families also had several members who held land separately. Mildred Campbell comments that there was much buying and selling of land in the sixteenth century, some of which was associated with efforts to consolidate holdings into homogeneous blocks. This was a slow process and it is impossible to tell whether it led to a man's land being in a block or not.[68] It would be useful to know how far Richard Everarde's holdings were scattered or in one or several blocks, but the fact that so many individual rents were paid at varying rates makes it likely that they were scattered. The complex pattern of land owning and holding revealed by the survey of 1577 suggests there was active buying, selling and sub letting of land in Great Waltham.

Comparisons with other research

These help to understand the Great Waltham picture better. The thesis of Felix Hull is important as it was based on several case studies of different parishes in Essex which included Great Waltham, the others being West Ham, Heydon, Crishall, and Witham.[69] The findings obtained from this study of Great Waltham correlate well with Hull's overall conclusions. For example Hull found the average proportion of freehold to copyhold tenants across his five case studies to be 43 per cent to 57 per cent which compares closely with 45 per cent and 55 per cent obtained from the 1577 survey of Great Waltham. A similar correlation exists for rents charged. This study has found annual freehold rents at Great Waltham ranged from 1¾d to 6d an acre and on average were 3½d an acre. This was one of the highest rates in Hull's case studies, although at West Ham it was much more, at 6d. Copyhold rents at Great Waltham were quite a lot higher at an average of 6½d an acre, but they were much less variable, and fell in the middle of Hull's case study findings, a rate that is quite common everywhere. All of these rent levels had been more or less fixed for many years and were uneconomic. Hull states that sometimes owners took payments in kind from leaseholders where their rents were low, but there is no evidence that this happened to free and copyholders.[70] Hull also detected a tendency for rents to cluster locally around one or more levels. This certainly happened for copyhold rents at Great Waltham, where the main cluster was 3½d and the smaller one was 9d, which outside West Ham was the second highest.[71] Hull did not find everything in Great Waltham to be exactly the same as elsewhere: freehold tenants held more land than in other places and more people held both freehold and copyhold land than anywhere else. Holdings also tended to be larger.[72] So it can be concluded patterns of land holding in Great Waltham were relatively similar to those in the other case studies, and that rent levels were comparable with elsewhere, but on the high side. Hull found no evidence in Essex of eviction or handing over of copies to be replaced by short term leases in the sixteenth century which happened in some areas, and he found no reference in Great Waltham to copyholds of 'inheritance' and 'for years' that reduced the independence of copyholders. There are very few records of disputes over tenure involving copyholders in Essex and they seem to have enjoyed relative security.[73]

Another source of comparison is a detailed study of Terling, a village only about five miles away from Great Waltham, that covers almost exactly the same period as this chapter. It draws on a range of records to examine in detail religious life, social affairs, economic and demographic structures and court litigation in relation to religion and class. It notes four important features which influenced the development of the Essex village economy in the sixteenth and seventeenth centuries. Firstly, the topography and soil type, secondly the agricultural technology available and associated husbandry practices, thirdly the system of land holding, and fourthly the influence of market opportunities. The writers believe that during the sixteenth and seventeenth centuries factors governing the first three features altered very little in Essex as a whole, but there were changes in marketing under the influence of the expansion of towns, particularly London.[74] The present study of Great Waltham, has shown up some differences in land holding practice compared with that outlined in the Terling study, where the claim is made that, 'From at least the late sixteenth century, most (Essex) land was held in large units by leasehold and let at market rents. Copyhold tenure remained as a minor element in landholding'.[75] This was clearly not the case at Great Waltham as the surveys show, and Hull did not find much evidence of commercial land leasing in Essex during Elizabethan times.[76] Even in Terling there is evidence that leasehold practice was not well established until the mid seventeenth century.[77]

The Lay Subsidy returns of 1523-26 raise the possibility of further differences between Great Waltham and Terling. Application of the socio-economic categories used by the Terling researchers to the Great Waltham data produces different results. There is a bigger range of wealth and higher upper levels of wealth at Terling compared with Great Waltham where a flatter profile is produced. The findings are discussed fully in the previous chapter, and the differences may be due to low returns at Great Waltham.[78] But there is also the possibility that the profiles at Terling and Great Waltham reflect true differences.

A third study, this time of Havering, is relevant, but less so because it is concerned about an area much more open to London influences, especially in the form of sizeable land purchases.[79] Land holding patterns were rather different to those at Great Waltham, and it is difficult to make comparisons because it is not clear from the Havering information quoted for 1617 whether tenancies were freehold, copyhold, or leasehold, or what rents were charged. The majority of the holdings were under thirty acres, just over 20 per cent were between 100 and 199 acres, and 17 per cent were over 200 acres. At Great Waltham in 1577 the majority of holdings were also under thirty acres, but the overall profile of landholding was much flatter and the proportion of large holders was much lower. The sub tenants at Havering, who on average only held 5-6 acres, were not listed, but their rents are known and in 1590 were about 7d an acre. Sub tenants were not listed in the Great Waltham surveys either and no information is available about their rent levels, but if it assumed these were higher than ordinary freehold and copyhold rents freehold and copyhold rents at Havering may not have been all that different to those at Great Waltham.[80]

There are recognisable similarities in the way new people of substance appeared in Havering and Great Waltham. In Great Waltham Richard Rich (mid 16C), a lawyer who was much involved nationally in the dissolution of the monasteries, bought Walthambury Manor and much other land in Essex, and in Havering a number of families bought land after making money from commercial enterprise in London, but on a much smaller scale than Richard Rich. Yeoman farmers became raised into the gentry in both places through large scale land acquisition – by renting rather than outright purchase. The Wright family in Havering rented land from the Rich family, and in Great Waltham, the Everardes, gradually achieved gentry status during the sixteenth and seventeenth centuries through a mixture of inheritance and building up a large holding of land by renting.

A major conclusion to be drawn for these comparisons is that the modernising tendencies of the time were less strong in Great Waltham than in Havering or Terling, which were both near to the main road between London and the bigger towns in Essex and East Anglia. It may be that the greater remoteness of Great Waltham served to weaken the forces of change somewhat. Compared with Terling land holding practice remained traditional considerably longer. Overall, it is likely Great Waltham was similar to other places in the neighbouring central parts of Essex and had a stable and relatively secure economic environment, especially for the farmers who were large enough to earn profits, but was not in the forefront of economic and related social change.

Do the differences that have been identified between Great Waltham, Havering, and Terling suggest that there was significant local variation in the character of social and economic life between parishes, as well as rates and timing of change, even though geographically close together? The authors of the Terling book themselves accept that there may be variations around a baseline. '… some of the general influences that shaped Terling's experience – demographic, economic, administrative, religious, and educational – were undoubtedly at work in the nation at large.….Our expectation would be that Terling provides one example, one variant, of a social process that was active elsewhere, though subject to considerable local variation in chronology and consequences'.[81] The overall findings of this study affirm what the writers of the Terling book say about the need for caution in making generalisations from one detailed example. If there was a large amount of variation the overall social and economic picture may be more complex that we sometimes present it to be.

The internal dynamics of the Ram family

Three distinct nuclear Ram families are mentioned in the 1577 survey, which almost certainly sprang from common forebears. These families are the beginnings of the three branches of the family that are discussed from now on, and are charted under the letters A, B, and C. The male heads of each of them were either siblings or cousins of some kind, although it is impossible to be precise. They all lived in South End, which lies around Great Waltham village, and formed what to us seems a very large number of family members in one location. The information about them in this chapter provides a quite detailed insight into the life of a middling sort of family. The general importance of wills in putting the family story together has already been discussed, and there is a particularly rich series of family wills from the mid sixteenth century until the first part of the nineteenth century. Many of the heads of family units left wills, and during Elizabethan and Stuart times they are particularly detailed. In the same period a number of references are made to family members in other people's wills.

One of the three nuclear families was headed by John 1C (d. 1568) who described himself as a yeoman 'late of Pleshey' in his will, although he also held land in Great Waltham and High Easter. He was a widower and probably lived in his son-in-law's house at the time he died. John is mentioned in the survey of 1563 but by the time of the next survey in 1577 his sons had left the village and formed two other branches which figure prominently in the later story, but not in Great Waltham. One son, William, who was probably the eldest, was left most of the family lands, and still retained 7 acres in 1577 when he was listed as a 'gent' living in Colchester. From other sources it is known he had become an attorney and also Deputy Town Clerk of Colchester. Another son, Christopher became a Church of England priest, and a third son became agent to the Cooke family in Havering, Deputy Steward of Havering and an Essex magistrate. This family is covered by the C charts.[82]

The second nuclear family, covered by the A charts, was that of Robert Ram who died in 1576, and his descendants were active in the parish until the late seventeenth century, when the male line died out. Many of the very detailed wills were left by members of this branch. The immediate family of Robert, including grandchildren is shown in Chart A1. How old Robert was when he died is not known, but his children were grown up and he had a number of grandchildren, so he could not have been born much later than 1510. His will describes him as a yeoman. There must have been some wealth in this family as Robert willed that 3¾d should be given to the poor 'on the day of my funeral', and when Agnes, his widow, died five years later she left 20/- to 'the poor people'. She also instructed how it should be spent. 'I will that a quarter of wheat be bought, baked and given, with one lead of cheese, to them on the day of my burial'. Such benefactions were commonly made at the time. During the reformation years significant efforts were made by officialdom to persuade better off people to give gifts to the poor as their numbers were growing, and such gifts did increase rapidly during this period. In 1547 clergy were instructed to exhort their neighbours to give money to the parish poor chest.[83] Robert also had three servants, a woman who was left

10/- and two men, one of whom was left ¾d. The other one received a quarter of barley. The wills of yeoman farmers often mention three, four or five servants, although the average may have been nearer one. Marjorie McIntosh found this to be roughly the case when she made an analysis of the number of servants per Romford household in 1562, for the main occupational groups. Only gentlemen and innkeepers had appreciably more than this, and those at inns were probably more involved with running them than acting as personal servants.[84] A manservant of the best sort had to be paid 33/- to 80/- a year, although a woman equivalent cost only about 13/- a year. In Essex a manservant of the second sort cost 60/10d and of the third sort 16/8d. Mostly yeoman would pay lower rates. Servants hired for the year lived in the yeoman's own household. In addition to such servants yeomen frequently had apprentices in 'husbandry' living with them. These young servants received no wage.[85] The smaller yeoman, or one who had several sons, had no need to hire labour, but the better off ones did.

Much of Robert's property, which amounted to between thirty and forty acres of land and three tenements, was copyhold. He willed these properties as if he owned them outright, as was the custom of the times. It will be seen that a main concern of heads of nuclear families in disposing of the land they held was to provide for any sons on a more or less equal basis. This ensured they all had a reasonable start in life. It was usual practice, particularly among family members who had pretensions to be yeomen, and women were not usually left any land. In medieval times the custom of widow's free bench was observed in Great Waltham, whereby a widow kept all her husband's land for her lifetime. [86] This practice had clearly fallen into abeyance among the Ram family by the time family wills become available from the mid sixteenth century onwards. But Robert did not follow general practice entirely, for a special reason. The first person mentioned is Thomas (d. 1611), presumably the eldest son, and he was left two tenements, a piece of pasture and £5. Because this is a minor inheritance he was almost certainly provided for by an earlier settlement, which may have been an inheritance of land in High Easter from another member of the family. It is known from other sources that Thomas lived at least part of his life at High Easter, and the whole tenor of Robert's will suggests Thomas did not live in Great Waltham at that time. Thomas still held his Great Waltham inheritances at the time of the 1577 survey and he paid rents amounting to 5d, so they could not have been very large. The wording of the will makes it clear that both tenements were occupied by others, who were presumably sub tenants since their family names do not appear in the 1577 survey. The rising population of the times and a related need for property meant there was increased opportunity for sub letting of surplus properties. Such rents were higher than those paid by the copyhold and freehold tenants who sometimes enjoyed rent levels dating back to before the Black Death. So Robert Ram and

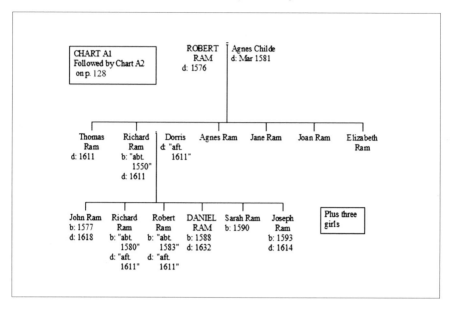

his family, who had three such properties may have made a good income from them.

Robert then leaves the main family lands jointly to his wife Agnes and his second son Richard. They inherited Rothes half yard which descended down the family until 1689. They were also left some additional pasture and meadow, plus a tenement, which like those left to Thomas was sub let. Richard also gained nearly all Robert's goods and chattels. There were all the animals and farm implements, '...four of my best horses, four of my best milch kine, and ten of my best ewe sheep' – (were the others sold since no other animals are mentioned?). The farm implements included one load cart, two dung carts, one pair of iron harrows, cart harness, plough harness, plough irons and one plough. This list was almost certainly an effective inventory of Robert's farm capital investment. The household goods included '... my best brass pot, two long pots, one great pair of cobirons, one copper in the kitchen, my great cauldron, six pewter platters, six pewter dishes, and six saucers of the best', besides 'two of my best bedsteads' (no others are mentioned). Agnes was left the residue. Presumably Thomas and the four married daughters did not need any of these items. It is possible Richard appears as such a major beneficiary because he was the younger son and not yet working on his own. A very similar situation, discussed below, occurred when one of his sons, Daniel (1588-1632), died.

Several issues are raised by the will. The fact that Agnes and Richard share Rothes reinforces the probability that Richard was a minor, for a more usual way to provide for a widow was to give her the use of a small cottage or hold a grown up son responsible for maintenance in his home. The implication is that Richard was not old enough to take sole charge and that meanwhile Agnes took responsibility. The will also makes no reference to where Robert lived or where Agnes and Richard resided after his death. Presumably they stayed on in the family home, using the household goods left to Richard.

Most of Robert's other bequests were in the form of cash. To Agnes, Jane, Joan, and Elizabeth, his four daughters, who were all married with children of their own, he gave 5/- each. Most of their children were also given 5/- each. There were two exceptions. Alice, the daughter of son Thomas, got 'one black milch cow' and so did Robert son of Jane, although in this case the colour was not specified!

Whilst Robert makes detailed reference in his will to domestic goods like pots, pans, plates, and bed steads, he says nothing about linen, mattresses and blankets. Was this because they were all kept by Agnes in 'the residue', and it was not masculine to be concerned about such things? In her own will five years later Agnes in her womanly way went into much more detail about these items, leaving sheets, blankets, feather and other mattresses, kerchiefs, and coverlets, to each woman in the family. Robert's perspective about such matters was not shared by everyone for his eldest son, Thomas, who died in 1611, went into great detail about the leaving of domestic items.

The executors of Robert's will were his wife and Richard, but Thomas had a main part to play as he was made overseer, along with Richard Ponde (late 16C), the husband of daughter Jane, and a member of a long standing Great Waltham family. The appointment of executors and overseers was done in a way which maximised what would now be called transparency. All interested parties were included. There were also three witnesses, two of whose identity cannot be traced. The third was Richard Everarde, a neighbour, and the largest landholder by far in the parish. Was he a friend of Robert or just an impressive name to be drawn on?

When Agnes came to write her will she appointed Thomas Ram, her son, an executor along with Richard Ponde, who appears to have been a trusted family member. The fact that Agnes selected her 'loving' brother Thomas Childe (late 16C) as overseer tells us her family name which provides information about the family Robert married into. Like the Rams and the Pondes the Childe family was long resident in the village. In the 1523 lay subsidy a Thomas Ram (mid 16C) is described as being 'at Childes', which points to a younger family member serving some sort of apprenticeship with that family. Two members of the Childe family held land in 1577, both in North End, so they lived some way away from the Rams in South End. Thomas Childe was one of the larger parish landholders, with about twenty five acres of freehold land and another twenty five acres copyhold, whilst John Childe (late 16C), presumably a relative, held about twenty acres of freehold land and eight of copyhold. The family was the fourth biggest land holder in the parish and had somewhat more than the Rams.

As the years passed Robert's son Richard added new holdings to his original Rothes halfyard so that at the time of his death he held about eighty acres. He became a substantial farmer, certainly of yeoman status, and had enough land to leave holdings to all his five sons. He was rich enough to leave £10 'to the poor people of Much Waltham', to be distributed to them at the discretion of his executors. Chart A1 shows he had nine children baptised of whom seven are known to have reached adulthood. Nothing is known about three of his daughters, Dorris, Susan, and Elizabeth, who probably died young, but Sarah (b. 1590), one of his youngest children, made what must have been a good marriage to Robert Everarde (early 17C), possibly the third son of Richard Everarde, who became a baronet in 1628.[87]

Richard provided carefully for each of his sons. To John, probably the eldest who he describes as his 'natural' son, he left 'a customary messuage in Great Waltham where he (it is not clear whether this refers to John (1577-1618) or Richard (d. aft.1611)) lived with all the copyhold and freeland belonging'. Unfortunately the size of this holding is not given, but it is reasonable to assume it was as large as holdings given to the other sons – between ten and twenty acres. Why John is referred to as 'natural' and the others are not is unclear. To Richard the second son, who probably remained unmarried, he left a messuage called Larkes in the nearby parish of Broomfield and Checknell, again with an unspecified amount of land. Robert (n. d.), the third son, was left several small holdings amounting to about ten acres – a customary tenement called Fletchers with an adjoining acre of land, some freehold land called Wistocke, and other freehold land, plus three acres of the Rothes Halfyard. The heart of the Ram holdings, Rothes halfyard – minus three acres – went to the fourth son Daniel (1588-1632), so he had about twenty two acres. One wonders why this land went to Daniel rather than John. The fifth son Joseph (1593-1614), who was dead when the 1616 survey was made, got a messuage called Motte with fourteen acres of land.

This record of how Richard provided for his five sons is the most detailed information to come to light about how the Ram family approached inheritance issues. Two other interesting examples of property disposal are to be found in the wills of this small family group. When Joseph died unmarried in 1614 at the young age of 20 or 21 he made a will that left all his land to his mother Dorris for her lifetime and then to his eldest brother John after her death. By

1614 Dorris was a widow, and as her husband's will had made no specific provision for her support Joseph's bequest served to improve her economic situation in the later years of her life. Joseph, who was one of the younger children, was made an executor of his father's will, together with Dorris, which suggests a close connection with his mother, and the provision Joseph made for her when he died hints they may have lived together. John was dead by 1622, when the next survey of Great Waltham shows that Joseph's land had ended up with his only surviving brother Daniel. Two of Richard's sons, John and Robert did not make wills so what happened to their land when they died is not known. There is no record of any being passed to brother Daniel, so it was presumably sold out of the family, or passed on to their wives. It is quite clear from this information that in this family group property and land was willed to family members, almost entirely sons or widows, flexibly, and in the fairest and most beneficial ways. Other Ram wills show that this was usual family practice. Such an approach to inheritance was common among the middling sort, being distinctively different to the practice followed by the aristocracy and gentry of leaving all the land to a single nominee, usually the eldest son if there was one.[88]

The Daniel whose family is shown in chart A2 inherited the Rothes halfyard in 1611. He was the last of his immediate family to be styled yeoman in his will, and he followed the inheritance practices of his father when he died aged forty two leaving a young family. He left all lands and tenements to his wife Clemenc during her natural life on condition she paid sons Daniel (1617-1689) and Richard)1618-1669) 40/- a year after they reached the age of twenty four. As will be seen shortly this amount did not compare well with general labourers' pay of about £9 a year, although they had to maintain a family on this income with no prospect of inheritance. When Clemenc died Rothes was to go to Daniel, the eldest son and stipulated parcels of land were to go to the younger sons, Richard and John (1625-1683). Under the will Daniel and Richard, who were fifteen and fourteen at the time, were effectively apprenticed to work the family lands for their mother until they inherited them when she died. John was only seven at the time and was too young to be involved. Joseph, the second eldest son is not mentioned in the will. Daniel, the eldest of the brothers, died last in 1689. He had no sons and possibly all his four daughters were dead, which raised the significant question of what to do with the Rothes halfyard, the major inheritance in this branch of the family. He chose to sell it rather than pass it on down the family line to nephews, sons of his younger brothers, Richard and John. His brother in law, William Marrion or Maryon, married to his sister Mary (b. 1631), was required to organise the sale of all his lands, and divide the proceeds equally between his brother Joseph (d. 1726), and his sister Mary. Why was this decision taken? There is evidence from the family wills as a whole that major bequests were only made within nuclear

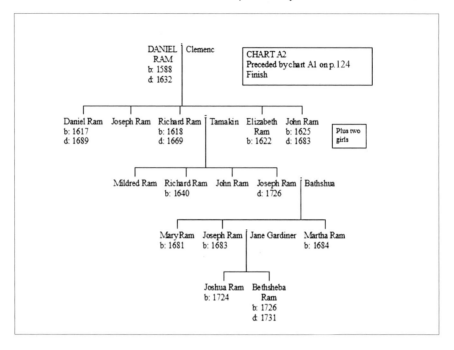

families, and clearly this process was followed here regardless of the loss of this land to the family. Maybe Joseph and Mary needed the money, or perhaps Daniel did not get on with the families of his brothers. It may even have happened because changes in farming practice were bringing traditional copy hold farming to an end. Joseph may have been a consideration too. A certain mystery surrounds him. He was not mentioned in his father's will and was probably never left any land holding, neither his birth or death was registered, which was unusual in the family, and he never seems to have married. He did not leave a will of his own. He may have been handicapped in some way or even illegitimate. Notwithstanding this mystery there seems to have been concern among his brothers to make provision for him. Whatever the family circumstances were on the death of Daniel the sale of Rothes resulted in the loss to this branch of the family of its core land holding along with the status of being a yardland tenant.

There are records of three more generations of this branch of the family in Great Waltham and then the male line ends. The last known family member to die in the parish was Joseph (d. 1726), when his will shows that he only held a dwelling house with yards and gardens. In the will he is described as a husbandman, and he left his house to Mary(b. 1681) his daughter, '... to use and dispose of as she sees fit'. Under its terms the house was to be divided so that his son Joseph (b. 1683) could live there, and Mary was charged to maintain her mother, which might involve selling it. All his son got was one shilling with permission to live in part of the house. Between the death of

Daniel (d. 1632) styled a yeoman and this Joseph a total of 11 wills were written by family members and all of them give occupation as husbandman.

These wills show that the later generations of this branch did not build up their inheritances during their lifetimes, and that its overall history was one of gradual decline. The reasons are not known, and the general economic situation, which is discussed below, may have played a part.[89] The failure of Daniel (d. 1689) to have any sons must also have been a factor, for it led to a major land holding passing out of family control. The court roll of Walthambury Manor has a number of confusing references in the late seventeenth and eighteenth centuries about the Rothes halfyard, and other land held historically by the descendants of Robert Ram, which are in conflict with contemporary family wills, the last of them being in 1749. In general terms all these records support the understanding that this branch of the family declined during the later part of the seventeenth century and died out sometime in the middle part of the eighteenth century.

The third nuclear unit of the Ram family that lived in Great Waltham descended from Thomas Ram (d. 1556) and is covered by the B charts. He may have been a half brother of Robert (d. 1576), and his family continued as farmers in the local area until the mid nineteenth century and then moved to London. I belong to this branch. The main line of descent in the next four generations is shown in Chart B1. So many of the sons are called John that they are numbered to aid identification. Thomas bequeathed the use of his farm to William (mid 16C) and John 1 (d.1588), his sons, on condition that they supported his wife during her lifetime. On his wife's death the home and lands were to be sold, but if William and John I wanted them they could purchase at a predetermined price. If the holding was sold the proceeds of sale were to be divided between heirs alive at the time. It looks as though Thomas, who married a second time, and incidentally repeated the sons' names, was providing for a situation in which there were older sons and a young second wife with children.

The fortunes of the next few generations of this family provide an example of just how complicated property and land holding could be in a place like Great Waltham. The pattern described is typical of the random purchase and sale of land that happened at Terling[90] and contrasts with the more ordered regime of Robert's family when they were prosperous. The pattern may derive from the more marginal position this part of the family occupied, which is indicated by the simpler content and poorer drafting of their wills.

At the time of the 1577 survey two people from Thomas' side of the family were living in Great Waltham. One was Sabyan, the widow of a John Ram, who was dead by the time the earliest survey of Great Waltham was made in 1563, and who may have been Thomas' elder brother. But because neither John or Sabyan is recorded in any of the new registers of baptisms, marriages, and burials and they did not leave wills the exact relationship with Thomas is unclear. For this reason they do not appear in chart B1. However quite a lot is known about Sabyan because her name appears in all the surveys up to that of 1583. In 1563 she held a half yard of freehold land, possibly as John's widow, which was a sizeable holding, but by 1577 when she must have been well into mid life, she had given up the half yard to hold a copyhold cottage called Kates in Church End with a garden of about half an acre, for which she paid rent of 3d. She was still living in the same cottage at the time of the 1583 survey. Here is an example of independent female retirement in the sixteenth century.

The other representative of this part of the family in 1577 was John Ram 1B, probably Thomas' son, and he had a copyhold house and croft of about two acres at Brades (Green) in South End. He held another croft of three acres, and a further four acres of land called Penden Gren, for all of which he paid 3/2d. rent. In 1588 he willed this property to his wife Rose (d. 1593) during her lifetime, and then to his son Thomas (b.1575), provided Rose redeemed a mortgage of £30 to Richard Ram, a son of Robert.[91] In addition he left a small amount of freehold land and waste ground adjoining one of his holdings to his wife, to be split among the children after her death.[92] The waste was probably unenclosed land. Many yeoman farmers made enclosures, 'but usually the

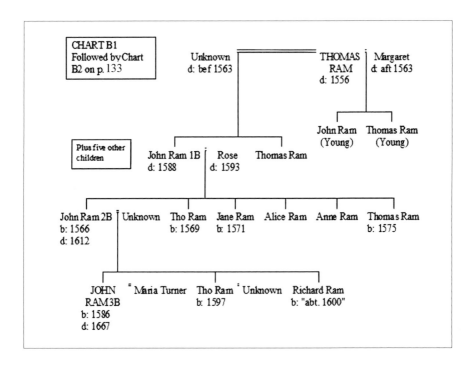

yeomen were among the land nibblers… and they converted the waste to tillage rather than pasture'.[93]

John 1B's branch of the family continued through to John 2B (1566-1612), who was a weaver with three sons who were under twenty six when he died – John 3B (1586-1667), Thomas (b.1597), and Richard (n. d.). John 2B did not appear in any of the surveys, but this was possibly because of the long gap between those of 1583 and 1616, which covered the bulk of his lifetime. Although his will says he was a weaver he probably held some land as well, which he was due to receive from his father upon his mother's death. Many yeomen exercised a craft or ran a business on the side. Sometimes the head of the house did this himself. But more frequently it was carried out by another member of the family under his supervision, or an outsider hired to do the work.[94] A Thomas Ram (b. 1569?) recorded in the 1616 survey as holding ten acres freehold called Elman's Field was almost certainly John 2B's brother. Elman's Field must have come to Thomas through the family because it was once the property of Geoffrey Ram a relative of this branch, who held land in both High Easter and Great Waltham in the early sixteenth century.

In his will John 2B mentions 'the house I now dwell in' is called Purley Castle which was in Great Waltham village. According to the survey of 1563 both Sabyan and Robert Ram had an interest in this house, and it seems to have passed down through several generations, possibly including transfers between the families of Robert and Thomas. In the 1577 and 1583 surveys the house was held by Robert's family, but sometime during John 2B's lifetime it came to him, and his son who died in 1667, the third of a series of Johns, also lived at Purleigh Castle. Although property was mostly left only within nuclear families the way Purleigh Castle was transferred shows that was not always the case.

The genealogy of the family is continued on from John 3B in chart B2 who made several touching bequests to grandchildren. 'I give and bequeath to my grandchild Mary (b.1660), the daughter of Richard Ram (1634-1714) my son, the little table standing by my bedside, and to John Ram (b. bef. 1667 – who must have died young), his son, my grandchild our little table, and to Hannah Ram (b. bef. 1667) his daughter, my grandchild, a little hanging cupboard.[95] Richard married twice and had five children, including three boys, but only one, also named Richard (1668-1710), survived and he predeceased his father aged 42. John 3B had several different landholdings during his lifetime, although in his will he is described as a weaver. The 1646 survey states he held a quarter yard called Eastgate.[96] Neither of the Richards left wills which makes the history of the family at this time rather obscure, and there is a degree of uncertainty about the line of descent. As far as in known the younger of them only had one child John 4B (1688-1762), but he had a very large family and reinvigorated the family line in the eighteenth century.

The story of the three generations depicted in Chart B2 is about very obscure people whose family fortunes are quite difficult to follow. The only reason for discussing them in some detail is to show the pattern of their lives and just how tenuous life was. Large numbers of their children died as infants, but just at the weakest point in the family descent, and remember this was the time when Robert Ram's branch died out, John 4B had fifteen children, including six boys who lived to maturity, which assured family survival for another period of time.

As in the medieval period not all of the family lived in Great Waltham, and those who did had links in nearby places with their kin and other families. A John Ram lived at Writtle later in the sixteenth century and held ten freehold acres in Great Waltham called Eldersfield, land which once belonged to the Geoffrey Ram who died in 1530. He must have been a member of the family but how he was related is not known. One of the descendants of the same Geoffrey Ram, also called Geoffrey (d. 1584), farmed in Nevendon about fifteen miles from Great Waltham. He was a contemporary of John 1B who lived at Brades Green in Great Waltham, so they must have been kinsmen. When he died he had a family of young children, and John 1B died in Nevendon in 1588, although his home was clearly in Great Waltham. It is possible that he was present in Nevendon helping out.

Some references have already been made to the many relationships that existed with other local families but the most detail available about these is provided by the will of Robert Marshe (d. 1561/2) who lived at Felsted, about five miles north of Great Waltham. Presumably as a widower he left £40 to his daughter Elizabeth '...which shall remain in the hands of my loving friend Robert Ramme of Great Waltham to the use of Elizabeth'.[97] The will goes on to stipulate 'Elizabeth shall be brought up under the governance of Robert Ram', so he effectively became her guardian. It is clear from the will of Agnes, Robert Ram's widow, that the relationship between the families was even more extensive, for it reveals her daughter Elizabeth married John Marshe, who was almost certainly the son of Robert Ram's friend. The fact that Robert Marshe appointed Thomas Childe the elder supervisor of his estate shows there was a triangular relationship between the Rams, Marshes and Childes.

Power and status in the community II
In medieval times Great Waltham farmers were free to grow crops as they wished but they also provided feudal services, mainly to Pleshey castle.[98] Although a significant local focus point it was one among many as far as the

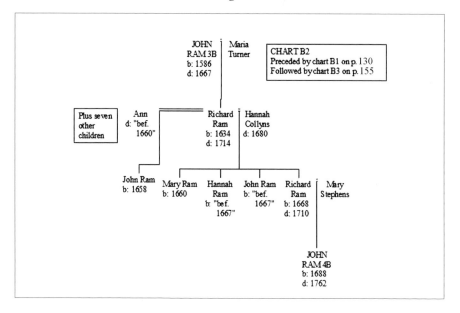

de Bohun family was concerned, for they held enormous estates in Essex and elsewhere. By the sixteenth century this castle had ceased to be of importance, and with the Reformation it disappeared altogether. The sixteenth century was a time of great change in the ownership of property. There was much selling of church and crown lands, and new types of proprietor emerged. Some, usually the largest, were the actual owners but there was also a second tier of people who rented from them. The richer ones might become peers and the lesser ones rise to be gentry. Some of them had made money through the professions or commerce, and others emerged from the yeomanry. Some of the new proprietors were institutions like hospitals, colleges and livery companies.[99] There was a hunger for land, and 'Buying and selling were particularly active in the south and east where the agrarian situation came earliest under commercial influences'.[100] There was frequent resale of land with associated rises in value during the period 1550-1620.[101]

In Great Waltham two new major land holders appeared in the sixteenth century, one being a large external proprietor and the other a home grown ex-yeoman who rented more land than he owned. The external proprietor was Richard Rich, a lawyer and national official closely involved with the disposal of monastic estates, who bought many for himself. He became one of the biggest land owners in Essex, and Walthambury Manor was one of his purchases, but his family came and disappeared in less than two hundred years. The other was the Everarde family who lived in Great Waltham. How they acquired Langleys Manor which only comprised about fifty acres in the fifteenth century, and gradually built up a large rented holding in Walthambury

Manor has already been described. After they established their position they remained a leading family well into the seventeenth century.

Influence in the running of the local community was exerted through holding office and giving leadership in the manor courts and related institutions. At Great Waltham only the main manor of Walthambury was functioning by early modern times, although even it gradually declined from the seventeenth century as its powers were taken over by other bodies, or ceased to be important. David Eastwood stresses the fact that the quarter sessions increasingly dominated local government in unreformed England. The Magistrate's Clerk became effectively the manager of county administration, which was controlled by a number of active magistrates, the sheriffs, and the deputy and full County Lieutenants. This development, together with the growing role of the overseers of the poor helped to make the manor courts redundant.[102]

Of the two largest land holders in Great Waltham only the Everarde family is known to have played a significant and regular part in parish government. Richard Rich lived in Chatham Hall near Great Waltham and it was said that when he took control of this manor he arrayed all the tenants before him.[103] He also owned Walthambury Manor at the time of the 1577 survey, and his name appears in the dedication to the first of the surveys in 1563. It is unfortunate that the listing of the jury or head men stops in 1543 but the types of people who appear in the list when it starts again in the seventeenth century are very similar to those present earlier, and some of the names are the same. The only clue to the people and families who were significant in the second half of the sixteenth century is in the list of 44 names in the dedication to the 1563 survey.[104] There is sufficient continuity across all these lists to suggest the middling people always had a major voice. The general impression gained from the material about Great Waltham is that the Rich family did not play an active part in parish life.

Who exerted power and influence in the local community was considerably affected by the pattern of landholding. This is clearly revealed from the 1577 survey of Great Waltham in Table 7. Many tenancies were of moderate size. Such a pattern no doubt encouraged the existence of a relatively open community run by the villagers themselves, especially those who had ten acres or more. These can be divided into two groups. One of them constituted fourteen families among whom two or more family members, and in eight cases three or more, were tenants. The average family holding among this group was 110 acres. The potential concentration of resources open to such families may have helped to boost their power and status in the community. The second group contained twenty nine families represented by only one family member. As would be expected, the average holding, of 52 acres, was considerably smaller than in the first group, although the number of large individual holdings – over 100 acres – was about the same in each. Seven of the families in the first group, who were not all among the largest land holders, were present two or more times in the lists of tything men for 1509-11. Far fewer of the singleton families were in these lists, or the 1563 dedication list, only making up 6 of the 28 decipherable names who also appear in the 1577 survey. About 1/3 of the singleton families were non resident, whilst all but one of those in the group with multiple representation had at least two resident tenants. This analysis suggests that social status in the parish was not determined solely by economic weight as measured by size of land holding, and that it was probably influenced by several other factors.

Non residence, was one of them, as this would have inevitably affected local standing in a negative way. Two other factors in particular may have enhanced social status. One was long association with the village. Status coming from this source would tend to be reinforced over the generations, especially if the number of family members increased and several of them had land holdings. Although only about a quarter of the families in the tything lists of 1509-1511 were still present as tenants at the time of the 1577 survey nearly half of those that remained had multiple individual tenancies – the Barnardes with eleven, and the Rams, Everardes and Sorrells with seven each. The third factor was large numerical presence, which of course meant there were several individual voices from a single family. At least six families had two or more resident tenants.

The concentrated presence of some families also affected the distribution of power and influence. Because there is much more scattering of families today we tend to overlook the extent that large numbers of family members sometimes lived in a single village community. The Ram family can be taken as an example. In 1577 it held seven tenancies four of which were occupied by families living in or very near Great Waltham. Agnes, Robert's widow, was one with five of her children – Richard, Agnes, Jane, Joan and Elizabeth. All the daughters were married with children. Three of them were married to men whose family names appear in the 1577 survey. One of them is mentioned as having a very small personal holding and the others belonged to families which had 19 and 29 acres respectively, although they are not mentioned directly. The wills of Robert and his wife do not make it clear exactly how many children their daughters had all told, but the wording suggests they each had at least two. Thomas the eldest child had children of his own, but once again it is not clear how many. Richard was either unmarried at the time, or had no children. Sabyan lived with another female member of the family, Margaret, and John I had six grown up children when he died in 1588. All this information indicates that at least 28 family members, including spouses, lived in, or very near, Great

Waltham in the 1570s, covering at least three generations. This was perhaps the most dense representation of family members in one place throughout the history of the family.

The number of individual land holdings in the Everarde and Barnarde families were such that their overall family size was almost certainly bigger than that of the Rams and there were three other families broadly comparable to them. This group of families were all significant land holders, some of them being among the largest. They were also long resident, and it was highly likely that all three aspects served to reinforce local social status. Yet another factor probably served to enhance influence. The Ram family in addition to having a large presence was intermarried with other influential families. The family of Robert Ram, discussed earlier in some detail, illustrates this phenomena. The same was probably true of the other long resident and influential families.

These findings about the nature of local society in Great Waltham are broadly supported in Felix Hull's thesis which found that Essex tended to be a fairly open society of relatively small estates and holdings, and that there was a marked absence of very large estates. Factors that might show up changing forms of land holding, especially payment of a fine on death or surrender, were not in evidence.[105] As rents were more or less fixed increasing this fine could be significant. In Essex there is not much information about whether these fines were fixed or not. 'But the lack of serious disputes and the continuous report of the well-being of the county .. makes it unwise to consider that the majority of Essex copyholders were other than satisfied with their position by 1600'[106] Hull found no evidence of eviction or handing over of copies to be replaced by short term leases in the sixteenth century, and there is no reference in Great Waltham to copyholds of 'inheritance' and 'for years'. Copyholders enjoyed relative security and there are very few records of disputes over tenure.[107] Hull found that lease holding was not common in Essex in Elizabethan times but when it occurred holdings were quite large – the average size being 53.5 acres, 70 acres if the packet of small leaseholds in Coggeshall is excluded. In the South and centre of the county average leaseholds were about 130 acres and in other areas about 20 acres. Sometimes whole manors were leased, e.g., of Woodham Ferrers to Walter Fysshe, citizen and Merchant Taylor of London. Such leases could be very large and were subject to various conditions, e.g., about payments in kind, maintaining the condition of buildings and the land, and forestry. Rents were not generally extortionate and the owners were mainly concerned to keep the soil well maintained.[108] Hull also found that by the seventeenth century the number of larger farms let at commercial rates had increased, although a significant if indeterminate amount of traditional free and copyhold land remained.[109] All the evidence available about Great Waltham points to traditional land holding practice continuing until the end of the seventeenth century. But in some places not far away change came earlier. A study of Terling, only about five miles away, found in that parish that during the seventeenth century larger farms came to be predominant.[110]

Social involvement was not only realised through leadership in the manor and parish. Being a respected and helpful neighbour was also important and F G Emmison's volumes of cross referenced Essex wills, covering roughly the years 1558-1603, are very helpful for identifying neighbourly associations.[111] Robert Ram was a regular witness of wills from 1588 onwards. Some of the people involved were among the more important members of the village, for example, Thomas Everarde (d. 1557/8), father of the Richard Everarde who acquired Langleys Manor by marriage settlements between 1520 and 1529 and William Sorrell of Great Leighs (d. 1556), but there were others of lesser status, like John Smeth (d. 1562) and a carpenter Geoffrey Crowe (d. 1566). Robert also acted as overseer for Humphrey Horsenaile (d. 1574) a member of a long resident Great Waltham family. In the 1577 survey Thomas Horsnaile, presumably the son or brother of Humphrey, held a half yard of land in Fourth End. The will of John Arwaker the elder (d. 1572), of which Robert was a witness, revealed something of the networking that lay behind such involvements. This John left two bushels of wheat at Christmas and two at Easter for bread to be baked for the poor and they were '... to be delivered by John my son for ever'. He also left his godsons, John Billyreca and John Ram '... my best coat to the intent that they shall yearly see the bread delivered'. In the 1577 survey John Billyrica held about 35 acres of land in Romhey End, presumably the John Billyreca mentioned in the will. It is clear from another will, of Joan Arwaker (d. 1576/7), was a widow of High Easter, shows that this family and the Rams were closely connected. She leaves '... to William Ramme my eldest son one of my best beasts, six sheep, and all corn and other fruit growing at my decease in Byrdes Croft in Leaden Roothing'. She had clearly been married to a Ram and then afterwards to an Arwaker as she leaves her best horse to John Arwaker 'my second son'. It is likely that a major reason for Robert being a witness to John Arwaker's will was close relationship, presumably by marriage. In 1586 Richard Ram was appointed supervisor of the estate of Henry Barnard (late 16 C) a member of an important Great Waltham family, who is described as being a yeoman and had a very large inventory of £250 7sh. and 9d.

Such involvements illustrate the closely interlocked nature of community life in the village and parish. Although the nuclear family unit was the basic building block in social life these were not isolated, either from their own families or their peers. The evidence suggests that social networks were complex and sophisticated, and that people provided neighbourly services to one another. Presumably there was a relationship between the extent people were asked to fulfil neighbourly acts and the confidence their neighbours had in their abilities. Another factor no doubt at work was that some people made themselves more readily available than others.

A picture of the Ram family in early modern times

Many of the public happenings in which members of the family were involved are reported in Table 8. As in the medieval period there are involvements in land deals, but not to the same extent, and those that did occur were mainly early in the period. Thomas, who participated with his wife Joyce in the deal of 1598 with John Goodeve, was almost certainly the eldest son of Robert Ram. The John Ram mentioned in the dealings at South Hanningfield in 1594 and 1595 could be John 1B, as no other adult John was alive at this time in Great Waltham. The contributions to community life through office holding in the manor, and in other ways, continued and will be discussed in more detail later. Table 8 provides a few fleeting personal glimpses of people, as does Table 4 for the medieval period. Several family members were required to help with road repairs in 1627. It also seems that some of the family were not all that community minded and were brought before the manor court for misdemeanours. Henry Ram must have been a bit of a tearaway. His connection with the family is unclear but it is possible he was a grandson of the Geoffrey Ram who died at Nevendon in 1584.[115] The list indicates there

Table 8. Public events in the Ram family at Great Waltham – 1550-1650.

1568	William Ram constable in petty sessions Great Lyeghs.
1580	John Ram – constable, Great Waltham.
1586	Richard Ram juror in quarter sessions.
1587	Charter of William Ram of Colchester son of John of Pleacey deceased granting lands he held by the will of his father to Nicholas Eve of High Easter.
1594	Robt. Cradock and Jn. Rame, pl. Jn. Tyrell esq. def. 12a.ar. 12a. pa and 8 a. wood in S Hanningfield. £60.[112]
1595	Jn. Pascall, gent. pl. Jn. Ram[m]e, gent. And wife Alice and Robert Cradock and w. Mary def. 12 a.ar. I a. pa. And 8 a. wood in S Hanningfield. £40.[113]
1598	Sale from Thomas Ramme, yeoman of Great Waltham, to John Goodeve of Little Edcombe and 4 acres. This deal also appears in the feet of fines in the following terms – Jn. Goodeve, pl. Thomas Ramme and wife Joyce def. 5a. ar. In Great Waltham £40.[114]
1621	John Ram indicted for not completing his share in mending roads.
1622	Daniel Ram, husbandman in Great Waltham indicted for killing deer in the park.
1622	Daniel Ram was juror of Walthambury Manor.

1627	Record of people liable for highway duty in Great Waltham. Some people had to provide carts, and the Rams were not required to do this. Others were called upon to be labourers and the following members of the family are listed: John Ram (weaver), Daniel Ram, Thomas Ram, and Henry Ram.
1639	Thomas Ram was juror of Walthambury Manor.
1641	Daniel Ram was Constable.
1641	Henry Ram gives evidence in (manor?) court.
1641	Henry Ram a witness in (manor court?).
?	Recognisances of Henry Ram, jun., farmer, and Henry Ram, senior, barber.
1643	Thomas Ram was juror of Walthambury Manor.
1646	Thomas Ram was juror of Walthambury Manor.
1647	Henry Ram in goal for non payment of sureties.
1647	Thomas Ram was juror of Walthambury Manor.
1650	Thomas Ram was juror of Walthambury Manor.

are two Henrys, father and son, who may be the father and son who were connected with Raleigh, about fifteen miles away, in the mid seventeenth century.

Many of the Ram family were farmers, and without doubt some of them were of yeoman status, but how many of them were and what did it mean in economic and social terms? How much land yeomen held is difficult to know. But Mildred Campbell ventures to say that in arable areas it was mainly from 25 to 200 acres. The yeoman was clearly to be identified with larger farmers who were developing farming on a commercial basis.[116] A helpful guide to where the Ram family fitted in is a table in volume four of *The Agrarian History of England and Wales* which shows the expenditure and output pattern of a hypothetical arable farm of 30 acres for the period 1600-1620, based on general knowledge of costs and earnings. The picture given there is set out here in Table 9[117] and it may not be too far removed from the situation on Ram farms at this time, although some of them had more land than this. Regional variations have to be allowed for in using this information. Central Essex probably did well out of being a wheat and barley growing area, with mixed farming, that had access to the rapidly growing metropolitan market. But although it was fairly near London it was not near enough to be affected overmuch by its high wage economy.[118] Moreover Great Waltham rents were much lower than those quoted in the Table 9 example. In 1568 Robert Ram's rents in total were only 14sh. and 2d for around thirty acres of land. Rents were also stable and there is no reason to suppose they increased much by 1600. Such a rental difference would increase the profit margin quoted in the example by over 35 per cent. If earnings differentials between Great Waltham and London are taken into account Robert Ram almost certainly exceeded the £50 which Peter Earle estimates to have been the lower limit of middle class income.[119] In addition he possessed and sub let several small properties. The will of Robert's son Richard reveals he held about eighty acres at the time of his death and must have been more wealthy than his father, perhaps significantly so.

The economic scale of the model described would not have normally required hired workers. Costs on seed were very high by modern standards and reflected their wasteful use at that time, but other costs like manure and equipment were lower. Farm implements were quite rudimentary.

Table 9. Expenditure and output pattern of a hypothetical arable farm of 30 acres for the period 1600-1620.

Item	cost (£/s/p)	output (£/s/p)	
Seed (wheat and barley)	09/13/09	10 acres fallow	
		20 acres crops	42/10/00
Rent (30 acres @ 4/-)	06/00/00	Minus Tithes	04/05/00
Manure	01/02/06		
Feed for oxen	02/12/00		
Interest and capital depreciation on stock and equipment	04/17/06		
Miscellaneous costs	10/00		
Totals	23/15/09		38/05/00
Profit	£38/05/00 - £23/15/09 = £14/09/03		

W G Hoskins found in sixteenth century Leicestershire that the average farmer above the poorest possessed a plough, one or two carts, and two or three harrows, plus spades, scythes and rakes. Much of it was made from timber and could be home produced. The most expensive item was the cart or wain, especially if the wheel rims were made of iron. Ploughs were cheap. Altogether it seems doubtful that the small farmer's capital equipment was worth more than about £3. Many farmers had some animals which produced income, and used horses, but oxen were cheaper to feed in the winter.

A thirty acre farm did not bring riches but the profit of about £14 was significantly more than farm labourers earned at the time – a maximum of £10 and 8sh. a year based on 10d a day. Allowing for some non working time it seems unlikely that the earnings of labourers were much above £9. Thus the farmer's income would have been some 60-70 per cent higher.[120] However, the figures presented here could be very markedly affected by adverse harvest conditions, and a farmer with a thirty acre holding would always tend to be 'on the margin'.

Though much obscurity still exists about the origins, extent and even the nature of agrarian changes in the Tudor and early Stuart periods, certain generalisations can be made. After the Black Death much land reverted to waste, land rents fell, owners withdrew from active farming, labour services were commuted, and the size of the labour force fell. Peasant holdings grew in size at the expense of commercial undertakings and there was a general upgrading of the village community.[121] But in the sixteenth and seventeenth centuries, under the stimulus of growing population, rising agricultural prices, and mounting land values, the demand for land became more intense and its use more efficient. The area under cultivation was extended. Large estates were built up at the expense of small holdings, and subsistence farming lost ground to commercialised agriculture. Changes in the balance of land distribution were accompanied by an increase in the number of agricultural wage-earners and a decline in their standard of living. In 1641 it was estimated a quarter of the population were poor and towards the end of the seventeenth century the poor may have been nearly half of everyone. Wage levels became lower to a significant extent.[122] There was a growing inequality of income among the different classes of rural society.[123]

From 1400 to 1650 there was a long and large rise in prices generally. Within this long term trend agricultural prices, particularly for grain, were subject to wild short term fluctuations. There tended to be sequences of bad and good harvests. The weather seems to have had a significant and basic influence, affecting output and indirectly population, so much so that a long run of good harvests meant a rise in the demand for clothing. There were also trade cycle fluctuations. Apart from these it is possible to discern periods of ten years or more when grain prices rose against other prices or vice versa.[124] Overall prices rose more in agricultural commodities than other products, although this was not continuous and the biggest increases by far were from 1540-1590. In the second half of the seventeenth century the general trend of agricultural prices was in fact downwards. This came about because of improved efficiency combined with the use of an increased cultivated land area. Monetary factors, like debasement of the coinage and imports of bullion from South America cannot account for all of the rises, and a significant proportion of them must have been due to a positive balance in overseas trade. Another factor was population growth, and then relative decline from about 1620. Overall the population may have more or less doubled between 1500 and 1700. Since agricultural processes keep ahead of others the people who benefited most in these general circumstances would have been agricultural producers who farmed for the market. This group showed a tendency to save and not spend lavishly and the most marked gains would have been made in the second half of the sixteenth century and early years of the seventeenth.[125]

These background trends help to put the economic position of the Rams in context. The wills of Thomas Ram (d. 1556) and Robert Ram (d.1576) show a rather similar scale of operation and capital investment to that of the model – the lists of tools contained in them match it fairly closely, although allowance has to be made for the fact that the model relates directly to a time fifty years later than they lived. What is quite clear is that in the period covered by the model, 1600-1620, Robert Ram's family was operating above the level described in it and that the other Rams in Great Waltham were probably on the lower side of it. Perhaps the family as a whole could be classified among what Mildred Campbell describes as '... a group of ambitious, aggressive, small capitalists, aware that they had not enough surplus to take great risks, mindful that the gain is often as much in the saving as in the spending, but determined to take advantage of every opportunity, whatever their origins, for increasing their profits'.[126] It is unlikely they behaved exactly according to the caricature but they were almost certainly like it to a degree.

The general impression obtained from the family records is that the second half of the sixteenth century was a time of prosperity and that the second half of the seventeenth century was quite a lot harder. It has been seen that at the time of 1523-26 lay subsidy, their status position was mostly in the upper middle of the four taxation categories in that subsidy, whilst in the seventeenth century hearth taxes they were not more than lower middle, and may have been below that. Very few, if any, of them at the later time were on the upper side of the thirty acre divide. The number of children born in families certainly became smaller and the wills convey a lesser sense of prosperity. In one sense the family trend of increased prosperity followed by relative decline fits well with the general picture of agricultural and economic change during the sixteenth and seventeenth centuries.[127] These general forces must have affected many families to a lesser or greater extent, and how they coped with them would have had an impact too. The Rams showed signs of different capacities to cope. Robert Ram's family declined in the seventeenth century and eventually died out, whilst the other, which was originally less prosperous, survived and then prospered. But the question of coping was complex. It could be influenced by chance, and the failure of Daniel (d. 1689) to have surviving sons was at least one factor affecting the fate of that part of the family.

In the 1662 hearth tax five family members are listed at Great Waltham – John, Richard, Thomas, Daniel and another John. All but Thomas had one hearth who had two.[128] In 1671, which is regarded as the best documented of these taxes, there were three family members – Daniel, John and Richard, all of whom had one hearth.[129] It is difficult to identify these men precisely but some of them belonged to the family descended from Thomas and others from Robert's. However, it seems clear that in the latter part of the seventeenth century the social status of both parts of the family in Great Waltham was more less the same, and is further evidence of the decline of Robert's descendants.

In 1662 there were 128 people who paid the tax, of whom 37 had more than two hearths, so the Rams were nearly all among the 93 payers at the lower end. Their position was more or less the same in 1671 when there were 46 payers with more than 2 hearths out of a total of 127. The 1671 tax returns are particularly interesting because they list 65 people who were excused payment because of poverty, so there was still quite a large raft of people in the parish below the level occupied by the Rams.

Wrightson and Levine in their book on Terling divided up the hearth tax payers using the same socio-economic categories devised for the lay subsidy of 1523-26. People with one hearth were considered to be labourers and the poor.[130] It is difficult to relate such a categorisation to the Ram family. Their economic status was clearly not that low even though their houses only had one hearth. Margaret Spufford believes there are potential problems with these generalised categorisations when it comes to relating them to individual people. Although they make sense in the round they do not necessarily tell the whole story. In her work on Cambridgeshire she collected quite a lot of information about the wealth of householders through inventories, which are not available at Great Waltham. She believed this information showed there is an overall relationship between wealth and the number of hearths, but she also found that the range of wealth among people with the same number of hearths varied considerably, particularly as the number of hearths increased. The range was smallest with people who had one hearth – four fifths of such people had under £50 in wealth and the median level was £25. When it came to three hearths the range in wealth was from just under £30 to £500, which at that time was a very large difference.[131] She says '... the extent of the economic and social overlap shown by the inventories, and the blurring of economic and social divisions caused by inheritance and personal preference mean that although the tax may be used as a guide to status and wealth in general, it may not be safely used in any individual example'.[132] But it was probably more of a guide at the lower end than the higher. Recent examination of national hearth tax payments suggests consistently more houses paid for three hearths in the south and east of the country, and because they were the richer areas, it supports the idea that the number of hearths in a house is a predictor of its occupants' wealth. Nonetheless the author concludes with a cautionary note.

'There clearly was correlation between hearths, house size, wealth and social standing, but how close it was and by how much it varied between regions and between town and countryside remains to be established'.[133]

Perhaps the Rams lived a simple life. But even if they were not among the labouring poor in the second half of the seventeenth century there is no doubt they were economically among the lower status groups. It might be imagined that along with relative economic decline there would be an equivalent fall in social status in the community, and a lesser participation in public office holding. But this is not apparent. It has been seen in the previous chapter how the manor records early in the sixteenth century show the Ram family was among the most active of families in Great Waltham's public life. Such activity continued during the prosperous years in the remainder of the sixteenth century. An example is John Ram, presumably John IB who lived at Brades, who was one of three village constables in 1580. Being constable was important and onerous.[134] Another example is Richard Ram, presumably Robert's son, being a juror on the quarter sessions in 1586. There were various sorts of jury that had to be filled. The panels of trial or petty jury were chosen from names of all the freeholders in the Sheriff's book. A statute of 1584 says the lists should include all men with an income of £4 per annum in land, or £40 in goods, which was a wider base, and it is likely that people other than freeholders served on juries. The other juries were the grand or presenting jury which was county wide. There was also another form of the second kind of jury called a Hundred Jury, but did not speak for the county as a whole. There was a strong tendency for many people who actually served on these juries to be yeomen.[135] Community services provided by yeomen were mainly local. In the county and the hundred when they were involved they assisted the gentry. They only had two national involvements, voting in county elections, if a freeholder, and participation in the trained bands, which were a sort of army reserve.[136] Until the civil war there was no great interest in elections.[137]

The manor court of Walthambury was a significant body in the later middle ages and continued to record land and property transactions into the early nineteenth century. The part played by the Ram family at the earlier period has already been discussed. In 1532 Robert Ram, jun., probably the Robert who died in 1576, is listed as a head man, but his name does not appear again. The Thomas who served every year from 1534 to 1543 was almost certainly the Thomas who died in 1556. After that time the rolls of the manor court stop listing the head men. Involvements of this kind continued in the first half of the seventeenth century, and beyond, in company with other villagers who constituted a community leadership group. Rams appear regularly in a list of names that appeared at the head of the court roll, along with about fifteen others. The exact function of this group is not clear, but it probably fulfilled a similar role to the head men of the early sixteenth century. Some members of the family were very active. Thomas, who it has not been possible to identify in the family record was on this list in 1639, 1643, and then most years from 1646 to 1657, and Daniel (d. 1632) was on it in 1622.[138]

There is a pattern in this involvement during the mid seventeenth century which possibly throws light on the family's political allegiances. Although participation in parish affairs was quite regular in Tudor times it tailed off during the reigns of James I and Charles I and then became very strong during the Commonwealth, from 1639 onwards. At the restoration involvement ceased suddenly for twenty years. It is possible the fluctuations were due to generational patterns in the family but it may indicate strong Parliamentary leanings.

Part of the status enjoyed by the Ram family derived from their position within the farming community both inside and outside Great Waltham. Opportunities came their way which brought gain but also involved supporting others at the same time, as the following example shows. Richard Aylett (d. 1599) of Doddinghurst, a nearby village, was a yeoman of some substance and must have died quite young. In his will he leaves '... to my wife my messuage and land called Halls and Coles in High Easter in the occupation of Robert Ram for eight years from Michaelmas 1602 until Richard [Richard Aylett's son] be gone out of his years of apprenticeship for eight years from thence next ensuing'.[139] This arrangement was made between Richard Ram of Great Waltham and Richard Aylett, possibly when the latter was ailing, and would have given his son Robert, then in his early twenties, experience of running a farm and at the same time helped Richard Aylett's widow cope with a minority situation. It is possible Richard Aylett served his apprenticeship with Richard Ram. This story is a good example of mutuality in a small rural community.

XIII
Tenant Farmers, 1650-1850

The 1805 survey

This is the second anchor point, along with the survey of 1577, to the documentation of events in Great Waltham. It was decided in 1805 to 'survey and value all the land and houses within the parish in order to make and settle an equal poor rate'[140] in anticipation that a workhouse would be set up. This happened in many parishes at the turn of the nineteenth century, but records show that another thirteen years passed before one was actually built in Great Waltham.[141] From an historical point of view the two surveys are important documents because they show just how much land holding practice, and the farming environment of the parish, changed over more than two hundred years.

All the holdings are listed by acreage, and in the case of the larger farms their names and occupants are often identified. A total of 104 are recorded, together with the tithe paid. Also listed are the names of 118 cottagers, who are described as 'necessitous poor'. None of the available information provides a complete picture of the total population and social makeup of Great Waltham at this time. The survey only lists the number of farms and the necessitous poor, without making clear what exactly this group comprised. The only other information is in a small book by H E Flight which says the total population in 1805 was 1475.[142] and that 328 people were 'in farming' and 118 'in trade'.[143] This too fails to provide a full social picture of the parish. However, Flight's overall figure fits quite well with later ones from the censuses of 1881 and 1901 in which the population was 2349 and 2222 respectively.[144]

Table 10 shows how the number and size of landholdings changed between 1577 and 1805. Compared with the earlier time they have grown larger, but the change is not revolutionary. The number over 50 acres has more or less doubled, and the number under 50 acres has fallen. The number of holdings of under 10 acres has halved and it seems likely the others grew at their expense. Obviously as the farms grew larger there would be less overall and the total number is down by about 25 per cent.

Table 10. Changes in size of landholdings at Great Waltham between 1577 and 1805.

Landholding (acres).	1805.		1577.	
	Number.	Per cent.	Number.	Per cent.
200+.	4	03.8	2	2.2
100-199.	14	13.5	7	5.1
50-99.	18	17.3	10	7.4
10-49.	42	40.4	46	33.8
Under 10.	26	25.0	71	52.2
Totals.	104	100	136?	100.7

At the end of the survey is a statement, shown in Figure. 6, which details how it was conducted and who made it. 'We the following parishioners being chosen as a committee to survey and value all the land and houses within the parish in order to make and settle an equal poor rate, and after having valued and surveyed the said houses and lands did publicly expose for the examination of the overseers and occupiers of the lands and houses valued as aforesaid a copy of the valuation and assessment, that any owner or occupier thereby thinking themselves aggrieved might appeal to the said committee, a day being publicly appointed for that purpose when the aforesaid appellants were heard, and their complaints duly attended to and relieved as the committee thought fit – have examined and do allow of the estimations as are here stated in this book'.

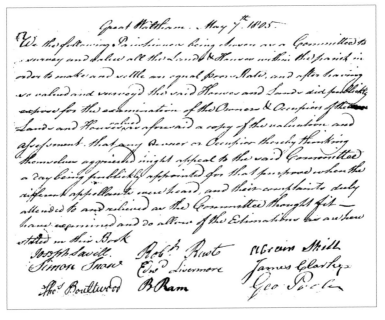

Figure 6. Great Waltham survey committee, 1805.

The people who formed the committee were no doubt representative of the more important parishioners, and nearly all of them were farmers or landowners. Three of the nine men ran farms of over 200 acres, four ones of over 100 acres and only one had a relatively small farm of 79 acres. So the committee was drawn almost exclusively from the larger farmers. It is well known that during the eighteenth and nineteenth centuries this group came generally to dominate the running of village life, but the reasons are not particularly clear. In fact why such a situation came about is rather puzzling. Why should village life be less egalitarian in the nineteenth than it was in the sixteenth century? There was no real incentive for the larger farmers to claim dominance, because the administrative powers of the parish had become progressively weaker since the seventeenth century. The apparent elitism may simply have been a consequence of the growth in average farm size, which meant that the relative importance of middle ranking farmers in the community was reduced, although the desire to control rate-funded expenditure could also have played a part.

In the 228 years between the two surveys there was a great turnover among the tenants and family names frequently died out. Only three families are present in both of them, the Sorrells, the Goodeves and the Rams. This level of population change was similar to that which happened in the period from 1300 to the middle of the sixteenth century. But whether it represented people coming and going from the parish or was simply the result of the male line dying out is uncertain. In 1805, as in 1577, some families – twelve in the later survey – had several holdings, and one or two individuals also had more than one. The Tufnell family, who initially held Langleys Manor had become by 1805 the dominant local landowner. They are shown in the survey as having two small holdings, but these must have been those not let out to tenants, and the true position was very different. During the eighteenth century they gradually bought more and more land – mostly copyhold, and then around 1780 obtained Walthambury Manor.[145] Several other families held very large tenanted holdings. The Poole family held two farms with a total acreage of 835 acres, and the Emberson family had four holdings which totalled 357 acres. Benjamin Ram 2 (1765-1825) probably had two holdings in Great Waltham and another in Roxwell. Other people may also have held bigger total holdings than is revealed by the survey because some of them were outside Great Waltham.

The great changes in farming between 1650 and 1850
Although the Ram family had a long history in Great Waltham, as yeomen and husbandmen, it only just survived in the mid seventeenth century and this crisis may have been related to changes in land holding patterns. Prior to then the farming system in the parish had been stable for two hundred years, in a way which secured the position of the small and medium sized landholder. But in the hundred years from the mid 1600s there were major changes in

agricultural practice that had a significant impact on the farming community. In a well documented study of Terling, a village very near Great Waltham, the social and economic climate became significantly more extreme. The village population grew appreciably in size, whilst the number of farmers stayed more or less the same. Farms grew larger so that the men who controlled them made good profits, as did the craftsmen who serviced their needs. The increase in numbers was almost wholly of landless labourers, who, whilst they could find employment on the larger farms, did not share in the growing prosperity of the farmers. In 1671 perhaps a third of Terling's population needed charitable support.[146] Earlier discussion has shown that developments at Terling were somewhat different from those at Great Waltham, but the trend was similar.[147]

Landowners were participants in the agricultural system. In the Elizabethan and Stuart periods several factors helped them. The value of land as an investment, and the social status attached to it, raised demand and this offered possibilities for increasing rents —though some owners realised capital by selling land and commodities such as timber. But no less important were the rising profits that could be obtained by owners through farming their own land directly. Population growth was increasing requirements for food, and real costs were falling because of a combination of improvements in productivity and relative decreases in other costs. In many areas rural populations grew faster than the availability of industrial employment, so labour was easy to obtain and cheap. But part, or all of this margin, often went to the tenant as much as to the owner.[148]

The extent that owners generally benefited from social and economic changes depended to a large part on the tenancy terms prevailing. In the sixteenth century tenure was still influenced by the land surplus of the fourteenth and fifteenth centuries. While demesne lands were sometimes leased on a short term basis customary holdings were usually subject to long term leases, or to a very high degree of tenant security, e.g., copyhold, which was often little different to freehold ownership as we now know it. Freehold rents were fixed and could not be increased. Some copyholders might not do so well where there were constraints on their security. For example, entry fines could be very high, so high that they could not be paid and the land was lost. If tenants were forced to give up historic holdings the owner was able to increase rents or bring in shorter fixed leases. How much this happened is not known.[149] There is no doubt that on many manors the acreage under lease was growing at the expense of copyhold, but the change of tenure did not necessarily imply a change of tenant. Other factors came into play as a result of land shortage and rising prices. Tenants could sub-let. '... tenants who occupied under rented holdings were well placed to sub-let all or part of their property at enhanced rates'.[150] These rents did not appear as official tenancies. Movements in rents during Tudor and early Stuart times cannot be measured with any exactness, but it is clear that those for large leasehold farms on private estates went up significantly. There was also a narrowing of differences between rent for poor land and better land. There were, moreover, other ways in which a landowner could earn income from his land. Even if rents could not be increased maintenance costs traditionally borne by the owner were increasingly passed on to the tenant, like repairs and estate improvements.[151]

How profit margins on larger and smaller farms compared in the seventeenth century is not really known. There was though a difference which arose from the larger farmer having a proportionately greater surplus for sale, and that he could be more selective about when produce was allowed onto the market. However the small farmer had certain cost advantages, as the larger ones had to hire labour.[152] The trend towards larger farms let at an economic rent gathered pace in the seventeenth and eighteenth centuries. It happened at the expense of yeoman farmers and husbandmen, whose opportunities in the sixteenth and early seventeenth centuries to expand horizons were curtailed, although the reasons were complex and not all that clear. Many yeoman and husbandman families disappeared.[153]

There is a lack of clear information about how and when major changes took place in Great Waltham, although the indication is that they happened in the eighteenth century rather than the seventeenth. By this period the manor functioned purely as a mechanism for transferring land.[154] Three major influences contributed to changing landholding practices: accidents of ownership; the owners' personal preferences; and a general trend towards leasing at commercial rents. The Everardes were the dominant local family during the seventeenth century and farmed most of the demesne at Walthambury Manor themselves. In 1643 a survey showed it amounted in total to 789 acres, and 505 were farmed personally. A relatively small portion of 284 acres was rented to others.[155] In fact although the Everarde family were made baronets by James I they never owned Walthambury Manor. Their position was established by buying up the freehold and copyhold titles of other tenants over a long period and farming them personally as tenants. They were always lessees of the manor of Walthambury, owned by the earls of Essex from the Dissolution until 1701 (when it was sold to Herman Olmius, a Dutch merchant). The Tufnell family came to Great Waltham in 1710 when they bought Langleys from the Everardes. They continued the practice of buying up freehold and copyhold titles but instead of farming these holdings themselves consolidated them into larger farms and let them at commercial rents. During the eighteenth century they gradually bought more land—mostly copyhold—and in about 1780 acquired Walthambury Manor. The Tufnell family eventually owned over 5000 acres of the parish as well as other estates beyond its boundaries. At the end of his life John Joliffe Tufnell (d. 1793) had a total rental income of about £18,000 a year plus ready money of £150,000. Alterations in the way land was let in Great Waltham during the seventeenth and eighteenth centuries went hand in hand with changes in ownership.

The end of the Napoleonic War brought a crisis to Essex agriculture, which included a depression that lasted on and off for many years. Farmers with land bought or rented at war time levels faced steep decreases in wheat prices while paying nearly as much for rent, poor rates, and manufactured goods as during the war. After a brief recovery in 1824-25 the depression was renewed. By 1830 things were even worse, and farmers were petitioning for rent reductions, which only came through after 1834.[156] In the period 1785 to 1854 national average wheat prices were at their highest in 1810-1814 at 102.4 shillings a quarter but were only just over half this level throughout the years from 1835 to 1854. They were at their lowest in 1850 to 1854 at 49.03 shillings a quarter.[157] There was sporadic unrest among agricultural workers during this period[158] which led in the late thirties and forties to incendrism.[159] In Essex 452 incendiary attacks were reported in the newspapers during the nineteenth century and 211 of them happened in the decade 1840-1849 which was by far the worst period.[160] Together this information suggests the 1840s and early 1850s were bad years for both farmers and farm labourers.

The farmers who did worst in the post war depression were newcomers who took on high rents.[161] It is likely that those who were more experienced and kept the same farm and landlord for many years did best, since it was in such circumstances that supportive understanding in difficult times was likely to be obtained. By 1855 Essex farming was moving towards a modest prosperity, and despite some bad seasons, this continued up to 1874.[162]

Power and status in the community III
Ram family involvement in the local community that has been observed at Great Waltham in Tudor and early Stuart times continued in a similar way during the later seventeenth and eighteenth centuries, notwithstanding their economic decline. Daniel (d. 1689) was Constable in 1641 and on the list of jurors in the 1650s and again quite regularly in the 1680s. Richard (d. 1669) was a juror in 1652, 1654 and 1658, and Joseph (d. 1726) was constable in 1707 and juror in 1707, 1708, 1709, and 1711. Daniel (d. 1722) was Constable in 1711 and on the juror's list in 1717, 1720 and 1722.

I have attempted to establish the general status level of the jury group in the years, 1639, 1651, and 1685, by examining the number of hearths recorded in the 1671 hearth tax returns for the families which served as jurors in those three years. Even though many of the names are illegible and it is difficult to identify individual people precisely, about a quarter of the jurors came from wealthy families and the remainder from middling ones, not unlike the Rams of that time. There was a tendency for the same individuals and families to serve repeatedly. Most of the family names present in 1639 were also involved in 1647, although there are more new names in 1685. But half are still the same as in the earlier years. Another feature of the names is that on each occasion between a third and a half of them are from families who were long resident in Great Waltham, like the Sorrells, Eves, Goodeves, Everardes, Barnards, Knightsbridges and Rams. All the Ram involvements after 1650 are listed in Table 11.

The continued presence of Robert Ram's descendants in this group is another example of power and status in the village community not being confined to the wealthy. The Ram family had been important in Great Waltham for a long time over which it had established a status niche that almost certainly enabled rentention of social place while economic fortunes ran down. This was a sort of living off the past, which is not uncommon. The social position of the family was also enhanced by their being yardland tenants. 'At Great Waltham, Felsted and High Easter there were definite indications of 'class' distinctions between copyholders. Those who still held ancient 'yardland', 'half yardland', and 'quarter yardland' holdings formed an aristocracy among copyhold tenants, whilst the bulk of the copyholders were 'Ancient Customary Tenantes' at Felsted or just 'other' customary tenants at High Easter'.[163] Such status also brought responsibilities and in Great Waltham the yardland tenants were liable to be Beadle.[164]

Members of the other Ram family in Great Waltham, descended from Thomas, were also involved as jurors, and seem to increase their role as the economic position of Robert's family declined. Richard was a juror in 1685, 1686, 1687, and 1688 and John 4B, his grandson was one quite regularly in the first half of the eighteenth century. John 4B's son Daniel was also a juror in 1720, 1722, and 1748.[165] Except for the Court Roll few parish records for Great Waltham are available until after the Ram family left in the 1820s. At the beginning of one of the overseers' rate books there is a list of parish officers for the years 1836-1846 – the Church wardens, overseers and surveyors – and the bigger landholders appear again and again.[166] The Vestry minutes from 1839-1862 make it clear that the major landowners and landholders dominated proceedings and office holding. None of the names dominant in the eighteenth century appear, except that of Tufnell. The post of constable was increasingly filled by tradesmen. The occupations of people becoming constable were first noted for the period from 1842-1846, when they were carpenter, baker, farmer, butcher, shoemaker, and veterinary surgeon. The practice of naming occupations continued until 1847 and the pattern of 1842 was similar throughout. Far fewer farmers were appointed to this post than had been the case in earlier times.[167]

Table 11. Members of the Ram family who served as jurors and constables 1650-1756.

1650	#Thomas Ramme.
	Court roll written in English from 1651.
1651	#Thomas Ram.
1652	*Richard Rame_ (probably 1618-1669 son of Daniel who was juror in 1622).
1653	#Thomas and *Daniel Rame** (probably 1617-1689 elder brother of Richard).
1654	#Thomas and *_Richard Rame._
1655	#Thomas and *Daniel Rame.**
1656	#Thomas Ramme.
1657	#Thomas Ram.
1658	*_Richard Ram._
1660	*Daniel Ram.**
1660	**Court roll written in Latin again.**
1681	*DANIEL RAM(probably 1659-1722 – nephew of _Richard_ and **Daniel**).
1683	*DANIEL RAM.
1684	*DANIEL RAMME.
1685	#'RICHARD RAMME (probably 1634-1714 descendant of #Thomas) and *_DANIEL RAME._
1686	*_DANIEL RAME_ and #RICHARD RAM.
1687	#RICHARD RAM and *_DANIEL RAME._
1688	#RICHARD RAM one of three constables.
1707	*Joseph Ram Constable.
1708	*Joseph Ram (probably d. 1726, or son b.1683 – son or grandson of _Richard._
1709	*Joseph Ram.
1711	*Joseph Ram.
1711	*_DANIEL RAME_ Constable (one of three).
1717	*_DANIEL RAME._
1733	**Court roll again written in English.**
1717	#JOHN RAM Constable (one of three) (1686-1762) grandson of #RICHARD).
1719	#JOHN RAME.
1720	**#DANIEL RAME.**
1721	#JOHN RAME one of three constables.
1722	#JOHN and **#DANIEL RAME.**
1727	#JOHN RAME.
1734	#JOHN RAMM one of three constables.
1740	#JOHN RAMM.
1749	**#DANIEL RAME** (1728-? son of JOHN).
1756	#JOHN RAM.

\# Descendant of Thomas Ram.

* Descendant of Robert Ram.

A picture of the Ram family in modern times

The sources of Information about what happened to the Ram family are not entirely the same as those used previously. Wills, for example, stop detailing how land and property was left – often there is just a bald statement saying all the property is left to a particular person, or outstanding leases are left to children without them being detailed. Perhaps as the copyhold system died out and leases became the norm there was less property to treat as inheritances. Fortunately the census returns compensate for these shortcomings, especially from 1841 onwards.

Over this period the Rams changed first from a family of several relatively small copyhold/freehold farmers with from 15 to 50 acres into one where a few leaseholders worked up to 450 acres, who were probably wealthier than their forebears but had no pretensions to being owners of land. Then, by the late nineteenth century, the whole family became landless and had removed from the Great Waltham area to become absorbed into the growing mass of employed people. These developments probably represented the biggest changes ever to affect the farming members of the family.

The person who sets the scene for these changes is John Ram 4B. He had fifteen children and it was through him that the family in the male line survived in Great Waltham. Chart B3 shows how this happened. Among all his children five boys survived to become adults, but only one of them, Benjamin 1 (1729-89) the youngest, became a farmer, but from him sprang three further generations of large tenant farmers. Both of his sons became farmers, Benjamin Ram 2 and John Ram 6B (1768-1835). Although all Benjamin Ram 2's children were baptised in Great Waltham, the last of them being born in 1797, he was the final farming member of the family to

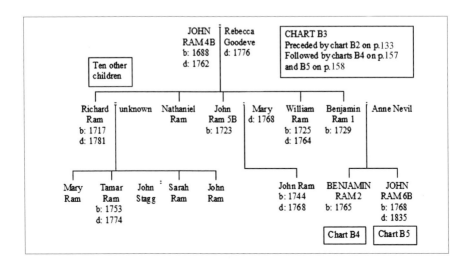

be closely associated with Great Waltham. Even so in later life he lived at Roxwell, a few miles from Great Waltham. His son William Ram 2 (1797-abt. 1881) took over his father's farm at Roxwell. Benjamin 2's brother John 6B moved to Steeple about fifteen miles away and his sons continued farming in that area until the mid nineteenth century. Most of the other sons of John Ram 4B, including Richard (1717-1781), John Ram 5B (1723-1785), and William Ram 1 (1725-1764) took up other occupations, and moved away from Great Waltham.

Not a great deal is known about John 4B, and that comes from his will and the account books of Samuel Tufnell (mid 18C) who was the largest local landowner. He had some interest in the Glebe of Great Waltham, which possibly contained around 125 acres, and in Hill Farm in North End, which amounted to about 150 acres. He also owned a malting business in Great Waltham which was left to Richard, his eldest son. Information about Benjamin 1 is also scrappy as his will does not make clear how much land he farmed or where it was. However it was probably quite a lot, which he wanted to pass on to his sons, Benjamin 2 and John 6B. His will states interest in several unspecified leases are to go to them equally. 'I give and bequeath unto my two sons Benjamin and John Ram the several leases and terms for years of and in my leases and lands which I shall die possessed of or with title unto and all my estate rights and interest in the several farms and lands respectively to hold the same to them their executors administrators and assignees for the remainder of the several terms therein respectively audit'.[168] He wanted the two sons to take over these leases jointly, perhaps because John 6B was not quite twenty one at the time of his death. However if they chose not to do this the shared interest could be divided with the guidance of disinterested third parties, and one of them could move elsewhere, which is what happened, although not for several years.

That Benjamin 2 remained associated with Great Waltham is clear from the contribution he made to the 1805 survey, and the land tax return of 1813/14 shows he leased a farm of 108 acres in Howe Street and Chatham End in Great Waltham parish from Trinity College Oxford, probably Rectory Farm.[169] In a booklet about the history of Rectory Manor in the Essex Review Revd Andrew Clark explained its history.[170] The Abbey of Waldon, which owned the Rectory prior to the dissolution, got the agreement of the Lord of Walthambury Manor in the late middle ages to make the Rectory lands a separate manor. These included the Glebe land, which became the demesne of the new manor. At the dissolution the Rectory and its manor remained united, and were ultimately bought by Trinity College, Oxford. A survey of it was made in the years 1573-6 and is still possessed by Trinity College. Although Benjamin 2 was active in Great Waltham his will states he lived at Newland Hall in Roxwell, about three miles away. Newland Hall was the rather grand farmhouse of Newland

Farm of about 200 acres which he leased. He probably also had an interest in
the Glebe at Great Waltham as there is a note in the 1805 survey by Benjamin's
name to say that the rents for the Glebe are to be deducted. It is known that
the Ram family held the Glebe earlier during the eighteenth century and this
note may indicate Benjamin was sub letting. A document in the Essex Record
Office has a drawing of the Glebe in 1817 which says it comprised 124 acres
and that it was let to Henry Sanford.[171] If Benjamin was holding all three
properties his total holding was around 427 acres.

Chart B4 shows that Benjamin 2 had two sons Benjamin 3 (1795- ?), who was
identified in his father's will to take over at Newland Hall, and William 2 (1797-
about 1880). What William 2 inherited on his father's death is not all that clear.
'I give and bequeath unto my son William Ram all my share and profit which
may appear in the lease of little Boyton Hall my name being put there at the
request of Lord Peter but not that I ever intended taking any share in the profits
that might arise from it'.[172] Little Boyton Hall was a neighbouring farm of 269
acres also owned by the Bramston family who lived in Roxwell from 1639,
when they bought the Screens estate, well into the nineteenth century.[173] What
happened in 1825 is unclear but the tithe map of 1842 shows that William
2 was renting Newland Hall farm at that time.[174] He remained there until his
death after 1881.[175] Benjamin 3 must have had personal problems for in the
1851 census he is described as a farm labourer living in Chelmsford.[176] There is
no reference to him in the 1861 census, although he had five young children in
1851. The tithe map shows that Newland Farm formed a compact block of land
with Newland Hall virtually in the centre, which the accompanying field list
shows was mostly given over to arable use with 32.5 acres of pasture.

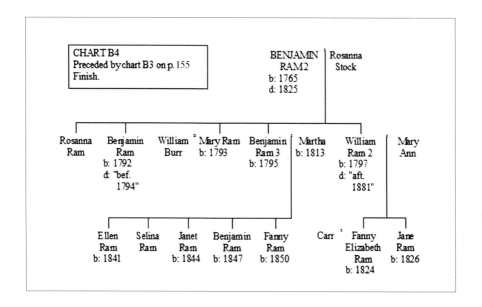

John 6B did not move away from Great Waltham until around 1804, for his first two children were baptised there in 1800 and 1803 but his third, Anne (b. 1804), was baptised at Purleigh, as were all his subsequent children. His association with a farm in Steeple near Purleigh, which he leased from John Tuffnell must have begun then. Besides being the major landowner in Great Waltham, John Tufnell owned land elsewhere, including Steeple, and John 6's move was almost certainly made with his support. Chart B5 contains an outline of John 6's family and that of his eldest son, John Ram 7B (1806-1852).

Two sources allow analysis of John 6B's economic position. Arthur Young wrote an *Agricultural Survey of Essex* in 1807, only three years before an estate steward valued John's Steeple farm and praised his stewardship: 'The whole has been very well managed and does the tenant credit'.[177] Young found that Essex farms varied greatly in size but 400-500 acres was considered large, many were of 200-300 acres, and there were large numbers of smaller holdings. Thus the farm of John 6B was among the largest. Rents varied considerably but according to Arthur Young were, on average about £1 an acre, and had doubled in the past 50 years.[178] The estate steward's survey showed the rent of John 6B's farm was £1 8sh. an acre so it may have been on the high side. On the other hand the farm was mostly tithe free, which were about 5/- an acre,[179] a factor that could account for a relatively high rent. The survey does not mention poor rates but presumably they also had to be paid. There is no doubt that between 1701 and 1835 rent levels increased substantially.

Colin Shrimpton in his more recent book on landed society and the farming community in Essex gives figures for five different areas and they are similar to Arthur Young's, as shown in Table 12. Shrimpton's estimates quoted

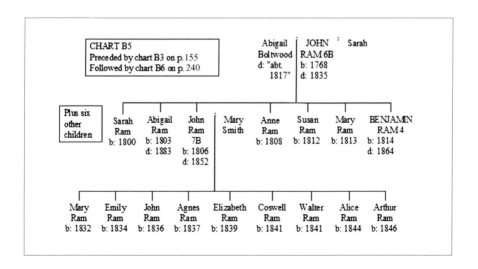

immediately below for central Essex cover Great Waltham, and are quite close to the overall average. Those for S E Essex cover Steeple and Purleigh, and although initially among the lowest increased more rapidly than most. Shrimpton's comments on the south east of the county are also relevant because of the moves of family members to Purleigh and Steeple in the nineteenth century.

Table 12. Rent levels in Central and S E Essex, 1700-1835.

	1701-50	1751-90	1791-1815	1816-35
Central Essex	9/1 (100)	14/9 (162)	20/7 (226)	30/8 (338)
S E Essex.	7/5 (100)	10/9 (145)	20/3 (274)	31/- (419)[180]

He says farmers came to value this area more and more as the profitability of wheat increased, for it grew the best wheat in the county, so the move of members of the Ram family to this area may have been calculated to bring gains and profits. If this was the case the outcome was mixed for the area suffered badly from poor harvests and the effects of agricultural depression, and although rents were abated by as much as 50 per cent for a time, they do not appear to have been permanently reduced.[181] Arthur Young used the accounts of a 200 acre farm to show the kind of profitability that could be obtained – around £1 13sh. per acre per annum, excluding rent, see Table 13. If this calculation is applied to John 7B's farm the result is an annual surplus of just over £770 and a profit of around £300 – which does not take account of either the economies of scale that would accrue on a much larger farm, the larger number of labourers that would be required, or the above average rent he paid.[182] A farm labourer at the time earned – very roughly – about £26 a year.[183]

Arthur Young believed most leases were effectively for 21 years, and that longer ones were going out of fashion. He lamented this on the grounds that they encouraged tenants to invest for profit and good farmers to stay with their farms.[184] Shrimpton also writes about the pattern of lease holding which developed in Essex. He makes clear that not all farms were on leases. Many were simply let from year to year, and some people farmed one farm for 40 years or more on that basis. There were different views about which approach was best. Short leases or no leases at all could lead to poor land management and over cropping of profitable crops, whilst leases as a whole tended to encourage tenants to be conservative, – to stop bad practice rather than make innovations. Owners nonetheless looked for tenants who would make improvements.[185] In the eighteenth century 21 year leases which had break options at 7 and 14 years were the most common in Essex. By the 1820s the leases grew shorter, with 7 or 14 years becoming more common.[186]

Table 13. Annual accounts in 1807 for a 200 acre farm near Felix Hall, Kelvedon, Essex.

Debits	£	s	d.	Credits	£	s	d.
Labour: 5 men @ £36/12.	183	0	0	25 acres of wheat.	350	0	0
Keep for 5 horses.	177	2	6	25 acres of soft corn.	243	15	0
Horse duty @ 12/- each.	3	0	0	12.5 acres of beans.	96	16	0
Poor rate & tithe.	66	0	0	12.5 acres of clover.	87	10	0
Wear and tear.	50	0	0	Profit of 4 cows @ 10/- each.	40	0	0
Seed.	70	12	6	Profit of 30 ewes @ 40/- each.	60	0	0
Interest on capital employed.	70	3	0	Profit of 30 lambs @ 30/- each.	45	0	0
Sundries.	10	0	0	Profit of 30 fleece of wool.	9	0	0
30 ewes @ 30/- each.	45	0	0	Profit of 20 hogs @ 40/- each.	40	0	0
20 pigs @ 20/- each.	20	0	0	Profit of 60 pigs from 4 sows @ 20/- each.	60	0	0
Feed for pigs.	20	0	0	Poultry.	10	0	0
Totals.	714	18	0		1042	1	0

Surplus: £327   3   0.

Profit: £127   3   0 (Assume rent to be £1 an acre). Profit is approximately .65 £ per acre.

The Rams certainly had leases because left over portions of them are passed on to sons in the wills of the period, and the impression gained is that most of them were for twenty one years. John Ram 6B's lease was for this length of time.[187]

The comments of Arthur Young two hundred years ago, and Colin Shrimpton in our own time, concerning the length of leases and the resulting attitudes of the tenant, raise an interesting issue. John 6B's father, Benjamin 1, left his sons the residue of his leases, probably in anticipation that they would be renewed. It seems as though the old copyhold rights of the sixteenth and seventeenth centuries were not forgotten quickly. It will shortly be seen that John 6B's approach to writing his will was very similar to that of his father. It is quite clear from the history of the Ram family in this period that interests in farms and local areas were retained over many years and several generations, just as in earlier times. Relationships between tenants and landowners were often long term and went a good deal beyond contractual obligations. Landlords were concerned about the well-being of tenants, for there was a strong spirit of independence among the farming community.[188] Landlords paid the greatest possible attention to the careful selection of tenants, especially in relation to their skill and capital resources, and were not beyond trying to exercise political influence over them. In general there was a good deal of mutuality in the shared interests of tenant and landowner. The tenant might want to preserve his lease interest whilst the owner would almost certainly want to keep good tenants. Although the theory and legal basis of the contract had changed, was there, in practice, some similarity with what had gone before? Of course there had to be renegotiation at the end of leases, when the owner had the right to increase rents, but if the tenant was a good one he had some bargaining power. By and large 'Essex tenants enjoyed a remarkably fine reputation as farmers ... especially for the great skill they had in the management of heavy land farming ... and praise from many quarters came to be heaped on the county's farming regions'.[189]

From 1750 onwards there was a sustained advance in farming which gathered pace up to the onset of the French Wars, when high wheat prices provided farmers with further prosperity. The ever continuing expansion of the London market fed this growth throughout.[190] Several of the Ram family, particularly in the late eighteenth and early nineteenth centuries ran big farms, and were what came to be called 'high' farmers. Analysis of the 1851 census shows that in England as a whole about half of all farms were between 100 and 300 acres and there were only 5,000 farms over 300 acres in the whole country.[191] Figures prepared by the *Essex Standard* in 1874 and based on the 1871 census show that this pattern was still true for Essex. Farmers were then more influential than ever before, some becoming businessmen and employers on a large scale. 39 farmed over 1000 acres, 351 had between 400-999 acres, 859 had between 200-399 acres. 256 farmers employed twenty or more men and 678 between 10 and 19.[192]

But tantalising questions remain about how some of the Rams became large leasehold farmers in the eighteenth century, whilst so many of them left farming. How did people come to obtain leases on larger farms as the more traditional smaller copyhold system declined? A fair amount of capital was required to make the initial agricultural investment. Capital requirements in central Essex in 1815 were put at £5 an acre, which went ever upwards. They had perhaps been about £3 an acre in 1770.[193] How was it that the only one of John 5B's five sons to become a farmer was the youngest? Where did Benjamin 1's capital come from? It does not appear to be his father's will for he only received £20 from it.

Most of John 4B's sons did not go into serious farming at all. Was this because there was more opportunity in the second half of the eighteenth century to do other things, or were they squeezed out of a more competitive system? The eldest, Richard Ram inherited all John 4B's property after a small provision was made for his mother Rebecca. '... and the rest of my house, heriditaments and real estate I leave to descend to my eldest son Richard and his heirs'.[194] This property was probably a malt house and kiln, and was in Richard's hands certainly from 1763 until 1777. In that year the Great Waltham court roll notes the following. 'The surrender by Richard Ram, maltser, to Thomas Bush, maltser of tenement with garden adjoining. All in How Street being now one messuage, a kitchen, malt house and kiln, and a yard and garden and the appurtenances to which Richard Ram was admitted in 1763'.[195] Presumably he sold the interest in the malt house at this time to retire. It also seems unlikely that Richard lived in Great Waltham for his children were born in Chelmsford and he married into a Chelmsford family. He appears to leave money in trust for his granddaughter Sarah Stagg, but this is uncertain for his will is almost illegible.[196] If it is assumed Richard followed the trade of a maltser through most of his adult life he would have been active during the period 1760-77. At this time the production of malt was fairly stable, and Essex was not as renowned for this trade as Hertfordshire and Bedfordshire. Even so there were presumably many local requirements for malt as Chelmsford was a regional brewing centre. Moreover with rising population the general volume of beer consumed increased almost continuously from the mid eighteenth century onwards.[197] It was a reasonably secure business to be involved in. Information about John 4's other sons is restricted to John Ram 5B and William Ram 1. John 5B also moved to Chelmsford where he became a Cordwainer. His will, in which he is styled gentleman, shows he was part of the circle in Chelmsford which linked the Rams and the Stagg family, for he left £150 to Sarah Stagg widow of John Stagg of Chelmsford, who was also a Cordwainer. Sarah Stagg was John 6B's niece and the daughter of Richard. There was another Cordwainer in John 5B's circle, Thomas Dance, of Chelmsford, and his wife was left £20. John 5 left many legacies to nephews and nieces and was probably a childless widower when he died.[198] All that is known about William 1 is that in his father's will he was left the lease of Great Waltham Parsonage Glebe. This must have been sublet to the Tufnell family for in the Langleys rent receipts book there a number of entries starting in 1761 concerning payments to William 1, and then after 1764, the year he died, to Richard. Each year the rent and land tax amounted to around £13.[199]

The high farmers in the family were prosperous people. John 6B's will shows him to have been a substantial man.[200] He left his wife £600, whom he married as a widower quite late in life, his eldest son £1500, and his two married daughters marriage portions of £900 and £500. The will shows how provision was made to safeguard the ongoing interests of the family. Like his father, Benjamin 1, and his brother Benjamin 2, he had a strong desire to sustain the family as an organic unit through the carrying on of the family business. This concern was very like that of his forebears in the sixteenth and seventeenth centuries, though it was expressed now in the context of leasehold farming. He willed that the executors, Abigail (1803-1883), his second and unmarried daughter, John Chapman, the husband of his eldest child Sarah (b. 1800), and his cousin William 2 of Roxwell, then aged thirty six, should carry on his business in the form of a trust, at least until the existing leases expired, and that each of his seven children should have access to the profits in the form of an annuity of £40. Benjamin 4, still a minor, was to receive his share in the form of maintenance. The eldest son, John 7B then aged twenty seven, was established on his own farm at Purleigh between Steeple and Maldon, so was presumably not a major concern. The other five children were daughters, two of whom were unmarried.

What kind of a social group did the large leasehold farmers form and what sort of lifestyle did they lead? Very little personal information about the Ram family is available outside wills and the account books of Samuel Tufnell. The Tufnell family steadily became the dominant land-owning family in Great Waltham during the eighteenth century. They lived in the parish and were not a remote family, as their account books show. They made purchases from villagers and drew on their services. In 1726 Samuel Tufnell paid several members of the Ram family to clear weeds, burn heaps of earth and break stones, although it is not entirely clear who these family members were.[201] Relationships were not all one way. John 4B owned Parsonage Meadow and rented it to Samuel Tufnell, whose account books show that other parcels of land were rented from John 4B.[202] In his will John 4B left £500 to provide an annual income for his wife and he ensured the capital was kept secure by lending it to Samuel Tufnell who paid out the interest. On February 5 1763 Samuel Tufnell records that he 'paid Mr Ram (£25) for interest on £500 borrowed'[203] and there are further records of annual payments to John 4B's sons. It is not known what happened to this capital sum when John 4B's wife died. Was it repaid to the family, for Samuel Tufnell had had the use of it for several years, or was it ceded to the provider, as it would be in a modern annuity?

Susanna Martins in a book about farming during this period offers some more general insights into the social life of the farming community.[204] By and large the living in of farm labourers had died out by the eighteenth century. If a farm was over about 70 acres labourers were employed and the farmer became more of a manager, although most of them rode round the farm each day to watch over progress. Farmers often travelled, partly to visit other farmers to talk about and to look at potential new farming developments, and to go to market. They had to deal with the commercial side of their business and made visits connected with the buying and selling of goods and produce. They were also entertainers of family and friends. The continuation of involvement in farming from father to son down several generations was quite common, and extended working relationships could develop with landowners, who were particularly interested in the tenant's ability to raise capital, his politics and his religion. By the end of the eighteenth century farmers' sons were tolerably well educated. The first Ram who signed his name in the Tufnell receipt books was William 1 in 1760. In bountiful years the bigger farmers made good profits, and most felt they were doing well enough if they met their bills, paid their rent, and kept a reasonable balance in hand. Most were happy if they could live well off the farm, go to market, give and receive visits, go shooting, and keep ponies and horses for the children. Some farmers were 'scientific' and kept good accounts while others just muddled through. Some enjoyed new social innovations like sending their daughters away to school, having their children taught to play the piano, and drinking sherry, whilst others continued much as their fathers had done before them. Some ran other businesses or property investments on the side. John 6B was praised by the estate valuer in 1810 for running a good farm, and several of the family reveal in their wills that they ran their farm as a business and had additional investments in shops and property.

Another way of obtaining a view into their lifestyle is by looking at the houses they lived in, for three of them still exist. Although Benjamin 2 continued to farm in Great Waltham he lived in the farmhouse of Newland Farm in Roxwell, and his son William 2 still lived there in 1881. Newland Hall is today a leisure centre that hosts weddings, training courses, conferences, and outdoor pursuits, including fishing and clay shooting. The House is a wonderful half timbered Elizabethan building with a moat and a grand avenue of trees leading to it. It must be one of the grandest houses ever lived in by a member of the Ram family. Another house is at Steeple Grange Farm on the edge of Steeple where John 6B lived and Benjamin 4, my great great grandfather, was born and lived for over thirty years. The current house may have been built since those times but it is on the same site. It faces the extensive farm buildings with a good garden behind, and this layout is shown on an earlier map. It is not comparable to Newland Hall. The third house is in Purleigh where John 7B farmed. It is a substantial building, now faced with cement that is painted white. It is located at the end of a drive which sweeps up to the front door in a semi-circular fashion within a large lawn which has a sizeable cedar tree planted on it. The large farm buildings, some of traditional Essex wooden construction, are off to one side. How much of the layout and buildings were there when John 7B lived there is not known but the house looks as though it is early nineteenth century, and might therefore have been his home.

As often in the family records wives and women tend to be shadowy figures. Fewer of them in this period left wills of their own than their Tudor and Stuart predecessors, which makes them all the more illusive. But Abigail Ram, an elder daughter of John 6B who was unmarried, did write a will in 1877 which like those of her predecessors focused in detail on personal items and bequests.[205] The will is summarised here to convey an impression of her life and times. She appoints friend William Humphreys, of Maldon, Essex Draper as Sole executor and trustee, leaving him an immediate legacy of £30. The West Essex Auxiliary Bible Society was given £10. Items of clothing were given to Ada Fanny, daughter of nephew John Sewell and Minnie Maria daughter of nephew Edward Sewell and linen and jewellery were left to niece Maria, wife of the said Edward Sewell. She gave all her books to Edward John Chapman Sewell, son of the said Edward Sewell, together with all her plate and plated articles, a pair of silver candlesticks, snuffers and a tray. Everything else was left in trust to the Executor to sell and then pass on proceeds, which totalled £606 6sh. and 11d.) in ten equal parts to the following relations: Sister Ann Sewell, sister Susannah Smith (b.1812), widow, sister Mary Ram (b.1813), spinster, nephew John Sewell, nephew Edward Sewell, nephew Arthur Ram (b. 1846), children of my late brother John, including the said Arthur Ram, children of late brother Benjamin Ram, children of late sister Sarah Chapman including the said Maria, and Edward John Chapman Sewell. In a codicil £10 was given to Anne Jane Coleman wife of Septimus Coleman, Ironfounder. As in earlier times, women still held land if they did not usually own it outright. Sarah Ram the eldest child of John 6B was left a half yard of copyhold land and a house at Great Waltham under the will of her maternal grandfather Thomas Boltwood (d. 1822) when she was twenty two.[206] In fact most is learned about them through their husbands' wills, by way of the provision that was made for them. The £600 John 4B left to his widow Rebecca was in the form of a bond that paid her an annual income of around £25 rising to £29. In addition he provided for Rebecca in a longstanding way by allowing her '... the use of my parlour for and during the term of her natural life'...'Also I give to my said wife Rebecca the furniture of the parlour aforesaid in order that she may lodge and inhabit therein. Such of my goods as she shall make choice of the same to be for her own use...' This effectively meant that his eldest son Richard had to look after his mother since he was left the house as a whole. John 4B left £20 in trust for the benefit of his daughter Rebecca, who was married to Henry Gage, 'exclusive of her husband'. Provision was similarly made for the two children of Richard, and this time the sum involved was £100. As has been seen John 6B left a complicated will which made fair provision for seven living children, five of them daughters. He also left £600 to his widow and was insistent in the will that if the product of the sale of his property was not enough to provide fully the sums he has specified, his wife was still to receive her £600 in full. In addition she was left the '... household furniture that belonged to her previous to our marriage', which was a second one for John 6B.

Most of the wives were from farming families. Some of them came from backgrounds similar to that of the Rams and from families of equally long residence in Great Waltham. The wife of John 4B was from the Goodeve

family, which appears in the 1577 survey, and had lived in Great Waltham
from medieval times. In 1819 L T Goodeve (early 19C) was overseer of the
poor in South End at Great Waltham and was paid £25. He carried on this
role for several years.[207] John 6B's first wife was a member of the Boltwood
family, who were described by H E Flight as prosperous gentry below the
topmost level.[208] The Boltwoods rented several farms in Great Waltham at
different times; the Hyde, of 160 acres, Palmer's Farm, acreage not known,
and Israel's Farm of 135 acres. In 1805 Thomas Boltwood held Hill House
Farm of 109 acres, whilst Edward Boltwood (early 19C) occupied the Hyde.
These farms were in the layer immediately below the very largest.[209] Many of
the Ram daughters married into local farming families.

The end of a long tradition.

When John 6B died in 1835 none of the family lived in Great Waltham but
at least fifteen immediate family members lived close by, at Roxwell, Purleigh
and Steeple, running three large farms. By 1881 there were only six left and
they were all elderly and mostly women. William 2 still lived at Newland Hall
in Roxwell, as a retired farmer in his eighties. His wife was still alive and a
widowed daughter, Fanny Elizabeth Carr (b. 1824), lived with them. In the
1881 census she is recorded as having an income from stocks and shares. In the
same census three of the daughters of John 6B lived together in Prospect Place,
Maldon. They were Abigail, one of the executors of her father's will, and two
younger sisters, Mary and Susan. Only Susan had married and she was now a
widow. The other local reference to the family in 1881 is that Edith (b. 1870)
and Walter Ram (b. 1876), both children of one of John Ram 7B's younger sons,
were visitors on census night at Little Hayes Farm, of 400 acres, in Stow Maries,
a small village near Purleigh. This was run by a George Green.

All the men and members of the younger generation present in 1833, or who
were born in the years between then and about 1850 had gone.[210] What
happened to them is described in chapter XVII. The drift away from farming
that started in the Great Waltham branch of the family in the previous century
turned into an exodus. How or why this happened is undocumented, but
three factors were almost certainly involved – the poor economic climate of
farming in the 1840s, personal capacities to cope, and a changing cultural
climate in which farming became less attractive. The difficult times that
economic developments after the Napoleonic Wars brought for farmers has
been outlined earlier in the chapter. The 1840s and early 1850s were the worst
years for wheat prices since 1815 and they were preceded by a very long lean
period which started in the 1830s. William Sewell the farming husband of one
of the daughters of John 6B went bankrupt in 1846.[211] The depressed times
would have made things very challenging for those who lacked commitment
or ability. Wives must have also found the situations very difficult.

The family presence in Purleigh was weakened, or ended, by the early death of John 7B aged 46 in 1852, possibly caused by economic circumstances. The fact that he made his will as early as 1839 suggests he may have been ill a long time before he died. In 1852 he had nine children aged between twenty and six, with the eldest son being sixteen. His wife Mary (b. 1810) was left to run their farm at the age of forty two, and to provide single handedly for a number of small children. He attempted to provide for family interests in a similar way to his father John 6B, willing that his business was to be carried on by a group of executors which included his wife Mary and John Chapman, the husband of John 6's eldest daughter, Sarah, and two other farmers. John Chapman held a similar role in the administration of John 6B's will.[212] Profits were to go to his wife until she married again, and after that she was to get £40 a year for life. He stipulated that the trustees provide training as required for his children. He was anxious that the leases on the farm should be extended, or another farm taken, to continue the trust until all the children had reached the age of twenty one. Then the business could be wound up and the proceeds divided equally, including his wife if she had not married again. He had 'a particular wish' that his eldest son John (b. 1836) should take possession of the farm, although he was only two at the time the will was written and only sixteen when his father died. What actually happened is not known but It is highly likely that John 7B's hopes were unrealised, even though, as chapter XVII shows, his younger son Walter (b. 1841) probably farmed in the area for a time.

The baby of John 6B's family, Benjamin 4 (1814-1864), took over the running of Steeple Grange Farm sometime before 1841 as the census of that year shows. In the 1851 census he is still listed as a farmer employing twenty men, although his address is in Chelmsford. But he left farming between then and the 1861 Census because in that he is recorded as being a clerk in Ipswich. Why Benjamin 4 gave up farming is not known, but it is likely the general climate of the times was a major cause.

SECTION 3 PROFESSIONAL AND ENTREPRENEURIAL RAMS

XIV

Francis Ram and his Family in Havering and London, 1550-1700

The Ram coat of arms

Francis Ram was the only member of the Ram family who obtained the right to a coat of arms, granted in 1590 and pictured in Figure 7.[213] No further use of them was made by later members of the family except Willett Ram in the 1920s, a descendent of Francis' brother William, who, according to a report in a local newspaper, had it put on the front of his carriage. The only reference to the arms by Francis' immediate family is in the will of his son John who left brother Samuel a 'ring engraved with my father's arms'.[214] It is interesting to speculate about the significance of this grant for Francis. His origins were among fairly humble farming stock, he became at least fairly wealthy, and was appointed a magistrate. Certainly this development would have marked him out in local society as being special. Most of the people who were fellow magistrates were at least local gentry and nearly all of them had coats of arms. John Wright of Wrightsbridge, of a gentrified family of yeoman stock and a close associate of Francis, obtained the same right in the same year, and they must have discussed the progress of their applications together.[215] The coat of arms has been chosen as a start point for this chapter because it communicates something important about Francis and how he viewed himself and his hopes for his family. Almost certainly he would have seen it as an outward sign of his status. The arms were coloured azure (blue) on a chevron (ermine) between three Ram's heads argent (silver). The drawing shown here is the one held by the College of Arms which intriguingly quarters Francis' arms with those of the Rushbrooke family.[216] This normally happens when families are connected through the female line, but in this case there is no known connection.

A father's influence

John Ram 1C (d.1568) of Pleshey and Great Waltham named four adult children in his will – William, probably the eldest, Francis I the main subject of this chapter, Christopher and Joan (mid 16C).[217] In the middle of the sixteenth century he was head of one of the three nuclear Ram families who lived in and around Great Waltham, as shown in Chart C1. He was a widower at the time of his death and lived with Joan and her husband John Welles, probably in

Figure 7.
Francis Ram's
coat of arms.

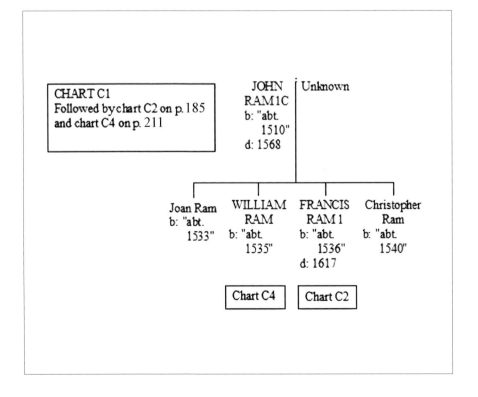

Great Waltham. Francis' father was presumably retired when he died but had been a farmer, and in his will he is styled 'yeoman'. He farmed land in Pleshey, Great Waltham and High Easter. Pleshey is mid way between these places, Great Waltham and High Easter. His land was a mixture of freehold and copyhold, with most of it being in Pleshey and Great Waltham. It is unclear in his will exactly how much land he had, because some of the holdings are not quantified, but it was probably around 30 acres on 6 sites. He must have been quite old when he died, since some of his grandchildren were born in the 1560s. This means he cannot have been born much after 1500. It is not possible to identify how he was related to other Rams in Great Waltham and High Easter, but he may have been a sibling of one or more of them, and was almost certainly a cousin of several of them. He is an interesting man for at least two reasons.

Firstly he fathered three sons of more than usual ability, and provided all of them with an education that led on to professional careers and moves away from their birthplace into a wider world. Christopher became a priest and held livings in Essex and Suffolk, and William became an attorney and Deputy Town Clerk of Colchester. Francis worked as agent for the Cooke family at Hornchurch, becoming, through the influence of Sir Anthony Cooke Deputy Steward for Havering, a magistrate, and Essex Clerk of the Peace. In all he served the Cooke family for about fifty years. They held large estates in Essex and elsewhere and Sir Anthony Cooke worked in the service of the crown at national level. His son in law was William Burleigh (1520-1598), Queen Elizabeth's chief minister. All three of John's sons lived in a distinctly different setting to family members who remained in Great Waltham, and from William there developed the third family branch. Many of their children and grandchildren lost their rural roots, and became genteel in the process. They may well have thought of themselves as more sophisticated than their Great Waltham cousins. We will never know whether this was the case or not.

Secondly, John's religious leanings were radically Protestant. The extremely long preamble of his will makes this very clear.

> First and principally I commend my soul unto the mercy of almighty god my maker redeemer and justifier and do believe assuredly that by the death and blood shedding of Jesus Christ the son of god my saviour I shall have free remission of all my sins and be made (illegible) of the heavenly (illegible) amongst the elect of god. Item I will that my body be committed to the earth (illegible) where it shall please god there to remain unto the most glorious coming of my lord Jesus Christ to indight? the quick and dead at the last? day. I do believe that the same my mortal and corruptible body shall arise again and be (illegible) from corruption and mortality and that I shall behold my lord and saviour Jesus Christ Without end? and through his mercy (the

(illegible) of sin death and hell notwithstanding) I shall be made partaker of his most glorious and triumphant kingdom.

There is much more in this preamble than a formal deference to the Elizabethan Protestant settlement that began only nine years before he died. It reads as a heartfelt statement of religious beliefs, which presumably he held to during the Marian years, and shows strong Calvinist traits.

There is significant circumstantial evidence that his sons had similar religious outlooks, which in part may well have come from their parents. The preamble to Francis' own will was very similar to that of his father.[218] Francis worked for Sir Anthony Cooke, a man of firm Protestant views, for nearly twenty years until his death. Francis' friends in Hornchurch were nearly all strong Protestant sympathisers. Francis' brother William worked in an extremely Protestant environment in Colchester, and was on friendly terms with leading Protestants there.[219] One of the parishes where Christopher served, in 1562, was Boxted, which had a long tradition of religious radicalism. In the early part of the fifteenth century some Boxted parishioners were Lollards, several of them being condemned and burnt for these beliefs. Related troubles and difficulties occurred in the parish throughout the sixteenth century[220] and in the 1570s and 1580s it was a centre of the classis movement, which aimed to establish a Presbyterian system of Church government.[221] It seems unlikely that Christopher would have been drawn to Boxted, or been acceptable there, unless he too was a radical Protestant.

All this information suggests a twofold tendency in this branch of the family, on the one hand to Calvinistic Protestantism, and on the other to a desire to better themselves. All John's sons were literate and he may have been as well. William went to Cambridge University, although he did not stay long enough to obtain a degree. In his book on the middling sort in Colchester during the period 1570-1640 Richard Smith notes the records of the town show there to have been a positive connection between a higher than usual degree of literacy and Calvinist beliefs.[222] The existence of such a link may have played a major part in enabling this branch of the family to break out of the traditional pattern of farming into a new and potentially more economically rewarding and socially sophisticated milieu. In doing this it met mixed fortunes, but in the longer term it was this branch that made a prosperous entry into modern times rather than the one that continued in farming.

Francis Ram's world

Francis' work for Sir Anthony Cooke led him into a new environment, not just an occupation different from farming. New horizons were opened up which led to personal fortune and a real step up the social ladder. As a by-product of the posts he occupied he was accepted as a social equal by local gentry and

mixed with elite Essex society. Francis' social world was a sort of miniature
version of that occupied by the Cooke family. Hornchurch in the second half
of the sixteenth century was near enough to London to be open to influences
that were not present at Great Waltham. Francis joined the world of the 'urban
yeoman' where there was active involvement in land and property speculation.
Hornchurch was a cosmopolitan society subject to two way traffic with
London. There was much coming and going and Londoners made their homes
in the area, or made investments there.[223] Families tended to make a mark and
disappear again in two, three or four generations. As with much of Essex at that
time it was a popular place for wealthy London families to buy country estates.
Francis obtained his employment from one of them and was well known in the
homes of smaller local gentry families, particularly the Wrights, Greenes, and
Atwoods, who lived in the hilly and pretty north west part of Havering, or just
outside its boundary. It is important to realise that Havering had considerable
administrative autonomy, and that Francis' role as Deputy Steward was an
important one. In 1465 the local tenants obtained a royal charter which made
the area a formal liberty, known officially as the Royal Manor and Liberty of
Havering-atte-Bower. See map in Figure 8. For most of the sixteenth century
Havering had powers equivalent to a county, and probably gained this status
because the Manor of Havering atte Bower was a Royal manor – usually part
of the dower of the King's wife. The Liberty had its own justices, one of them
elected by the tenants and inhabitants, its own coroner and clerk of the market.

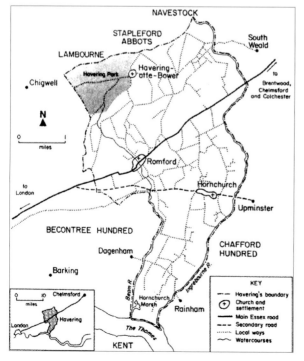

Figure. 8. The Royal
Manor and Liberty of
Havering atte Bower.

These officials had all the functions normally carried out by regional or county bodies.[224] When Francis became Deputy Steward he held overall day to day responsibility for local administrative matters.

Havering covered an area about six miles long and at it widest was just over three miles wide. It ran from the River Thames up into the low Essex hills at Havering atte Bower, and was divided into nine wards, six in the 'Romford Side' and three in the 'Hornchurch Side'. Romford was probably the biggest centre of population and lay across the main road from London to Colchester and East Anglia, whilst Hornchurch was the other town. In Elizabethan times the area was predominantly agricultural, although its economy was much influenced by London, whilst today the southern part of Havering has been mostly built over. During the years 1575-1620 the population of Havering increased from about 2000 to 2750, that of Romford parish from 1500 to 1800 and Hornchurch parish from 600 to 950.[225]

An impression of the sort of people Francis mixed with socially can be obtained by looking at the biographies and family backgrounds of the two men who were appointed to oversee the indenture he made in 1617, probably to hold property and distribute income after his death in stipulated ways.[226] This practice was widely used at the time to protect against alienation by the crown during minorities – of which there were a lot – and to overcome domestic uncertainty – people often died young and in difficult circumstances. The people he chose were Nicholas Cotton (early 17C) and John Wright, called by Francis 'the younger'. They must both have been men he trusted and knew intimately, and in his will Francis describes Nicholas Cotton as 'my loving friend'.[227] The term 'loving friend' occurs quite often in contemporary wills and was obviously a phrase of the time. It was no doubt sometimes used rather loosely, but in most cases in wills related to the Rams the general feeling conveyed suggests it did reflect a special bond of affection. This Nicholas Cotton was almost certainly related to the elder Nicholas Cotton (d. 1584), but although the family prospered in the Hornchurch and Romford area for some time, there is no clear line of descent.[228] A Nicholas Cotton was buried at Hornchurch in 1652, who may have married Elizabeth the daughter of Sir Richard Weston, a resident of Roxwell, nearly twenty miles from Hornchurch on the way to Chelmsford. Sir Richard was Chancellor of the Exchequer in 1622 and ambassador to Germany in 1629.[229] Elizabeth was buried at Hornchurch in 1614.

Francis knew the elder Nicholas Cotton very well – so much so that he was called 'a loving friend' in Nicholas' will, and appointed overseer of the estate.[230] The will also reveals that Nicholas, Francis, his brother William and their wives all knew each other socially, for it mentions William Ram and his wife Marion as his 'loving friends'. McIntosh says the older Nicholas Cotton was a self made man who came to Hornchurch from outside. Once established, although by no means affluent, he was chosen as a churchwarden, a post he continued to hold for several years. He was what McIntosh calls an 'urban yeoman', being involved in property speculation and money lending as well as agriculture. It was the money lending and property dealing which made him financially prosperous. By 1567 he was assessed in the subsidy for £30 in goods, the highest in Romford town and only exceeded in the whole of Havering by five others, all of whom were large landholders. Nicholas Cotton was also involved in Havering administration, being a regular attender at the manor court, as well as at various times working bailiff, chief constable for the Romford side, and the Havering coroner.[231] All these duties brought him into a working relationship with Francis in his own roles of Deputy Steward and magistrate, which was perhaps how they became friends. The Cottons' roots were not unlike those of Francis.

John Wright, 'the younger', belonged to a family with more pedigree than the Cottons, although it was not closely involved in Havering affairs until about 1607.[232] Francis would have come into contact with it through his work as Deputy Steward long before. The Wrights had lived locally since the thirteenth century, had become yeomen, and by the mid sixteenth century one of them, John Wright (d. 1551), had climbed into the gentry. In his will he still described himself as a yeoman, even though he became a knight and built a family mansion at Kelvedon Hall.[233] He called three of his sons John, whom he referred to as Eldest John (b. 1510), Middle John (1522-1558) and Young John (b. 1524). Middle John inherited Dagenhams Manor, Wrightsbridge, and this branch was the one active in Havering. It is difficult to tell one of these Johns from another, but from genealogical charts in an unpublished manuscript in the Essex Record Office it looks as though John Wright, 'the younger' was the grandson of Middle John and son of the 'elder John' of Francis' day.[234] John Wright, 'the younger' was approximately 45 in 1616. He was a barrister, a Member of Parliament and Clerk of Parliament. Two step brothers who were young men during Francis' later years became prominent people in the City of London, Nathaniel (b. 1581), was a merchant and member of the Common Council whilst Lawrence (1590-1657), was a prominent London doctor. In 1617 the senior branch of the family held 650 acres at Weald Hall and John Wright, 'the younger' had 116 acres at Dagenhams. Both estates were between Romford and Brentwood, about five miles north of Hornchurch. Francis and John Wright may have got on because both their families had common roots as yeoman farmers with long histories in villages only about ten miles apart. Other things happened to help bring them together, which perhaps grew out of this basic identity. Both had connections with Gray's Inn and intermarriage with the Greene family, which will be discussed later. It is possible Francis appreciated that the Ram family was not as prosperous as the Wrights, and the history of Francis' immediate family suggests there was desire to emulate them.

Professional life

Nothing is known about Francis' early years, his education, or how he came to work for the Cooke family, a relationship which started around 1558.[235] McIntosh says he began working for them as bailiff to their manors in Essex. By 1563 he had also become Deputy Steward for Havering, taking over day to day responsibilities from Sir Anthony Cooke who was Steward, a post he continued to hold until 1604. The stewardship of Havering was held by a member of the Cooke family throughout Francis' tenure of the deputy position. In her thesis on the Cooke family McIntosh writes, 'He (Francis Ram) must be given a major credit for the supervision of the Cooke lands and the functioning of Havering during these years'.[236] As the holder of the position of Deputy Steward he was also one of three magistrates for the Liberty. So, within Havering and to a certain extent in Essex as a whole Francis grew to exert influence through working for the Cooke family. The appointment of a Deputy Steward was customary by the end of Henry VIII's reign with the main functions being responsibility to the Crown for the satisfactory operation of the manor, presiding at sessions of the manor court, maintenance of the court rolls, management of military affairs and review of the turnout of local musters. Francis may also have been responsible for collecting royal rents in Havering through local assistants, as between 1553 and 1618 the office of High Bailiff was joined with the Stewardship of Havering.[237] The magistrates of Havering carried out all the duties completed by county magistrates, although the volume of activities dropped off significantly after Sir Anthony Cooke died in 1576, when Havering became increasingly subject to county authority. They had exclusive jurisdiction over all offences committed, they approved the arrest of suspects and questioned them, but they could not try felonies alone and had to consult with outsiders, usually lawyers. People found guilty of a felony with no extenuating circumstances were hanged on the local gallows.

When Sir Anthony Cooke became *Custos Rotulorum* (keeper of the rolls) for the County of Essex at a general session in Chelmsford on 17 April 1572 Francis was named Clerk of the Peace for Essex,[238] which involved administering the Justice system throughout the county. It was permissible by law for the *Custos Rotulorum* to act through an agent in completing his three major functions; the guarding of the records of the sessions, production of writs and indictments, and other formal papers. Francis took these functions over and Sir Anthony Cooke did not attend a single session after his appointment as *Custos Rotulorum*. Although he nominally witnessed writs after 1572 the signature on the document is invariably that of Francis. Francis' duties as Clerk of the Peace covered the following matters – to enrol proceedings of sessions, to read indictments, to draw up the procedures, to record proclamations of servants' wages, to register licenses, and to certify transcripts of indictments, outlawries, attainders and convictions, to keep a record of the justices' proceedings and to attend to general clerical work.[239] Francis is recorded as being Clerk of the Peace as late as 1606.[240] His experience as Deputy Steward of Havering must have provided an invaluable background to taking on the broader role.

Francis was also an Essex magistrate, but when he became one is unclear. In a book about legal affairs in Essex at this period he is not among a list of the justices printed in it.[241] But McIntosh states quite clearly he was an Essex magistrate. 'In 1590 Sir Henry Grey (1547- bef.1619), Francis Ram, and George Hervy (d. 1605), all Essex JPs who lived in Havering, questioned Katherine Atkinson, formerly servant to John Hale of Collier Row, about the father of her illegitimate child'.[242] According to the records of a Session of the Peace held at Chelmsford in 1608 Francis was acting as Justice of the Peace.[243] Perhaps the clinching information comes from the Calendar of Assize records. There are two volumes of these in the Essex Record Office for this period.[244] Each assize is headed by a list of the county magistrates and in the volume which relates to Elizabeth I Francis does not appear among them, but in that which covers the years of James I he is listed regularly from the time it starts in 1607 until his own death in 1617.

Francis also did much work for the Cookes in his capacity as the family agent. The Cooke fortunes were founded on land and property purchases by Thomas Cook(e) (later 15C), especially in Essex. Sir Anthony Cooke inherited these properties, and augmented them by further purchases and inheritances. Following his death the estates were gradually sold, especially during the time of young Anthony (1559- 1604). An account of the lands held in 1580, shortly after the death of Sir Anthony's son Richard (1531-1579), shows there were over twenty manors and other properties in Essex, plus more in Warwickshire and London, together with a scattering elsewhere in England. The income in that year – which did not include that from the estates of Gidea Hall and Bedford's Manor, both in Havering and not valued – was nearly £1377.[245]

No details have been found about Francis' estate management duties but McIntosh provides a little picture of what this aspect of Francis' work involved.

> The Family had exceptionally capable assistants. Francis Ram, the principal figure, had served as general steward and legal assistant to the elder Sir Anthony Cooke and, to young Anthony's great good fortune, he lived on until 1617. During most of his life Ram continued to supervise the Cooke estates, acting as Anthony's agent in his various financial transactions ... He also managed the routine administration of the Liberty of Havering. Had it not been for the loyal and financially astute Ram, the Cookes would certainly have come to utter ruin much more quickly.[246]

Francis managed the estates for three Cookes, probably ceasing to do so in 1604 when Edward Cooke (1580-1625) became head of the family. Each of them raised different demands and challenges. Francis was recruited by Sir Anthony and worked for him until his death in 1576. Anthony was an able person who built up the estates and kept Francis busy because of this. Further demands on Francis probably arose as a result of the part Anthony played in national affairs. He moved in the royal circle of Henry VIII and near the end of Henry's reign was made a Gentleman of the Privy Chamber, an office which he held until the death of Edward VI. He took part in many commissions on behalf of the king, was created a Knight of the Bath and entertained the royal court at his Essex home, Gidea Hall. He was also probably involved with the tutoring of Edward VI in his youth. During this period Anthony became a strong Protestant 'of a dark and unforgiving colour',[247] and throughout Mary's reign he was in exile, although his wife and family remained at Gidea Hall. During these years Francis presumably took on a lot of responsibility for the estates. In Elizabeth's reign Anthony continued to participate in royal commissions but was not given an important position at court. 'The Queen did not warm to his instructions, issued immediately upon her accession, that she should become a new Judith or Deborah, nor did she like his offensively dogmatic manner about every other subject as well'.[248] So, towards the end of his life Anthony may have been more free to spend time on the running of his estates. It is also possible these received personal attention from the next head of the family, Richard Cooke, who was more like his grandfather and great grandfather than his father, being a quiet country gentleman. Anthony must have overshadowed him and Richard, who in any case, only lived for three years after his father died.

Francis' later years were almost certainly burdened by the character and lifestyle of Young Sir Anthony who inherited the Cooke estates in 1579. He was Richard Cooke's only son, who immediately had financial problems because his mother who controlled a significant portion of the estate income was a spendthrift. But he himself did not lead a quiet country life. He joined the court in London – in the process running down the family resources, taking on big loans, and building up heavy debts. He spent some time in the Fleet Prison for debt. To cope with the debts he started selling off land. In addition he was often away from Essex and his middle years were very chaotic. During the last four years of his life he was in Ireland a great deal, as captain of a company of troops.

McIntosh writes that Sir Edward Cooke, who took over the estates in 1604 resented Francis' influence so removed him from being Deputy Steward. How far Francis played any further part in the management of the Cooke estates is not known. He was in any case an elderly man by that time. Edward came into possession of the Cooke lands when they were very run down. The dominant concern of his life was keeping his head above water financially, but in the end he failed to do this.[249]

McIntosh concludes her statement about Francis' qualities and the effort he put into running the Cooke estates in the following way. 'After reading of the many loans and land sales which Ram handled in person, travelling around the country to make the necessary arrangements we are comforted to find that he purchased several rich Cooke holdings himself'.[250] How much land and property Francis owned or rented is unclear. In the 1570s he held the title of a large Havering estate in company with the older Nicholas Cotton together with several other people.[251] More property was obtained from the Cooke family. Larkestock Manor on the edges of Gloucestershire and Warwickshire, worth £16 at the time, was 'licensed' from the Cooke family to Francis in 1579 together with some other unspecified lands in Gloucestershire.[252] What exactly 'licensed' meant is not clear. Sir Anthony paid £1200 for Larkestock Manor in 1564[253] and if Francis bought it he must have paid significantly more than that 16 years later. In 1581 he obtained lands in Warwickshire from the Cooke family, at Nuneaton and nearby Chilvers Cotton. These investments, in areas favourable to sheep rearing, were possibly made to take advantage of the great sixteenth century boom in the wool trade, although it was past its peak by this time.[254] If the indenture referred to in Francis' will could be found it would throw interesting light on these matters. Francis was also involved in land purchases in Essex, seemingly in partnership with others. In 1585 together with Andrew Somner he acquired four messuages, four gardens, sixty acres of arable, twenty-five acres of meadow, fifty acres of pasture, as well as three acres of wood in Magdalen Laver, Moreton, Bobbingworth, and North Weald Bassett for £240.[255] He was again involved in a deal in 1585 at Little Warley worth £80.[256] With his brother William Ram he was involved in several smaller deals.

How wealthy Francis Ram became is not known either. He would have had incomes from his various roles, and probably earned fees from performing tasks associated with some of them. It is not known how much income he obtained from property holdings, although it is clear he had some. It is, however, obvious from the position he held, the fact that he was granted the right to a coat of arms in 1590, and his general standing, that he was a man of some substance.

Social, political, and religious relationships
Francis was involved in a complex of contacts based on Havering and the Cooke connection but developed around it in independent ways. These extended into London, where his wife came from, and about half his sons lived and worked. But his sphere of interest was always local. Of central importance for Francis were links with four wealthy families. These were the Cottons of Romford and Hornchurch, the Wrights of Kelvedon Hall, the Greenes of Bois Hall in Navestock, and the Atwoods of Littlebury Hall near Stanford Rivers.

The Cottons and the Wrights, mentioned earlier, had origins that had a lot in common with Francis' own background, but they had both done financially better in the earlier part of the sixteenth century than the Rams. This was particularly true of the Wrights. The builder of the Wright fortune, John Wright was from the generation before Francis. This family closely resembled the Everardes in Great Waltham, who had been local yeomen farmers, had made useful marriages, and were in Francis' day by far the largest landholders there. They finally obtained a knighthood in Stuart times. Yet Francis was much more of a social equal of the Wrights than were his Great Waltham cousins of the Everardes. Although Francis was closing the social gap he was in many ways a generation behind the Wrights. The Greenes and the Atwoods were different kinds of families, in that they did not have local roots, having moved to Havering through the acquisition of a country estate after making money in London, mainly through commercial activity and involvements in the legal and medical professions. No doubt Francis' links, and later social relationships, with these families originated from work related contacts, particularly with Nicholas Cotton and the Wrights, whether they were to do with estate management, the running of Havering Liberty, or the magistracy.

The Wrights and the Greenes knew each other independently of Francis. Their connections probably started when Robert Wright (b. 1516), an elder son of Sir John Wright, married Mary Greene in 1541. The link was reinforced by the marriage of Katherine Wright (b. 1513), a younger sister of Robert, to John Greene (d.1594) in 1550 and then by his purchase of Bois Hall in 1565, which was only a mile away from where the Wrights lived. There were further marriages between the two families over the next four generations, some based on Essex contacts and others on London connections. The Greenes probably opened up London opportunities for the Wrights because they were well established there before the beginning of the sixteenth century. 'Younger John' Wright's father married Bennett Greene as his second wife in 1580, whose mother had a strong city base, and two of their sons, Nathaniel (b. 1581) and Lawrence, (1590-1657) became prominent figures in London. Francis possibly became friendly with the Greene family through his contacts with the Wrights.

Francis almost certainly obtained useful social and business links through these families, for himself and his family as a whole. John Wright 'the Younger', for example, was a London barrister who had attended Gray's Inn in 1587, and so did his son, another John Wright in 1616. He was familiar with the Inns of Court in a way Francis could not have been as a younger man, and no doubt provided help to Francis in securing a place there for his eldest son Francis (abt 1575-1610?) in 1605, presumably with the intention of him becoming a lawyer. Several of Francis' other sons went to work in London and one of them, called William (abt. 1574-1612) married Margaret Greene in 1606 at St Stephen's

Walbrook, a church with which her parents, Christian Greene (d. 1639) and
husband Reynauld Greene. (b. 1575?) were long associated. Christian Greene's
will of 1639 confirms the family links with this parish, as does the baptism of
Margaret Greene (b. 1586). Reynauld was a son of the John Greene who bought
Bois Hall. The marriage of William Ram and Margaret Greene shows there was
general mutual socialising between the families. In fact, several people from all
three families were linked with St Stephen's Walbrook in the late sixteenth and
early seventeenth centuries. In addition to William Ram and Margaret Greene,
Lawrence Greene, possibly a son of Reynauld Greene's younger brother Robert,
baptised two children there, one in 1600 and another in 1603. Moreover, a step-
brother of 'younger John' Wright called Nathaniel Wright married in the same
church in 1612 and the marriage license says he is of that parish. A Thomas
Greene baptised a daughter, Margaret there in 1598.

It would appear that St Stephen's Walbrook was a gathering point for a
number of the younger members of all three families. They formed a group
which was effectively an extension of the Havering network in London, a
development that may have been encouraged by one Henry Wright who was
vicar there in the sixteenth century, and Robert Greene (b. 1576) who was a
churchwarden in the late sixteenth century. It is possible he was the younger
brother of Reynauld Greene and was married to Friswolde Wright. There are
signs in the registers of baptisms, marriages and deaths that similar networks
existed at other London churches, particularly at St Lawrence Jewry and
St Mary Aldermanbury. But it is impossible to document the linkages fully
because all the families were very large. For example the John Greene who
bought Bois Hall in 1565, had at least thirteen children who in turn provided
him with seventy one or more grandchildren!

The basis of the connection with the Atwood family is less clear. This family
lived at the manor of Littlebury at Stamford Rivers near Kelvedon Hall and
Ongar for four generations from about 1553 until the property was sold in
1701. They were socially of some standing because their genealogy is listed
in the visitations of Essex,[257] but little is known about their origins or the
part they played in local life. McIntosh mentions that a William Atwood was
a member of the Parliamentary divisional committee for southern Essex and
that he married someone from the Wright family, but she says he comes from
Noak Hill not Stamford Rivers.[258] This person could be the William Atwood
(b. 1596) who was active in the 1640s. He would have been the brother in
law of one of Francis' grandsons, Francis Ram (1607-1644), who married
William's sister Katherine (b. 1603-d. abt. 1675) in 1629. The only specific
information about Atwood activities concerns William's younger brother John
Atwood (b. 1599) who was a lawyer of Gray's Inn and lived at Broomfield.

There was probably a religious element in the connections forging Francis' social circle. The Cottons, at least the elder Nicholas Cotton, along with most of the Wrights were strongly sympathetic to Protestantism and to Parliament. Francis was as radically Protestant as his father if the preamble to his own will is any guide. In fact they are extremely similar!

> I commend my soul to the most merciful custody of Almighty God most assuredly believing through the most precious death and passion of my only Saviour and Redeemer Jesus Christ to have full and free pardon of all my sins and after this transitory life indeed so become partaker of all such blessings as are prepared for all the elect and chosen saints and servants of God in the life to come. And I believe that in the general resurrection my body shall rise again and be united into my soul and shall hear that most joyful statement pronounced to me among others come ye blessed of my Father inherit the kingdom prepared for you before the beginning of the World And thenceforth shall continue in eternal bliss amongst the dear Saints and Servants of Almighty God.[259]

The period covered by Francis' life witnessed some of the most dramatic changes in Church life ever to happen in England and related struggles were still going on when he died. Exactly how ordinary people responded locally to the events at national level is unclear, but one suspects many wearily conformed to developments and changes as they happened. Perhaps those who embraced Protestantism most strongly were among the more significant beneficiaries of the Reformation. It was undoubtedly true that the Reformation period provided great economic opportunities for ambitious, able, and adventurous people to do well for themselves by acquiring property and land that became available as a result of the closure of the monasteries. This was as true for people of the yeoman class as for the very rich. Sir John Wright founded his family fortune on renting manors from the Rich family, which itself became one of the largest landowners in Essex on the back of purchases of monastic lands. Clearly the older Nicholas Cotton did well from property dealings. Many of the up and coming people of the day, like the Cottons, Wrights, and Francis Ram, promoted their interests and wealth by such means.

But the interest in Protestantism was not necessarily purely economic. People who are able and of the fringe often join processes which offer a way of making a mark. Protestantism was also ideologically rooted in the eastern parts of England and in London. Essex villagers in Boxted were among early Lollards, and Colchester, where William Ram the attorney worked, was a centre of Protestant fervour. Numbers of these people suffered for their beliefs. Many of the early settlers in the Americas went there for religious reasons, and came from Essex. The Protestantism of Francis was probably influenced by a number of things, including his father's outlook, but, one way or another, it almost certainly helped to create and sustain his circle of relationships, particularly with the Cottons and the Wrights.

The elder Nicholas Cotton and Francis certainly had Calvinistic ideas in common. Nicholas' will was long and strongly Calvinist in tone, expressing hope to be among the elect and chosen.[260] Although not all the Wrights were fervent Protestants the branch which Francis knew was strongly Protestant and a supporter of Parliament in the Civil War. Robert Wright (late 16 C), an uncle of 'the younger' John was an extreme Presbyterian who became rector of Dennington in Suffolk and as a young man held religious classes near Great Waltham in the late 1570s. In the 1640s and 50s control of Havering affairs was in the hands of the Parliamentary divisional committee for southern Essex of which John Wright 'the younger' was a prominent member, being its first chairman. Two step-brothers of John Wright 'the younger' were young men during Francis' later years. One was Nathaniel Wright, who became a London merchant as well as being a central figure in the Massachusetts Bay Company. He was also a Common Councilman in the City of London. He was elected to the Militia Committee in 1642 when the tension between Charles I and Parliament backed by the City was coming to a head. Many of the members of the Militia Committee were among the more radical members of the Common Council.[261] The other was Lawrence Wright, later an eminent London doctor who treated Oliver Cromwell. The Greene family do not appear to have had such a strong identity with Protestantism, and were not much involved in Havering politics during Francis' prime years, but the friendly relationships that existed with the Wrights and the Rams suggests all three families had at the very least a fairly similar outlook about politics and religion.

The range of Francis' associations suggests he was able to manage religious relationships on a broad front, which was perhaps an important part of his role as Deputy Steward. He was for example one of two overseers to the will of the conservative vicar of Hornchurch, William Lambert and one of the witnesses. Another friend was Marscelin Owtred, (d. 1592), a London based member of an important Hornchurch family, who nominated my 'friend Mr Francis Ram' overseer of his will. This had a very long Protestant biased preamble.[262] One member of this family preceded Francis as Deputy Steward of Havering and others were elected bailiff. Francis was also a witness to the will of Thomas Latham of Langtons in Hornchurch (d. 1593), who was obviously very wealthy. McIntosh says he was 'one of Hornchurch's wealthiest gentlemen'.[263] Under the terms of his will lands were to be sold by Francis and Thomas' own brother in law. As coroner of Havering in 1576-77, he would certainly have worked with Francis. There is, however, another potential angle on the relationship with Thomas Latham, because he was a strong Protestant who was in open disagreement with William Lambert (d. 1592) the conservative vicar of Hornchurch, and friendly with John Leeche, teacher and radical Protestant preacher in Hornchurch.[264] And of course Francis worked for Sir Anthony Cooke, who was, as has been seen a deeply religious man.

Little direct information has been found about Francis' political involvements. The only time he emerges publicly into political life is over the disputed justice's election at Havering in 1607, by which time he had ceased to be Deputy Steward and was an elderly man.[265] But the role Francis played indicates he was a conciliator and it is clear from events at this time that Francis still remained concerned with local affairs. In the early seventeenth century there were five gentry families in Havering – the Cookes, Ayloffes, Quarles, Greys, and Legatts – which increasingly competed with one another for local power as the authority of the Cooke family declined. Animosity was especially strong between Sir William Ayloffe (early 17C) and successive heads of the Legatt family in the decades around 1600, and this came to a head over this disputed election. In addition to highlighting personal disputes, it brought into focus tensions between the principal families and the more middling ones. The documentation of the 1607 events shows how the leading families manipulated traditional procedures for their own advantage over and against people of more intermediate status, who had played a more important role than them in Havering affairs during the sixteenth century.

In that year John Leggatt (early 17C), an antagonist of the leading families, became the elected justice but died soon afterwards. In the election which followed there was no obvious candidate, which led to a great deal of confusion as well as a disputed outcome – was the victor a Legatt or an Ayloffe? At a new meeting to hold the election all went well until the jury was sworn, when the dispute between the middling people and the principal tenants broke out again. Chaos followed as the jury could not agree who should be elected as justice, so the chairman gave the choice to the entire assembly. Francis was one of six people who took action to involve central government to help resolve the problem judicially. A letter and petition was sent to Robert Cecil, the Queen's minister, signed by Francis and five other important tenants of Havering – Robert Quarles (d. 1639), 'Senior' John Wright, William Courtman (early 17C), Gawen Harvey (mid 17C) and James Harvey (late 16C). Robert Cecil passed the petition to the Lord Chancellor who issued a writ in November 1607 empowering Francis, Gawen Harvey and James Harvey to swear in the person who was victor at the open election. However the dispute ran on to nobody's credit. It was fed partly by inability in Havering to agree a common approach. The leading families would not accept the authority of the lesser people who had directed affairs previously, but were divided among themselves.

The early years of the seventeenth century in Havering were complicated by the increasing efforts of the Stuart kings to restore lapsed money raising powers.

It was a period of growing uncertainty in which leading families that failed to stand against the impositions of the crown lost out heavily when it was defeated in the Civil War. It was also a period in which the long resident Wright family gradually emerged to play a greater part in local affairs, starting around the time of the disputed election. 'Senior' John Wright was one of the signatories of the letter to Cecil, and he together with his son 'younger' John were both members of the election jury of the manor from 1608 to 1613. 'Younger' John Wright took on the role of Deputy Steward in 1618 and then from 1625 to 1633. The part Francis Ram played in these affairs reveals something of his position and situation. He was obviously an important and influential figure, being able, even as an old man, to be a leader in the moves to resolve the disputed election. He was socially connected with the other signatories. Richard Cotton (b. 1599?-1635/6) was the son of the younger Nicholas Cotton, friend and confidant of Francis, 'younger' John Wright was one of the overseers of the indenture connected with Francis' will, and Francis' youngest son, Benjamin, married a daughter of Sir Simon Harvey, who was most likely related to the James Harvey who lived in Hornchurch.[266] Perhaps it was Francis who encouraged the Wright family to exert local leadership. But he cannot have had status equal to the other signatories because he did not own or occupy equivalent estates or rank as a member of the gentry. He was part of their group because of the important official roles he had filled for many years, and appears more in the role of a conciliator, administrator, and facilitator, than that of a main player.

Family life

The first certainly known fact about Francis is the date and place of his marriage and the name of his wife, although there is even a little doubt about that. He was married in 1573, in London at the parish church of St Lawrence Jewry and St Mary Magdalene, Milk Street, to Helen, or Ellen Foxe (b. 1555) (or Sope as her name appears on her marriage license). She was eighteen at the time. In the will of Nicholas Cotton, senior, Helen Ram, the wife of Francis, was left thirty shillings to buy a ring to remember him by, so this forename will be used. it is also assumed the maiden name of Francis' wife was Foxe as in his own will Francis made a small bequest to his brother in law, John Foxe. Helen was born in London. The first recorded baptism of a child of their marriage is of Samuel (1583- 1624) at Hornchurch, after which there followed five other baptisms at Hornchurch – Elizabeth(1585-1586), Nathaniel (1588-1606), Edward (1590- 1617), Joseph (b. 1593) and Benjamin (1594-1623). Helen died in 1613 and was buried at Hornchurch. At least four children were born before Samuel but no baptismal record of them has been found – Francis (d. 1610), John (d. 1617), William (d. 1612) and Anthony (d. 1616). The first three of the latter group of names occur many times in the Ram family, but Anthony on no other occasion. Was he named after Sir Anthony Cooke? Chart C2 shows how the family of Francis and Helen grew over the years.

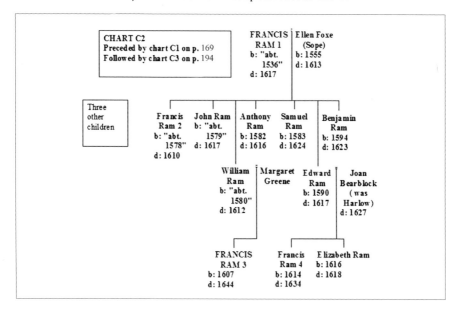

CHART C2
Preceded by chart C1 on p. 169
Followed by chart C3 on p. 194

FRANCIS RAM 1
b: "abt. 1536"
d: 1617

Ellen Foxe (Sope)
b: 1555
d: 1613

Three other children

Francis Ram 2
b: "abt. 1578"
d: 1610

John Ram
b: "abt. 1579"
d: 1617

Anthony Ram
b: 1582
d: 1616

Samuel Ram
b: 1583
d: 1624

Benjamin Ram
b: 1594
d: 1623

William Ram
b: "abt. 1580"
d: 1612

Margaret Greene

Edward Ram
b: 1590
d: 1617

Joan Bearblock (was Harlow)
d: 1627

FRANCIS RAM 3
b: 1607
d: 1644

Francis Ram 4
b: 1614
d: 1634

Elizabeth Ram
b: 1616
d: 1618

Francis worked for Sir Anthony Cooke from the late 1550s most likely living in Hornchurch from about 1563 when he became the Deputy Steward of Havering. However, his marriage license says he was of the London parish of Holborn, so he may have lived in various places in his young adult life.[267] His work for Sir Anthony Cooke certainly took him to various locations including London. From 1559 to 1566 Cooke maintained a London residence, 'Aburgeny' or 'Burgeyne' Place on Warwick Lane, near Blackfriars and St Paul's.[268] Perhaps it was through trips to see Sir Anthony in London that he got to know Helen, or by way of friendships that were beginning to develop with the Greene and Wright families. When the Ram family went to live in Hornchurch they attended the parish church, where there is still a fine wall mounted monument to them. A number of children and grandchildren were buried at Hornchurch, even though several lived elsewhere. It is possible that family members who lived in London went to Hornchurch when they were sick to recover, and sometimes died there. Francis and his family may have lived at Hornchurch Lodge, that was in all probability built some time in the sixteenth century, and in the early twentieth century was said to be a beautiful ivy-covered old house in the middle of Church Hill. A local charity, known as the Ram Charity originated in a cottage near to the Lodge, which has led people to connect the Rams with it.[269] This charity began in 1616 when Francis' son Anthony left £40 to his father to be put in a trust for the poor of Hornchurch. In 1618 the executor of Francis' will agreed to give a house to Hornchurch parish instead of the £40. The rent from this house was to be used to employ the poor. In 1621 a deed of settlement confirmed the gift of Poynters (Painters) in the High Street that was let on lease from 1623. By

1837 it had been replaced by two cottages, the rent from which was used to maintain charity houses in the parish. In 1862 it was said the rents had been used to employ the parish poor on the roads, and to provide coal for the poor in the hard winter of 1860. In 1968 the site was let on a seventy five year building lease and in 1971 the annual income was £1,575.[270]

Francis and some of his descendants built up many contacts and friendships during a long association with Havering, Hornchurch, and Romford. The range of these is revealed by mentions in around thirty wills between around 1570 and 1600. Some of them no doubt derived directly from Francis' professional roles, but others must have been the product of personal friendships. Francis was mentioned by name in sixteen local wills, as beneficiary, executor, overseer or witness, and his wife Helen was witness to the will of Geoffrey Tyman, a Hornchurch husbandman, in 1594. In a substantial number of cases Francis was executor or overseer. A further sixteen wills were witnessed between 1590 and 1602 by a William Ram, at least six of which can be identified to Francis' brother, the attorney based in Colchester. The others almost certainly involve this William's son, another William Ram (abt 1560-1620) who lived in Romford and was an urban yeoman and innkeeper.

Maud Hulke of Great Baddow (d. 1570/71) was a widow when she died leaving to a Mary Ram one cupboard, to Ellen Ram 'three sheets that shall lie on me at the day of my burial', and to Francis Ram's two children twelve pence each. Francis Ram, her 'son in law' shares the residue with one other person and he is also appointed an executor.[271] There is a problem with this will because although the Ellen referred to appears to be Francis' wife it is dated several years before they were married. It is possible dates have been confused. Maud's relationship with Helen is also unclear. The tone of the will does not suggest she was her mother, but she may have been an aunt. The term 'son in law' was then used more loosely as a term of relationship than it is today. Assuming the Ellen and Francis referred to in Maud Hulke's will are the ones in the book, and no other similar couple has been traced, this will is the only example of Francis and his wife being beneficiaries in a family will outside his own nuclear family.

The following example illustrates how professional relationships turned into friendships. George Malle or Mawlem, (d.1575), a substantial Hornchurch yeoman, was the manorial (elected) bailiff of Havering from 1557 to 1560 and must have known Francis professionally. But a deeper relationship developed for he made 'my loving friend' Francis Ram one of two overseers of his will, for which he received twenty shillings. In addition 'Once a year when my executors and overseers shall assemble for taking the account (managing the estate) they shall have a competent dinner and each of my overseers 20 pence apiece for their pains'.[272]

Sometimes friendships continued over many years with the same family. Francis was a witness to the will of John Bright (d. 1578) of Romford, innkeeper and yeoman, who sent his stepson to Oxford University, one of only two Havering boys not of wealthy families to attend university during this period.[273] This association continued with his widow Elizabeth Bright, (d. 1595). She left small sums to Francis' eight children, and to her god daughter Catherine Ram. She left 'To master Francis Ram, for his good advice and friendship bestowed on me forty shillings, one long bow and one sheaf of arrows, and to his wife two gold angels'. In addition 'her loving friend' Francis Ram is made executor.[274] The tone of this will suggests Elizabeth Bright held Francis and his family in affection.

References to Francis in wills also reveal that his friendships and contacts extended beyond the rich and influential. In 1581 and 1582 there was a local landholding dispute. Unhappiness with progress led six Hornchurch men from old established middling families of no great wealth to remove the current tenant by force. This prompted a dispute with the Essex Quarter Sessions and its Sheriff, in which the Sheriff's bailiff was assaulted. The Havering men concerned were eventually outlawed.[275] The six men involved included two members of the Uphavering family, who were tanners, and John Bushe, a yeoman. Francis would have played a part in this dispute as Deputy Steward and as a magistrate, but, as several wills show, he was associated personally with the Uphavering family and, probably along with his nephew William the innkeeper of Romford, had at least some connection with John Bushe. When William Uphavering, (d. 1575) either the father or elder brother of those involved in the affair just described, 'my loving friend' Francis Ram was one of four supervisors nominated in his will. Francis was the senior of them because he was given five shillings whilst the others got three and four pence![276] Thomas Uphavering (d. 1595) left a will in which William Ram was a witness, who performed a similar function for John Bushe.

The involvements of William Ram, the innkeeper son of Francis' brother William of Colchester, may have been professional rather than social however, because he was an inveterate drafter of other people's wills. Reference has been made elsewhere to him writing a will for a Romford plague victim in 1603.[277] The local wills witnessed by him and his father may well have been drafted by them for a fee. The fact that their involvement was almost always as a witness and nothing more substantial suggests personal connections were less strong than was the case with Francis. William Ram the innkeeper is also a beneficiary in one will. Joan Worthington (d. 1586), was a servant in Hornchurch who came from the North of England. She had accumulated money and goods and left ten shillings to William Ram, who was a fellow servant. She also left 'the rest of my goods to William Ram, desiring him to see me buried'.[278] William would have been about twenty at the time and had presumably come to Hornchurch from Colchester by arrangement between Francis and his father.

The general picture obtained from the wills is that Francis was friendly with a number of middling local people as well as the better off, and was able to mix the roles of a senior local official with such relationships. But his standing with the townsmen and yeomen farmers was different to that with the gentry and landowners. He was not asked to be overseer or witness of wills by members of the Greene, Wright, or Atwood families. Perhaps he was not looked up to by them in the same way as the more middling people who asked him to look after the final settlement of their affairs. One gets the impression his circle was, for him, a rich and pleasing one, and the fact that he lived such a long life inevitably led to it becoming quite extended over time.

Relationships with family members are most clearly revealed in Francis' own will. He left quite a large number of small sums which included family members outside his immediate nuclear family. For example he left four shillings each to the sons of his deceased sister Joan Welles, and other amounts to the daughters of his long dead brother Christopher, to his brother in law John Foxe, to Lady Elizabeth Mewys, the remarried widow of his eldest son Francis, and to the children of his brother William. He seems to have been especially fond of Robert Ram (1564-1638) who was rector at Copford, near Colchester, his wife, Elizabeth (d. 1639) and one of their daughters called Rebecca Ram (b. 1596), 'formerly my servant'.[279] Rebecca was a great niece of Francis. There is another example of a servant being a family member in the will of John Ram, Francis' son, who left £5 to a servant called Sarah Berblock, most likely a member of the family married into by brothers Anthony and Edward.[280] The biggest bequest Francis made was to his grandson Francis 3 (1607-1643), who was left land in Hornchurch to be held in trust until he reached his majority. This may have been prompted by the fact that his father William had died not long before in 1612 when young Francis was five years old. All other property questions were dealt with in the indenture referred to previously. The range of these bequests shows Francis to have maintained a wide number of family contacts.

It is clear Francis and his brother William had mutual friendships with people in Havering, as the will of Nicholas Cotton senior shows. In addition to bequests to 'loving friends' Francis and his wife there is a small gift to William, brother of Francis, and Marion his wife (d. 1602) who he also calls his 'loving friends'.[281] The tone of the will suggests that there was mutual friendship between Nicholas Cotton, Francis Ram and William Ram, probably centred on Havering. Although brother William lived in Colchester he probably travelled about in Essex on legal business and his acting as witness to Havering wills is evidence of this. The inclusion of the wives suggests they were also part of the friendship circle.

Occupational and marital openings were no doubt found at the turn of the seventeenth century in various ways, as still happens, but family contacts probably played a considerably bigger part then than they do now. Although Francis clearly made his own way in the world family links played an important part in providing for his sons, and probably his daughters, either directly by way of Francis' own initiative, or through them becoming involved informally in his own network of relationships. The semi automatic process that applied in Great Waltham of each generation following the other on the land, was obviously not possible.

Around 1600 Francis had seven young grown up sons and, no doubt, looked happily to the future, but a cloud came over his family life as he got older and in the years immediately after his death. Although he lived to about the age of 80, his children and grandchildren suffered a truly terrible morbidity. Only two of his sons, John and Samuel, survived to be over forty, and only one, William, had children who grew up to have families of their own. It is possible that four sons pre-deceased him. The paragraphs that follow tell the story of Francis' sons. Because of the frequent appearance of the name Francis until the end of this chapter they are now numbered as in the charts.

The sons who went to London were associated with the following parishes, by way of being married, buried, or baptising children – St Benet Sherehog, St Lawrence Jewry, St Margaret Friday Street, St Mary Aldermanbury, St Mary Magdalene Milk Street, St Matthew, St Stephen Coleman Street, and St Vedast. These parishes were all within the city wall, in the western half, to the north and south of Cheapside, and made up one of the areas where the prosperous citizens lived. However, not everyone living in these parishes was well off, as the rich and the poor lived more cheek by jowl than they do now. Statistical evidence for 1693 shows that some of London's highest land and rental values were in these parts of London, which adds to the impression that Francis' family living there were well connected.[282]

As I made a final reading of the whole text prior to publication an impression came to me that the paragraphs which follow about Francis' children are disjointed and at times almost impossible to make sense of. At first I thought it must be because they are poorly written but then on deeper reflection another idea came to me. There are three traumatic episodes in the history of the Ram family, two of them to be told later – the bankruptcy of John Ram 5C (1739-1810) of Colchester in 1796 with the effect it had on the fortunes of his family, followed by the collapse in the 1850's of the farming side of the family's involvement with agriculture. But the one that stands out is what happened to Francis Ram's family in the early years of the seventeenth century. My reflection led me to believe there is a significant difference between this and the other episodes. It is simply impossible to write in a structured way about the terrible fortunes that befell Francis' family. Hardly any of his children were able to establish families, develop occupations, or build for the future. They were literally wiped out, with one hammer blow following another in rapid succession, most tragically through the experiences of the family of Francis' youngest son Benjamin. One wonders how the family lived through what happened to them. The little pen pictures which follow tell their stories simply. It is important to wrestle with them because they are real and people actually experienced them. They are an important part of the overall story. Nearly all these events happened between 1610 and 1625, during which time over twenty family members died. The stories tell about the doggedness of human life. An irony is that Francis' own death at the ripe old age of about eighty happened in the midst of the carnage, which destroyed so quickly the achievements he built up during his lifetime.

The eldest, Francis 2 went to Gray's Inn, whether with a view to him becoming a lawyer or to simply to receive a rounded education is unclear. Many sons of wealthy parents at that time went to the Inns of court to obtain a general education, although this was rather unlikely in his case because he was in his late twenties when he went there. Several of Francis' sons were apprenticed to city companies at an older age so perhaps there was a special arrangement for older men. He was admitted to Gray's Inn on November 1 1605 'by C Yelverton without a fine'.[283] It is not known if Francis worked as a lawyer. Land worth £460 was transferred from the Cooke family to him in 1603.[284] He married Elizabeth Gerard (early 17C) in 1602 at Harrow on the Hill in Middlesex, a daughter, probably the youngest, of William Gerard (d. 1583) of Flamberds , Harrow on the Hill,[285] who most likely rented the estate from around 1566. It was a sub- manor of Rectory Manor and its size was originally 320 acres. Over the years the Gerards extended their holdings and in 1583 these were described as being 610 acres in several parishes. In 1664 Flamberds was the largest house in Harrow parish with 25 hearths.[286] This marriage may well have come about through an association of the Rams with John Gerard (1545-1612) the Botanist, a member of the family. This is a separate story which will be told later.[287] Francis 2 died at Hornchurch aged about 36. He left no will, so exactly when he died is not known, but his brother Anthony, who died in 1616, left £100 to each of his surviving brothers – John, Samuel, Edward and Benjamin, and £5 to Lady Elizabeth Mewys wife of brother Francis 2 – so he was dead by that time. They probably had a daughter Elizabeth (b. 1609), but there is no record of her as an adult so she probably died in infancy.

John Ram probably the second son retained connections with Hornchurch, but his occupation is not known and it is uncertain whether he married. He died aged about 50 making a will in which he left two houses in the parish of Hornchurch to his brother Benjamin.[288]

William Ram, the third son, married Margaret Greene in 1606 at St Stephen and St Bewet Sherehog, Walbrook, in the City of London. Where William and Margaret lived, and what his occupation was, is not known, but a number of Margaret's uncles and cousins worked in the city as merchants, grocers, haberdashers, and lawyers and may have provided work related openings. William died aged about 33 leaving his wife with four small children to bring up – Francis 3 and 3 daughters whose names are not known. They were given support by the wider family because John Ram, who died in 1617, left £20 to Francis 3, to be paid at the age of 21, plus £2 a year towards his maintenance until he attained 21 years,[289] and grandfather Francis willed lands to him in 1617.

Anthony Ram married Susan Williamson nee Bearblock (d. bef. 1616) in 1610. In the marriage license he is described as a goldsmith.[290] He was apprenticed to the Goldsmith's Company, being presented in 1611 by John Chalkhill, and apprenticed to Thomas Maddox in 1614. He gave a gold cup and cover to the Company just before he died. At that time it was quite common for people to be apprenticed to the famous livery companies and then to follow unrelated, or loosely related, occupations, so it cannot be assumed any of the Ram family who were apprenticed to livery companies followed that profession.[291] Anthony died young aged 35. In his will he leaves £10 to William Bearblock his father in law, who in 1610 was a Goldsmith of St Foster's Lane, and died in 1620.[292] His wife and a child died before him as he requests to be buried at St Matthew Friday Street, London, 'near to late wife Susan and daughter Susan', who was baptised in 1613 at the same church. The inter-relationships between the Ram, Bearblock and Harlow families are difficult to disentangle, especially as several of the women involved had been previously married. Anthony's wife Susan was almost certainly the sister of the Joan Bearblock (d. 1627) who married Edward, his younger brother, as the widow of Mr Harlow. Susan herself had previously been married to a Mr Williamson and Anthony clearly had affection for a member of this family. In his will he leaves to Mrs Margaret Williamson (a possible relation of Susan's first husband), the lease of a house and shop called the Wheatsheafe with eight acres of land in Hornchurch, referring somewhat ambiguously to her as 'the wife which I should have married'. He may have known her while his wife was alive, and even secretly preferred her to Susan!

Samuel Ram was a farmer in Dagenham, close to Hornchurch. He left several farms to Mary (m. 1617) his wife – Bin (en)trees in Dagenham 'wherein I now dwell', a farm in Hornchurch lived in by Mr Cotton, a farm called Harrolds Wood lived in by John Collins, a farm in Bushe Elms, and others in Hornchurch.[293] He was buried in Hornchurch in 1624 aged 41.

Edward Ram had a house in Clapham, south of London. His occupation is not known but he is described as a 'gent' in his will. He was only 26 or 27 when he died. He left the Clapham house to his wife Joan nee Bearblock, plus £385 owing to him. He left to his daughter Elizabeth (1617-1618) £100 at 21 and his son Francis 4 (1614-1634) £40. Elizabeth was a tiny baby in the year her father died, and she herself was dead and buried at Hornchurch sometime during the following year. This Francis was apprenticed to the Drapers' Company in 1629. He died in London four or five years later and was buried at St Vedast Church. Edward also left £50 to each of Joan's three children by a previous marriage to Mr Harlow. £10 was left to Francis 3, son of deceased brother William,[294] and £3 to his father in Law William Bearblock the elder (early 17C). After Edward's death Joan lived in Egham, Surrey, and died in 1627. In her will she left £5 to brother William Bearblock, to son John Harlow £100, to son William Harlow, £150, and to son Francis 4 £50. She also left £2 to an uncle Sir John Benham.[295] A relation of Joan's named James Bearblock completed the probate of the will of her son Francis 4 in 1636, describing himself as a merchant, of Olave Jewry.[296]

Benjamin Ram, the youngest of Francis' sons also appears in the Goldsmith Company's records – presented by Mr Bearblock in 1613 and apprenticed to him in 1615. Benjamin was made free by redemption in 1616 and admitted a freeman in 1616.[297] Benjamin married Jane Harvey, daughter of Sir Simon Harvey, a family the eldest Francis had connections with in Havering. He died aged 29, presumably in London as he was buried at Aldermanbury. He made a will in which he left all he owned to his wife Jane and their child Francis 5 (abt 1620-1625).[298] Their youngest child, John (1623-1623) was already dead and all the other members of the family died in 1623 or shortly afterwards. Jane was dead a month after Benjamin in August of that year, leaving a will which gave everything to her son Francis 5,[299] who died at Hornchurch in 1625. Thus Benjamin, Jane, John, and Francis 5 all died in swift succession. Benjamin's immediate family story is perhaps the most tragic illustration of the misfortunes that befell Francis 1's children.

Other Rams outside the immediate family obtained openings in Havering, probably as a result of the influence of the eldest Francis. A young relative was made bailiff to the Bacon family, which was related by marriage to the Cookes, during their short tenure of the Havering manor of Marks. In the Essex Record Office there is an undated list of documents relating to Marks manor, in which two references are made to members of the Ram family.[300] They are both about legal matters. The tasks described could be part of the young bailiff's duties, or perhaps be one off services provided by the eldest Francis. Another young family member, or perhaps the same one, became under-clerk of the market for Havering.[301] The eldest Francis may have been responsible for collecting royal rents in Havering through local assistants, and if this was the case he recruited a family member to be one of them. William Ram collected payments as Deputy Bailiff for the manor of Havering from 1607 to 1616,[302] who was either the eldest Francis' nephew, the urban yeoman from Romford, or his son also called William (b. 1589).

Without doubt the story of what happened to the family of the Francis who came to live in Hornchurch from Great Waltham appears tragic to us, but perhaps was quite common at the time. By 1630 only two male members of the Hornchurch Rams were left. One was the son of Edward, called Francis 4, and he died unmarried a few years later in 1634. The other, Francis 3, was the eldest child of William and his genealogy is shown in Chart C3.

He lived most of his life at Navestock, Essex, but was buried at Hornchurch in 1644. He was presumably a farmer, possibly on some, or all, of the lands acquired by the eldest Francis in 1585. Christian Greene, his maternal grandmother, left '£10 to grandchild Francis Ram 3 of Hornchurch and £50 to Katherine 'his wife' in 1639. Christian Greene also left copyhold land in trust for the two younger children of Francis 3 until they were 21, plus £50 each. Katherine was to receive income from this land meanwhile.[303]

These two children, John (abt 1632-1713) and William (1634-1712) were probably the last surviving male members of the Hornchurch family. John never married and seems to have lived all his life around Stanford Rivers. William went to the Charter House School from 1648 to 1653, and was apprenticed to the Merchant Taylor's Company in 1651, becoming a freeman in 1658. It is not known whether he was linked by occupation to this company. Membership of a livery company, especially the older and more prestigious ones was more status symbol than anything else. William lived in London for a time, as he and his wife Penelope baptised their fourth child Penelope (b. 1672) there, at the church of St Vedast Foster Lane, and another child, Mary, (b. 1681) at Highgate, just north of London. He was buried in Hornchurch, although his will says he is of the parish of Broomfield, where John Atwood, a lawyer and maternal uncle had lived. Perhaps he retired there. This village is very close to Great Waltham the home of the farming Rams. An elder brother of William and John, another Francis 6 (1630-1683), died before them and he married Dorothy Spencer in 1656, presumably a relative of Christian Greene, whose maiden name was Spencer. There is no record of them having any children.

How things ended

Although there is scattered evidence the family continued to be associated with the Hornchurch area into the eighteenth century little information is

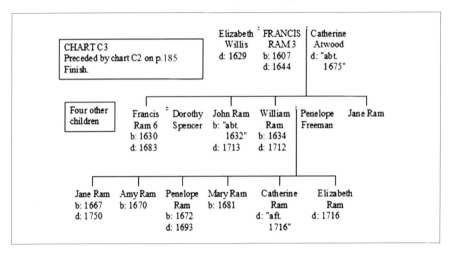

known about it, and after the 1730s individuals cannot be linked together anymore. The many deaths of young family members in the early seventeenth century no doubt caused the family fortunes founded by the original Francis to suffer a setback, and there was no recovery. The other family branches, in Great Waltham and Colchester, continued, even though both of them also nearly died out during the seventeenth century. Was the failure in Hornchurch just bad luck, the product of an unhealthy family, or the outcome of a greater risk of early death which living in London or its environs involved?

Population as a whole in England grew appreciably between 1560 and 1620.[304] But of course there were marked variations in different local places. London's population nearly doubled in this period but such growth was only sustained by much immigration. In Hornchurch and Romford the population also increased but the number of burials exceeded baptisms, so this growth also happened as a result of immigration.[305] This obviously means death rates were high. Circumstances in Great Waltham are not known, but Wrigley and Schofield found in the parishes they studied that only three to seven per cent of them had more deaths than births, and all of those were in or near urban areas.[306] The rural situation of Great Waltham means it was probably like the majority, so life expectancy was better than in Hornchurch or London. This would not have made much difference however, for people generally died early by our standards. It has been estimated the average expectation of life for men was 30-35 in the wealthier parts of London, with many prosperous men surviving into their fifties.[307] Thomas Paynel wrote in 1541, '... nowadays, alas, if a man may approach to forty or sixty years men repute him happy and fortunate'.[308] So, relatively early death was a common experience in many families, but it is possible Francis' family suffered worse than some.

Without doubt the Hornchurch Rams lived a different kind of life to that of their Great Waltham cousins, and to a lesser extent those in Colchester. The initial Francis and his elder brother William were probably the first members of the family not to live by farming, and from then on agricultural links gradually diminished in their families. But the change was not sudden and farming connections continued until the nineteenth century. The last of the Hornchurch family to be documented, the William who died in 1712, was in many ways typical of them. He lived and worked in London during his middle years, owned property in Hornchurch, was buried there, although he lived in the country in 'the parish of Broomfield' at the time of his death.[309]

The presence of William in Broomfield raises an interesting question about wider family relationships. Broomfield and Great Waltham parishes abut each other and it is very unlikely that William did not know about the many Great Waltham Rams and his inter-relatedness. In 1700 there were seven distinct Ram families in the second parish, and the Hornchurch Rams originated from there only 150 years earlier. But the only mention of contacts between the Hornchurch and Great Waltham Rams is in the will of the original Francis, who left four shillings each to the sons of his deceased sister Joan Welles, who probably lived in Great Waltham. What did they think of each other? Their worlds had drifted apart, and they probably had increasingly less in common. Francis would not have left Great Waltham unless he wanted a different kind of world, and none of the descendants of the Rams who moved away from Great Waltham in the sixteenth century ever went back there again to live.

XV

Professionals, Farmers, and Merchants in Colchester, 1550-1800

The will and bankruptcy of John Ram 5C (1739-1810)
John Ram 5C was probably the wealthiest member of the Ram family, and he was possibly one of the richest people in Colchester before his bankruptcy in 1796. He was also the only person in the family who is known to have become a bankrupt. This event and the will he wrote in 1793 tell us a lot about the Ram family, the middling sort of people, and their values at that time.

His will was the most spectacular one made by a member of the Ram family. It was even more detailed than some of those of the sixteenth and seventeenth centuries, ran to ten pages, and was written shortly after the deaths of his wife aged 46 and eldest daughter, aged 21.[310] When he wrote his will, at the age of 54, John had six surviving children: John 6C (b. 1776-d. bef. 1810) was 17, Nicholas (b. abt. 1779- 1816) was about 14, Jane (b. abt 1781) about 12, James (1787-1804) was 11 and William (1785-1798) was 8. The only beneficiaries were John and Nicholas, and their inheritances were conditional upon them making certain provisions for their younger brothers and sisters. John is charged to give each of them £600 when they reach 21 plus yearly payments of £24 until then towards education and maintenance. Nicholas is required to do the same but the lump sums are £500 and the maintenance allowances are only £7. 1793 was almost certainly a tragic year for John and he was no doubt concerned about what would happen to his family if he died shortly afterwards. Maybe he was also ill that year or wrote the will as an insurance policy to cope with extreme family uncertainty – a frequent occurrence at the time. If he had died shortly after making the will, special provision would have been required to administer it as his eldest son did not become 21 until 1797. However, he survived for another eighteen years and there is no evidence that he made a later will. For details about John Ram's family see chart C9. In earlier years John Ram had been in partnership with Thomas Dixon and Alex Carter in the coal trade, but in 1791 he began trading on his own from a yard opposite the Goat's Head.[311] From this yard at the Hythe, the main dock area of Colchester, timber, chalk and reeds were shipped and there was also a granary. As a coal merchant, miller, dealer and chapman, John had quite

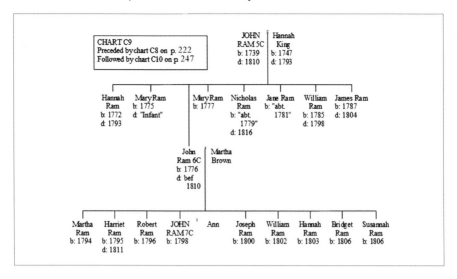

wide ranging commercial interests. He additionally held about 85 acres of land in Colchester, some freehold and some copyhold, and owned about 14 houses and tenements. Although he withdrew from other land holdings at Berechurch in the early 1790s, he may still have retained some landed interests outside Colchester. Thomas Dixon, more or less a contemporary of John Ram, continued in the coal trade from the Hythe after their partnership ended. Both men were active at St Leonard's Church. John became a regular attender at the Vestry meeting from 1791[312] whilst Thomas Dixon (d. 1810) acted as overseer in 1780 and 1790, becoming a churchwarden from 1785 to 1791.[313] Another man active in the vestry, J C Tabor (early 19C), was one of the assignees who oversaw John's bankruptcy.[314]

In 1790 John Ram bought a house in Love Hill, now Hythe Hill, from a Mr Taylor for £1000.[315] It was the sort of house, in which he could reflect his ambitions and his growing social and financial position. Perhaps its purchase was part of an over reaching that ended in bankruptcy six years later. The house is portrayed inside the box in Figure 9 although the map it is taken from dates from 1923.[316] It was next door to the rectory, presumably of St Leonard's Church which was just down the hill, set in four acres of gardens, and was only about ten minutes' walk from the Hythe. The drive way ran in from the left hand front side, then round to the back and finally out to the road again at the other side of the house. At the back the view looked out across open fields to the River Colne. In the notice of bankruptcy in 1796 there was a detailed description of the house. On the ground floor there was a parlour and counting house to the front, a drawing room eighteen feet square '... commanding a beautiful prospect', plus a good kitchen. There were four good bedrooms, four garret rooms, three cellars, a wash house, brewhouse,

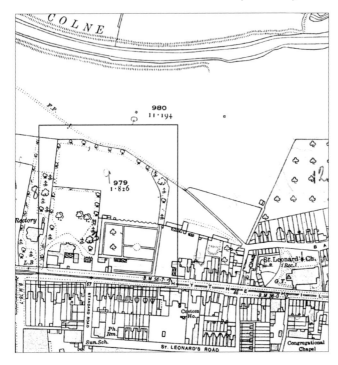

Figure 9. Plan of the Colchester house of John Ram 5C (d. 1810).

laundry, coach house, granary, three pumps, two pleasure gardens, a field and orchard adjoining and four acres,' situated in the pleasantest part of the Hythe'.[317]

John Ram was 57 at the time of his bankruptcy. The *Biographical Dictionary* of John Bensusan Butt, a manuscript in the Colchester branch of the Essex Record Office, now transferred to the record office in Chelmsford, makes the following comments about it. 'In 1796 Ram was the subject of one of the more spectacular of the rash of bankruptcies amongst Hythe merchants and other traders during the 1790s. These were occasioned largely by overstretching of credit due to the rapid wartime inflation and the disruption of shipping by the French wars'.[318] John Ram's reference in the *Biographical Dictionary* details the terms and conditions of the bankruptcy. It is very interesting to compare this and his will with what seems to have actually happened. Table 14 spells out a complicated story. Although the formal provisions of the bankruptcy stipulated that John Ram's possessions were to be sold for the life of the bankrupt[319] there is evidence that what actually happened was more complicated. Not all of the items mentioned in the will are recognisable in the statement of bankruptcy, which may be due to a variety of reasons – they were just not included, they had been disposed of between the writing of the will and the bankruptcy, or they became confused with other items in the listing. None of the properties that did appear in both were sold randomly, and in fact they were all let. Some of them continued to be in the hands of the family, but on what terms is not known. What seems likely is that the assignees bought or held the properties and sub let them, but it is not clear who benefited from the rents. The assignees met as a group from time to time to deal with related business and John Ram was a member. It appears that a sort of trust was being operated and there are definite signs that during John Ram's lifetime the interests of the Ram family were safeguarded. Moreover his will was proved

Table 14. The bankruptcy of John Ram in 1796.

Will item: **To son John Ram.**	Terms of bankruptcy.	Apparent outcomes.
Own freehold house – Love Hill (4 acres).	To be sold by assignees.	Bought by J C Tabor, one of the assignees, before 1809.[320]
Golden Noble Hill. Used to have a windmill. House. Flour shop and garden, etc.	To be sold by assignees ?	In 1809 in the occupation of Nicholas Ram or under-tenants.[321]
Burned? House Farm (10 acres).	Not identifiable in bankruptcy.	Not known.
Kiln in St Giles parish (2.5 acres).	Not identifiable in bankruptcy.	Not known.
Peacock's Garden, Battleswick Manor (52 acres).	Sayer's Farm and quay plus 52 acres from Battleswick manor. To be sold by assignees.	Let to un-named person.
Old Hythe in St Giles Parish.	See above.	Not known.
Fields called upper and lower Broomfield in St Giles Parish (8 acres).	Not identifiable in bankruptcy.	Not known.
Borsham or Borshall – a tenement.	Not identifiable in bankruptcy.	Not known.
Field called Homefield. (4 acres).	Not identifiable in bankruptcy.	Not known.
To son Nicholas Ram.		
Middle Mill plus adjoining King's meadow (1 acre).	To be sold by assignees.	In 1796 occupied by Mrs Mary King and William Abbott on 4 yr. lease at £50 a year. This was still the case in 1809.[322] The son of John Ram, another John, rented the mill from Joseph Green, one of the assignees from 1796 to 1799.[323]

New Rise Gate. Meadow near Middle Mill leading to North St (Middleborough St) (1 acre).	Not identifiable in bankruptcy.	Not known.
Pasture close by above (1 or 2.5 acres).	To be sold by assignees.	Not known.
Five tenements in St Giles Parish.	10 tenements to be sold by assignees.	Let to un-named persons.
Four or five tenements in St Botolph's Street.	2 tenements to be sold by assignees.	Let to un-named persons.
House that belonged to John's father Nicholas in Angel Lane.		Not known.

when he died which suggests there remained some items not covered by the bankruptcy, although probably not many. At the time of John Ram's death the newspapers said the life interests expired and all the lots were then sold outright, with the exception of the house in Love Hill which was previously purchased by J C Tabor, one of the assignees.[324] What actually happened is not known.

At the close of the eighteenth century Colchester was in economic transition, being in the process of declining as a cloth town to become mainly a commercial and service centre for the surrounding area. The social and economic group to which John Ram belonged was part of the controlling elite in the town, about which John Bensusan Butt writes in the following terms.

> ...the Colchester elite, politically and socially as well as economically is composed of a group of affluent middle class men from a variety of trades.... There is also an increasing group of professional men, mainly attorneys, included in the elite....Generally speaking the wealth of the town is focused around this Cabal of prosperous tradesmen, professionals and merchants from the Hythe. Family linkages are strong in these groups....Though the Hythe group tend to be outside the immediate circle of Corporation politics they are much better represented on the Channel Commissioners – a body equally important and clearly nearer their immediate needs.[325]

He concludes with a list of the Colchester Corporation in December 1788 which includes the occupation of the people listed. John King (d. 1790 or 1794), John Ram's father in law, is in it.[326] He became successively a councillor, alderman and Mayor. A potential source of association between the two men was that they were both millers.

John's bankruptcy must be seen in the context of the times. Business was then very dependent on the bill of exchange and the development of mortgages and trusts. This fostered an economy based on credit, which some saw as eroding the social fabric. Bills and credit were a substitute for money, which moderated the demand for cash at a time of slow growth in the economy. It was also a mechanism that helped to make up for the problems met with before the existence of a readily available banking system in transferring money from one person to another, but excessive reliance on credit made business failure an ever present possibility because of the lack of readily available money to pay debts. It also has to be remembered that in business at that time there was no way of limiting liability, and that risk could only be ameliorated through partnership. In this situation government had to decide how to view bankrupts. 'Were they men of overreaching ambition and avarice who were dishonestly evading their creditors and deserving of punishment; or were they enterprising men who deserved sympathy'.[327] The law of bankruptcy covered all bankrupts although it was really intended to deal with defaulters who were trying to avoid their creditors, but from 1706 some protection was given to honest bankrupts. 'The bankrupt surrendered his estate, which was divided amongst his creditors; he was discharged from his debts when four fifths of the creditors by number and value agreed; and if he paid 8s in the pound, he received 5 per cent of the realised estate to start life anew'.[328] The intention was to encourage enterprise in an environment which was highly dependent upon credit, but this liberalisation of practice only related to wholesalers and manufacturers – retailers and artisans were not covered.

No direct information has come to hand about the impact of the bankruptcy on John or his immediate family. It is possible he was released from it and started in business again, but this would have been difficult for someone then in his sixties. Most of his children did not survive, only two of the sons mentioned in his will, John 5 and Nicholas, living into adult life, and Nicholas died in 1815 without any children. John Bensusan Butt's *Biographical Dictionary*, states that John senior married again in 1794, to Martha Brown. Although this event is recorded in the local newspapers and the *Ipswich Journal* clearly says the John Ram involved is a coal merchant at the Hythe, Colchester,[329] there is no evidence of this marriage in the family papers. It is highly likely there was confusion with John 5 who may have worked in the family business at that time. Separate information about the son shows he married someone called Martha around 1794, and that his first child was called Martha (b. 1794).[330] From further information known about him it is clear he lived in relatively straightened circumstances, and was never more than a small farmer in Fingringhoe, near Berechurch and Colchester. Between 1796 and 1799 he rented the mill mentioned in his father's will from Joseph Green, one of the assignees to the bankruptcy, and then moved on, probably to Fingringhoe.

John Ram, merchant and bankrupt, has provided a start point for this chapter but he was one of many of a long line of Rams in Colchester who went back at least to the middle of the sixteenth century. This part of the Ram story is perhaps the most complicated to write and to understand. It covers a very long period – from the mid sixteenth to early nineteenth centuries – containing considerable diversity of social and economic involvements. The people described are more varied than those in Great Waltham, or for that matter Havering. Colchester was, and is, a more complex society than Great Waltham, but unfortunately there are relatively few publications that help to put the Ram family in context.[331] However, one of the major upsides of the Colchester story is that it shows how the Rams accommodated themselves successfully to a truly urban society for the first time. The involvements of Francis Ram's family with Stuart London never really produced a positive outcome.

William Ram (abt. 1535-1602)

There are scattered references to Rams in Colchester in the middle ages, but they cannot be connected directly with the family. For example Richard Ram (mid 14C) paid rents to the Borough, appears in its records,[332] and had probably been in Colchester from mid century onwards.[333] He seems to have been most active in the 1350s.[334] The same is true of two other people with the family name, Richard in 1434-35 and Henry in 1444-45, who were both admitted to Colchester as free Burgesses,[335] There are references to Rams in the early registers of baptisms, marriages, and deaths which cannot be placed, for example to John Ram son of Nicholas Ram (d. 1561) who was buried at Copford. But Luke Ram (late 16C) who married Jane Read at St Botolph's in 1574, Catherine Ram (late 16C) who married John Wynter there in 1579, and Dorothy Ram (late 16C) who was baptised the daughter of an unknown John Ram in 1598 probably did have connections with the family. This is because William Ram, the first known member of the family to live in Colchester from the middle 1560s onwards, had close connections with the same parish. He was buried at St Botolph's Church on 27 July 1602 and his wife, Marion (d. 1602), was buried at St Nicholas' Church on 27 July, although the entry says she was of St Botolph's parish. Rather mystifyingly, a John Ram baptised three children, at St Nicholas' Church in 1566, 1567, and 1569. With the entry for the last of these, Elizabeth (b. 1569), there is a note which says John is an under sheriff of Colchester. This was at the time when William Ram was baptising children of his own at the same church. It is extremely unlikely they were not from the same family, but no relationship has been proven. This conundrum is possibly sorted out by the will of Joan Potter (d. 1584), of Great Burstead near Billericay who might be the Joan listed in chart C1. She left to 'John Rame my brother 30sh., to Thomas Rame my brother, my sister Rose Rame, my brother Francis Rame, and my sister Goodin? 6/8 each. To my brother's son the son of William Ram 6/8 at 21'.[336.]The last person mentioned is almost certainly the William who went to Colchester from Great Waltham and his son, who lived in Romford. Joan's will suggests that the John she mentions and the John in

Colchester are one and the same person, but why he is left out of his father's will, along with Rose and Thomas, is a mystery.

William Ram's origins in Great Waltham have been mentioned earlier.[337] He is recorded as being a student at Cambridge University who matriculated, a preliminary stage examination, but did not stay on to take a degree. The entry for him reads, 'Matric. Pens. From Trinity Hall, Easter, 1551'.[338.] This means he was admitted as an undergraduate in 1551 as a 'pensioner', i.e., someone who paid for their 'commons' or daily food supplied at a fixed charge. He was probably between sixteen and eighteen at the time, which would mean he was born between about 1535 and 1537. Most likely he first went to Colchester not long before 1559-60 when a William Ram of Pleshey, very near Great Waltham, was admitted a free Burgess.[339] During the second half of the sixteenth century he baptised a number of children at St Nicholas' Parish, Colchester starting in the 1560s. The first to be registered was Robert (1564-1638), and at least a further nine followed between 1564 and about 1581. When he married his wife Marion is not known, but he had at least two sons, William (abt. 1560-1620) and Richard (b. abt. 1562 -1640) who were born before Robert.

A summary of his career has to be put together by compiling fragments of information from various sources. He is mentioned in a 1577 survey of Great Waltham as still having seven acres of land there, and in this survey is listed as a 'gent' living in Colchester. There is a documentary reference in the Essex Record Office that he was an attorney and Deputy Town Clerk of Colchester in 1562.[340] He was still holding this post in 1576 because he is referred to in a letter dated 25 September 1576, from Francis Walsingham, Principal Secretary of State, to the Bailiffs, Commonality and electors of Colchester commending William Ram, the Deputy Town Clerk.[341] Whether this post was salaried, full or part time is not clear, nor is it known how long he held it for. There is information in the Assize Records which indicates he had other professional involvements. In March 1582 Henry Nicholles of East Doneyland near Colchester was indicted for grand larceny at a view of frankpledge before William Ram steward of Edward Dobson, esq., lord of the manor.[342] William is also referred to as Under Sheriff of Essex in two more references during 1577.[343] He was still in Colchester in 1587 because a charter dated that year which grants lands which he inherited from his father in 1567, to Nicholas Eve of High Easter mentions he is from Colchester.[344] It is probable he combined tasks as Deputy Town Clerk with the general work of an attorney, acting as steward at East Doneyland, or holding other public offices. It is also clear that he wrote and witnessed wills, both in Colchester and in other places.

It is impossible to say how wealthy William was, but he may not have all that well off. Between 1582 and 1589 he is recorded in the *Collectors of the Poor Book* as paying one penny each year towards the Poor Rate in St Nicholas Parish. He is always called a 'gent' and usually appears about fifth in the list of contributors which clearly reflects status. The aldermen and bailiffs at the top usually pay four pence or more whilst William appears below them at the head of a large number of people who pay one penny. So, although he had high status he was not a high payer, and this might mean he was not able to make such a big contribution as the other more important people, or was not required to do so.[345]

It is important to view William in the context of the Colchester of his day. The town was a significant city in Roman times. In the Middle Ages and on into the early modern period it was partly an administrative centre, partly a market town, partly a port and also an in industrial centre. In the sixteenth century the wool export trade grew very significantly in which Colchester participated through the carriage of wool to the continent and the weaving of cloth for export. In 1500 the town was still mainly contained within the old walls that formed a rectangle to the south of the castle. The population was around 4500.[346] Main roads ran North, South, East, and West, and the River Colne went roughly from East to West between the town and the castle. There were five mills on the river, and three bridges across it. The port was a little way off from the town at The Hythe, where there was a separate community and church, St Leonard's. The merchants tended to live close to the Hythe. In the later Middle Ages the richer people lived mainly in the part of the High street that was in the parishes of St Runwald and St Nicholas, and in East and West Stockwell Streets. The west end of the High street and perhaps North Hill in St Peter's parish was probably also a wealthy area. The southern part of the town was poorer.[347] Presumably William lived in St Nicholas parish which was probably still one of the more prosperous parts of the town.

One of the main sources of personal information about his official life and position in Colchester are local records which give information about him and reveal the sort of people he knew and associated with. Most of it comes from wills in which he is mentioned.[348] Some of them were written by aldermen of whom there were ten and they comprised, along with two councils of sixteen members each, the governing body of Colchester in the sixteenth and seventeenth centuries. All these bodies were elected annually.[349] William is also mentioned in wills made by bailiffs, of which two were elected each year and they were the town's chief executives prior to the introduction of mayors in 1624.[350] One was the Chamberlain, the most senior fiscal officer.[351]

Thomas Turner (d. 1575), gentleman, an alderman, and bailiff in 1574 and 1567[352] left 'To William Ram, of Colchester, my gelding, with the saddle etc to the same belonging I used to ride, or my colt at Bremstens which he likes best'. He also willed that 'upon the full finishing of my account of my chamberlainship in Colchester, £5, part of that due to me from the town, shall be bestowed towards the finishing of the new building in the new hall, 40 shillings, the rest I give to William Ram, deputy town clerk, for his painstaking about the same, and the residue I will shall be divided among the now four sergeants of the same town.' He appointed 'William Ram of Colchester, gentleman, the elder, and John Pye, one of the aldermen of Colchester (bailiff in 1581 and 1586)[353], and Edward Coker, my wife's brother, and my brother, John Turner, overseers. In his will George Sayer , the elder, (d. 1573) bailiff at least six times between in 1540 and 1567, refers to John Pye as a son in law. This links William with George Sayer through his shared role of overseer of the will of Thomas Turner. William Markaunt (d. 1582), of St John's in the Parish of St Giles besides Colchester, made a large number of quite small bequests in his will including the following. 'To everyone of the following persons a ring of fine gold, to be made for them, and to be of the finest fashion' to the value specified. Each ring was to be enamelled and engraved. 25 people are listed, including family and friends. Twelfth and thirteenth on the list are Mr William Ram of Colchester, the elder, and Mrs Marian Ram, his wife. Their rings were for the value of 30sh. and 20 sh. respectively, which was a typical value. A goldsmith is to be paid £4 for making each ring. He also leaves 'to my friend, Mr John Ram the elder, of Colchester, gentleman, £10, to mistress Marion Ram, his wife, 20sh., and to Wiston Ram, my Godson, 40sh. (Wiston was a child of William Ram), who was also given a tawney livery coat. Perhaps this John Ram is the mysterious John mentioned earlier, although it is unlikely that both John and William had wives with the same name. This difficulty may be because of an error in the published transcription of the will. William is mentioned again later in William Markaunt's will in the following terms. 'To my very (good) friend and gossip Mr William Ram, the elder, of Colchester, my black morning gown, a doublet of black satin, etc'...'. William Markaunt came from a prosperous background for his father John (d. 1583) is described in his will as a gentleman, and William's elder brother Edmund (d. 1578) is similarly designated in his will. John Griffith of St Botolph's in Colchester (d. 1590), gentleman, left 40sh. 'To friend William Ramme of Colchester'. He also left to his 'loving brother Richard Griffith of London, all my bookes that are here in Colchester and at London'.

This information shows that William Ram was associated with the ruling group in Colchester, which, since he was Deputy Town Clerk, is hardly remarkable. But some of the wills include references to William that suggest more than formal professional relationships with people who were intellectually aware. John Griffith and William Markaunt possessed books at a time when they were only just becoming widely available, and regarded them sufficiently highly to leave to named individuals. William's association with the ruling group in Colchester got him into trouble with the law on one occasion in

March 1567.[354] He was indicted with other notables of Colchester of riot and assault. They attacked Henry Morrant on the river at Rowhedge Reach in East Doneyland, and carried off boats belonging to various people, at the instigation of Thomas Lucas, Town Clerk.

The wills in which William is mentioned show him not only to have been an associate of leading people in Colchester but also ones who were sympathisers with radical Protestantism. William Markaunt was certainly of such a mind and made a long introductory statement in his will, which included a dissertation about death. He was the brother of John Markaunt vicar of Great Clacton from 1559-1586[355] and left money to several clergy – Mr Loe, Mr Lewis, Mr Serles, Mr Farrow, Mr Morse, and especially George Northey 'our general preacher and pastor of our congregation', who received £4 and was an extreme Protestant.[356] He left a book called 'Master Calvin's Institutions' to Sir Thomas Lucas – who William worked for as Deputy Town Clerk. Thomas Turner asked Mr Challenor, preacher in Colchester, 'to preach four sermons to the people of Colchester after my death'. These bequests suggest a sympathy for the common preachers, although it has to be said it was common at the time to support the preachers in this way.

During the Elizabethan period it was traditional in Colchester to appoint 'common preachers' as part of the Corporation's policy. They were usually quite eminent clergy from Cambridge University who had advanced Protestant views. One of the most renowned was George Northey, who was imprisoned for non conformity in 1583 soon after his appointment, but then released. The common preachers played a pivotal part in the religious and community life of Colchester and bore much responsibility for the town's continuing tradition of non conformity. Their presence also led to political tensions between the more radical members of the Corporation who supported them and the more conservative elements who did not.[357] The period during which William was active in Colchester was a turbulent time in which social reform, religious beliefs and politics became inextricably entwined. From early in Elizabeth's reign Colchester was almost entirely Protestant, there being a sympathy for Calvinist ideas among all social levels, but there was also a desire among some for a more gradualist approach, particularly about the social reform of manners. During most of William's life significant efforts were made to reconcile different views, but after 1600 there was so much confusion that it was almost impossible to get agreement among the divergent groups, with tensions becoming particularly bad after 1620.[358] It is reasonable to assume that alongside William's friendship with radical sympathisers also went common interests about religion. It is also impossible to review William's religious position without taking account of the close relationship he had with his brother Francis, which is discussed in chapter XIV and in the following paragraphs.

One of the surprising things about William, and probably the most interesting and best documented, concerns the botany book that he wrote, and was posthumously published and printed in 1606 by Simon Stafford, 'dwelling in the Cloth Fayre, at the sign of the three crowns' in London.[359] At least two copies of the book still exist, in the British Library and in the pre-Linnaean collection of the Royal Botanic Garden at Kew. A botanical reference book written in 1993 mentions that William Ram a public notary of Colchester wrote '*Little Dodeon*' in 1606, which was an epitome, that is summary, of Lyte's Herbal.[360] William's book was written in the context of the great interest which developed in plants and botany during the latter part of the sixteenth century, originally in Mainland Europe. Henry Lyte (1529-1607) popularised the continental work by translating and publishing a famous herbal written by a Dutch doctor Rembert Dodonaeus in 1578, under the title of '*A New Herball or Historie of Plants*'. John Gerard a famous Elizabethan botanist wrote his own book, '*The Herball or General History of Plants*' in 1597, which is one of the best known botanical books ever to have been written. Gerard was originally a barber surgeon who had his own garden in Holborn, London, and travelled widely at home and abroad on plant collecting trips. He was the superintendent of several gardens, including those of William Cecil. William's book was therefore part of a growing general interest in botany and herbal remedies.

The book has six sections. It starts with 'The corrections of dangerous plants and herbs', that is plants which are medicinally important but can have ill effects, and there follows a 'Calendar of the Year' which includes the gardening year with details of what to eat and drink in different seasons. The next three sections consist of helpful hints on the subjects of 'Observations for Gathering Herbs', including the time to do so, 'Observations for Gardening', about garden tasks for different times of the year, and 'Observations for Diet' which offers guidance for the whole year on what food is good to eat at different times. The last section, 'Incidentia' takes up three quarters of the book and lists many herbal remedies for every imaginable illness and unpleasant condition. The cures listed are typical of the day, from which the following two have been randomly chosen. 'For the byting of a spider, rub the place well with flyes', and '...to provoke sleep, Take lettice seeds and Smallage seed: Stamp them and temper them with the white of an Egg, and lay it on the forehead. Take powder of Smallage, Penbare and Pynts, tempered with oyle or greace, and anoynt the temples, etc. Stamp Leek seeds and temper them with woman's milk, and the white of an egge bound to the temples'.[361] Although it is called an 'epitome' it is nonetheless nearly 250 pages long! It is a mixture of medical herbal remedies, health and dietary care, together with gardening advice.

Although the title implies William's book is like its predecessors, but in summary form, in reality it is structured quite differently. In the Henry Lyte translation the basic pattern is to list and describe each plant under several headings which include a description, places where it grows, and its virtues. The plants are grouped into six parts, depending on the characteristics, e.g., ones which are sweet smelling, which have medicinal properties, and are used in cooking meat. The sixth part is about trees and shrubs. William Ram's book is more practical in its orientation and lays emphasis on gardening and the use of plants in herbal remedies rather than the botanical description of plants. There is also a difference in aim. Whereas William dedicates his book to the ordinary people Henry Lyte dedicated his to Queen Elizabeth.[362] What William says in his preface, entitled 'The Author to the Reader', is worth quoting at some length as it brings out the difference and reveals why he wrote the book, which in turn tells us something about what sort of person he was.

> So as where the great booke at large (i.e., the full version) is not to be had but at great price, which cannot be procured by the poorer sort, my endeavour herein hath bin chiefly, to make the benefit of so good, necessary and profitable a worke, to be brought within the reach and compasse as well of you my poore countrymen and women, whose lives, health, ease and welfare is to be regarded with the rest' ... Whilst doing this '... my onely and greatest care hath byn of long time, to know or thinke, how and upon whome to bestow the dedication of this my very small labor: And in the penning of this my letter, my Affections are satisfied with the dedication thereof to thee my poore and loving Countryman ... for whose sake I have desired publication of the same, beseeching Almighty God to blesse us all.

This is the only known piece of writing by a member of the family which reveals social attitudes. It appears that the book was, to some extent, written out of a social concern.

But how did William come to write the book, for his workaday world was far removed from botany? He was evidently part of a social circle in which it is most likely botanical and other affiliations overlapped and inter-linked. It has been seen elsewhere that William came from a strong Protestant background and mixed with people of a similar mind in Colchester. He also had much experience of public administration in the town. Did these involvements encourage social concern? He was also part of his brother Francis' circle in Havering, and this may have merged with a botanical circle of which John Gerard was a member, or even the centre.

The botanical circle is extremely interesting in its own right and as an example of social networking. We are familiar with plant hunters and cataloguers who in later centuries made their names in the Pyrenees, the Alps, or the Himalayas, but people of Gerard's time did the same in their own homelands.

It so happens that many of them were doctors and apothecaries, probably because of the association of plants and herbs with homeopathic remedies. An interesting source of information about these developments is a book about the friends of John Gerard.[363] In his younger years Gerard developed plant related contacts with a number of people including Matthias de L'Obel a native of Lille and a qualified physician who came to London in 1569. In 1570 he and a Frenchman, Pierre Pena (also a doctor) printed a book about plants called *Stirpium Adversaria Nova* in London. Matthias stayed in London and practised as a doctor. He may have met Gerard between 1569 and 1574. He made plant collections in England, and Gerard did the same, particularly in Kent and Essex. Henry Lyte, Gerard and Matthias either knew, or knew of each other, and incorporated material from each other into their own books.

On his plant collecting trips John Gerard met many people, who were also interested in plants and botany. Colchester was among the places he visited. In wondering why a Colchester lawyer like William Ram wrote his book, it is natural to make a potential link between this and Gerard going there. Was there an inter-connection? Surely an unusual combination of circumstances led to William writing his book. In Gerard's famous 'Herball' he referred to the people he met on his journeys as well as the botanical aspects. A summary of visits made to Colchester appears in 'The Friends of John Gerard' that is based on material in 'The Herball'.

> It may be that Gerard was in Colchester on more than one occasion, as he was acquainted with several people in and around the town .... He was acquainted with Thomas Buxton, apothecary there, and he may have had intelligence (from him) of some medical details recorded in 'The Herball'. The first of these is particularly instructive. It concerns William Ram, Notary Public of Colchester, who was for a time Town Clerk (*sic*), and who successfully treated Mrs Marie de L'Obel after she had been burned by lightning. It is uncertain if Gerard actually met William Ram, who was sufficiently interested in plants as to publish an abridged version of Henry Lyte's 'Niewe Herball'. His patient, Mrs Marie de L'Obel was the wife of Hugh de L'Obel, merchant of Colchester, whom she survived. Matthias de L'Obel visited Colchester in 1596 and it is reasonable to infer that the occasion for this visit was to call upon Paul and Marie, who were probably his relatives.[364]

In this report a potential circle is discernible between William Ram, the de L'Obels, Thomas Buxton, and John Gerard.

Further possible figures in the circle are suggested in *The Friends of John Gerard* when it is stated that 'The Herball' links Robert (Thomas ?) Buxton with John Duke, MD, a physician in the parish of All Saints Colchester, whose wife was a member of the Winthrop family, and that John Duke's daughter Mary married Lawrence Wright, the half brother of 'Younger' John Wright.[365] The Winthrop family were prominent among the founding fathers in New England, and Nathaniel the brother of Lawrence Wright was a leading London member of the Massachusetts Bay Company. Several of these people were well know by the family of Francis Ram of Havering, especially the 'Younger John Wright.[366]

Even more significantly some intriguing questions can be asked about the relationships of John Gerard with the Ram and Wright families. William obviously knew the de L'Obels, and must have known Thomas (Robert)[367] Buxton and John Duke. He would probably have known the Wrights through his brother Francis. How did John Duke's daughter get introduced to Laurence Wright? William Cecil was interested in plants and had gardens at his London residence in the Strand, besides those at Theobalds, an estate in Hertfordshire which he purchased in 1564. Sometime before 1577 he had been looking for someone to look after them. By then John Gerard had become superintendent of these gardens[368] and remained associated with Cecil for 21 years.[369] Is it possible that the Rams might have facilitated Gerard's relationship with William Cecil since he was the son in law of Francis Ram's employer, Anthony Cooke? John Gerard was a junior member of the Gerard family of Ince, although how he fits into the family genealogy is not clearly documented.[370] At this time one branch of the family lived at Harrow on the Hill in Middlesex. Francis Ram's eldest son married Elizabeth Gerard of Harrow on the Hill and how did they meet each other?

This is not the end of the possible interconnections. John Gerard may have been helped on his plant collecting trips to Kent by Hugh Morgan, who was a London apothecary practising in and around the parish of St Vedast Foster Lane. The name of Hugh Morgan appears in the registers there. He is mentioned in 1570 and 1571 by Pena and L'obel, and he later became apothecary to Queen Elizabeth. Not far away he had a garden in St Stephen's parish, Coleman Street which Pena and L'obel had visited. Hugh was the son of John Morgan, of Great Bardfield in Essex, a village only a few miles from Great Waltham. His uncle, Richard Morgan was incumbent of Great Bardfield.[371] Was Hugh Morgan known to the Rams as well as John Gerard? He was a contemporary of both Francis and William, living from 1530 to 1616, and they all came from the same local area.

Another issue in this story is why botany became so important to William. The book he wrote must have taken him a lot of time, reflecting a major personal interest. If he treated Mrs Marie de L'Obel medically, did he treat people more generally by means of herbal remedies? There was a close, and indistinct relationship at the time between an interest in plants, herbal remedies and medical treatment. Although Gerard's main concern was with plants he was closely connected with the medical profession and practised medicine himself.[372] He treated John Dee, the philosopher, scientist and magician in 1594.

William Ram's family

Only two of William's large family, shown in Chart C4 have left much information about themselves. One was William, probably the eldest, the urban yeoman and innkeeper of Romford who figures in the snapshot about Francis Ram.[373] He lived most of his life in Romford and died there in 1620. He married Judith Nooth in 1586 and they had nine children. Judging from the registration records for Romford the family continued to live in the area for at least three generations, but the male line gradually died out.

The other is the third eldest son Robert, who was probably the first person in the family to obtain a university degree. He graduated B A from Jesus College, Cambridge in 1583-84, M A in 1587, B D in 1595, and D D in 1602.[374] The Ordination Register of the Guildhall Library states he was ordained in 1588 and constituted to serve at Little Horkesley, a village very near to where his uncle Christopher served as priest in the mid sixteenth century.[375] He later became rector of Copford, just on the western edge of Colchester and vicar of Great Birch nearby at an unknown date, continuing to hold these livings for the rest of his life. Robert's second child, Richard Ram (1588-1640), was baptised in Colchester in 1588 and it is likely Robert married his wife Elizabeth (d. 1639) not long before. The first child known to be born at Copford was John Ram (1591-bef. 1675), which means Robert was rector at Copford for at least forty six years. Between about 1587 and 1610 Robert and Elizabeth had sixteen children who survived infancy, and there may have been others that

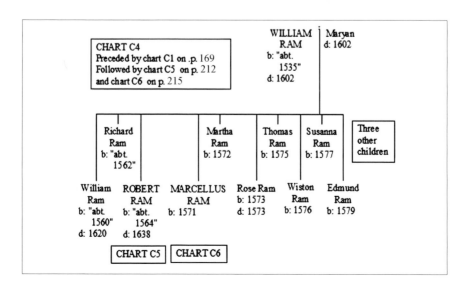

did not. This is the largest number of children known to have been born to a couple in the Ram family. Chart C5 shows the male members of his family, but the girls are omitted because of lack of space. However they are included in Appendix 1 – the family timeline.

The church at Copford is very beautiful and is almost wholly a Norman building dating from the twelfth century. Originally it was most likely to have been the chapel to the nearby medieval manor house, now Copford Hall, which in the middle ages was held by the Bishop of London and regularly used by the bishops as a rural retreat.[376] In modern times its glorious and famous medieval wall paintings have been uncovered and restored, but in Robert's day they would have been invisible under a coat of whitewash applied in 1547. They were not rediscovered until around 1690. The quality of livings at his period varied greatly, and Copford appears to have been one of the better ones.[377] In 1650 the glebe was worth £30 plus tithes of £83/17/0. In 1887 the living was worth £749, quite a large amount for the time, but whether its value had remained constant over the years is not known. In 1610 the rectory house was 'sufficient and complete' and 'very spacious' whilst nearly thirty years later in 1637 was said to be in 'very good repair'. In the hearth tax return of 1662 it counted ten hearths, which was the same number as the manor house.[378]

Having such a large family no doubt involved Robert in many domestic matters. But he was also a learned man, who, during his earlier years must have devoted considerable time to his studies, certainly up to his forties. The information in *Alumni Cantabrigienses* shows he completed theological studies after he

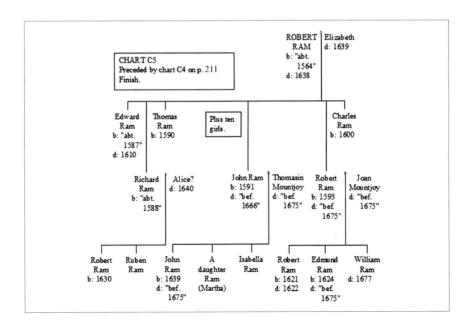

graduated, which led to being awarded a D D. This achievement is confirmed in a notebook held by Jesus College called *Register of Fellows, 1497-1618* that was compiled by A Gray, but it does not actually say he was a fellow. It has been seen already that Colchester during the later part of the sixteenth century and into the seventeenth was a centre of radical Protestantism and religious ferment, in which the Corporation of Colchester offered bright and radical clergy from Cambridge University opportunities to be 'common preachers'. Robert must have visited Colchester frequently and been well connected with events there, certainly until the death of his father. With his family background and learning it might be expected he would have had radical religious tendencies, leading to participation in Colchester's religious life, but practically nothing is known about his religious outlook, and there is no evidence of radical involvements. No records about his activities have been found in Colchester, or at Jesus College, which would not have encouraged radical religious involvements. The college was never a centre of Puritanism, and took the royalist side during the Civil War. The Master, Richard Sterne, and the former Master, William Beale were arrested and imprisoned in the Tower of London by Oliver Cromwell towards the end of Robert's life. All the other fellows, except two, were ejected from their posts. The only clues available about Robert's religious practice are that he gave a monthly lecture in each of the parishes and assured (Archbishop Laud of his conformity in 1633.[379] One or two insights about his personal views are revealed in his will of 1635.[380] He left his Book of Martyrs to daughter Sarah (b.1610), and to daughter Susan (b. 1607) his best English Bible 'lately bound in London'. 'The rest of my books to my sons Richard and Robert'.(b. 1593-bef. 1675) It would be interesting to have a list of these. The special mention of Foxe's famous book may indicate an identification with radical Protestantism, but on the other hand his falling in with the Laudian reforms suggests he was a cautious man, and possibly a conservative one, who kept a low profile in the country and did not get involved in controversy.

Robert became closely associated with the owners of the Copford manor through the marriages of two of his younger sons. John Ram (1591-bef. 1666) married Thomasin Mountjoy and Robert Ram (1593-bef. 1675) married Joan Mountjoy whose family owned the manor from around 1612 to 1626 when it was sold to John Haynes.[381] Several children were born in Copford to the two sons, to John between 1639 and 1642 and to Robert between 1621 and 1625. John appears to have lived locally until he died, sometime between 1649 and 1666. Robert went to Jesus College, Cambridge, graduated B A in 1611,[382] and was ordained in 1622 at St James, Colchester. His presence in Copford in the early 1620s suggests he was assisting his father, who by that time, was quite elderly, although in what capacity is unknown. What happened to Robert in the longer run is not known either.

Robert's, second son, Richard, also became a priest in the Church of England a few years before Robert. He graduated B A at Queen's College, Cambridge in 1606 and M A in 1610. He was ordained deacon in London in 1610 and priest in 1612. He was first curate of Great Birch, where his father was rector, afterwards becoming vicar of Great Bentley, Essex, 1613-1615, and rector of Peldon, Essex, 1615-1640, where he died. He married Alice and had two children, Robert and Reuben, both baptised in 1630 at Great Burstead in Essex.

The most colourful aspect of Robert are his daughters and their marriages. Ten of his children were girls, and all but two of them are known to have married – seven of them at Copford, presumably by their father. Two were over thirty when they married, two were in their middle twenties and three were under 20. As three of them married Anglican clergy, and two of Robert's sons were clergy, there were six clergy in the family, including Robert. The clerical husbands of his daughters all held livings in Essex, and were all ejected from their livings, either in 1647 or 1662. Two of them were Parliamentary sympathisers and the other was a royalist.[383]

In his will Robert left small sums to the poor in Copford and Birch plus about £400 in legacies to family members. The advowson of Hockley Magna was left to his son Robert. Richard was left 'his house' that has not been identified, who could also buy unspecified lands £40 cheaper than others. The later records of Robert's family suggest some of it remained in the Copford area for about fifty years after his death, perhaps as small landholders. The eldest son John was certainly there and is referred to in several local documents as 'gent'. In 1649 he and his wife made a conveyance of various copyhold properties worth £3500 belonging to Copford Manor, to his brother in law Israel Edwards vicar of East Mersea and husband of his sister Elizabeth (b. 1594).[384] In 1666 the same Elizabeth, by this time a widow, made an annuity of £35 to Martha Ram daughter of John Ram, gent, deceased, 'for natural love and affection'.[385] The References to the family in Copford die out in the last quarter of the seventeenth century. Edmund Ram (1575-1628), a younger brother of Robert, the rector of Copford, had associations with the place, although probably living in Colchester. He left a house there called Fordes in trust to pay to 'Margaret my wife the rents and profits thereof and after her death to Martha my daughter'. By a codicil 47 acres bought in Copford was left to his wife. He additionally left tenements, legacies, and goods to people including 'my nephew Robert's son of my brother Robert D D' in his will of 1620.[386]

Difficulties in the seventeenth century

Robert Ram's family lost its identity in the male line just like that of his uncle Francis Ram, who lived in Hornchurch, and the longer history of the Ram family in Colchester was carried on through another son of William called Marcellus (b. 1571), who was baptised in St Nicholas' parish. Chart C6 shows the descendants of Marcellus for the next four generations. He married a Colchester woman, Ann Mannock and had at least three children in the last years of the sixteenth and the early years of the seventeenth centuries, all born in Colchester. The only other thing known about him is that he was set upon in Colchester in 1617 because of the legal case that arose from the attack.[387] The history of the family in the Colchester area is quite obscure during most of the seventeenth century, and making sense of it is not helped by there being a large number of sons called John. To help keep track of them those in successive generations are marked sequentially. The eldest child of Marcellus was John Ram 2C (1598-bef. 1646) who was baptised at St Botolph's, a parish that had earlier connections with the family. In 1653 the marriage certificate of John Ram 3C (1626-1666) and Mary Place records not only their marriage at St Mary the Virgin at the Walls but also says his parents were John and Marie Ram, and that his father (John Ram 2C) was a weaver. John and Marie had a son Edward Ram (b. 1633) who was born in London and admitted to Colchester Grammar School in 1646 as an orphan. The admission record says he is the only son of John Ram 2C, but family records show this to be incorrect.[388]

At some point in his life Edward's elder brother, John Ram 3C, went to live at Stoke by Nayland where he died in 1666. This village is about five miles to the north of Colchester in the scenic valley of the River Stour, which

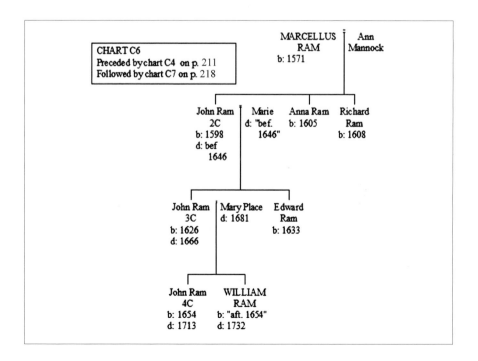

marks the boundary between Essex and Suffolk. He may, or may not, have been aware that Christopher Ram, a brother of his great great grandfather William Ram (d. 1602) was vicar of Bures and Boxted, two nearby villages, in the third quarter of the sixteenth century. Several children were born to John 3C at Stoke by Nayland, including John Ram 4C (1654- 1713). Another son, William Ram (aft. 1654-1732), definitely died in this village and was probably born there. As the baptismal and burial registers of both Colchester and Stoke by Nayland have serious gaps in them at this time, and there is a lack of wills among the key people, the line of descent described above cannot be proved. However, *The Ram Family*, which was very thoroughly researched, says the circumstantial evidence for the accuracy of the line described here is very high.[389] What John Ram 3C did for a living is unclear, but he may have combined being a merchant in Colchester with farming. It is through his children that the Ram family begins to reappear from its seventeenth century obscurity.

Renewed prosperity

John Ram 4C was described as a merchant in 1695, when '... at the request of the aldermen and some of the members of this corporation Mr John Ram was admitted and sworn a free burgess upon payment of £15.[390] What sort of merchant he was is not known. The connection with the Corporation lasted some years for he is listed as a member in 1693 and served until 1702. Although born in Stoke by Nayland he died in Colchester and was buried in St Runwald's parish. None of his children seem to have survived into adult life. In 1698 he married a second time when he was forty four, at Berechurch a very small village about five miles to the South East of Colchester, when he was noted to be a widower of St Nicholas' Church. Berechurch was to remain a favourite location of the family until it left Colchester at the beginning of the nineteenth century. His new wife was Elizabeth Goddard, herself a widow of a merchant called John Goddard. The Goddards were quite wealthy, owning two manors near Berechurch – Fingringhoe and Peate, both about five miles further out from Colchester. They were left to John Goddard, gent. by an uncle, George Frere or Freer, who was a London merchant. The manors then passed to John Goddard's son, another John, who sold Fingringhoe in 1707 to Marmarduke Rawdon – a Colchester lawyer.[391] In 1808 the Fingringhoe estate contained 769 acres – 412 being uplands and 356 salt marshes. There were three farms – Hall, Hay and Wick plus one or two other small parcels of land – so it was a sizeable property. The Goddards kept Peete manor, and the grandson of the first John Goddard, a further John, married Elizabeth daughter of Francis Gardiner, Mayor of Norwich, in 1685. A son that he had by her died an infant, and he devised the estate to be sold after his wife's death for payment of his debts, giving the remainder to Thomas Bayles of Colchester. The latter sold it in 1728 to Jacob Browne.

John Ram 4C, the Goddards and the Bayles families were linked in property transactions, and probably had social connections. In 1704 John Ram, Elizabeth his wife and Thomas Bayles, grocer, were associated in a mortgage connected with Fingringhoe Manor.[392] In 1703 John Ram, merchant, was one of three parties to a mortgage on a property to be held in trust for Thomas Bayles, grocer.[393] The Bayles family came to Colchester from Suffolk and their genealogy is included in *The Visitation of Essex*.[394] They became quite prominent in Colchester, and a grandson of the Thomas Bayles associated in the mortgage with John Ram, another Thomas, (d.1775), was Mayor of Colchester in 1762 and 1766. Presumably these later members of the Bayles family were know to the Rams living in Colchester at the time.

William, the younger son of John Ram 3C seems to have remained in Stoke by Nayland all his life. In 1697, probably in his forties, he bought a farm there for £222 and in the title deed he is described as a yeoman. He had a large family which is shown in chart C7 in outline. How much land William farmed at or near Stoke by Nayland is unclear. He called his purchase Stoke Farm but it has not been identified by that name and does not appear on any local maps that have been seen. All the available information suggests this farm had several names during the period the Ram family had an interest in it. The earliest was perhaps Stoke Farm, or this may just have been a generalised way of referring to it. The others were Porters Farm and Rams Farm. The latter name is on the current sheet of the 2½ inches to the mile Ordnance Survey map, and the farm is about one mile to the east of Stoke by Nayland.[395] A farm in this village figures in several family marriage and inheritance settlements during the eighteenth and nineteenth centuries which was eventually sold in 1871, back to the local manor for £1500.[396] There is a map with the sale papers that shows clearly it is the same farm as the one called Rams Farm on the Ordnance Survey map. In 1871 the farm had 43 acres and was probably always about this size. It was a mixture of freehold and copyhold land. The farm house is still there but may have been rebuilt or refaced as it looks to be of nineteenth century style and the site is on a south facing hillside with a stream running along below it. When the family first occupied Ram's or Stoke Farm it was probably worked directly by the family and in time it was added to, in 1739 by Francis Ram (abt. 1694-1750), a son of William, who leased 114 acres at Thorington Street within half a mile of the original farm. This land was rented for 23 years for £180 a year which increased the family interest to about 150 acres[397] Even though Rams Farm stayed in the family after Francis died no more Rams lived in Stoke by Nayland and the farm then became a source of rental income.

Four documents have been used to draw up a reasonable, if not perfect, picture of William's family in the mid eighteenth century. They are the deeds relating to Stoke or Rams Farm,[398] another deed relating to the Tendering Hall Estate

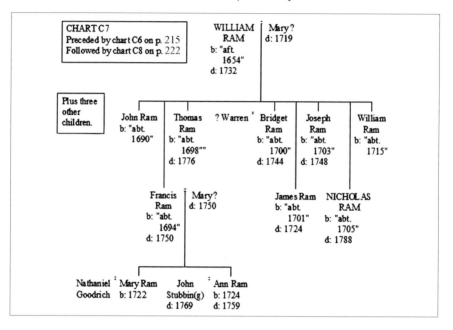

at Stoke by Nayland,[399] and two wills. From them a picture emerges of how a family of middling status managed its affairs, both internally and in alliance with other families. The most helpful of the wills is that of Bridget Warren (abt. 1700-1747) of Great Bromley, a daughter of William Ram.[400] Great Bromley is to the East of Colchester and about ten miles from Stoke by Nayland. Her bequests provide one of the few examples there are in the family history of women leaving property in their own right, albeit as a widow. Bridget appears to have married quite well and to have had no children of her own who survived. She left a house and some unspecified land to others, but the remainder of the land, called 'Raylins', went to '...John Ram 5C son of Nicholas of Monkwick, farmer (abt. 1705-1788), and William Pearson, yeoman, son of John Pearson of Berechurch, farmer', as tenants in common. How all the Pearsons were related is not clear. John 4 was Bridget's grandson and was only five when she died, so his holding was effectively in the custody of Nicholas who secured a greater interest in 1757 when John Pearson surrendered his share to him. The inclusion of the Pearson family probably arose through Nicholas' connection with that family after he moved to Monkwick Farm at Berechurch, to be reinforced by his second marriage to Elizabeth Pearson (1718-1773) in 1748. In a separate bequest Bridget Warren left land called 'Spencers' in Great Bromley to Nicholas. In all about 35 acres was involved, and when Nicholas made his will in 1779 he spoke as though he held both Raylins and Spicers.

Bridget also made some cash bequests to her surviving brothers which reveal what most of them were doing and where they lived in 1744. She left £40 to

Francis Ram of Stoke, farmer; £40 to William Ram (b. abt. 1688) of Fingringhoe, farmer; and £10 to Joseph Ram (b. abt. 1703) of Fingringhoe, single man. The birth dates of none of these men are known for definite but circumstantial evidence suggests that Francis was the eldest, since he farmed in Stoke by Nayland, presumably on the main holding. Other references in Bridget's will make it clear that Nicholas had also moved away from Stoke by Nayland and was farming about three miles from William at Monkwick. Both places are to the South East of Colchester. Thus by the mid eighteenth century the Ram family had spread around Colchester as farmers and, in a small way, rentiers. The occupancy of the Fingringhoe farm may have come through the connection John 4C had with the Goddard estate early in the eighteenth century. These moves also show how land was acquired by marriage and through friendships – especially with the Pearson family. The will of Francis who was given £40 by Bridget reveals he had made a marriage settlement of £1000 in the form of a bond to his wife Mary (d.1750), presumably to support her in old age, but she died shortly before him, and the will was changed so that the £1000 was split equally between their two daughters, Mary (b. 1722), then married to Nathaniel Goodrich, and Ann (1724-1759) married to John Stubb(in)s. Ann also got £300 whilst her husband was left the 'leases of my farms, etc, etc', which presumably included Stoke or Rams Farm and the 114 acres rented in Thorington Street.[401]

These deeds and wills show that the sons of William Ram were linked in a mutually supportive network, that involved families connected with them by marriage. It was cemented by three elements; by shares in family property; by elder brothers taking responsibility for younger ones, including formal guardianship arrangements; and by the farmers among them working in co-operative ways. Francis, probably William's eldest son, farmed in Stoke by Nayland, William, another older son, was farming in 1732 at Wormingford and by 1744 at Fingringhoe where he had help from Joseph (abt 1703-1748). Joseph was a younger brother who may have been handicapped in some way because he never participated in the property sharing arrangements enjoyed by the other brothers. Later on he possibly lived with Nicholas for he died at Berechurch. Nicholas, probably the youngest of the children, was helping out at Stoke by Nayland in 1732, but around 1735 moved to Monkwick Farm at Berechurch. Another elder brother, John, went to live in Eye, Suffolk and Thomas (d. 1776) did not go into farming, but became a surgeon after attending Colchester Grammar School.[402] Francis had no sons and his daughters both married, one of them to John Stubb(in)s, who took over most of Francis' holdings in Stoke by Nayland on his death. All the brothers, bar Joseph, were given shares in Stoke or Rams Farm as children or young men, and as time went by some brothers surrendered their shares to others. It is possible there was a business arrangement between John Stubb(in)s, William, Nicholas and another brother Thomas about the farming business at Stoke by Nayland as a whole. Thomas and William were admitted to Stoke or Rams Farm in 1699, and Nicholas in 1725 after the death of another brother James (abt. 1701-1724). In the same year Francis was given guardianship of Nicholas. In 1732 William ceded his share to Nicholas. After 1732 Nicholas had a significant share in the farm and clearly kept in touch with the daughters of Francis and the Stubb(in)s family because two of the witnesses to his will in 1782 were Mary Goodrick and John Stubbin.

The complicated way that interests in Stoke or Rams Farm were shared among members of the family is, in some ways, rather puzzling, for its material significance was not great. It contained no more than 45 acres that were only partly freehold and the annual income when sub-let by Nicholas was not more than £40. If available to one person £40 a year was a moderate sum in the mid eighteenth century, especially if it was a second income, but sub divided it was not worth a great deal. What lay behind these elaborate arrangements? Was there a desire to keep the family, and family by marriage, together for mutual advantage, support, and safety? Did the ownership of this farm seem more important to them than it really was? Was their careful sharing of proportional interests in the farm a reflection of the importance they attached to property rights? Was it a necessary way of obtaining wider co-operation among the family? The inheritance patterns described reflect strongly those used by farming family members in Great Waltham, and are typical of practice among the middling sort.

Nicholas Ram (Abt 1705-1788) and his family
It was through Nicholas, one of the younger sons of William, that the upswing in family fortunes gathered pace. Although, like most of his male siblings he was rooted in farming there was a certain difference between him and the others. Whilst they remained relatively small scale yeomen he acquired more land and sub-let some of it, which produced income over and above what he earned himself. He also enjoyed a long life and was married three times. He had many children and built up around him a new network of relationships that was only partly based on farming.

It is noticeable throughout the family story that increasing family fortunes are often associated with a father who lives a long time and has a large family. Such upswings tend to happen at times of general prosperity, whilst downswings are more associated with difficult periods. But more personal elements, like ability, luck, and good health must also have played a part because not all the nuclear units within the Ram family enjoyed prosperity during the upswings, and not all of them succumbed during the downswings. It is most likely that features particular to the family were stimulated in different ways by background economic and social trends. Nicholas' longevity, his prosperity, and his three marriages certainly helped to widen the family network and social circle in Colchester.

There were seven children in Nicholas' family, born of two wives, and the main details are given in chart C8. His first wife was Abigail Sayer (d. 1747) and they were married in 1735. She was the brother of John Sayer (d. 1732), of a well known Colchester family, who traded in the town as a merchant. His will makes clear he owned property there including a quay and a coal yard.[403] The will also shows that he was connected by marriage with two other substantial Colchester families – the Osbornes and the Solleys. He left to Abigail a freehold property with tenements and ten acres known as Burnthouse Farm in St Giles Parish, in the occupation of Edward Osborne. Abigail and Nicholas had three children before she died and Nicholas had four more who grew to adulthood by his second wife Elizabeth Pearson. The long term inter-connectedness of the Ram and Pearson families has already been mentioned. The Pearsons were a farming family from Layer de la Haye, a village very near Monkwick farm where Nicholas lived.[404] Nicholas' third wife was Mary Sollery (1723-1788) whom he married in 1778, but nothing is known about her. Nicholas came to farm in Berechurch at Monkwick Farm around 1735 and died there in 1788. The original Ordnance Survey map for the Colchester area dates from around 1800 and both Monkwick Farm and Reed Hall, the home of the Ward family which owned Monkwick Farm are shown on it.[405] The Ward estate was of about 620 acres, mostly let on fairly long term leases. Nearly all of the estate has now been swallowed up by the development of Colchester, but It was then about three miles from the town centre. The Ward family were wealthy merchants who lived partly on their Colchester estate and partly in London. A letter found in the Essex record Office from Nicholas, dated 11 September 1735, and addressed to John Ward at Great Kirby Street, Hatton Garden, London, seems to relate to the negotiation of an agreement between them and suggests the association of Nicolas with the Wards began about that time.

> Sir,
> I put a letter into the Office for Mr Bowle with yours accordingly as you desired me and when you have Got the Report it would be the Best way to come to the Wick and conclude upon everything that you would make a reserve of, that there might be no difference between us and then I should the better know what to do for I should be vary sorre to live under a landlord where there was anything of that sort, but I hope everything will be put upon a fair footing and if things be not concluded upon between this and Michaelmas Please to send word about bid bank lands upon the account of Paying the Poore Rates.
> From your Humble Servant to Command,
> Nich Ram.[406]

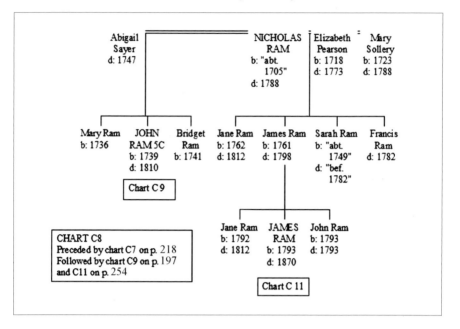

The relationship between Nicholas and the Ward family lasted for over fifty years and achieved a certain degree of intimacy, illustrated in two letters exchanged at Christmas 1773.[407] The first is from Nicholas, dated 16 December 1773 and addressed to Ralph Ward at Wimpole Street, London.

> Sir,
> I hope you received a hare and brace of pheasants which I sent you last week and would be glad to know what day you would be pleased to have your Turkey and Oysters. .... Shall be glad to see you downe when agreable. Our complyments Attend on you and Mrs Ward and all friends.
> Your Humble Servant,
> Nich Ram'.

In reply Ralph Ward wrote,

> Mr Ram
> Sir,
> The pheasants and hare came in secure and very safe and much obliged to you for them. ....My wife joins with me in wishing you and family the compts of the approaching season. I am.
> R W.

There is another letter around the same time which suggests some of the children of the two families met socially. It is dated December 16 1774 and is from Maria Ward, at Portman Street London, to her mother, in copybook writing. It mentions the Ram family.

> Dear Mama
> This is to let you know that the Holydays begin next Thursday. I hope to have the pleasure of seeing you on that day. Pray give my Duty to Papa, compl: to Miss Ram, and love to my sister. I am.
> Dear Mama,
> Your dutiful daughter,
> Maria ward.[408]

Someone has written 'aged 12' on the letter which shows Maria was the same age as Jane Ram (1762-1812), one of Nicholas' daughters.

There are several splendid deeds in the Essex Record Office at Colchester detailing the leases between Nicholas, his sons, and the Ward family.[409] They effectively tell the story of the Ram family and Monkwick for over sixty years. The first one makes it clear Nicholas was leasing Monkwick Farm by 1735. The lease was renewed in September 1753 for 21 years, which included an extra 60 acres, subject to payment of annual rent of £112 plus rates and taxes. It was then extended further to 1782, with an increased yearly rental of £130. On the related deed there is written a note that Monkwick Farm had for many years '... been in the occupation of Nicholas Ram, his under-tenants or assigns', so Nicholas did not farm all the land himself and sub let at least some of it.

A number of conditions applied to Nicholas' leases from the Ward family. Rent had to be paid within 40 days of being due. Nicholas could only sub-let with permission from Ralph Ward. Also he had to '... plough, sow, and till dung and manure the lands...in a husbandlike manner'. In the last year of the lease these items and straw are to be left available. Nicholas was also required to carry materials for the maintenance and repair of buildings, and he had to keep gates, styles, and fences in repair, although he was able to use wood from the estate to do this. Nicholas had use of the barns on the farm.

In 1780 the Monkwick leases were taken over by Nicholas' elder son John 5C, presumably as he aged and retired. This is the John who became bankrupt and is discussed in detail at the beginning of the chapter. The original lease to John from Ralph Ward ran from 1780 to 1795, and included Monkwick Farm of 110 acres together with additional lands of 65 acres known as Lordswood, plus about another 57 acres formerly in the hands of Daniel Cock and latterly in the occupation of Nicholas Ram. In the lease John Ram is stated to be of Monkwick and a farmer and the rent charged was £150. He probably held further land not owned by the Ward family because he paid land tax on Sheldricks Farm in 1780, which has not been identified.[410] He, like his father, had under-tenants, and it is highly unlikely that John was involved directly in farming. In the Colchester trade directory of 1793 he is described as a merchant[411] and this is confirmed from other records about him. He also lived in Colchester, not at Berechurch, but Nicholas presumably lived at the Monkwick farmhouse until his death.

In 1792 the Monkwick leases were transferred to James Ram (1761-1798), John's younger step brother, for 11 years.[412] He is listed in the 1793 Colchester Directory as a farmer.[413] It is possible a decision was made in the early 1790s for John to concentrate on his business activities and to pass the family's farming interests to James who was around thirty at that time. He was certainly left most of the farms owned by the family under his father's will: the property at Great Bromley of about 35 acres which had a rental value of about £35, the farm at Stoke by Nayland that had a rental value of £30, the Key in Colchester of 37 acres with a rental value of £20 and the Tan Office of six acres in Colchester with a rental of £15, including the house. These were a mixture of freehold and copyhold properties and when he took over the leases on Ward family lands in Monkwick in 1792 James held in all just over 300 acres. He almost certainly rented out the four smaller farms which produced an annual income of around £100 and probably farmed the other land himself. He married Jane Meades (d. 1810) of London around 1790 and had three children of whom the only survivor was a son James (1793-1870).

Various documents enable a good picture of Monkwick Farm to be put together. An 1806 plan of the Ward estate shows it to be bisected by a minor road leading from Colchester to Berechurch. On the larger western side is Reed Hall, where the Wards lived and on the other is the Monkwick farmhouse and farm.[414] On the plan Monkwick farm totals roughly the 230-240 acres rented by the Rams. The Monkwick farmhouse was away from the main road and lay across a small stream along which was pasture land and some ponds. In a small book on the history of Berechurch Leonard Grant wrote a paragraph about the history of the farm.

> The farm of Monkwick (or Monkwyck) derives its name from St John's Abbey, and means 'Monk Farm'. It was given to the Abbey of St John, Colchester as an appendage to the Manor of W Donyland by Eudo, and the farm helped to supply the needs of that institution until the suppression, when the lands reverted to the crown. The Duke of Northumberland took the W Donyland manor in 1543 with all its lands. He gave the manor and Monkwick to Sir Francis Jobson. In 1592 the manor was purchased by Robert Barker who died in 1618, but the lands were held by this family until

1718. The estate then came to Thomas Perry, who sold it to Knox Ward, esq. At the present day (the late 19C) the owners are the Ward-Tomlinson Trust.[415]

Comments are also made about the farm in the Victoria County History.

The manor house at Monkwick originated as a farmhouse, possibly moated, built by St John's Abbey before 1523. Sir Francis Jobson apparently rebuilt the house and enclosed a park there. The interior of the house was refitted in the mid seventeenth century: panelling and an overmantel of that date survived in 1989 in Colchester Museum. By 1662 the house had eleven hearths. By 1735 it was dilapidated, and the eastern part was demolished to provide material to repair the rest. (See Grant History of Berechurch). The two storied, timber-framed and plastered house, with a projecting upper storey and two gables on the south side was occupied as a farm house from that time until its demolition in 1963. Medieval fish ponds south of the house, fed by Birch Brook, survived until the brook was piped in the twentieth century. A dovecote recorded in 1814 may have been on the site of that built c. 1543.[416]

Ralph Ward kept rooms in the house for a servant – a bed chamber accessed by a pair of stairs and a parlour. He had the use of all but one of the fishponds and free pasture for two horses, freedom for sport, access, and timber, and in addition Nicholas had to keep available for him stabling for five horses.

From what is known about Nicholas it is possible to put together an overview of his economic interests. He was mainly a farmer, but he almost certainly sub let some or all of his smaller holdings. In his will he is styled a gentleman and in the Essex County Poll Book for 1768 he is listed as a freeholder in the Colchester constituency. His total landholding amounted to around 300 acres. Notes he wrote at the time his will was drawn up show he had an income of about £100 from the sub-let farms, which he presumably lived on in his old age. Nicholas died a wealthy man, as his will of 1782 shows. How he disposed of his farms and his land holdings has already been recounted but there were also more personal bequests. He left the house where he lived to his wife and then to John Ram 4 after her death. This was presumably Monkwick farmhouse, which of course he only rented as part of the Monkwick Farm. He also directed that James should allow his widow £20 a year from the income of the Great Bromley farm unless she married again. He gave £1600 to his daughter Jane (1762-1812) and £1200 to his younger son James. The residue of the estate went to John 4 which included 'monies, bills, bonds, notes and other securities', and may have come to a further significant sum. John 4 was made sole executor.

How rich were Colchester Rams at this period? In a Ph D thesis of 1990 Shani D'Cruze made an estimate of personal wealth in Colchester between 1730-1830 broken down into three periods and based on all wills proved for Colchester individuals, so they include all social levels. She took a sample of 35 out of 221 for the first period from 1735-1750, there were 201 wills in the second period from 1780-1799, and the third period from 1800-1829 included 204 wills. Three types of bequest were identified: real estate, monies and securities, and household goods. Table 15 is a summary of Figure 1:14 in the thesis.[417] These findings show John 5C and his father Nicholas were among the top 5 per cent, and it will be seen that this is true of John 5C's brother James. Yet they were probably not among the very richest. When Edward Morley, who belonged to a family of Hythe merchants spanning at least two generations, died in 1786, he left over £20000 in money and business property.[418] John Ram's brother in law, John Bawtree 2, was a partner in the Colchester and Essex Bank and in wealth easily eclipsed all of the Rams.[419] Over the next few pages there will be many references to the Bawtree family.

Table 15. Personal wealth in Colchester 1730-1830

	1735-1750.	1780-1799.	1800-1829.
Real estate:			
I house/ land.	22.9% of wills	26.4%	23.1%
2-5 houses/ land.	21.4% of wills	21.4%	17.2%
5+ houses/ land.	14.3% of wills	5%	4.9%
Monies/securities:			
up to £100.	45.7%	16.9%	13.2%
£101-500.	25.7%	11.9%	11.8%
£501-1000.	2.9%	6.5%	9.3%
£1000+.	0.0%	4.5%	3.9%

Family networks in the late eighteenth and early nineteenth centuries

Social historians have been aware of interest networks which involve marriages between several families for some time. Perhaps it first came to notice through the extensive Quaker intermarriages that occurred in the eighteenth and nineteenth centuries. My own Ph D research on Birmingham showed the extent of this.[420] It might be thought Quakers were exceptional, because of their requirement that marriage had to be within the Quaker fold, but similar networks existed among middle class Presbyterian and Unitarian families in Birmingham.[421] More recently several books have shown such networks were not confined to religious groups. Leonora Davidoff and Catherine Hall have especially drawn attention to these features among middle class eighteenth and nineteenth century families, which they have linked with efforts to create family security in a profoundly insecure world.[422] Table 16 presents what happened to the Ram family between 1750 and 1825 in a tabular way whilst Appendix 3 does the same in the form of a genealogical chart. A complex pattern evolved which included six inter-marriages among four families over three generations. Three of the marriages were between cousins, which must have stimulated and reinforced the intimacy of the circle. Sarah (b. 1749), a daughter of Elizabeth and Nicholas married her cousin John Pearson (b.1742). A second marriage of cousins linked the Rams and the Bawtrees when Jane Ram, another daughter of Nicholas, married John Bawtree 2 (1762-1824). In the last generation James Ram and Elizabeth Adye were married.

Four significant figures emerged in the circle created. One was Nicholas' eldest son by his first wife, John Ram 5C a wealthy Colchester merchant and then bankrupt, whose story has already been told, another was his son in law John Bawtree 2, who was a banker and reformer in Colchester. The third was his grandson James Ram who achieved a national reputation as a writer on the law – he appears in the Dictionary of National Biography – and the fourth was Major Ralph Adye (d. 1804), who is also mentioned in the Dictionary of National Biography in an article about his father Stephen Adye. Ralph Adye wrote a famous artillery book *The Pocket Gunner,* that was a standard army gunnery manual of the British Army for much of the nineteenth century.[423]

Table 16. Intermarriages between the Ram, Pearson, Bawtree and Adye families.

Generation	Marriage date	Name of man	Occupation	Name of woman	Occupational background
1	1748	Nicholas Ram	Farmer & rentier	Elizabeth Pearson	Farming
2	1759	John Bawtree 1	Brewer	Sarah Pearson	Farming
2	1770?	John Pearson	Farmer?	Sarah Ram	Farming
2	1788	John Bawtree 2	Banking & commerce	Jane Ram	Farming
2	1799	R W Adye	Military	Elizabeth Sarah Bawtree	Brewing
3	1826	James Ram	Lawyer	Elizabeth Jane Adye (only daughter of Elizabeth Sarah Bawtree)	Military & commerce

He married Elizabeth Sarah Bawtree (1771-1857), the younger sister of John Bawtree 2. Presumably Elizabeth Sarah and Ralph met in Colchester which has always been a base for the Royal Artillery. Ralph died quite young in 1804 when their daughter Elizabeth Jane (1801-abt. 1881) was two. Her mother never remarried and died in Colchester in 1857, so it is likely that she lived mainly in the Bawtree circle. She was buried in the parish church at Abberton, near Berechurch, where the Bawtree family lived.[424] She married Nicholas' grandson James.

How did these families come into association? Perhaps there was a creative thread that attracted people to each other. John Bawtree 2 was an innovative and energetic man, Ralph Adye was a writer of some ability about military matters, whilst James Ram the younger was one of the more original writers about the law in the first half of the nineteenth century. There must also have been a strong social focus to the relationships for so many marriages to occur. But more mundane reasons may have been of equal or basic importance. Apart from the Adye connection all the families were entrepreneurs in some way, with farming providing a common link. In an unpublished essay about the drinks trade in Colchester John Bensusan Butt makes the following relevant comments.

> In the eighteenth century the brewing industry ceased to be a domestic industry. Before the middle of the century (in Colchester) brewing seemed to be an extension of the activities of the Hythe merchants who would already have the necessary working capital as well as working premises and a knowledge of the trade in grain.[425]

The Rams and Pearsons were farmers, the Bawtrees were brewers, and John Ram 5C was a merchant who traded in grain. John Bensusan Butt also states in this essay that brewers at this time were beginning to develop chains of inns in which they could find outlets for their products, and as will be seen the Bawtrees were involved in this development. So it is quite possible the families were brought together by common interests in the growing brewing trade and related activities.

The network most likely began when Nicholas Ram went to farm at Monkwick in the 1730s where he met the Pearson family which farmed close by at Layer de la Haye. There was certainly a connection by the 1740s for Nicholas was an executor of the will of William Pearson (d. 1740), a yeoman farmer.[426] The Pearson family was important in the parish as John Pearson was Churchwarden in 1769 and William Pearson was so in the 1790s.[427] In 1747 Nicholas married Elizabeth Pearson, probably a niece of the William who died in 1740, and definitely the sister of Sarah Pearson (d. 1782) who married into the Bawtree family in 1759. It has already been seen how relationships between the Rams and the Pearsons were cemented in property grants connected with the will of Bridget Warren in 1747, an aunt of Nicholas.[428] The area around Berechurch was much favoured by the Ram family and their associates, and they seem to have had a special liking for Layer de la Haye, as many of them were married or buried there in the eighteenth century. The Pearson family may well have prompted or promoted this association. The Bawtree family acquired a farm at Abberton three miles away in the late eighteenth or early nineteenth century. However, the origin of the Ram family connection with the area is much older, for Robert Ram and his sons were clergy in the sixteenth and seventeenth centuries, in the nearby villages of Copford, Great Birch and Peldon. The husband of one of Robert's daughters, John Algar, started his career as Priest in Charge of Layer de la Haye. John Ram 4C was married for the second time at Berechurch, very close to Layer de la Haye, and had connections with the local area in the early eighteenth century.

The Network between the Rams and the Pearsons was extended to include the Bawtree family when Sarah Pearson, the sister of Nicholas' wife Elizabeth, married John Bawtree 1 in 1759. This John Bawtree was a brewer at Wivenhoe, who also ran several inns in the area. In his will of 1773 he left property to three sons. John Bawtree 2, the eldest and the future husband of Jane Ram, obtained land and premises in Brightlingsea together with an inn called the 'White Lion'. The middle son, Samuel was given granaries, warehouses, a wharf and a quay called 'woodyard' in Wivenhoe, whilst the youngest brother, William, got two inns, the 'Red Lion' in Wivenhoe and the 'Duke's Head' in Walton le Soken.[429]

The wider story of the Bawtree family is told here in some detail because it reveals the social world in which the Rams mixed. Although Jane, the daughter of Nicholas and first wife of John Bawtree 2, died in 1812 and he married again the following year, the other members of the immediate Ram family must still have been part of his circle. All John Bawtree 2's children were mothered by Jane and there were special reasons why the connection would have continued, for when Jane's brother James died very young in 1798 at the age of 37 John Bawtree 2 was appointed guardian if James' son, also called James, became an orphan. This in fact happened because the wife of Jane's brother died in 1810. So there was a period, from the age of seventeen when James' development would have been in the special care of his uncle by marriage. During his later teens James' life must have centred around the Bawtree family. This may have been how he was drawn into marriage with John Bawtree 2's cousin Elizabeth Jane Adye, whose mother was a Bawtree. Although she and James moved to London and then Ipswich, she returned to Colchester on James' death in 1870 and lived the rest of her life in Colchester.

Two of the three sons of the Wivenhoe brewer developed commercial interests in Colchester. John Bawtree 2 owned property, shown by the lease he made in 1813 of Badcocks Farm to messrs Whitmore and John Pearson, which included a number of properties in Colchester.[430] He was also involved with one of his brothers in commercial ventures in the brewing trade, but his main interest was banking. Early banking facilities in Colchester were provided by John Mills (d. 1822). In 1766 he set up as a tea merchant in the town in association with Richard and John Twining who were cousins by marriage. In addition to the tea business they negotiated customers' bills and accounts through a London bank connected with the Twining family. This banking facility was one of the earliest to be started in Essex. In 1787 he opened the Colchester and Essex Bank in partnership with them.[431] This partnership was dissolved in 1797, but John Mills continued the bank for in the property settlement he made in 1821 on his son he calls himself a banker.[432] When John Bawtree 2 became involved in the bank is not known, but it could have been around the time of the dissolution of the original partnership. When he died John Mills left most of his property, which was the bulk of his wealth, to his son John Fletcher Mills.[433] The bank survived in the hands of this son in partnership with John Bawtree 2 and then 3. In 1848 Mills, Bawtree, and Errington was one of two small private banks in Colchester. The nature of the Errington connection is not clear but it may have been a member of the family of George Errington (1756-1795), a barrister and landowner of Grays, Thurrock and Chadwell St Mary.[434] By 1891 the bank was called Mills, Bawtree, Dawnay and Co. It collapsed in that year and was taken over by Gurney's and Round, Green and Co. of Norwich, which was itself taken over by Barclays Bank in 1896.[435] All the directors of the bank must have been wealthy men. John Bawtree 2 in his will of 1822 left Badcocks Farm at Abberton to his son John Bawtree 3. In addition he left £10000 to his daughter and his stock in trade capital at the bank to her husband.[436] The Mills family who were partners in the bank over several generations was very wealthy. J F Mills, the son of John Mills, acquired the Lexden Park estate in Lexden village, just outside the western edge of Colchester, in about 1821. He enlarged this and it passed, after the death of his wife in 1840, to his son in Law G H Errington (d. 1883), who, also was a partner in the Bank and lived at Lexden Park. When he died his estate was valued at £110285. This was made up of property, £101213, and rental income, £8473. He also had £10000 invested at 4 per cent which brought in £601.[437] At the time this was a very large estate.

The younger brothers of John Bawtree 2 and their families were also active in the town. Samuel Bawtree, with George Savill bought Hull (or Distillery) Mill in 1811, demolished it, and built a distillery on the site as well as a rectifying house in Culver Street.[438] The distillery went out of business about 1841 when the buildings were sold.[439] William seems to have moved to the London area, but one of his sons, George, played an important part in the public life of Colchester. He was a conservative mayor of the town in 1838-39, as well as being Borough Treasurer and Secretary of the Stour Valley Railway Company.

He was also a director and for some years Secretary of the Fire Office founded by his uncle John Bawtree 2. His wife was a daughter of Dr Roger Nunn who was Mayor of Colchester in 1834-35, and 1842-43.

John Bawtree 2 was more than a banker for he made innovative contributions to the development of Colchester. The Essex Equitable Insurance Society was founded in 1802 at his instigation, and was among the earliest provincial fire insurance companies to be set up in competition with the old established London bodies. Its 24 directors, drawn equally from Colchester and the county, acquired a lease of the Corn Exchange in 1803, buying its first fire engine in 1812. In 1819 an office was built on the site of the Corn Exchange, and in 1820 the Society was formed into the Essex Life Insurance Society. John Bawtree 2 was additionally a founding father of the Essex County Hospital, that was the idea of Archdeacon Joseph Jepherson, vicar of Witham and Rector of Weeley. There were some false starts but eventually the availability of redundant army hospital buildings made the vision seem a real possibility.[440] The money required was raised by eight men – H N Jarrett, George Round, John Bawtree 2, R W Cox, J Mills Jun (d. 1840), who became treasurer until his death, H Cock, G Savill and Revd J Jefferson. There was no guarantee that the subscribers to this completely private venture would get their money back. A wing of the army hospital was purchased for £1181 and 12sh., a sum which was later paid back to the subscribers by means of a successful public subscription. A public meeting was called to launch this and the eight purchasers were elected as an executive committee. Three of them, George Round, John Bawtree 2 and Mr Savill were requested to find a fresh site for the re-erection of the hospital. John Bawtree 2 was also on a three man committee to agree the rules for running the hospital.

The Bawtree family first acquired a landed interest when John Bawtree 2 took a share in Badcocks Farm, of 183 acres, in Abberton near Berechurch. When he died he owned the farm outright.[441] This farm may have become known as Layer House at a later date. Exactly when the Bawtree connection with Abberton started is unclear but the burial stone of Philip Fenning (1779-1848) in the churchyard at Abberton shows it was sometime in the late eighteenth or early nineteenth century, as it says he was bailiff to the late and present John Bawtree for 36 years.[442] The family continued to live at Abberton for many years. John 2's son, John Bawtree 3, went to Cambridge University in 1810, three years before James Ram. Although he spent most of his life working in the family bank, he was ordained a deacon of the Church of England in 1818 and spent a time as curate in a Kent parish before joining the bank. In later life he became a J P. played a part in Corn Law reform, and became Deputy Lieutenant of Essex.

Through all these achievements the Bawtree family became very much part of Colchester's establishment in the later nineteenth century, about which the Victoria County History comments in the following way.

> [Borough Council] ... members often had vested interests which might seem to threaten their impartiality ... Most council members of both parties were merchants and traders, or professional men; a few were gentlemen of private means; many had family or business connections with other members or officials, and prominent men often served on other bodies. Of the 24 council members 7 in 1857 and 9 in 1865 were also improvement commissioners. Charles H Hawkins, (1818?-1898) a borough councillor 1844-89, mayor four times, poor law guardian, improvement commissioner, Chairman of the Essex and Stour Valley Railway, and leader of the Colchester Conservative Party illustrates the power of a local family network: he was the son of William, a council member, son in Law of John Bawtree, a prominent citizen, and younger brother an business partner of William Warwick Hawkins MP, who was himself the son-in-law of Francis Smythies the elder a former town clerk.[443]

Besides raising the issue of vested interests this comment gives a good picture of the world of the Bawtree family in the later nineteenth century.

Providing for widows

The kinds of provision made to support widows by Nicholas' parents and brothers, which was described earlier, continued in a more sophisticated form in the marriage settlements between John Bawtree II and Jane Ram in 1788, James Ram and Jane Meades in 1791, R W Adye and Elizabeth Sarah Bawtree in 1799, and James Ram and Elizabeth Jane Adye in 1826.

The first of these involved the £1600 cash inheritance of Jane Ram which she acquired in 1788 on the death of her father. She married John Bawtree 2 in the same year and under the terms of the marriage settlement Jane surrendered her inheritance to him. In return he settled copyhold and other property in Wivenhoe and Brightlingsea, presumably of equivalent value to the £1600 inheritance, on her brother James. On John Bawtree's death Jane was to benefit from this property for life, exactly how is not clear, but in fact he outlived her and her brother James died before either of them. This was a sort of life insurance policy which the woman could access if her husband died before her, but what is not clear from the documents is what would happen to the assets if, as happened, she and brother James died before her husband. Were they retained in a trust to support other Ram widows at a later time or just absorbed into John Bawtree 2's own estate?[444]

The other three settlements were also, in some way, based on property. In the case of Ralph Willett Adye and Elizabeth Bawtree the 1799 settlement took the form of an indenture between Ralph Willett Adye, Elizabeth Sarah Bawtree, John Willett Willett (of Dorset), John Bawtree 2 (of Colchester), and Samuel Bawtree (of Colchester). Part of some property possessed by Elizabeth Bawtree, but in the hands of her brother John Bawtree 2, which amounted in value to £1000, was formed into a trust to provide the marriage settlement. This trust and its capital was to be available for later heirs.[445] In the event the marriage did not last long for Ralph Adye died in 1804 and his wife spent a long widowhood within the Bawtree family circle. Only two of their children reached maturity and their son Stephen Bawtree died unmarried in 1832, so the sole beneficiary was the other child, Jane Elizabeth who married the younger James Ram. Their marriage settlement also involved using property as a means of providing for his widow in the event of his earlier death and is discussed more fully in chapter XVIII.[446] The marriage settlement of James Ram senior and Jane Meades was very like that between Jane Ram and John Bawtree 2, except that a specific covenant was made to provide for the widow. A tripartite indenture was agreed in which property of Jane Meades – houses in Silver Street London – were settled on her husband and he in return covenanted to surrender the proceeds of the Ram farm in Bromley to Jane for her lifetime.[447]

The administration of the various assets and trusts was quite complicated and sometimes related arrangements were entered into which did not follow the original agreement to the letter. For example in 1857 the only beneficiary of the 1799 indenture then living was Elizabeth Jane Adye, now Ram, and she was entitled to the trust income for life. John Bawtree 3, who was the executor of his mother's will, paid part of his debt to her in that year, but it was quite a long time before she received the money, for there is a note in the Essex Record Office by Elizabeth Jane Ram and dated May 16 1871 that she has received from John Bawtree and James Inglis – executors of her mother's will – £1000 part of her estate by transfer.[448] The money was in reality not paid until her husband died, so it may have been kept back to provide a pension. Monies could be rolled over and made available to new beneficiaries, and also added to. This happened in the case of Elizabeth Jane, for on her husband's death the trust was augmented by including all her estate of just over £2200, and this new trust was to benefit a surviving unmarried daughter, Jane Elizabeth Ram. These examples of providing for widows have to be set in the context of the time. An underlying issue difficult to understand today, is that at this period under common law, all of a woman's cash, unlike land, became her husband's property at marriage.[449] If a trust of some kind was not established the whole of a woman's assets were open to be taken to pay a husband's debts. The arrangements described above formed a way of protecting women's money and property and were increasingly used by the upper middle classes. The use of trusts indicates that there were sufficient resources to provide adequately for women and children. At the same time however the dependence of women was emphasised, since husbands were effectively given charge of women's material resources. In the first two of the four instances referred to here Jane Ram and Elizabeth Sarah Bawtree become very dependent on their husbands, but there is greater mutuality in the second two. The nature of the settlement seems to be affected by the type of assets brought to the situation and possibly also by the desires and values of the parties involved. There also appears to have been a trend over time to making more specific provision for widows.

The end of the connection with Colchester

The fortunes and interests of families can change very quickly. After almost disappearing in the seventeenth century to be followed a great expansion in the eighteenth century, the male line of the Ram family had disappeared from Colchester by the 1820s.

Something of what happened to the bankrupt John 5C's family is discussed in detail elsewhere.[450] They clearly lost out heavily as a result of the bankruptcy. John 6C the eldest son became a small farmer and had several children, including a number of girls who may have married and lived locally. One of his sons, Joseph (b. 1800) was a husbandman or shepherd in Layer de la Haye in 1819.[451] It is possible he and two brothers John 6C and Robert (b. 1796) were all living and working in London by 1827.[452] John certainly was. Nicholas, the other surviving son of John the bankrupt, had possession in 1809 of one of the properties included in the bankruptcy, Golden Noble Hill. This property was once a windmill and contained a house, flour shop and garden. Nicholas died childless in 1815 leaving all his unspecified property to his wife, Mary.[453] Whether he still had possession of Golden Noble Hill at the time is not known.

By the early nineteenth century the male line in Nicholas Ram's family by his second marriage to Elizabeth Pearson had also died out in Colchester. There were two sons of the marriage, and the younger of them, Francis (d. 1782) only had one child, a daughter called Joan. He left all his unspecified property to his wife Elizabeth. Francis probably married Elizabeth in 1781 because there was a settlement of that year in which the Stoke or Rams Farm title was conveyed to Elizabeth for life. She married again and kept the farm until she died, after which it returned to Nicholas' grandson James the younger. Francis left some property which is apparent from Besusan Butt's *Biographical Dictionary*. This refers to the sale of the substantial family house in Bear Lane, which was described in some detail in a sale advertisement in the *Ipswich Journal* during 1782. The advertisement was inserted by Sarah Pearson of Layer de la Haye, either the sister or a niece of Francis. In 1783 Francis' stock was advertised for sale, including 130 gallons of Rum, so he was probably building up a business as a wine merchant, possibly with help from his Bawtree relations.[454]

The elder of the two sons, the older James, had children but the only boy to survive, was younger James, who trained as a lawyer, moving first to London and then Ipswich. On James' death his widow moved back to Colchester, presumably to be near her Bawtree relations, and In 1881 was living in West Lodge Road, off Lexden Road, which was one of the smartest areas of Colchester. On census night two unmarried daughters, Jane (1832-1905) and Clara (1834-1910) were at the same address, who almost certainly lived with her. One of her young grandsons, a child of Stephen, was visiting. This little group made up the only people bearing the Ram name known to have lived in Colchester into the later nineteenth century.

SECTION 4
LIFE WITHOUT LAND, 1800-1900

XVI
Family structure in the nineteenth century

Two of the original branches, B and C, survived into the nineteenth century although they were very different compared with what they had been like two hundred years earlier. The break from farming lay at the root of the change and affected all the family, but in different ways. Socially and occupationally there was greater diversity, in which one branch lost its middling status. The story of each of them is told separately. Although they appear to have mostly lived their own lives, some happenings occurred which show that the branches knew of each other and that occasionally there was interaction between them, at a level not very much different to that which occurred in earlier times. Although all of the family lived in London and its environs for a time in the nineteenth century there was a tendency among the better off members to migrate back to earlier geographical roots.

Branch B continued in farming until the second half of the nineteenth century but then nearly everyone who belonged to it drifted to London, mostly to take unskilled jobs, one of the first to go being my great grandfather, Charles Harry Ram. As large tenant farmers they had been quite wealthy, but they did not own their land and when they gave up farming they were effectively forced to start all over again. How poor they were is unclear but they were certainly at the lower end of the social ladder. One cannot but wonder what they made of this downturn in fortunes.

Branch C continued the part of the family established by William Ram in Colchester in the mid sixteenth century. In the 1780s it became large, quite rich and part of the topmost ranks of Colchester society, yet by the 1830s only a few scattered individuals remained. There were no external economic events to explain what happened to family members at Colchester, as in the case of the Great Waltham farmers, and the two obvious reasons for their decline stem from internal family happenings. The first was John Ram 5C's bankruptcy in 1796 which almost certainly had a devastating impact on the prosperity of his immediate family, and the second misfortune was that a lot of the male adults died young, or without children, towards the end of the eighteenth century.

The scale to what happened was quite similar to the sufferings of Francis Ram's family in Havering during the seventeenth century.

The remnant of the Colchester Rams continued as two relatively distinct families in London. One was made up of the descendants of John Ram the bankrupt. His grandson, John 7C, was in London in the 1820s, living there for the rest of his life. Several of his uncles may also have migrated to London. The social status of this branch was lower middle class. The other one was formed by James Ram the son of the bankrupt's half brother, also called James. As a young man he became an orphan but through his abilities effectively salvaged the middling identity of the family. The pattern of his life was a throw back to his direct ancestors in the sixteenth and early seventeenth centuries for he went to Cambridge University and became a lawyer. He was admitted to the Inner Temple and practised in the area of conveyancing, originally in London but in Ipswich during his later years. He also wrote a number of books about the law, one of which in particular, *The Science of Legal Judgement*, was of some legal importance.

James Ram established a new middle class dynasty although some of his children were more successful than others. His eldest son, James, who was not one of the higher achievers among them, became a private tutor who crammed candidates for entry to Sandhurst, and other military academies. His second son Stephen was a London solicitor and almost certainly became the most materially successful. A younger son, Willett, became a solicitor in Halesworth, Suffolk. This is a small market town about twenty five miles north of Ipswich. Two younger sons, Edward and Ralph became Anglican clergymen. Edward was a colourful figure who spent all his professional life as vicar of the parish of St John Timberhill in Norwich, whilst also holding the post of chaplain to the Norfolk County Asylum. Ralph became headmaster of Holbeach Grammar School in Lincolnshire, and later held country benefices in Cambridgeshire. Many of James Ram's grandchildren were professional people of some kind – solicitors, teachers, clergymen, and architects.

Each of the three chapters which follow, like all the others on the family, starts with a focus that provides special insight into the family group concerned. In the case of Charles Harry Ram and his family it is the army book of the author's grandfather, in the case of James Ram's family it is a photograph of Stephen Ram – the first family picture to have come to hand – and in the case of the descendants of John Ram of Colchester it is the baptismal records of James' and John's children at St Luke's Church in Chelsea during the 1820s and 30s.

XVII

The Less Well Off

William Ram's army book

There is a small book with a hard red cover in my possession that contains the basic record of the time my grandfather, William Richard Ram (1877-1940), regimental number 4094, spent in the British army from 1893 to 1902. He served in the First Battalion of the Kings Royal Lancaster Infantry Regiment which was raised in 1680 by Charles II to often serve abroad and taken part in major campaigns.[455] The Regiment's long history contains many vicissitudes. During the American War of Independence almost the whole regiment were captured at the Battle of Saratoga, whilst just after the Battle of Waterloo ships carrying it home were wrecked off Ireland. Many of the men, wives and children who had gone out to Belgium to celebrate the defeat of Napoleon were drowned. In the opening action of the Battle of the Somme 584 out of 700 men were killed. Today the Lancashires are a mechanised infantry battalion much used for overseas postings such as Cyprus and Bosnia.[456]

Figure 10 shows the page in his army book which contains his personal details.[457] It reveals he joined the army under age using a false name, Raine, saying he was nineteen when he was really fifteen. His signature at the bottom of the page is clear and fluent. His occupation is described as labourer. That he joined the army under age is known within the family and has always been linked with wanting to avoid an unhappy home background, although I have no knowledge of the exact circumstances. He was a short man, like all the known members of the family. In 1893 he lived with his parents and four brothers and sisters, Thomas, Charles, Susan, and Leo just off New North Road, Hoxton, in London. They seem to have moved around a lot in the locality for three different addresses appear in my grandfather's army book. One, Wimbourne Street, still exists, being a little north of the junction of Old Street and the City Road, but the others, Bookham Street and Reetham Street have disappeared, although they were nearby. In 1835 this area was on the edge of London but by 1900 swathes of new suburbs had grown up and it was becoming inner suburbia. The original houses in Wimbourne Street have been demolished to be replaced by blocks of flats. There are however still some early to mid nineteenth century terraced houses close by on New North Road where it crosses the Grand Union Canal, which are possibly typical of other houses that existed in the area in the 1890s.

The other information in the book is about the clothes issued to him and details of his savings account and postings. During the years 1895 to 1897 he made deposits in the regimental savings bank building up a balance of £20/4/6 by September 1895, but held just over £2 in the other years. He was overseas for nearly all his time in the army – in India for the whole of 1895, in Malta for 1896 and from January to September 1902, in Hong Kong for 1897, and in Singapore for 1899. The rest of the time he was at Aldershot, in 1900 and 1901. There are group photographs of him during this time, together with two rather gruesome pictures which must have been taken on his foreign travels. One of them shows a row of kneeling blindfolded men on a beach, presumably convicted criminals, and the other is of them all decapitated.[458] My grandfather was a private in the army, becoming servant to one of the majors from the middle of 1896 to the end of 1897. Then from February 1900 to the time, in mid 1902, when he left the army he was servant to the battalion commander, Lt. Colonel Rowlandson. Correspondence between them suggests they got on well.[459] More will be said later about contacts with army colleagues after he left. The fact that my

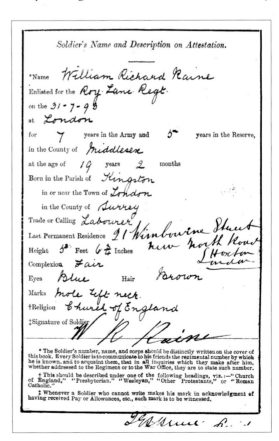

Figure 10. Personal details page from William Ram's Army Book, 31 July 1893.

grandfather held these posts indicates he was not without presence, and stories about him within the family show him to have been a warm sociable man. Later photographs show him to have had a military bearing.

Benjamin 4 and the end of a line of farmers

Charles Harry Ram who was born at Steeple Grange Farm, which the family had farmed as leaseholders since about 1800, was the youngest son of Benjamin 4. An earlier chapter has told the story of how Benjamin 4 left farming when my great grandfather was a boy.[460] It was probably because of related disruption that Charles Harry went to London as a young man. There is no doubt that the events which overtook Charles Harry's father had a very significant influence on the material fortunes of this branch of the family up to and including my father's generation.

There are many Benjamins and Johns during this period and the earlier practice of numbering each generation is continued here. This part of the story of the farming Rams starts with Benjamin Ram 4 who took over his father's leases on Steeple Grange Farm, Steeple, in the later 1830s, probably under some sort of family guidance organised as a trust. He would have hardly been twenty five years old, and running what was then a very large farm of nearly 500 acres must have been a daunting task, especially as the hard times that followed the Napoleonic Wars had still not run their full course. In the 1841 census Benjamin 4 is listed as farming at Steeple Grange, and employing twenty men and two servants. In the 1851 census he is similarly recorded, but is now living in Chelmsford – around ten miles from Steeple. This development many or may not indicate a break from farming, for farmers at this time quite often

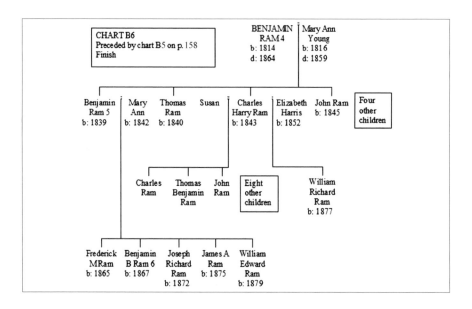

lived away from their farm. But the insecurity revealed by the pattern of family baptisms during the 1840s and 50s suggests there was some family turbulence. They may have lived away from Steeple for some time because a child was born to Benjamin 4 in Terling, Essex in 1845, and two more in Chelmsford in 1850 and 1853. The last of his children was born in Ipswich in 1858. By the time of the 1861 census he was working as a clerk in a foundry in Ipswich, and his burial record says he was an accountant.[461] So the break with farming must have occurred during the mid fifties. The company he was working with was almost certainly Ransome's, the famous Quaker agricultural machinery business. It was set up in 1789 by Robert Ransome and produced ploughs, threshing machines, other agricultural equipment and railway goods. The 1850s and 1860s were decades of expansion, so there must have been a requirement for staff of various kinds and his farming background may have been useful.[462] Benjamin 4 and his wife lived in Ipswich for the rest of their lives.

The immediate reasons for this upheaval are not known. It could be Benjamin 4 became tired of farming and wanted a change, but there was probably some economic pressure involved, as it has been seen that the 1850s was a very bad time for farmers.[463] The last of his children to be born in Steeple was Charles Harry in 1843 when he would have only been in charge of the farm for a few years, and he himself was only in his mid thirties. It has been possible to trace four of Benjamin 4's children with certainty in the 1881 census. They are all boys: Benjamin 5 (b. 1839), Thomas (b. 1840), Charles Harry (b. 1843) and John (b. 1845). Their stories will be told shortly.

But why did he and his family go to Ipswich? There is some interesting circumstantial evidence about why this happened. James Ram, about whom we shall learn more later, worked as a law writer and conveyancer initially in London but moved to Ipswich in the mid 1830s. He died there in 1870. He was a professional man who almost certainly gave Benjamin 4 some support. The only other family member who had the resources to help was William Ram, a cousin of Benjamin 4, who still farmed near Great Waltham. He had been involved in the trust established by Benjamin 4s father John Ram to manage Steeple Grange Farm in the immediate period after his death in 1835, before Benjamin 4 took over full responsibility. In many ways it would have been more natural for him to give help than James, but perhaps he was also suffering in the farming malaise of the time.

There is clear evidence of connection between the families of Benjamin 4 and James in Ipswich because a child of Benjamin 4, Jenny Maria, was baptised at St Nicholas' Church on 18 July in 1858, the church attended by James and his family, where all his own children born in Ipswich were baptised. There is the family memory that Benjamin 4 lived in Ipswich and that there were some wealthy relations who gave help, which generated tensions.

Benjamin 5 and his family

In 1881 Benjamin 5 was married, worked as a porter, and lived at 113, Blenheim Court, Kensington, London. At that time he had five children, all boys, between the ages of sixteen and two. Benjamin and his family moved around a great deal for the children were all born in different places; Frederick Ram (b. 1865) in Pimlico Middlesex, Benjamin Baker Ram 6 (b. 1867) in Little Ilford Middlesex, Joseph Ram (b. 1872) in Acton Middlesex, James (b. 1875) in New Maldon, Surrey, and William (b. 1879) in Barnes, Surrey. Frederick was an errand boy but nothing is said as to whether the others were at school or in jobs. Blenheim Court no longer exists but in 1881 the area appears to have been quite mixed socially. Many of Benjamin 5's neighbours had servants. The immediate neighbour at 111 was a married banker's clerk with two servants and on the other side at 115 there lived a graduate Anglican clergyman without a living who had one servant. In 1901 Benjamin 5 was now an auctioneer's porter living with his wife and youngest son, also a porter, in 3, Colville Square Terrace. This was listed in the census as a boot repair shop. There were six other heads of household at the same address, two of whom had wives. They gave their occupations as charwoman, dressmaker, man on own means, car man, and coachman/groom. This street still exists, being near to Westbourne Park Road in Notting Hill. His other children had grown up and left home. There is no record of Frederick or James in the 1901 census and they may have died. Benjamin Baker was married with two small children, lived in Newington and worked as a stationary engine driver. Joseph was also married with a young family, and was a milk carrier.

Thomas Ram and his family

Thomas Ram (b. 1840) was the only known male member of the family at large to move away from Essex or London. In 1881 he worked as a house carpenter in Penarth Glamorgan and was married to Annie from Swansea. They did not have any children. Penarth was developing very rapidly in the 1870s and 1880s as a subsidiary port to Cardiff which was only about three miles away on the other side of the mouth of the River Taff. They lived at 6, Plassey Street, which still exists, in the centre of the town sharing a house with the family of Thomas Palmer. He was also a house carpenter but about half the age of Thomas, so presumably Thomas was the main occupier of the house. Thomas Palmer was also married with a young wife, and his mother lived with them. Plassey Street was occupied by people involved in the developing trades and business of the town: as masons, lime burners, engine drivers, a railway foreman, a coal trimmer, and labourer at the dock. They were mostly people of a lower middling sort. By 1901 Thomas was back in London where he lived in Sterndale Road, Hammersmith. This is just off Shepherds Bush Road about half way between Shepherds Bush and Hammersmith. He was now sixty with grown up children. He must have remarried because his wife is called Mary in the census return. He was still a carpenter, recorded as working on his own account, so presumably he ran his own small business. His three children aged between 23 and 19 had all been born in Glamorgan, at Penarth or Ferndale. His son, Ernest worked with him in the carpentry business while two daughters, Rhoda and Dottie, were both dressmakers, with a note that they worked on their own account at home.

Charles Harry and his family

Charles Harry Ram was working as a gardener in 1881 living at 2 Pump Court, St Sepulchre in the City of London – this was just north of Smithfield Market off Farringdon Road. Pump Court has gone but the neighbouring streets of Faulkner's Alley and White Horse Alley have survived. The people who lived in them must have been quite poor because they were nearly all manual workers and many were labourers. Lots of the houses had two families in them and some had three. At the time Charles Harry had at least eight children aged between sixteen and one, five of them by his first wife Susan and three by his second wife Elizabeth Harris. Only four of them were resident on census day 1881: Susan (b. 1873), the youngest of the children by his first wife was about seven, together with those of his second wife Elizabeth – William, my grandfather, Jane (b. 1878) and Alice (b. 1880). Charles Harry moved around a lot in London like his elder brother Benjamin V.

Charles Harry must have come to the capital by the age of twenty two for his eldest child Charles, (b. 1865), was born at Clapham. Two further children, Thomas B Ram (b. 1867) and John (b. 1869) were born in Kennington where they were baptised in St Mark's Church. He also had a brother John (b. 1845) who was three years younger than himself and they probably associated with each other in these early days in London, because John had a son called Cable baptised at St Mark's Church Kennington in 1872.[464] The entry in the 1881 census for John notes he lived with a young family in Newington where he worked as a house painter. There are no more references to John in the census records, but there is an intriguing one in the 1891 census to Cabbe Ram who was 22 years old and had been born in Kennington. The name is not exactly right, and the date of birth is three years out but Cabbe might well be a misspelling of Cable and dates of birth can get muddled! Cabbe in 1891 was a prisoner in Wandsworth jail.

The 1871 census shows that Charles Harry and his family moved on to Kingston on Thames, Surrey where all the children living at Pump Court in 1881 were born between 1873 and 1880, so he can only just have moved into the centre of London. In 1881 Charles (b. 1865) was a scholar on the 'Cornwall' at Purfleet, Essex and Susan and William are also described as scholars in the census return. It may be that he and Benjamin V were in contact during the 1870s because Kingston, New Maldon and Barnes are all quite close together to the south west of London, and sometimes they lived in the same town. A large amount of information about the 'Cornwall has come to hand with help from John

Matthews of Thurrock Local History Society.[465] The quote which follows provides the most detailed knowledge obtained about the education of any of the Rams.

> HMS *Wellesley* (later called the 'Cornwall') was built by the East India Company at Bombay and launched on 24th February 1815 as a 3rd rate 72 gun ship. She saw active service in the Far East on several occasions, being for a time Flag Ship of Rear-Admiral Sir Frederick Lewis-Maitland. When she returned from this service, some 27 cannon balls were found embedded in her sides. She was loaned to the School Ship Society by the Admiralty in 1868, fitted out as a training ship, moored off Purfleet in April of that year and re-named 'Cornwall'. Owing to industrial development at Purfleet, she was moved to Denton, below Gravesend in 1928. In 1940 she was severely damaged by enemy action and subsequently sank; she was raised in 1948, to be beached at Tilbury-Ness, where she was broken up. Her timbers were found to be still in good condition so were used in the rebuilding of the Law Courts in London. When the Cornwall was broken up, her figurehead was taken to Chatham Dockyard, where it still stands, just inside the Main Gate under her original name of Wellesley. Many souvenirs were made from her timber, to be made into ashtrays, candlesticks, serviette rings etc, each with a metal plate giving details of the ship. These can now be found in maritime antique shops and fairs.

Who or what the School Ship Society was is not known and no details about it have come to hand, or what the role of the 'Cornwall' was in 1881. It may still have been a training ship, in which case Charles, who was about sixteen at the time, may have been planning to become a sailor. But it could have been used a reformatory for delinquents because the reference in the census return says he was an 'inmate-scholar' which has a certain sinister tone. Even if Charles was a bit of a tearaway as a teenager he obviously settled down later. In 1901 he was married to Elizabeth and had four children between the ages of two and eleven – Emma, Elizabeth, Bertha, and Charles. He was an office porter living a few streets away from his parents, in one of the Peabody buildings at Roscoe Street just north of the Barbican.

In 1901 Charles Harry and his family lived at 37, Bookham Street, where they must have been in 1893 as we have seen my grandfather gave this as his home address when he joined the army. Charles Harry was not present on census night but he was probably still alive as we shall see he is mentioned by a correspondent of the author's grandfather at a date after 1901. On census day 1901 the household was made up entirely of women. Of the children who lived at home in 1881 only Alice remained and she was now twenty one. The others were Rose (b. 1883), Emily (b. 1887), Edith (b. 1888), Florrie (b. 1890), and Latey (b. 1893). Alice was a cigar maker, Rose a box maker, and Emily was a label printer. There was no mention of his three sons, Thomas, William, and John. William was away in the army, and Thomas was probably dead, for in the front of William's army book there are pasted two newspaper clippings about the sudden collapse and death of Thomas Ram aged thirty four in Gracechurch Street. His wife is named as Flora. The clippings are not dated but Thomas would have been thirty four in 1901, just before William left the army and the clippings have the appearance of being stuck in by him. There is reference in the 1901 census to Flora Ram, widow, who has four children aged from three to nine. She was looking after these children on the earnings of a charwoman.

After the time in the army William came back to London and married. The copy of the Kings Own Regimental Calendar which is in his papers was sent by him to his future wife Georgina Nicholls as a present. She lived in Brunswick Square, Haggerston. This does not now exist, but must have been only a few streets away from the New North Road area where William's parents lived. An army friend's letter dated 15 March 1903 reveals William was married by then and that he had left the army. The letter is mostly about old army associates and what they are now doing. Letters from his colonel, J Rowlandson, who he was servant to in the army, make it clear that William had difficulty finding work after leaving the army. In one, dated 31 December 1906, the colonel writes, 'I wish you could get some (illegible) work for you were a very good servant to me'.[466] Eventually he worked for the Gas Light and Coke Company in Haggerston, very near where he grew up and his wife lived before they were married, until he retired in the 1930s.

The Purleigh relations

These were mainly children and grandchildren of Benjamin 4's brother John 7 who farmed at Purleigh and died in 1852. Among them there was a similar move away from farming to live in London, but with some differences. By and large they did not become manual workers, like their cousins. Moreover a few of this family group stayed in the country, or went to London and then moved back to the country. There were clear interconnections between those in the country and in London. Two of John 7's sons, Walter (b. 1841) and Arthur (b. 1846) both lived near Purleigh in 1871. Walter married in the late sixties and had several children in the seventies. He married a woman named Ellen who came from nearby Stow Maries or Cold Norton. They had four children during these years: Mary, Edith (b. 1870?), a son who was so young it had not been named on census day 1871, and then another son Walter (b. 1876). But by the 1881 census Ellen was remarried to George Green, who had a large farm in Stow Maries. There were two children in this family, Edith, now aged eleven and Walter, born presumably before father Walter died. Arthur, the youngest of John 7's children was living in West Ham in 1871, then aged twenty four and it is likely that his elder sister, Agnes (b. 1837) was living with him, since she is also recorded as being in West Ham. Another elder sister, Elizabeth Ram had married and moved to London, for a daughter Mary Willett was born at Hampstead in 1868. Another child, Henry was born at West Ham in 1874.

In the years up to 1891 this group all moved around a good deal. By then Agnes, still unmarried, was back in Latchingdon, another village near Purleigh where she kept lodgers. In 1881 Elizabeth and her husband were in Hackney, where Arthur, now a bank clerk, lived with them.[467] By 1891 Arthur lived in Wallington, Surrey, and was married with three children: Arthur C, John B and Mary W. Ellen, now Green, still lived at Stow Maries together with Edith now aged twenty one. Mary Ram, almost certainly the widow of John 7 was present at the Green family farm on census night 1901 when she is described as Mother in Law. Another Mary Ram (b. 1813), a sister of John 7, was also at the Stow Maries farm on census night. In 1881 she is recorded as living with two of her sisters in Maldon. Clearly the Rams and the Greens intermarried on at least two occasions and met socially.

So it seems mobility did not lead to disintegration of identity within the family, for the picture just described shows significant connections were maintained. Contacts certainly occurred between my family and the Purleigh relations because the family memories include my grandfather being taken to visit aunts in Maldon, one of whom was almost certainly the Mary referred to above. Moreover In the 1901 census Walter, the son of Walter and Ellen who was then twenty five was a grocer's assistant in East Pitfield street, Shoreditch, which was only a few streets away from where Charles Harry and his family lived. It seems reasonable to think there was some social contact between them.

The descendants of John Ram 5C
The history of the family of John Ram 5C, merchant and bankrupt from Colchester during the years after his death in 1810 is not very clear.[468] Some of his descendants probably stayed in the Colchester area, at least for a time. But the story of this branch of the family only becomes clear again in 1827, when a grandson John 7C, was living in London. He clearly had links with a

Table 17. Ram family baptisms at St Luke's Church Chelsea, 1827-31.

Year baptised.	Children of James Ram.	Children of John Ram.
1827 - 21 January.		John Henry.
1828 - 14 December.		Caroline.
1830 -12 June.	Stephen Adye.	
1830 - 21 November.		William Brown.
1831 - 7 December.	Jane.	

cousin from Colchester named James Ram who moved to London in the 1820s as a lawyer. Table 17 shows how both John Ram and James Ram baptised children at St Luke's Church Chelsea in the 1820s and 1830s. On January 21 1827, John 7C and Ann Ram baptised a son John Henry (b. 1827) at St Luke's, followed by two other children in the succeeding two years, Caroline (b. 1828) and William Brown (b. 1830). Later census returns and baptismal records confirm that this John Ram was the grandson of the John who died in 1810, and that he was born in Colchester in 1798 or 1799. John and Ann were certainly in London by 1824 when their first child, William (b. 1824) was baptised at St James'. Another son, George (b. 1837) was baptised at Ranelagh Presbyterian Church, also in Chelsea. In 1871 John 7C was living in Kensington with his son George as a widower. John did not appear in the 1881 census, so was presumably dead by then. Two of John 7C's brothers, Robert (b. 1796) and William (b. 1802) with their families may also have been in London in the 1820s and 1830s but it has not been possible to confirm this.

John 7C's family, shown in chart C10, continued to live in London right up to 1900. The John Henry who was baptised at St Luke's Church Chelsea in 1827 is mentioned in the 1881 census, when he was married with six children living at home in 10, Newland Street, Hanover Square. This must have been renamed or new buildings put up, but the area is identifiable as near Sloane Square, between Cliveden Place and Pimlico Road. It is just round the Corner from Ranelagh Grove, where the Presbyterian Chapel was presumably

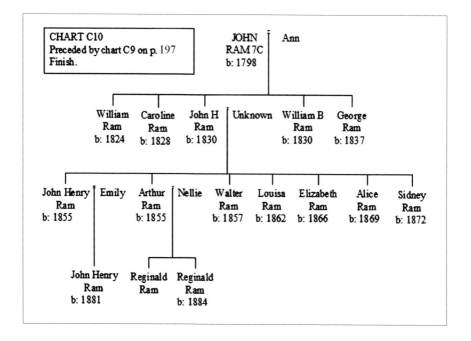

situated. John Henry is listed in the 1881 census as a 'Mechanical Engineer L T Boat Cy', and two of his children were old enough to be working. Arthur, (b. 1855), was an engine fitter and Walter, (b. 1857) a commercial clerk. The three younger children were still at school. In 1881 the area around 10, Newland Street was very mixed socially. Another married man without children, a Frenchman who worked as a cook, lived in the same house. A porter in the Bank of England lived at number 9, whilst at number 11 there were two small families – a harness maker and a builder's clerk. One of John Henry's sons, another John Henry (b. 1855), had recently married and left home. He worked as an ironmonger in Battersea, which of course is just at the end of Chelsea bridge on the South side of the River Thames. He had a son, yet another John Henry (b. 1881). This little family group does not appear in the 1901 census. But a younger son of the elder John Henry called Arthur does, who is aged 44 and married with two children, Reginald and Violet. Arthur is listed in the census as a Mechanical Engineer and Reginald appears as an Apprentice Mechanical Engineer. Arthur was living in Chelsea in Paulton's Square, so this family had lived in Chelsea for almost one hundred years.

The presence of John 7C in Chelsea and his connection with St Luke's Church cannot pass without comment. James Ram's father was step brother of John's grandfather and through St Luke's Church these two family groups were brought together again. When James came to London as a young lawyer he lived first in what today we call Bloomsbury, and baptised his eldest child at St Giles in the Fields Church in 1829. But he then moved to Chelsea for all his further children born in London were baptised at St Luke's in Chelsea, certainly those born between the years of 1831 and 1834. Judging from the baptismal records it looks as though the association with St Luke's Church started with John rather than James, but they probably both went to this church during the years from 1829 to the time James moved away to Ipswich. This is another example of how family members kept relationships together in new circumstances.

XVIII
The Professionals

Stephen Ram's photograph

In a manuscript document about the Ram family in the British Library there is a photograph of Stephen Adye Ram (b. 1831).[469] It is the only picture of a family member that exists before the taking of photo snapshots became common practice. This photograph is shown in figure 11. Stephen was probably aged between fifty and sixty when the picture was taken. If this assumption is correct it would have been in the 1880s. He looks a dignified person, who has authority but is not without warmth. At that time his family of eleven children – eight sons and three daughters – were growing up rapidly. His wife Susan Scott was thirteen years younger. As this part of the book develops it will be seen that Stephen and his immediate family were typical of the grander members of James Ram's family. Stephen was still alive at the time of the 1901 census so his life spanned the whole of the Victorian era. The picture is a good way to set the scene on James Ram's family because it helps to convey quite powerfully what the members of his family were probably like.

James Ram's legal achievements

It was Stephen's father James who established this branch as a modern professional family. James came from the Colchester branch of the Ram family which had a long history and included some wealthy members, but overall it was not dissimilar in social standing to the large leasehold farmers who emerged from the Great Waltham part of the family in the eighteenth and early nineteenth centuries. But he achieved something that had not been done in the family for nearly two hundred years through going to university. He was indentured to a London firm of solicitors and admitted to the Inner Temple in 1813.[470] From there he went to Pembroke College, Cambridge as a scholar in 1813 to obtain his B A degree in 1817. He was admitted M A in 1823 and called to the Bar in the same year. At the Inner Temple he was the pupil of an eminent conveyancer, Richard Preston.[471] and himself became a conveyancer.

From the seventeenth century onwards conveyancing became a distinct and specialised branch of the legal profession. By the later part of the eighteenth

Figure 11. Stephen Adye Ram.

century it was firmly established. Its development was prompted by the growing complexity of property law, which led to a small group of lawyers coming to have expert knowledge in this area, which other lawyers depended upon. Similar developments happened at this time in other branches of the law. As soon as the use of written documents grew up to create or transfer interests in land the need arose for rules of interpretation. Initially there was much confusion about their definition but clarity was gradually established during the nineteenth century. As in other areas of the law, reforms were made to accommodate practice to modern needs. Gradually in the nineteenth century solicitors took over much of the detailed work connected with conveyancing.[472] There were unsuccessful attempts during James Ram's lifetime to establish a register of deeds and titles.

Early in his career James Ram became a writer on legal matters beyond the sphere of conveyancing and it is his contribution in this respect that brought him some fame and an entry in the Dictionary of National Biography. He wrote six books in all on various topics of the law. The second one, published in 1825 was about the rights of parents to direct and control their children's education, the third one, also in 1825, was about the law of tenure and tenancy. In 1827 he wrote about wills and landed property, a book which had two editions, followed by another in 1832 about assets, debts, and encumbrances. Most of these books have long been forgotten, but two are still available, being reprinted as late as 1980. Amazon Books listed them in 2009 as available second hand.

The first of them, *The Science of Legal Judgement* was written about case law in 1822 when James was only twenty nine. It was initially published in England to be followed much later in New York in 1871. It is still used, particularly in

America.[473] In *A History of English Law,* the most recent authoritative book on the subject, written in 1938 by Sir William Holdsworth, there is detailed discussion about what James achieved in *The Science of Legal Judgement.* In volume twelve there are the following background comments on the history of case law reporting. Reports on cases began to be made in the seventeenth and eighteenth centuries, and collections of these were created – often for private use. Some were published. Towards the end of the eighteenth century there were important developments in the way cases were reported and listed. Reports were made and published as soon as possible after cases took place. A clearer separation of ones dealt with by different courts – particularly in regard to common law reports and the cases dealt with in the Court of Chancery was increasingly made. Separation also began of different classes of cases. The way of writing reports became more standardised.

The modern theory as to the authority of decided cases was reached substantially by the second half of the eighteenth century. This process was assisted by the better reporting and codification of cases described above. In the first instance codification appears to be simple. 'A decided case makes law for future cases, and will bind all inferior courts, and generally courts of co-ordinate jurisdiction. But the more closely the theory is examined the less simple does it appear. The decisions of courts sometimes conflicted, and the weight to be attached to their decisions was different. Decisions could be reversed at a later date if it was thought some other line of authority ought to be followed. This theory effectively requires careful explanation and understanding'.[474] Holdsworth continues further about the issues involved.

> But it was not till the early part of the nineteenth century that a lawyer set out to give a systematic explanation of the theory underlying the system of case law, and of the conditions under which it was accepted: and it was not until the same period that a lawyer attempted to compile a list, for the guidance of lawyers, of cases which had been doubted or over-ruled. Of the two books which were written in this period to fill this gap in our legal literature I must say few words.

> The first and by far the most important of these books is James Ram's very learned book on *The Science of Legal Judgement* ... The author sets out to explain the manner in which the system of case law is applied: the considerations which the judge must take into account in framing his judgement: the relative weight of the decisions in different courts: the relative weight of other sources of the law, such as the civil and canon law, textbooks, mercantile customs, and the opinions of conveyancers: the weight to be attached to arguments from public policy, inconvenience, absurdity, or analogy: the weight to be attached to different sets of reports: the weight to be attached to dicta: the limits within which cases could be distinguished:

considerations which might increase or lessen the authority of a decision: the various measures which a judge should take to inform himself in cases in which it was difficult to form a conclusion as to the facts of the law.

Holdsworth pays James Ram the following complement.

> The problems discussed are clearly stated, and they are solved with great skill by means of apposite quotations from other cases and other legal authorities. As the result of his discussion Ram, though he admits the system of case law has its defects, considers that its merits largely outweigh these defects.[475]

The second of James' books still available was his last, about the work of the jury, which appeared in 1851, and went through three editions in England and America.[476] It was liked by some but not by others. The *Solicitor's Journal* commented, 'A very amusing and readable book, and, one calculated to be of use to beginners in law'.[477] The *London Athenaeum* did not agree. 'Nor do we confine our disapproval to the general design of Mr Ram's treatise; for the style in which he carries out his plan of literary illustration is as careless and confused as the plan itself is ridiculous'.[478]

Various appraisals of the value of James Ram's writings still survive. A recent commentator, A W B Simpson, considers *The Science of Legal Judgement* to be 'a remarkable though now largely forgotten work which had some vogue in America. His other writings, which include the strangely titled *Treatise on Facts, as subjects of Inquiry by a Jury* (1861) remain in oblivion'.[479] But Sir William Holdsworth had a somewhat different view. 'One of the ablest books on this subject (the codification of case law), entitled *The Science of Legal Judgement*, was published by James Ram in 1822'.[480] The *Dictionary of National Biography* comments as follows. 'As a legal author Ram obtained a well founded reputation for painstaking research, methodical arrangement, and lucidity of style'.[481]

James Ram's work and his family life

The entry for James Ram in the *Dictionary of National Biography* gives a small amount of biographical information. It says he was first indentured to a firm of London solicitors and that he then went to University, around the age of twenty one. (We have already read that this was to Pembroke College at the University of Cambridge). After he finished at University he went on 'what was then the grand tour during 1818-22'.[482] *The Science of Legal Judgement* was published at the end of this period. There are several references about him in the Inner Temple records. Its accounts show that he paid £47.50 rent for chambers there in 1823, but unfortunately do not record where they were located. The minutes of the Bench Table (one of the Inn's governing bodies) for 2 Nov. 1832 record his gift to the Library of 'his treatise of assets, debts and encumbrances', and on the 7 Nov. 1834, the Bench Table thanked him for his present to the Library of his work 'The Science of Legal Judgment'. The annual Law List provides the following professional addresses for him: 1826: 10 Crown Office Row [Inner Temple], 1829: 77 Chancery Lane, 1837: Ipswich (conveyancer), 1851: 4 Stone Buildings [Lincoln's Inn] & Ipswich, 1854-70: Ipswich (conveyancer).[483] It is not clear whether this list of addresses provides a continuous picture of his working activities and locations, but at the very least it gives an outline. It looks as though he moved away from London in 1837 at the age of forty four, and then spent the rest of his working life in Ipswich, although in the early 1850s he also worked in London. Colchester became connected with London by train in 1843 whilst Ipswich was reached in 1846.[484] During the second half of the nineteenth century accessibility by train to London increased rapidly and by its end Ipswich was less than two hours from London and forty minutes from Colchester.

James Ram inherited two small farms that came into the family during the seventeenth and eighteenth centuries. One was at Great Bromley and came by inheritance to James' step uncle John in 1744. It was left to James on the death of his sister Jane in 1812. Although only 26 acres it was let during the nineteenth century for between £40 and £45, and it seems to have continued in the family after James' death. When James married Elizabeth Jane Adye in 1826 they made a marriage settlement that involved this farm. He was then aged thirty three and she was twenty five. James committed himself to surrender the farm for mutual use between him, Elizabeth and their heirs. He also covenanted to pay her £200 a year for life out of his income.[485] The other farm was at Stoke by Nayland, Suffolk, and was part of the Manor of Stoke next Nayland with Shardlows and Withermarsh, which he inherited through his grandfather Nicholas. Its earlier story is told elsewhere in the book.[486] He was admitted to the ownership in 1833 when the holdings were a messuage or tenement called Fyells or H(W)arreys, plus two pieces of meadow containing five acres, plus twenty further acres. A parcel of waste land called Levenheath (about three acres) by dint of an enclosure act was added in 1817, and at the time of James' death it was just over 43 acres in size.[487] This farm went by several names but it is called Rams Farms on the current two and a half inches to the mile Ordnance Survey map.

When James died Rams Farm was sold and the proceeds were invested and put in trust to provide an income for his widow during her lifetime. After her death three of their sons, James, Edward and Ralph, were each to have lump sums of £200. Half the residue on his wife's death was to be put in trust for the benefit of his daughter Jane, and the other half similarly for Clara. If they died the entire residue was to be split among the three sons just mentioned. Ram's Farm realised £1500 in 1871, but there is no indication of what other property James owned. What happened to the Great Bromley farm, and did James rent or own the sizeable house he had in Ipswich? The only other thing that is clear from the will is that household furniture and books were left to his widow and that two other sons, Stephen and Francis, were free to buy any of the properties sold at market rates.[488] The will effectively provided for the widow and the less financially secure children. Those like Stephen, Francis and Willett who had made sound careers of their own were not included, although some other provisions may have been made to accommodate them.

James and Elizabeth Jane's first child, James Ram was born two years after they were married in 1828, at St Giles in the Fields, London. Other children followed in the 1830s, Stephen, Jane, Clara, Francis and Mary, all of whom were baptised at St Luke's Church, Chelsea, but the address of their home is not known. More births followed the move to Ipswich, the first being that of Willett Ram in 1837. Edward was born in 1843, and Ralph in 1845, so in all James and Elizabeth had seven children. See chart C11 for details. They also had many grandchildren.

Although as a younger man his life centred on London, James had of course originally come from Colchester, as did his mother who lived there through a long widowhood which ended with her death in 1857. James' wife also came from this town and moved back there after his death. Why James moved away from London to Ipswich in mid life is not known, but one possible and obvious explanation was a desire to be near other family members who lived in Colchester. In Ipswich he lived in an old part of the town in Silent Street, not far from where Cardinal Wolsey spent his childhood, in a large Georgian House with a big garden, which is clearly visible on old maps, although it has now been pulled down. What he did in Ipswich is not entirely clear. Most of his books were written by that time, but the Law List says he worked as a

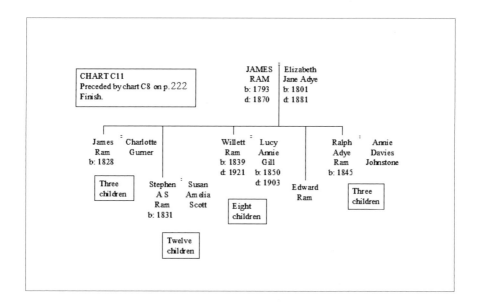

conveyancer. Ipswich grew very rapidly during the middle of the nineteenth century so there would have been plenty of this type of legal business, and it is possible he dealt with complicated cases from all over the country.

James and Elizabeth Jane cast a large influence over several generations of their family in at least two ways. They re-established the dynastic strength of this side of the family through the large number of children they had, who were mostly boys, and they also established an upper middle class professional way of life that lasted for at least three further generations. The phenomena of a large family developing around a successful man has been seen elsewhere in the Ram story. There are obvious comparisons with the William, a direct ancestor seven generations removed, who founded the Colchester branch of the family. He too was a lawyer, he too had a large family, he too had several sons who became clergy in the Church of England, and he too was a writer. On both occasions the legal profession provided the basis for a new start. The family image was most likely reinforced by Elizabeth Jane having a developed awareness of her own dynastic background, which has been mentioned already.[489] She certainly expressed it through the names given to her children. Many of them had the Adye surname as their second or third fore name or that of the Willett family. This was a family of gentry status which was related by marriage to the Adyes. The Adye family clearly meant much to Elizabeth Jane which had a distinguished connection with the Royal Artillery from the time her grandfather, Ralph Adye, wrote a famous treatise on courts martial.[490] In the nineteenth and twentieth centuries the connection was even more distinguished for three successive generations of the Adye family became generals in the Royal Artillery. Ralph's brother Stephen, who was a near contemporary of Elizabeth Jane became a Major General. In the next generation most of the Ram family would have known of General Sir John Adye (d. 1900), who was Governor of Gibraltar. In turn his son became Major General Sir John Adye.

Descendants in London

James' two eldest sons lived in the London area for the bulk of their lives, but they must have gone to Ipswich in the late 1830s with rest of the family as children. James (b. 1828) was nine at that time and Stephen about six. James went to Jesus College at Cambridge University, but does not seem to have graduated. He matriculated in 1847, and was certainly in London by the early 1850s. He married Charlotte Gurner of Bath in Somerset, and they lived in various places around London. Their first child, Charlotte Adye Ram (b. 1853), was born at St Giles in the Fields where he himself was born, a second child Jane (b. 1854) was born in Hammersmith, followed by a third Edward (b.1859), at Beckham in Kent. Once this early period of movement was over James and Charlotte settled in Waldegrave Road, Penge which was very near to Crystal Palace. The 1881 census says the girls were teachers who lived with their parents whilst Edward was a student of architecture. None of them are noted in the 1901 census, but it is known that Edward became an architect who worked abroad in Hong Kong. The daughters presumably married between 1881 and 1901. James and Charlotte must have died by then.

Although the career of James suggests he was not among the ablest of the sons it is ironical that more is known about what he did than for most of the others. This is because of a chance survival of a booklet in the British Library advertising a cramming school he ran for entrants to military colleges. The booklet could be obtained from 22, Devonshire Terrace, Notting-Hill Gate where the school operated, price 1/-.[491] Much of it is about how the various entrance examinations were conducted and what was tested. He describes himself as a military tutor who receives Gentlemen (either as Boarders or otherwise) to give them instruction in the subjects of the various Military and Naval examinations. He writes that he devotes himself especially to the 'Preparation of Pupils for entrance into the Military Colleges of Woolwich, Sandhurst, and Addiscombe, and for the General Examinations of Candidates for direct Commissions in the Queen's and Indian Services: also for the recently established Civil Service Examinations'.[492] It may be his mother's military connections helped to get his school known and recommended by the army. Terms for Boarders were by the year with three months notice of removal, £150; by the quarter, £42; or by the month, £15. For any shorter period an annual rate of £200 per annum applied. For pupils who paid by the day one half of the above terms were charged in each case. Pupils requiring temporary or partial instruction paid at the rate of 2/6 per hour. Teaching of German, provision of a seat in church, or washing were extra. The domestic arrangements were under the personal superintendence of Mrs James Ram. James also wrote a strange little book on the philosophy of war which maintains war has a valid function and defends it against the attacks of those who decry it. Perhaps he used it at his school.[493]

The general impression conveyed from what is know about James' second son Stephen is that he was a substantial and competent man. His picture conveys this, his life was stable, he had a big family and he lived in a large house. He was a solicitor, who by 1870 was a partner in the firm of Bridges, Sawtell, and Ram, 23 Red Lion Square, London. The winding up of father's estate in 1871 took place at this office, when his younger brother Willett Ram was a witness to the sale of Ram's Farm along with another brother, Francis. Documents related to this event say that Willett is a solicitor, who was likely to be working for his brother Stephen, or recently established in Halesworth in his own solicitor's practice.[494] Stephen's children filled middle class occupations and some of them went to University. Less is directly known about him than brother James, because nothing equivalent to James Ram's advertising booklet has ever come to hand. The first information about his adult life is the baptism of Gilbert Scott Ram (1864-1938) his eldest child, when he then lived in Mecklenburg Street, which runs parallel to the left of Grays Inn Road, being about fifteen minutes walk from most of the inns of court. The only reference in the Mormon lists is to the baptism of another son, Melville (b. 1867) at St Pancras Old Church. This was very near the house he lived in for many years at 32, Oakley Square. Although these references make it clear he was married and living in London from at least 1864 there is no reference to the family in the 1871 census. Perhaps the records relating to them were lost.

In 1881 all his family is recorded in the census, by which time he had nine children between the ages of fifteen and one. Three more were born in the eighties but cannot be traced in the 1891 census. It is possible they were staying elsewhere on census night, or had died, but the youngest Humphrey lived to marry. So in total Stephen had twelve children between 1865/6 and 1886 and ten are known to have grown to adulthood. In 1881 Gilbert the eldest, then aged fifteen/sixteen, was a boarder at Oakham Grammar School, which must have been quite sizeable for it then had 54 boarders. The next eldest, Stephen (b. 1867) was a boarder at a private school in Godalming. One of the others, John (1869-1939), was staying with his grandmother, Elizabeth Jane Ram on census night, whilst all of the others were at home in Oakleigh Square. This still exists and is between Euston Station and Camden Town, very near St Pancras Old Church where the family worshipped. The Rams lived on the South side of the square where unfortunately all the houses have gone, but the originals on the North side remain and give an idea of what Stephen's house was probably like. They form a long terrace of large Regency or early Victorian buildings. The 1881 census also lists neighbours who were a piano maker, an annuitant, an architect, a dental surgeon, and a builder by the name of Laing. There were four servants in the Ram household – a cook, two nurses, plus a housemaid. They were all women, their ages ranging from 36 to sixteen. All of them came from Eastern England – Lincolnshire, Northamptonshire, Huntingdon and Cambridge – from where Stephen's wife almost certainly found them on recommendations from her clergy relations, who it will be seen had parishes in these areas.

Stephen Adye was still alive in 1901, still listed in the census as a solicitor, although he was seventy by then. Four of the children are still living with their parents, John, aged 32 , was a solicitor's charge clerk, Susan (b. 1870) was a church worker, and Helen (b. 1877) a music teacher. John had gone to public school at Felstead in Essex, and before qualifying as a solicitor matriculated from Cambridge University on a non collegiate basis. After qualifying he practised in the company where his father was a partner.

Stephen Adye's wife Susan Scott, (b. 1844) was thirteen years younger than her husband, and also still alive in 1901. Many of the male members of her own family were Anglican clergy who formed a complex pattern of inter-relationships very like the one connected with the Colchester branch of the Ram family in the early Stuart period. In Susan's family there were Anglican clergy in four successive generations during the eighteenth and nineteenth centuries. Sometimes there was more than one in a generation. They included several able people. Thomas Scott (d. 1835) was Susan's grandfather, who after Cambridge University was a priest in Buckinghamshire for most of his life, but moved to be rector of Wappenham in Northamptonshire when he was quite elderly, from 1833 until his death in 1835. His eldest son Thomas (1807-80), Susan's father, went to the same College as his father, Queen's, where he was a scholar and a fellow. He also became a Church of England clergyman, holding simultaneous livings in Nether Broughton, Leicestershire, Isleham in Cambridge, and Onehouse in Suffolk between 1831 and 1846. He also became rector of Wappenham after his father died in 1835, but from 1846 until his death this was his sole living, where Susan was born. His younger brother was George Gilbert Scott (1811-1878) the famous architect, so Susan lived for many years just round the corner from her uncle's St Pancras Hotel which was built between 1865 and 1877. George Gilbert Scott, Junior (1839-1897), the architect of the Anglican Liverpool Cathedral was Susan's cousin and about five years older than her. Another younger brother of Susan's father, John (1809-1886), was a doctor in Buckingham until 1842 when he went to University after which he also became a clergyman, first in Cambridge, and then from 1867 to 1886 he was vicar at Wisbeech. Both Susan's father and uncle John became honorary canons at cathedrals, Thomas at Peterborough and John at Ely.

By 1901 Stephen Adye's other children had all gone their separate ways which are recorded in the census of that year. This involved a scattering that is typical of modern middle class families in which qualified young people have to be mobile to find suitable jobs. The eldest son, Gilbert, now aged 36 and unmarried had become an electrical engineer who lived in lodgings in the Cromwell Road, Kensington. The second son, Stephen who was slightly younger than Gilbert had become a clergyman. He went to St John's College Cambridge and was then a curate at Haslingden in Lancashire from 1887 to 1892. From 1893 to 1895 he was Assistant Diocesan Inspector of Schools in the Manchester Diocese. He remained in the North of England the whole of his life spending most of it as vicar of St Mary's Lowgate in Hull. Three of his mother's relations were vicar there during the nineteenth century, bringing both evangelical and high church influences, the latter being akin to the work Stephen's uncle, Edward Ram, did in Norwich, as will be seen shortly. George Gilbert Scott did much restoration work at this church. Later in life Stephen was also a Canon and Prebendary of York Minster. In 1901 he was married and lived with his wife Mary and family in the vicarage of St Mary's in Hull. they had three small children, Stephen (b. 1895), Percival (b. 1897), and Melville (b.1899). They had four servants – a cook, a maid and two nurses.

Margaret (b. 1870), probably the twin of Susan, was a nurse in Brighton.

James Ram had another son who lived in London who was named Francis. Neither his date of birth or death is known and the only family based information about him emerges from his role in the settlement of his father's estate in 1871. In the related indenture he is said to be 'of the War Office, London' and does not appear to have married. He was still alive in 1891 aged 65 when the census gives his occupation as living on own means, which presumably means he was retired. He lived in Reigate.

Descendants in Halesworth.

Halesworth is a small market town in Suffolk about thirty miles north of Ipswich where one of James' younger sons, who was born in Ipswich in 1839 became a solicitor in the 1870s. His name was Willett 1 (so numbered because of the way successive generations of the family were given the same name) and first appeared in the town's trade directory in 1868. In that of 1873 he is listed as living in London Road at *The Limes*, which is now part of a residential home complex. A law firm 'Frederick Cross, Solicitor, Clerk to the Magistrates and Commissioners of Taxes' was also recorded, to become Cross and Ram by 1879. In that year Willett Ram had a rather pompous personal entry as 'Ram, Willett, (firm Cross and Ram), solicitor and commissioner in the Supreme Court of the Judicature & Clerk to the Magistrates, Blything Division of Suffolk'. He also had a separate entry as Clerk to the County Magistrates (Blything Division).The entries for him are the same in 1883 and 1896. Willett's elder son, Willett 2 (b. 1875) appears as Willett jun. in the 1900 Directory and in 1904 the developing involvement of Willett's family in the firm is made clear by the following personal entries; 'Ram Willett (firm Cross, Ram and Sons)'; 'Ram, Willett, jun. Solicitor (firm Cross, Ram and Sons)'; and 'Ram. Francis Robert, Solicitor (firm Cross, Ram and Sons)'.[495]

Not a great deal is known about the younger life of Willett 1, or how he happened to go to Halesworth. In 1871 He signed documents connected with the settlement of his father's estate at the office of his elder brother Stephen in Red Lion Square London, but it is not clear whether he worked there for a period after qualifying as a solicitor, or whether he was just dealing with the paperwork connected with his father's death. He did not go to University. The Halesworth directories show he was established in Halesworth by his late thirties, which may have happened through a link his father had with the Cross family. In a book about a local hospital, called the Patrick Stead Hospital, it is mentioned that William Cross, rector of Halesworth when he died in 1821 at the age of 56, was also a fellow of Pembroke College, Cambridge. He would have been in his late forties when James Ram was a student at Pembroke College.[496] Frederick Cross, the solicitor with whom Willett I became a partner was his son. The Willett Rams remained connected with the same firm until 1953 when Willett 2 retired. In 2005 the firm of 'Cross Ram and Co Solicitors' still existed in Halesworth at 18, Thoroughfare where the name is etched in frosted glass in the front window of its office.

The book about the Patrick Stead Hospital also mentions Willett 1 and his wife being present at the opening of the hospital, commenting about them in the following way. He was a '... dapper little gentleman with silver white hair and moustache', who had the Ram coat of arms, presumably the one granted to Francis Ram of Hornchurch in 1590, embellished on the coach that his wife '... used for her drives into the country and about the Town'.[497] These were presumably the ones which appear at the front of *The Ram Family*, that Willett 2 and his son William (b. 1907) wrote in 1940.[498] This is the only known use of them in the family beyond the lifetime of Francis Ram. It is not clear what right Willett 1 had to use these arms, but in doing so he shows he was very conscious of his past history. Both he and his wife supported the life of the Parish Church. Mrs Ram was a sick visitor and Willett 1 led a Sunday afternoon Bible class at *The Limes*. In 1898 Willett 1 together with two members of the Cross family had a Mission Room built in Chediston Street, where Willett conducted services.[499]

In the 1881 census when Willett 1 was 42 and his wife Lucy was 31 their household contained four children between the ages of six and seven months, with four female servants between the young ages of fourteen and nineteen. One was a Nursery Governess, one a Cook and Domestic Servant, another a Housemaid and Domestic Servant, and the fourth was a Nurse Domestic Servant. Neighbours were a mixture of annuitants, often retired, trades people plus one or two professionals. Frederick Cross lived only a few houses away.

Willett 1's family had grown in several ways by the time of the 1901 census. He had two more children, both girls who were named Frances (b. 1882) and Emma (b. 1885), so in total he and Lucy had eight children, one of whom, Henry (1879), died young. The children were sent away to various private schools. Two went to Lowestoft, but Ernest (b. 1879) went to Brighton College before matriculating at Pembroke College, Cambridge and then taking his solicitor's articles. As Willett 1's family grew up his eldest son, Willett 2 joined the solicitor's business eventually managing it after his father retired in 1905. He himself worked on until he retired in 1950. Two younger sons, Francis (b. 1877) and Ernest were also working in the firm in 1901. Francis is described in the census as a Solicitor's Clerk and Ernest as an Articled Clerk. It is not known what happened to Francis in later life but Ernest was admitted as a solicitor in 1903 going on to work in London. Willett 1's eldest daughter, Lucy (b. 1876) had married in 1900, but three younger daughters, aged between 21 and 16 still lived at home. All of them married at later dates.

Descendants in Norwich

Edward, James' seventh child, born in Ipswich in 1843, was in some ways one of the more remarkable members of the family. Most of James' family seem to have been establishment minded but this was not true of Edward. For one thing he went to London University, and not Cambridge. Why this happened is not known, but he graduated with a first in theology from Kings College in 1865, almost certainly being one of the first students of the university. More significantly he devoted his career to reform and support of minority movements rather than the maintenance of the settled order. Also he married less conventionally than most of his relations, to Virginia Noverre, whose father must have come from aboard. In 1881 he was dead but his widow lived in Norwich being described in the census returns as a Professor of Dancing. A number of Noverre family members were involved in this venture. One was an unmarried son, Richard who was Virginia's younger brother, whilst another was a married younger brother, Frank, who was described in the census as a Dancing and Music Master. Edward and Virginia lived as near neighbours of Frank in Chantry Court, Norwich. Unusually for the Ram family of the time they had no children. But these differences did not cut him off from the rest of the family for he refers in his papers to getting wood for the rebuilding of the pulpit from Halesworth where his brother Willett lived and of modelling one of the restored windows in his Norwich church on one the Ipswich church that his parents attended.

Edward did though have one similarity with other males in his wider family – he became a Church of England clergyman, being ordained in 1866. Five years later he became vicar of St John's, Timberhill, in Norwich at the age of twenty eight. He also had another appointment in Norwich as chaplain to the Norfolk County Asylum. When he went to Timberhill it was decayed and literally falling down. 'The tower had collapsed nearly 80 years before, and the chancel arch and porch were shored up with timber so that they should not suffer the same fate. The thatched roof was in total disrepair and the lead on the aisle roofs was leaking badly ... Father Ramm (sic) set out to transform St John's into his vision of what a medieval church should look like'.[500] He did this over the next 47 years until his death in 1918, but he did more than that for he reinvigorated the life of the church and parish. He must also have been an exceptionally loved vicar. When I visited the church in 2003 asking after Edward the response was immediate and completely unexpected. 'Oh yes, Father Ram, yes we remember Father Ram', and it was clear that after a time lapse of over eighty years he was still remembered with love and affection. In a short book of four pages about the parish over two of them are taken up with his story.[501]

An important focus in Edward's ministry was the ritualist movement in the Church of England, the widest influences of which occurred during the years he

was active. G T Rimmington writing recently about this movement's influence
on Leicester comments about its reinvigorating power, and the same could
be said of many areas in England. 'An impressive feature of the first decade
of the twentieth century was the way in which Leicester, in particular, was
influenced by the Oxford Movement. This brought into the area a sprinkling
of zealous pastorally-minded men who acted as pioneers, encouraging others
to adopt a more caring style of ministry'. The Ritualists supported the poor
and Rimmington mentions particularly Donaldson, the incumbent at St Mark,
who though a son of a gentleman, accompanied unemployed shoe workers on
a march to London. Rimmington continues that Donaldson and several others,
'brought hope and colour into people's lives, [and was] one of the reasons why
Anglicanism competed well with Nonconformity in Leicester ... during the first
decade of the twentieth century'. [502] Clergy generally became more professional
during this period, and Edward was one of the pioneers in bringing this about.

Edward's career and his involvement in the ritualist movement deserves some
attention, based on a collection of his papers now in the Norfolk Record Office
in Norwich. [503] These relate to correspondences, dialogues and controversies he
was involved in together with a large number of related newspaper cuttings. One
of the papers is a personal memoir written near the end of his life about his
experiences at Timberhill. He says his involvement in the Ritualist Movement was
sparked by the imprisonment of Revd Sidney Fiathorne-Green of Manchester in
Lancaster Prison around 1883, for wearing vestments, which although correct
according to regulations in the vestments rubric, caused offence under the Public
Worship Regulations Act. 'I felt that by adopting the use of them (the rubric
regulations) ...I should be giving the best support I could in maintaining the
law of the Church'. [504] Edward apparently had the support of his parishioners in
doing this. To Edward the wearing of vestments in a particular way, as well as
the use of plainsong and incense, were of symbolic significance in a greater cause
of developing a more witnessing kind of Church. The introduction of ritualist
practices at Timberhill in the 1880s was accompanied by mission and community
based work. Sisters from A H D (Ditchingham Nuns) started working in the
parish in 1884 and continued to do so at least to the end of Edward's ministry.
The first mission was held in 1884, was succeeded by many more in the following
years. There was a growing emphasis on worship, instruction and intercession. [505]
In 1887 to raise money for the church its friends performed '*As You Like It*' in
the open air besides having a may pole, country dancing, an open air concert,
and a bazaar. The introduction of daily masses in 1889, brought psychological
relief to Edward, whose periodic attacks of what he called 'internal neuralgia'
stopped from that time. 'Through so personal a thing I am glad to record this as
a memorial of God's mercy to me, and I think also as a sign that he has accepted
the daily offering'. [506] This note suggests the actions of Edward at Timberhill
were not made without personal internal struggle and tension.

Edward got support from the Church authorities for some of his initiatives, but opposition for others. This was partly because of personal attitudes. To begin with the Bishop of Norwich supported the building of a rood screen at Timberhill, but when Bishop Sheepshankes came in 1893 it was opposed, ostensibly because no faculty had been given. This dispute lasted on and off for twelve years until 1905. Edward introduced the ritual of the Blessing of the Fire and the Pascal Candle in 1886, but it had to be stopped because of the opposition of Church institutions. Edward became involved in, or caused, local controversies with the Bishop of Norwich as well as with ordinary people. Services had to be held behind locked doors and there was crowd unrest at the church in 1880, 1888, 1894, 1898-99, 1901, and 1903. He believed three issues – the taking of the communion to the sick, the erection of the rood screen and the use of incense – were at the root of the problems. 'These were outwardly the cause of the difference, but that which underlay them all was the opposite ways in which he (Bishop Sheepshanks) and I viewed the ground on which they rested'.[507] Edward wrote a book about ritualism in 1888 which was based on a number of lectures he gave in his church about the history of the Church in England.[508] In the final lecture on the Catholic Revival in the Church he spells out his own views about the importance of the ritualist movement. It is clear he saw it as a source of renewal and revival. It led directly to the renewal of Convocation after a lapse of over a hundred years, diocesan conferences were established, new dioceses were created, old churches were restored and new ones built, regular communion services were restored, there was fuller and better teaching about the faith, morning and evening prayer was held regularly and churches were open for private prayer, seats were freely available, the holding of parochial missions developed, and the sick and the poor were visited.[509]

These thoughts about renewal are confirmed in a recent detailed book about the Ritualist Movement by W N Yates. 'The Church of England as it existed in the Nineteenth Century was very bound up with the state … Ritualism helped to shatter this, although it was not the only force working in this direction. They (ritualists) did not affect the liturgy but they did affect what people saw happening in Church.'[510] They were indeed a force for change, generally exerting influence beyond their numerical strength. Originally a movement among better educated and middle class groups, both clergy and laity, its influence spread as time went by. Originating in the 1840s the movement's high point was around 1900. Ritualism was part of a wider desire to resurrect the ideals and values of the past, as a way of coping with the economic, social and political upheaval of the period.

An important question which is not clear from the papers about Edward Ram in the Norfolk Record Office is the nature of the part he played in the ritualist movement. Was he simply a local enthusiast, or did he contribute at national levels as well? In 1903-05 there was a Royal Commission on Ecclesiastical Discipline into the use of incense, and Timberhill was one of two local churches visited by the commissioners. It is clear from a packet of papers in the Norwich Record Office that Edward was closely involved in the Commission, about which there was massive reporting in the national newspapers.[511] But in W N Yates' book there is only one reference to Edward[512] whilst in the lists of leading churches Timberhill is not mentioned. The book shows that there were quite a large number of local churches which contributed, and it is apparent from Edward's papers that he was in correspondence with a number of them. It may be there was no co-ordinating organisation and that ritualism really was a movement. But the failure of W N Yates to mention Edward's role in the Royal Commission, the absence of a reference to Timberhill as a local church of significance in the movement, and the fact that he does not appear to have known about Edward's papers in the Norfolk Record Office, suggests the part Edward played may not be fully recognised.

Descendants in Holbeach

Edward's younger brother Ralph, also became ordained into the Church of England, serving for a long time as headmaster of Holbeach Grammar School. He went to Queen Elizabeth's Grammar School in Ipswich, following on to Corpus Christie College Cambridge in 1863, first as a pensioner and then, after matriculation, as a scholar. He was ordained deacon in 1869 at Norwich, becoming priest in the following year, after which he served as curate at St Stephen's Church in Norwich from 1869 to 1873. He then became curate of St Peter's Church in Croydon, Surrey between 1873 and 1877. It was at that point that he became headmaster at Holbeach Grammar School in Lincolnshire and remained there until 1891. Holbeach was only a little town and in 1881 there were only four boarders at the school so its overall number of pupils must have been quite small. At the Master's Lodge in that year there were three servants, a cook, housemaid, and nursemaid. After leaving Holbeach he became Curate at Soham in Cambridgeshire from 1894 to 1903 and then Rector of a small village called Mepal in Cambridgeshire from 1903 till 1920. He died in 1926 at Cambridge.

In 1875 Ralph married Annie Johnstone the daughter of Revd William Johnstone (1820-1901), who he must have met whilst serving in Croydon. At that time her father was Professor of Mathematics and Classics at the Military College, Addiscombe as well as being Chaplain there. Later he was vicar of Berden in Essex, from 1875 until 1891, when he retired to Worthing. Ralph and Annie had two daughters , Mary (b. 1878) and Phyllis (b. 1880), who in 1901 were both teachers at Newcastle High School.

PART 4

HISTORY AND *THE THREAD*

SECTION 1   THE RAM FAMILY, *THE THREAD*, AND IDENTITY

XIX
Putting *The Thread* to practical use

Now that the Ram story has been told the next part of the book uses the concept of *The Thread of Identity*, explained earlier in Part 2, to detect patterns in that story which throw light on the content of human identity. These are difficult to plot because identity is an extremely complex phenomena and there is an enormous amount of detailed and diverse information about the Ram family. This is why the facilitating framework of *The Thread* is required. In this section information about the Ram Family is collated together within *The Thread's* framework. Then in Section 2 (chapters XXIII, XXIV, and XXV) a picture of identity derived from this analysis is presented.

The Ram information is fitted into *The Thread* framework on the 'best fit principle' so before this is done it is important to explain the slots the information is to be fitted into. These comprise three areas, or influences, described on page 82, which together contain nineteen yardsticks. The general content of each influence with the yardsticks they contain is now outlined.

Influence 1 – general forces in society
Economic, demographic, customary, political, and legal frameworks – (yardsticks 1a to e) – shape much of the change that occurs in society. They operate within a recognisable overarching relationship that has existed for hundreds of years, certainly since the beginning of this book. In it the influence of the economy appears to be predominant, and the driving force. Customary, political, and legal frameworks are in many ways subordinate influences which feed off the energy for change that emerges from the economy, although each is capable of initiating independent force.

Influence 2 – how individuals and groups express themselves
This includes seven yardsticks. One is called *freedom of choice among the middling sort* (2a). Four others are called arbiters of choice, which affect the availability of choice for individuals and groups – *life chance, wealth, influence, and power* – (2b to e). Today one of the biggest conveyors of life chance, i.e., freedom to make the most of abilities and opportunities, is education, which is

easier to obtain if your family is relatively wealthy, and also if your inheritance includes a high IQ. In the past there was almost certainly less life chance, but it has always existed. In the Middle Ages one avenue to education and enriched life chance for poor boys was to become a priest. Potential life chance, wealth, influence, and power are all enhanced by the extent individuals and groups inherit wealth, power, and property. The term access is used in preference to ownership because there was a long period when the benefits of property were available without actual ownership. In early modern times most people below the elite did not own land or property outright, but rented it, by copyhold or freehold title. This was still common practice in the nineteenth century. The derived wealth came from using the property to run an enterprise and make money.

Two other yardsticks are included in this influence because they contribute to how people make choices. The first is *individual beliefs and values* (2f), e.g., the principles and values people live by, social attitudes, and ideas about individual worth. In the modern world there are many ways of expressing views on a plethora of subjects. But in the past this was not so true. Moreover few records have survived which document individual beliefs and values in the Ram family or those like them. But people do reveal beliefs and values indirectly through the way they relate to, and treat, other people. The most obvious sources of this kind of information as far as the Ram family is concerned are wills, and how family members conducted their lives. The second is *religious practice* (2g).

Influence 3 – how individual and group formation occurs

This is based on the yardstick called *family influences* (3a). The Minnesota study of twins in the USA of twenty to thirty years ago found that inheritance and peer influences were more important sources of enculturation than the immediate family. But inheritance was clearly seen to play a part and this comes through the family, as does early enculturation. So the family cannot be eliminated as a source of influence. In contemporary society peer influences are seen as very important, partly because there are so many of them, relative to the family. But in the past these were more limited because family groups mostly lived close together in small stable communities.

Six other yardsticks are also included which deal with the handling of social interaction. *Dealing With people through citizenship* (3b), including camaraderie and friendship. This covers relationships where formality predominates over intimacy. It takes into account interpersonal dynamics, such as appropriate levels of assertiveness and behaving in a normal way within the group to preserve a workable degree of cohesion and coherence. Citizenship has regard to other people, and respects democratic and egalitarian principles, including the protection of minority views. *Dealing with people through mirroring* (3c) in psychiatric language is the process whereby each member of a group reflects themselves to other group members and learns how to develop successfully by incorporating parts of other members into themselves. It is about bonding with others. All human experience, positive and negative is involved. If an individual has a safe enough personal space, trust of others is developed together with an expanded belief in diversity and the ability to go on learning. A sense of belonging is derived through these experiences. *Dealing with people through exchange* (3d) is a key element in social and group dynamics. It means sharing without losing, or put another way the process of mutual learning and benefit. Within social groups it happens all the time, for example, finding a partner, who one shares personal information with, and who can be trusted with material goods. The family is a classic example of a social group within which exchange occurs. Exchange can also happen between social groups, e.g., the exploitation of the many by the few, and is very uneven in its form. Some aspects of *dealing with people through the interaction of body and mind* (3e) have to be actually experienced to be real, like the knot in the stomach caused by anxious feelings or the atmosphere created when people walk out of meetings in anger. Such aspects of interaction are not usually available for historical study, but some elements included in this yardstick can be discerned in historical documents. *Dealing with people through the management of diversity* (3f) *and the need for coming together within the group* (3g). Diversity is caused for example by the differences in experiences which group members have, and the need for coming together can arise as a device to help survive emptiness, loneliness or confusion. It may take the form of shared spiritual seeking. These forces are often handled by the formation of pairings and subgroups. They are not easy to uncover in historic contexts or in family life, but it is possible to gain some insights indirectly through observing actions and choices made by people about individual religious beliefs, social attitudes, belief in individual worth and many other things.

XX

Influence 1 – general forces in society

Economic frameworks

Even in late medieval times at Great Waltham farmers were free to husband their land in their own way, with which presumably went the facility to develop economic opportunity – together with an active land market, that certainly existed. There was also a certain amount of industrial and craft activity alongside farming. How far individual freedoms, socially and economically, were more extensive in the sixteenth and seventeenth centuries than earlier is not easily discernible, because of lack of documentation. Many ideas and theories, discussed in Part 2, have been identified about this question.

The holding of economic position or power of course helped to shape identity. In the later middle ages the Ram family were certainly landholders, being important enough to be involved in property dealings. They were part of the 'middling sort' so much so that their more prosperous members were among those farmers who could operate on a profit making basis in early modern times. Such family members were relatively prosperous people, belonging among the upper yeomen, who were effectively small scale capitalists. This standing no doubt coloured the estimation they had of themselves, their social position, and the people they mixed with. The impression obtained from the overall data available in the sixteenth and seventeenth centuries is that the first half was a time of expansion in which numbers of families, including the Rams, did well, but that later on economic influences were not so favourable. Life seems to have been generally harder after 1630 than before, and by the mid eighteenth century part of the Ram family in Great Waltham, once the most prosperous part of it, disappeared after a long decline. Following this setback prosperity increased generally in the eighteenth and nineteenth centuries, in which much of the Ram family shared, although those who remained in farming lost out heavily during the agricultural depression of the mid nineteenth century.

Considerable developments occurred in the economy across the whole period covered by the book, which included the world's first industrial revolution.

There were great changes in agriculture during the seventeenth and eighteenth centuries that had a big impact on the farming members of the Ram family in Great Waltham. The national economy became both more diversified and increasingly specialised which caused some new occupations to emerge, whilst some old ones expanded or changed. Havering, being a small place on the edge of urban influences, illustrates particularly clearly the changes that occurred in the sixteenth and seventeenth centuries. It was near enough to London to be affected strongly by the great growth of that city. A number of land purchases were made by wealthy people from London to set themselves up in the country. Francis Ram was employed by such a family and mixed with many of them. He almost certainly aspired to become like them. Perhaps the 'urban yeoman' of Havering described by Margaret McIntosh, illustrates most clearly the changing times. Nicholas Cotton, one of Francis Ram's friends was such a person. Francis' nephew, William Ram was another, if on a lesser scale. Basically these people merged the traditional farming role, like that typical at Great Waltham, with systematic property dealing and money lending. Such people flourished in the kind of fluid environment prevailing in Havering. In many ways the urban yeoman became a new expression of the 'middling sort'. What happened in Havering also occurred more generally. There was a large amount of buying and selling of land in Essex as a whole during this period. Richard Rich, a major government official bought large amounts of land in the county in the mid sixteenth century, including Great Waltham.

One of the most profound results of economic change was probably the impact it had on work patterns between early modern times and the nineteenth century. The professions grew particularly rapidly in the half century before the civil war. Both Francis and William Ram, the first members of the family to break away from farming, benefited from this development through their occupational involvement with the law. This provided three main types of occupation. The bar where top flight barristers could earn very large incomes was the professional pinnacle, but becoming a barrister was a great gamble as only the top small group really earned big money. The 'mechanic' work was done by attorneys and increasingly a new breed of solicitors. The third branch was that of the clerks – the bureaucracy that staffed the courts. William Ram was more engaged in 'mechanic work' than Francis but both of them linked their legal work with more general administrative and executive responsibilities.

Most people of the middling sort in the seventeenth and eighteenth centuries were not interested in profit in the modern sense of annual profit. There was then a much greater emphasis on accumulation. Once a year, or perhaps more irregularly, assets were valued and liabilities were deducted leading to a new figure for 'stock' being arrived at. Actual profit levels are difficult to determine and levels of from 6 per cent to 30 per cent may have been achieved. The rate of accumulation that was possible for many suggests that most rich people began as rich people. Rich people got better marriage settlements, and the age of death influenced fortune accumulation to a significant extent. Investment was a good way of making money, as the returns could equal those of running a business and were more easily obtained. Merchants and professionals were among the occupations that were able to make significant investments because of a low need to have assets tied up in stock. Clearly with emphasis on investment as a way of increasing wealth those people who managed against the odds to reach the age of sixty or seventy had the opportunity to build up a much bigger capital than those who died younger.[1]

Increasingly though people made investments in different ways. The figures which follow are provided by Earle for London[2] so although scale would obviously have been less in places like Colchester and Havering, trends and patterns were probably similar. Through the late seventeenth century and into the mid eighteenth century loans, mortgages, government debt, company stocks and bonds became increasingly important as investment outlets. The losers were leases and shipping. Loans and leases tended to be favourites with those having smaller fortunes whilst the other possibilities became increasingly important among people having £5000 or more. The really wealthy still tended to acquire real estate even though the return on land (5 per cent) was much lower than, for example leasehold property, which gave a return of between 8 per cent and 13 per cent. About 20 per cent of real state investment was in farms, 30 per cent in larger country estates, but over 50 per cent was in London property and suburban villas. The Ram family must have been influenced by these developments in pursuing their entrepreneurial activity and making investments.

As the nineteenth century wore on most of the Rams were swept up into the urban development of London. The majority of the ex-farmers had to manage as best they could and seek opportunity where it came, as their skills were not easily transferred to an urban situation especially if they had no local helpful contacts there. A good number of them became poor. But the Rams were probably not among the poorest, and all of them must have come to London in the hope of a better future. For the middle class professional members of the family there was probably less change, although they still came to London to seek opportunity. James Ram went there from Colchester as a young lawyer from the branch of the family that gradually adapted to the modern world over three hundred years by combining interests in farming, being merchants and making property investments. James and some of his family did not stay in London, going back later to locations nearer their roots. It is likely nearly all the middle class moves in the nineteenth century were related to the search for professional jobs.

The force of the economic changes described here briefly were enormous. The Ram family was much affected by them, but slowly, except perhaps in the nineteenth century. The farmers among them carried on as they had always done, but their way of working changed. Other family members seized new opportunities and in the end finished up more prosperous.

Demographic frameworks

Across England these were much in line with the general economic peaks and troughs. Although disagreements exist about actual national population levels at particular times there is general understanding that the following pattern occurred. After a medieval peak there was a large fall in population at the time of the Black Death in the mid fourteenth century, followed by relative stability until the sixteenth century. Then, during Tudor and early Stuart times the population of England more or less doubled. There was a setback in the later seventeenth century during a period of declining harvests, which brought considerable difficulties to farmers. It is also possible that as a result of greater economic insecurity there was a rise in the age of marriage, or more people never married at all.[3] It is unlikely that the check in population growth was due to famine for there was sufficient social support to prevent this.[4] But there was an increase in mortality after 1625 compared with previous years which were particularly settled. There was no really serious mortality crisis in England from 1560 to 1624.[5] or between 1681 and 1726. The last major mortality crisis was between 1727 and 1741,[6] which was followed in the later eighteenth and nineteenth centuries by an unprecedented explosion in population.[7] There is a clear national profile of two growth peaks with a trough in between, something which is equally clear in the history of the Ram family.[8] In such a large population as England it is natural to assume that the aggregated pattern of general demographic change would not be reflected all that closely in individual families because of the uneven ways in which general developments happened. Some variation in the pattern of numerical change in different branches of the Ram family is indeed discernible, but the most noticeable feature is the extreme similarity to the general pattern, and this was in a very small family. This raises a question. Might what happened to the Ram family have been typical of many families? Perhaps families were affected in a more uniform way by demographic change than might be thought.

Customary frameworks

Life in the medieval rural environment can be thought to have been very circumscribed, but that would be a mistake. By the fourteenth century in Essex there was considerable economic freedom, which allowed people to live and shape their own individual lives. Although modernising tendencies affected Great Waltham as well as other places, it changed less quickly than some neighbouring parishes, like Terling, which was only seven or eight miles away.

At Great Waltham nearly all the business connected with the running of the village and parish was dealt with internally. The manor court oversaw its governance, handled disputes about hedging, encroachments, and other matters. It had to maintain the roads. It also had to deal with much law and order, as only the most serious offences went before the magistrates at the assize court. Although this system was in gradual general decline, particularly from Tudor times onwards, it was intact at Great Waltham throughout the early modern period. Participation in community life through the manor court and the church was important in forming the identity of individual people and the groups they were part of.

Social change happened gradually over more than one generation rather than by sudden leaps, so important threads of continuity in the way people lived, like family and social networks, helped to bind them together. This was the case even though modernising tendencies became more noticeable in the second half of the sixteenth century, which was a creative and outgoing period – a time when people seem to have felt freer to do new and different things. Some of the change was probably stimulated by the growth in population, which in and around London was very great. Between 1550 and 1600 London's population increased by 67 per cent, whilst between 1600 and 1650 it rose a further 88 per cent. The eastern suburbs grew most rapidly between 1560 and 1640.[9] Essex farmers fed London and its expansion affected all the areas in which the Ram family lived, especially at Havering the home of Francis Ram. The occupational diversity that developed among the Ram family at this time was almost certainly a reflection of what was going on generally.

A very important aspect about customs in early modern times was an increasing interest in privacy. Houses ceased to have one main living room with just one or two smaller ones, and housing standards developed appreciably. Today we tend to think about improved housing standards in terms of increased facilities, but then they had a major impact on the way people lived. A detailed study about private life makes this point in the context of upper class Tuscan people just before the Renaissance.[10] Customs became generally more civilising making life more refined, especially for the better off. Changes like these would have helped to increase the importance of personal and individual identity.

During the nineteenth century customary practice changed rapidly, and was possibly the only time when it happened so rapidly that people in one generation were highly conscious of it. The forces of economic and demographic change became so strong that the cohesion of traditional communities began to break down as people migrated to form entirely new communities in the great cities. Society became much more global. Some of the measures taken to cope with the change, like Poor Law reform, only partly succeeded, as local communities reacted against them.[11] The decline in the importance of small communities created fundamental change. Jose Harris termed these changes in culture and customs the nationalisation of culture, and considered that local forces, although not overwhelmed, became less dominant in the nineteenth century than previously.[12] She also thought 'The result was increasingly a society in which rootlessness was endemic and in which people felt themselves to be living in many different layers of historic time'.[13] The force of change was so powerful that the Ram family was wholly caught up in it, whereas in previous times some had adapted gradually to modernising urban life with the majority remaining in a traditional environment. The complete break of family involvement with the land during the nineteenth century registers the shift most powerfully. It was during this century that the lifestyle of the Ram family was transformed into being thoroughly urban.

There is no doubt these changes had an impact on the shape of identity. As they moved away from their agricultural and local roots the family lost most of their community involvements. They seem to have had little corporate public identity in London. The previous involvements as local officers and as contributors to public ventures appear to have ended. Life became much more private except within occupational spheres. Nevertheless, as some of them, usually the more prosperous ones, moved back again into a country environment a semblance of earlier social involvement reappeared. The degree of social upheaval involved in these changes cannot be exaggerated, particularly for those who became the poorer members of the family. Quite new styles of living came into being. But the impression gained from the story of ongoing family life is that this did not lead to rootlessness, or loss of family identity. What happened was that this came to be expressed in modified ways.

As the vast majority of the Ram family moved to London they become recognisably modern. But it is difficult to pinpoint exactly what the essence of this development was. As far as the Ram family is concerned the feature that most easily makes them appear modern is that the jobs they did and general patterns of employment increasingly became like they are today. This was a period when class came to be seen by writers and theorists in a new light, in which conflict figured prominently. But it is questionable, as noted elsewhere, whether awareness of class division played a greater part than it had previously in the Ram family.

Political frameworks
In the middle ages life was primarily run locally, partly because social, economic, and political affairs were relatively undeveloped. The vast bulk of the population were rural agriculturists. In the early sixteenth century national politics still only imposed itself on local life at moments of crisis, but by Tudor

times administration was becoming more complex. Even so, throughout early modern times administrative change happened mostly in gradual piecemeal ways, except perhaps for the introduction of the Elizabethan poor law. This was a root and branch move to deal with the social problems caused by the growing number of rootless people. Gradually, though, the need for more management and control led to the greater involvement of the wider world in the local, and as this happened local responsibilities and powers were eroded. David Eastwood stresses that the quarter sessions increasingly dominated local government in unreformed England. The Magistrate's Clerk effectively became the bureaucratic head of county administration, which focused as a whole around a number of active magistrates, the sheriffs, and the deputy and full County Lieutenants. Francis Ram was the Magistrate's Clerk for Essex for quite a long period, at a time when these developments were beginning to have a significant effect on the role of the magistrate. These factors combined increasing to make the manor courts redundant in the seventeenth century and particularly in the eighteenth century.[14]

It is apparent from the records and writing available about late medieval Great Waltham that there was a considerable amount of local autonomy. Landowners and principal tenants were mainly absentee, and in the fourteenth century Walthambury Manor reverted to the Crown. It is unclear whether the Steward, who chaired court meetings and presumably had some contact with the owners, had detailed instructions about how to conduct affairs. In any case he was dependent upon village volunteers for administration to be carried out. In early modern times new owners bought Walthambury Manor but they too were either absentee, or non participative in day-to-day village affairs. In this circumstance the local community took on much responsibility for its own governance, and it is this absence of an elite in practical local politics that raises interesting issues for our own time.

The running of local administration in early modern times was distinctively different from what happens now, when there is very little real autonomy among local communities. Although democracy as we think of it did not exist in early modern times positions of authority in the parish and membership of leading groups in the manor court were open to election and nomination from among the villagers. So there was a form of local democracy. It seems almost certain that the more established and senior families took a lead in running affairs, but this group was not a cabal for it probably included a third of adult men. It tended to be made up of three categories of people: the largest tenant landholders, people from families of long residence, or families which had several resident nuclear units. The three categories tended to overlap. The inclusion of the Ram family in this group was assisted by long residence and large presence, as it was not among the largest landholders.

Up to the eighteenth century local governance was heavily influenced by a tighter sense of community than now, probably much tighter, taking into account the fact that most lives were led almost completely locally. It must have been very difficult to live in any parish without being known. With this way of life went advantages and possibly disadvantages. It would have encouraged mutual support and shared decision making, but there would also have been lack of privacy together with a high level of public knowledge about one's business, public and private. There can, however, be little doubt that sweeping centralisation in the nineteenth century diminished the role of the small community in maintaining mutuality of relationships in the local environment. In large urban contexts social mutuality may even have ceased to exist. Administrative change may have been inevitable because the frameworks of the past simply could not cope with the development of large scale communities, but the methods adopted caused far reaching social change. Social support became depersonalised along the professionalised and bureaucratic lines we now have, instead of being run in the local community by and for people who all knew each other.

There were certain ironies in these developments, often unappreciated today. Whilst men of the middling sort increasingly became part of the formal political framework in the nineteenth century, as they acquired voting rights, many of them lost their long held role in the functioning of local community, either as a result of the diminution of local powers because of reform, or because they themselves left traditional communities to live and work in huge and depersonalised settings. Their political involvements may have declined in real terms.

Legal frameworks

By the fourteenth century the agricultural system of the middle ages was in decline, and in Essex may never have been applied universally. As the medieval framework evolved the landholding system began to be more individualistically based. Even so it is clear from the Essex manorial rental of 1328 that feudal tasks were allocated to people in Great Waltham. Gradually the practice of customary holding land turned into copyhold land tenure, which by the sixteenth century became virtually the same as freehold tenure. Although initially this development was an informal system in the local manor it progressively became formally enshrined in the law during the sixteenth and seventeenth centuries. This change was of great significance to the Ram family which held much of its land by copyhold. In practice the Rams who held land were basically free to run it, use it, and dispose of it as they wished, in entrepreneurial ways. As the seventeenth century progressed a variety of practical pressures brought about further changes in the way land was held. There was an increasing tendency for land owners to buy out the smaller free and copy holders so as to be able to lease their land in larger farms for fixed terms at commercial rents. In practice farmers who were not landowners came to hold land on a commercial contractual basis. All these changes were driven by practical needs and developments, not conceptual changes in the legal system, which took a long time to catch up. It was not until the nineteenth century that statutes were enacted which encouraged the voluntary extinguishing of copyhold, and the copyhold system was not legally abolished until 1925.[15]

Members of the Ram family involved in farming were mainly concerned with the law as it affected property transactions, either that which they held themselves or in relation to partnership ventures they were part of. Occasionally they were connected with the direct buying or selling of property. Family members who lived outside Great Waltham in Hornchurch, Colchester and Stuart London also held, and in some instances bought and sold property, so they would have used the law in making related transactions. All these associations with the law were as users, but Francis and William Ram, who were legal professionals, would have looked at the law in a less background way. They valued it as a source of income derived from a system they served professionally. This perspective probably affected Francis the most, who as a magistrate was an agent of law enforcement, but William would have been concerned with how the law affected the administration of Colchester and his other professional activity.

Even though some property was bought and sold directly by the family it likely that much of the property occupied by the Ram family was rented rather than owned, even late into the nineteenth century. This was particularly the case among the farming members of the family who held land for hundreds of years as renters. The tensions in this situation became more clear as the old copyhold system was changed into one based on leases. In early modern times land in Great Waltham was passed from one generation to another in quite a seamless way, and it could be sold for cash, but under the leasehold system such freedom disappeared, all without any changes to the legal system. The tenant farmers at Purleigh and Steeple in the nineteenth century were less secure as a result and were forced to form trusts in the effort to continue family farming businesses when older members of the family died, attempts which ultimately failed.

Another example of how the law related to the Ram family is provided by the way it affected property rights of women. The law emasculated the position of women in a twofold way. It forced them to transfer to husbands on marriage any capital they held and in bankruptcy situations all the resources of the family could be taken to meet debts. Because of these constraints steps were taken to work round the legal system to safeguard family interests. Various devices were used by the middling sort to protect women's interests across the centuries. Sometimes husbands left a lump sum which was used to pay an annuity. Sometimes sons who acquired the family home were required in their father's will to allow their mother the use of a room during her lifetime, or until she married again. The use of trusts and settlements was always common, but the way they worked changed over the years. In the eighteenth and nineteenth centuries the favourite method was the marriage settlement whereby money or property belonging to the bride's family passed to the husband who set it aside to provide for his wife if he died first. Sometimes these settlements passed on from one generation to another. The potential financial insecurity of women among middling families is apparent in the marriage contracts drawn up by members of the Colchester branch of the family in the eighteenth and nineteenth centuries. Some contracts could be more favourable to women than others, depending on their spirit of independence, attitudes of their husbands, and views held within wider families. Detailed examples of practice in the family are mentioned at various points in the text of the book.

In the nineteenth century women began to hold jobs and earn money in their own right, which opened the prospect of a more general legal independence from husbands. Many of the poorer single women had jobs in nineteenth century London. Middle class women in the family of Stephen Ram became teachers or nurses, quite often living an independant life away from home. Married women only worked in support of their husband's business, like the wife of James Ram who helped to run the domestic side of his cramming academy in London during the mid nineteenth century.

As far as the Ram family was concerned the interaction of their interests with legal frameworks stayed much the same throughout. The main point of contact was with processes for dealing with property transactions, except for those who were legal professionals. As the family's involvement in copyhold and freehold land tenure diminished in the eighteenth and nineteenth centuries, to be replaced by renting for a fixed term of years with no long term rights, their interest in legal or semi-legal arrangements became less significant. The law was always important to the Ram family but in a background way. It certainly acted as a constraint on the shaping of identity, but because the areas of the law that were important to the family only changed slowly, and in formal terms usually only reflected what had long been common practice, or upheld what was dying out as common practice, it never had a dramatic impact.

XXI

Influence 2 – how individuals and groups express themselves

Freedom of choice among the middling sort
In the middle ages and early modern times many landholders, who made up the vast majority of the population, had few alternatives to working their land where, or near where, they were born. People did move about but mostly within a relatively local area, as families acquired land by inheritance or purchase, or made marriages. There was less constraint on the landless than the landholders for they had less investment in a local place. There seems little doubt that during the period covered by this book the number of landless people increased considerably, and that many of them became either farm labourers or migrated to towns and cities on whatever terms they could. The smaller farms in Great Waltham, with less than about 20 acres, probably did little more than provide subsistence for the farmer and his family, except perhaps in good years. But the genuine yeomen among them were able to build up reserves of capital and land that increased security, purchasing power, and choice. This was probably true of Robert Ram in the later sixteenth century and his son Richard in the early seventeenth.

One of the striking impressions to have emerged from researching life in Great Waltham during early modern times is that whilst there were considerable limitations on people they were not without freedom of choice. In fact being a land holder, however small, required entrepreneurial choices to be made. Farming the land has always required decisions about what to plant, what animals to keep, and how best to exploit opportunity. Failure might mean the family would starve. Moreover all landholders, not just freeholders, were able to leave land and other property to family members when they died. The overall impact this had is dealt with more fully in the yardstick below on family influences, but there is much evidence from Ram family wills that considerable thought went into partitioning inheritances in ways that met family needs fairly, which were often very different from generation to generation. Choice in family affairs was complicated by the fact that families were not simply based in one parish. They often had interests in several.

In 1577 there were 137 tenancies in Great Waltham, of which just under half were 10 acres or more. All the people involved in running these, about half of the total male population, must have been entrepreneurs of a sort. It has been seen how there was an active land market in fifteenth century Great Waltham and that the Ram family was involved in it. Entrepreneurialism, or earning a living by running a commercial enterprise, grew in the sixteenth century. The most striking example of this in Great Waltham was the growth of the interests of the Everarde family, but although they became a dominant family they only exemplified to a high degree what was true for many who held a reasonable amount of land. In fact such activity may have been commoner in early modern times than in the modern period when most people are employed by others. It is worth assessing this difference in relation to freedom to make choices. We like to think we have much freedom of choice today, tending to think of people in early modern times as having less choice. In some respects, this is undoubtedly correct, for example in terms of what we do with our lives, and what we spend money on, but it may not be true in relation to how we earn our living. With so many more people being employed by others may it be that significantly more people have less real choice in their work than their predecessors in early modern times?

There are many examples of entrepreneurial decision making among the principal male members of the Ram family. Most of those who lived in London or Colchester had business concerns of some kind, quite often linked with farming and the sub letting of farms. Those who worked as farmers in Great Waltham, were also entrepreneurial. Running a business could not have been easy. Without doubt risk was involved in making the choices involved, which even if they were sound, could be destroyed in the most cruel way by early death, the weather, or economic uncertainty. Business failure was an ever present possibility. John Ram 5C was a notable Colchester bankrupt in 1796, one of the richest men in Colchester at the time, an event that clearly had a fundamental and negative impact on the fortunes of his immediate family. One of the remarkable things is that not more family bankruptcies are known of, but perhaps some were covered up. All these uncertainties, coupled with the absence of any form of 'limited liability', encouraged, and perhaps made inevitable, the practice of various kinds of partnership. This in itself involved choice about who to make partnerships with, which would have been determined partly by the potential of a group of individuals to work together in a 'group' identity.

Another striking impression to have emerged from researching life in Great Waltham during early modern times is the extent that many middling men exercised choice through the part they played in running Walthambury Manor and the related parish. Because administration in medieval and early modern life was so decentralised, and owners were quite often absentees or not involved actively in communities, there was a great deal of freedom for local people to run affairs. As members of the middling sort the Ram family was very active in parish life at Great Waltham. Thus they exercised responsibility and choice, along with a sizeable portion of fellow parishioners, in ways unknown to many middling people today.

The development of two new branches in the Ram family during the middle and late sixteenth century increased dramatically the range of choices open to some of the family. Francis Ram became a land agent in Havering, an enterprise which created opportunity for himself and his family, some of whom moved in an upwardly mobile way into the urban environment of London. The other branch was founded by William Ram, Francis' brother, whose career was based on his involvement in the law and the niche he carved out as a law administrator in Colchester and its environs. His descendants lived on in Colchester for over three hundred years as a family of clergy, merchants, and rentier farmers. The two brothers shared two special characteristics that made them different from their farming cousins; they were formally and professionally educated and they were firm followers of radical Protestantism. Both of them were also 'big individuals' being two of several examples in the family of how such people enhanced the range and quality of potential choice.

The original farming branch in Great Waltham is not to be seen as full of dullards, for this way of life also required choices to be made, perhaps of adaptation to new circumstances rather than of making new initiatives, but choice was involved nonetheless. A great transformation occurred in landholding practice during the eighteenth century which led to farming becoming a much more commercial activity. The changes required a large adjustment among the families involved. Moreover, in this situation some of them ceased to be farmers, because there was just not room for so many. One part of the Ram family in Great Waltham, the historically less prosperous part, adjusted positively and the other did not, for reasons that are obscure. These economic developments affected choice and identity to a significant extent, either by extending or limiting it, depending on the way people reacted to change. There were gains for those who survived as large tenant farmers because they were almost certainly better off financially than most of their predecessors.

The story of the Ram family and its experience across the centuries has highlighted that the making of choices is a complex matter. Change is not straightforward or necessarily progressive. There is a strong tendency today to assume there was always less choice in the past than there is today, but that is not necessarily the case. The types of choice available to the Ram family and others like them in the middle ages were different to ones commonly made today simply because the framework within which life was lived was very different, but that does not mean there was less choice.

There are two particular spheres where choice may have decreased. One, the reduced role played by the middling sort in community governance, has already been discussed. The other is that of work. In the nineteenth century modern administrative and business practice developed to support a huge growth in population and new urban communities. These included new kinds of job, like school teaching and nursing for the middle classes. It became possible for women to achieve independence through work and a number of the children and grandchildren of Stephen Ram obtained jobs as teachers and nurses. The search for jobs led to increased geographical mobility. Most of the moves away from London among middle class family members in the nineteenth century involved a search for jobs. There was also a richer range of self employment for poorer people. Several of the Ram women and children in London were self employed seamstresses. But overall the changes in employment almost certainly also involved a reduction in the level of entrepreneurialism among the middling sort.

It is impossible to be precise about the level of entrepreneurial activity, both in the past and at the present time, but what information is available for Great Waltham in late medieval and early modern times, especially in the Lay Subsidy of 1523-26 suggests around 75 per cent of the adult male population were in tax categories I-III, almost wholly farmers and craftsmen, with the remainder in category IV being labourers. If these figures are anything like accurate the level of entrepreneurial activity must have been very high for the working patterns of the first two occupational groups, which accounted for over 40 per cent of the population, were based on self employment. However a proportion of category III may have had work in which self employment and working for others was mixed together. It is equally difficult to obtain current figures about the number of entrepreneurs today, that is people who run their own businesses and are self employed. Several related statistical indices are prepared by The Office for National Statistics.[16] However they are all based on self selection from a range of employment possibilities. Whilst the self employed is a good indicator of entrepreneurial activity, it is especially difficult to tell how far chief executives of larger companies put themselves down as self employed or salaried! Even so the broad picture is relatively clear. The level of entrepreneurs in the working population is now almost certainly below 20 per cent, a significant reduction.

In association with these changes in employment patterns traditional levels of independence and freedom of choice would have declined. The Ram farmers of

Great Waltham illustrate this development very clearly. For hundreds of years they enjoyed great freedom running farming businesses but when they gave up farming and went to London this way of life for them disappeared. Most of them became painters, gardeners, and porters. The same thing happened to many other families across the centuries, but the point it brings home is the loss of independence associated with modern employment practices.

Life chance as an arbiter of choice
Perhaps one of most powerful examples of chance in the Ram family story is the fact that the name survived for so long. This is all the more remarkable when its smallness and the large numbers of deaths that occurred generally among children and young adults are taken into account. Appendix 2 shows just how small the family has always been.[17] In 1600 there were 28 male members of all ages alive, the highest number ever identified before 1900 when there were 39, whilst in 1700 there were only 13. Having a long standing family name adds to an individual's sense of identity and means something to people, especially when the majority lived in small closely knit communities. Even in traditional communities having such an identity was unusual, for a considerable proportion of other families in Great Waltham died out completely over a period of about two hundred years, or the family name was lost because the male line ended. The high status attached to possession of medieval 'yardlands' in Great Waltham and other villages around during early modern times, was at least in part due to reverence of old institutions, on which the Rams may have played to gain advantage and influence, sometimes consciously but perhaps also unconsciously.

The vagaries of health and disease continued to have a potent impact on people into quite recent times. Whilst the decimation Francis Ram's family by deaths in the early and middle years of the seventeenth century might be expected, similar examples still occurred into the nineteenth century even among the better off. John Ram (d. 1810) the rich merchant of Colchester had eight children between 1772 and 1787 and nearly all of them were dead by 1816, with a lot of them dying in early childhood. It was during the seventeenth and early eighteenth centuries that the family presence in Great Waltham was only kept alive by the survival of two singleton boys. Whether such ups and down in the family were the result of pure chance, or partly due to some more personal characteristics, or were brought on by general economic circumstances, will never be known.

Another factor which affected life chance was family background, particularly the level of education achieved. Although members of the Ram family and their like had moderate wealth, influence, and power inside the local community the only way they could break out into a wider sphere, unless they were very lucky, was through becoming educated. Most yeomen had a fairly basic education although there was a tendency to seek improvement from one generation to the next.[18] There is no evidence that family members who were farmers in Great Waltham were literate until the middle of the eighteenth century. But occasionally they had a better education. 'To have a son in the church or in medicine or the law raised the position of the family in the community and made available more land for the others who remained at home'.[19] Before going to university or Inns of Court it would have been necessary to go to the nearest grammar or a village dame school, or be taught by the vicar, or at home.[20]

There are only three known examples from Great Waltham of boys from farming families like the Rams going to university in Tudor and Stuart times, and only one of them stayed on to take a degree. Most is known about William Sorrell through the will of his stepfather Thomas Griggell alias Griggs or Criggs (d. 1576), a yeoman farmer. The 1577 survey of Great Waltham records Alice Criggs, presumably his widow, as holding 143 acres, so he must have been a substantial farmer. His will contains a detailed bequest of several tenements and land in Great Waltham to his wife and Thomas Sorrell, brother of William, on condition that they paid William an annuity of 40s for six years '...so that William do remain a student at the University of Cambridge during the six years'. He also left to William '£10 within 1 month after he shall commence Bachelor of Art'. William was admitted sizar, or someone who received a food allowance, aged 23 at Caius College in 1571, but there is no record that he stayed on to graduate. His school is given as Bury. Another member of the Sorell family, Robert, also matriculated, that is enrolled as a student, at Magdalene College in 1597, receiving his BA in 1600-1. The third example is William Ram, the eldest son of John Ram 1C who matriculated as a pensioner – an undergraduate who lived at his own expense – from Trinity Hall, Cambridge, at Easter 1551, so he went to university a number of years before the others. He did not stay on to take a degree. The only other boys who are known to have gone to university from Great Waltham during early modern times were all Everardes, from the most important family of local origin in the parish. At least five Everardes over three generations, starting with Anthony in 1575, matriculated from Cambridge and then went on to one of the Inns of Court. One member of the family, Hugh (mid 17C) took a degree from St Catherine's in 1654.

William Ram had two brothers, and all three must all have been more highly educated than was usual among farming families, as they each had a professional career. William was an attorney, who lived in an urban environment at Colchester. Francis was an estate manager, administrator, and magistrate, whilst Christopher bcame a Church of England clergyman. These men provide the first examples of a widening of life chance in the Ram family. It may have simply occurred because they were all very able, but the times were particularly propitious. There was more opportunity, partly because the economy was becoming more diversified, linked with a general increase in prosperity. There is widespread evidence of new people making money and achieving raised social status as a result. Such changes must have had an impact on perceptions about identity, particularly by helping to raise horizons, often involving the introduction of people to a wider range of professional and social contacts outside the immediate village community. Such contacts helped to widen the formation of identity away from the family and village communities. It is noticeable that the expansion of the Ram family in both Havering and Colchester took place around the development of new networks and through patronage.

Wealth as an arbiter of choice

It is extremely difficult to convert monetary values of the past into modern equivalents. This is partly because so many purchased items either change their worth or disappear over time, to be replaced by others. Another problem arises because the way wealth is understood changes across the generations. For example in the seventeenth century wealth and assets measured a person's status rather than their income, not now the case except for the very rich.[21] In the period 1660-1730 people with wealth of £300 to £600 upwards were liable to surtax. A capital sum of this size would be enough to lease a house, furnish it in style, and still have plenty left. Personal wealth of a few hundred pounds and an annual income of about £50 set the lower middle class limit. This was three to five times more than the ordinary working man had. A fortune of £10,000 put one in the ranks of the wealthy. Some had over £100,000 and were 'millionaires'. It has been noted earlier that a farm labourer at the beginning of the nineteenth century earned – very roughly – about £26 a year, which provides a wealth marker for later times.

Even allowing for the difficulty of making wealth comparisons it is clear none of the Ram family were among the rich elite, but in the sixteenth century Robert Ram of Great Waltham almost certainly had an annual income of more than £50 and Francis Ram of Havering must have had much more, although how much 'wealth' either of them had is not known. Throughout the story of the Ram family many of heads of nuclear family units were middling people who ranged from modest husbandmen to the fringe of being rich. They were middling in the sense that they were clearly not poor and apart from one or two individuals definitely not rich. This spread is far wider than some people define as middling, and there is discussion elsewhere in the book about what sort of people were 'middling'.[22]

Wealth in the Ram family came from farming, working as professionals in the Church or the law, or indeed from a combination of farming, running businesses and being property owners as in Colchester. The wealthiest member of the family was probably John Ram 5C of Colchester who went bankrupt in 1796 six years after he bought a very fine house in the town for £1000. Prior to his bankruptcy he was almost certainly one of the wealthiest men in Colchester. But the family grew wealthy out of running businesses rather than owning land or property, for the available evidence suggests they rented more than they owned, certainly those of them who were farmers. This meant that if they fell on hard times there was little they could do but leave their farm, which might make them homeless, for their house was probably part of the farm. Only a few member of the family are known to have owned their own homes, besides John of Colchester. Among them were one or two of Francis Ram's sons in early seventeenth century London or Havering. As late as 1870 the will of James Ram the lawyer did not state how the house he lived in at Ipswich should be disposed of, which implies he did not own it. Almost certainly the poorer ones paid rent – for they moved around a great deal and had no capital with which to fund purchases.

A snapshot of male members of the whole family in 1881 shows seventeen of them were of working age of whom seven were of solid middle class professional or farming status, three were poor working men, whilst seven were shopkeepers, engineers, clerks, or artisans. None however seem to have been without work. As it has not been possible to identify the number of labouring family members in earlier generations it is not known if the 1881 snapshot of wealth was typical of other times. The 1577 and 1805 surveys of Great Waltham, augmented by information from wills provides the following occupational picture of the family. In 1577 there were seven adult male family members, of whom four were farmers – two yeoman and two husbandmen – one was an attorney, one was an Anglican clergyman, and the other was an estate manager and local administrator. In 1805 there were five adult men of whom two were entrepreneurs – one originally on a large scale but latterly bankrupt – and three were farmers, two of them on a large scale. Two events stand out in the history of the family as having an adverse impact on wealth. One is the bankruptcy of John Ram 5C in Colchester, which had a long term effect on the prospects of his descendants. The other was the break from the land in the nineteenth century by the farmers from around Great Waltham. It seems that their skills as agriculturalists were not easily transferable and they lost their middling status. Benjamin IV's descendants were hit particularly hard.

When a family member became noticeably wealthy there was a tendency for the status generated by this success to be retained for several generations, although on a diminishing scale. It seems that several generations were able to benefit from the achievements of an unusually successful person. With wealth goes the desire to conserve and protect what is held.

Influence as an arbiter of choice

A variety of records show the Ram family were influential members of the community in Great Waltham throughout its residence there. One factor that contributed to this was a significant overall land holding, but it was not by any means the only one. Two others counted as much, or even more. One was their numerical size – there were sometimes several separate nuclear family units living in and around the parish at the same time – and the other was its continuous presence in the area from 1327 to the 1880s. The fact that the family position was based on these three factors is a sign that influence and power were not necessarily solely derived from economic position, especially as the Rams were not among the most wealthy families in Great Waltham. The same phenomena occurred among a relatively small number of other families in their networks.

The sources of social standing in the community described here no doubt added to the family's sense of identity. They probably felt that certain standards were expected of them, particularly the main family members in each generation. It would also have given them confidence in a variety of ways: in the management of their affairs, in their assumption of leadership, and in belief in themselves. There would have been a practical impact on the quality of their marriages and other alliances they made. A further characteristic which stemmed from their social standing was the way they networked with others outside the family. It seems that this was a key part of the middling way of life, for many other families of similar status were involved. Such networks were a powerful way of exerting and gaining influence.

Francis Ram's relationship with Anthony Cooke and the network spawned by it provides one example. Once he had become employed by Anthony Cooke, and it is not known how this happened, his world expanded initially through the patronage of his employer. He must have been chosen as Deputy Steward of Havering on Anthony Cooke's nomination, and likewise took up the post of Clerk of the Peace for Essex when Anthony Cooke became *Custos Rotulorum* (keeper of the rolls) in 1572. No doubt from Anthony Cooke's point of view he was merely passing routine tasks into capable hands so that he was free to do other things. But for Francis this brought opportunities for economic and social enhancement together with potential for further patronage. Most probably he became an Essex magistrate through his work as Clerk of the Peace, as his general social background would not have enabled him to become part of the elite group of people who administered justice in Essex. Through his work as Deputy Steward he likewise would have come into contact with local gentry like the Greene, Wright and Atwood families, which led into social contacts and employment and marriage opportunities for members of his family.

Another example of the same period is the botany and gardening network that existed between Francis Ram, William Ram and John Gerard the botanist and botanical writer. The details have been discussed earlier and the point here is to draw out the fact that interest networks were not based entirely on economic self interest or marriage alliances. A recent book about the eighteenth century Lunar Society shows this club, for that is what it was, to have been of considerable importance and to have involved leading industrial and intellectual families like Watt, Wedgwood, Priestley, Galton, Darwin and Boulton. The 'Lunar' families socialised around interest in scientific and technological experiment but intermarriage does not seem to have occurred very much.[23] Nonetheless shared intellectual interests could become bound up with marriage as well as economic alliances. There is strong evidence that the botany circle linking Francis and William Ram and John Gerard included such relationships. John Gerard lived in Holborn where Francis Ram's wife came from, and where Francis lived at the time of his marriage. Gerard became gardener to William Cecil who was related by marriage to Francis Ram's employer, Anthony Cooke. William Ram and John Gerard had a botanical association based on Colchester that may have developed independently of Francis, but which could equally have been the product of introductions that came through Francis. Francis Ram's eldest son, another Francis, married into the branch of the Gerard family which lived at Harrow on the Hill. There are too many potential interconnections here to think that all these happenings were pure chance.

Such interconnections occur today but perhaps do not lead to the degree of patronage that happened here. If this story is typical, and there is no reason to suggest it is not, the general lesson is that networks among middling families in the sixteenth and seventeenth centuries were very similar to those detectable in the eighteenth century. The network that developed around Nicholas Ram, his parents, brothers, other families related by marriage, and their descendants provides an example from the later time. He was a farmer who lived on the outskirts of Colchester and belonged to the branch of the family which mixed agricultural interests with being merchants, and owning and sub-letting property of various kinds. The network he was part of linked people of various occupations in marriage, and probably business partnerships. In addition to farming the occupations involved were brewing and banking. It included four families in six intermarriages, and continued well into the nineteenth century. This story is told more fully elsewhere.[24]

The farming branch of the family provides examples of the same phenomena. In nineteenth century Steeple John 6B was a prosperous man who built up round him a large family and business network. In addition to running a very large farm he owned several properties and shops. When he died in 1835, aged sixty seven, he was at the centre of an agriculturally based network which included his eldest son aged twenty seven, John 7B, who was working a farm of over three hundred acres in nearby Purleigh, his nephew William 2, in his mid thirties, was working a slightly smaller farm at Roxwell, about twenty five miles away near to Great Waltham where John 6B was born, and two daughters married to farmers. His eldest daughter, Sarah, then aged thirty five, was the wife of John Chapman who ran a farm at Danbury which was about twelve miles away. Anne, another daughter was just over thirty and married to William Sewell who farmed at Latchingdon, a village mid way between Steeple and Purleigh.

The focus of this network without a doubt was securing and preserving the participants' interests in farming. This is made clear by John 6B's will. This established that his executors, Abigail, his second and unmarried daughter born in 1803, John Chapman, and his cousin William 2 of Roxwell, were to carry on his business in the form of a trust, at least until the existing leases expired, and that all his children should have access to the profits in the form of an annuity of £40. The trust was a defensive mechanism to safeguard the family financially. It must be remembered that whilst most of the farming members of the family at this time had large farms they were all tenants, and probably their main residences went with the tenancy. They actually owned very little property.

The Ram family has always formed, and been part of, networks, just as much in the sixteenth as in the nineteenth century, although they may not have taken exactly the same form. Such happenings over a long period of time cast doubts on the idea, sometimes expressed, that networkings of this kind are to be identified with the appearance of a modern middle class in the eighteenth century. The Rams used their networkings both defensively, to preserve interests already obtained, and as a vehicle for 'getting on'. Who you knew and how you got on with the people who mattered was of central importance in gaining influence, wealth and power, and safeguarding your own interests.

Power as an arbiter of choice

Power is sometimes difficult to differentiate from wealth and influence, two of the other arbiters of choice. But one of its distinguishing characteristics is occupancy of a formal position or office, and Great Waltham provides a clearer example of this happening than in any other local situations in which the Ram family was involved. If power is defined in terms of practical leadership enshrined by office holding then evidence suggests the powerful group in Great Waltham were almost certainly the middling local landholders and craftsmen, including the Ram family, but not the richer landowners. The recent detailed work of H R French on parish government in the seventeenth century comes to very similar conclusions, that parish government was controlled by the middling sort and that the yardstick for assessing eligibility to hold powerful positions and offices was annual worth or income.[25] In Great Waltham during early modern times the majority of farms were of middling size which encouraged power sharing among quite a large portion of village residents, who were mainly elected to their positions by fellow villagers. Such a way of working implies a sizeable portion of local males participated in choices which affected the running of their community. There is no evidence there was a highly defined and steep pyramid of power in Great Waltham at any time during the period covered by this study, although governance may have become more hierarchical in the eighteenth and nineteenth centuries.[26] It seems that those who ran parish government were chosen democratically from among their peers. Yet this was a society which today is considered undemocratic because there was no mass participation in representative elections.

Patronage is another way of exercising power, by exerting will over others or 'fixing things', although influence is also involved in this. Patronage was important right up to modern times in developing and preserving favourable networks and opportunities. Neither was it all top down for both junior and senior participants gave and received. The Rams went to farm in Purleigh and Steeple under the patronage of the predominant landowner in their Great Waltham home base, who also owned land in these two parishes, but he gained from the arrangement because he was assured of good and known tenants. Since there was no system of applying formally for jobs developing useful contacts was the only way of obtaining most openings. But by the nineteenth century the growing importance of formal qualifications for determining entry into the Church, and legal professions, which many of the middle class members of the Ram family chose for a career, together with other types of public employment, was weakening the influence of patronage.

Patronage was exercised in and through the networks the family belonged to. The interlocked relations between the Ram, Pearson, Bawtree, and Adye families in Colchester during the eighteenth and nineteenth centuries are a prime example. Susan, the wife of Stephen Ram – a London solicitor – was the daughter of an Anglican clergyman and related to other clergymen, who obtained most of her household servants from country places where they had livings. There was also a strong tendency among farmers for son to follow father in the same occupation, often on the same farm. The Ram farmers of Purleigh and Steeple used trusts which drew on other family members and neighbouring farmers as a way of managing affairs.

The status achieved by the Ram family in Great Waltham makes it clear that power in earlier times was not necessarily dependent on high social status or wealth. William Ram, the Colchester attorney, is an example of this from outside Great Waltham. He is the first member of the Ram family known to have been called a 'gent' – as early as 1577 in the Great Waltham survey, in various deeds, and in the *Colchester Book of the Poor*. This consists of annual lists of citizens who contributed to the support of the poor. But his father was a yeoman, and William had hardly any land. He was essentially a professional, and judging from his contributions to the Colchester poor rates from 1582-1589, not a particularly rich one. He paid one penny each year when the major figures, like the aldermen and bailiffs, almost always contributed four pence. Yet he was obviously respected enough to be called 'gent' by contemporaries, almost certainly because of his professional standing and his position as the Deputy Town Clerk of Colchester.

It is noticeable that the picture obtained about family involvement in power sharing at Great Waltham is not repeated in the larger places where they lived, in London and Colchester. Why this is the case is not entirely clear, but it is likely to have been connected with most family members becoming absorbed into London, where the opportunity to take part in community life, either by office holding or occupational influence was greatly reduced. When middle class family members lived in small towns, like Halesworth or Norwich, later in the nineteenth century echoes of previous involvements re-appeared, for the clergy and solicitors had a certain status in their communities. But in general terms family members almost certainly had less power and influence in the nineteenth century than before. They became more like the masses, even though more of the better off males had the right to vote by its end. A social factor which may have had a contributory impact on this was the way life became more privatised.

Individual beliefs and values

Mildred Campbell in her book on the yeoman farmer identifies a number of characteristics she believed were typical of that social group. Industry and thrift were important values in an insecure world but did not necessarily mean unremitting labour or meanness was predominant. It was certainly customary for them to recognise the poor in their wills during Tudor and early Stuart times.[27] She has a whole chapter on the 'Measure of the Man' in it describing the yeomen of the sixteenth and seventeenth centuries in the following terms. Life was still fairly rough and ready and there were local feuds. Yeomen exhibited quite a lot of independence, both locally to those above, and also in wider matters, e.g., petitions to central bodies on matters considered unjust.[28] Yeomen who sprang from the ancient freeholder group were very proud of their status, like the gentry.[29] She believed the more recently prosperous yeomen also wanted to pass on gains to children, and to establish them permanently. Passing on heirlooms was of great significance

– chests, beds, sheets, etc. Their general characteristic is '...that of a group of ambitious, aggressive, small capitalists, aware that they had not enough surplus to take great risks, mindful that the gain is often as much in the saving as in the spending, but determined to take advantage of every opportunity, whatever their origins, for increasing their profits'.[30]

The findings of Mildred Campbell are well reflected in the Ram family. Seeking opportunity is something that comes across quite strongly in the information that is available about them. However life was not always about ambition or self assertion. The wills of family members reveal the practical values people lived by in their daily lives along with the sort of relationships shared with others – through friendship patterns, working relationships and the sorts of voluntary networks people got involved in. At Great Waltham in the sixteenth century the family network obviously included other families in the village, as well as neighbouring villages. Some of these contacts were economically based whilst others were of a social character. One relationship, already discussed, started as a friendship which led to marriage bonds. It was between Robert Ram (d. 1576) and the family of Robert Marshe of Felsted, about five miles to the north of Great Waltham.[31] Other wider relationships also grew out of marriages. Robert Ram's wife Agnes was a member of the Childe family which like the Rams was long resident in Great Waltham. In the 1523 lay subsidy Robert's eldest son Thomas is described as being 'at Childes', which points to him serving some sort of apprenticeship with that family, that presumably came about through his parents' marriage. Commercial relations sometimes merged with neighbourliness. The contract agreed by Richard Aylett of Doddinghurst, a village not far from Great Waltham, and Richard Ram of Great Waltham in 1599 is a good illustration of this.[32] But, and most importantly, love within the family is apparent from a number of Ram wills. Most touchingly John Ram 3C left cupboards and tables to his grandchildren. The one he left to John, his grandson, he refers to as 'our little table' as though they used it together. Love is also apparent in the strong desire to provide for the next generation of the family. It is obvious from family wills in the sixteenth and seventeenth centuries that men who held a reasonable amount of land and had several sons went to considerable lengths to distribute it as fairly as possible. The major desire seems to have been to give each son enough land to provide a start in life which could be built on.

The only direct expression of beliefs in all the information available about the Ram family is in the preface to William Ram's book, *'Ram's Little Dodeon. A briefe Epitome of the new Herbal, or History of Plants'* where he confides he wrote the book so the poorer people could get access to the medical and other advice that was out of their reach in more expensive herbals. Both he and his brother Francis were influenced by radical Protestantism in Elizabethan times, and perhaps the social concern which underlay the writing of his book came from this source.

Numbers of family members showed themselves to be caring people, with concerns that are apparent through professional and work related circles, ones within their family, others in their local community, besides general friendship networks. One of the striking things about the family is the frequency with which this happens. Several examples have been written about in this text. Some of them were built around the more successful family members, but not exclusively so. The same kinds of circles are to be found among the poorer Ram relations who lived in nineteenth century London. All of them formed an essential framework which helped to forge identity, which was part social and part individual. The values involved are not the sort that could be described as moral or ethical, although there are these elements within them. They are rather unarticulated ways in which people establish social meaning. They often go unmentioned and undocumented, but that does not mean they are unimportant, and part of the intention here is to draw attention to their significance.

Religious practice

The evidence available suggests the Ram family by and large conformed to the religious practice of their day. The registers of baptism at all the places they lived show that members of the family were invariably baptised in the local parish church. Presumably this also happened before the registers began. Directly available information about religious views comes from the preambles of wills, which mainly show a perfunctory religious interest. The only one written before 1550 is that of Geoffrey Ram of High Easter, which dates from 1530, and he does no more than bequeath his soul to God and express a desire to be buried in the local churchyard. Between 1550 and 1650 there are twelve more wills. That of Thomas of 1556 is the only one to suggest Catholic sympathies. 'First I bequeath my soul to Almighty God and Lady St Mary and to all the holy company in heaven my body to be buried in the churchyard of Waltham aforesaid'. Most of them make no more than a formal deference to religious issues but have a Protestant orientation. A typical example from the sixteenth century is the will of Geoffrey Ram dating from 1584 where the preamble contains the following spiritual references. 'I bequeath my soul to almighty God my maker and redeemer'. Another illustration from 1611, the will of Thomas Ram, reads 'I bequeath my soul to Almighty God (and to Jesus Christ my Saviour) and my body to be buried in the churchyard of Much Waltham'. The words in brackets have been added, almost as an afterthought. Preambles of family wills gradually became progressively formal and brief, so much so that by the nineteenth century there was usually no religious reference of any kind. This reflected general practice.

The only exception to this stylised approach to religion is to be found in the family of John 1C. His will shows him to have been a radical Protestant and the preamble to his will is discussed in detail in chapter XIV.[33] His two sons, Francis and William, were similarly inclined. In Tudor and early Stuart times religious forces had a very strong impact on society at large. The lives of Francis and William Ram spanned this period, which revolved around the social and political developments that accompanied the growth of Protestantism in England, so it is difficult not to feel Protestant religion influenced them greatly. This probably happened in two ways – directly, through the beliefs they held and more indirectly through the opportunities related ways of life opened up for them. Francis and William were almost certainly the first members of the family to receive a good education, which their father, and possibly their mother, clearly valued. Support for the idea that there was a connection between education and Calvinism has come from recent work done by R D Smith on Colchester data. He found there was a close connection between literacy and Calvinistic belief. Between fifty and sixty percent of the people who had Calvinist inclined preambles in their wills signed them in the late sixteenth and early seventeenth centuries. As a whole there was a much higher level of will signing where testators were clearly Protestant than where they had traditional or neutral preambles.[34] This information lends support also to the understanding that there were inter-connections between a higher degree of literacy, firm Protestantism, and desire for personal achievement.

A succession of men in William Ram's family in Colchester became Church of England Clergy during this period, followed by another line of clergy in the nineteenth century in the same family branch. All together eleven of its members either became clergy, married clergy, or married into clerical families in the four hundred years between the late sixteenth and late nineteenth centuries. Why were there so many clergy in this one branch of the family when there were none in other branches? All of the associations with the clerical profession happened in late Tudor, early Stuart times, or in the nineteenth century, both periods of heightened interest in religion. Was the association borne of conviction or careerism? Either may have been possible, but certainly in the earlier period there is some evidence that this branch of the family were genuinely influenced by religious conviction, and the same may have been true later, though it is not so evident.

The only known association with non conformity is the baptism in 1837 of one member of the family at Ranelagh Presbyterian Church in Chelsea, London. Such staunch adherence of the family to the Church of England in itself says something about their beliefs and values. There is an assumption today that attachment to the Church of England would represent respectability, conformism, and links with the establishment. But there was of course no other Protestant Church to belong to until the seventeenth century. In the sixteenth century there was a strong tendency, against the background of the religious troubles that went on in mainland Europe with terrible results, to see supporting the national church as loyalty to the national community. Members of the family who became ordained clergy in the Church of England were part of the formal establishment, as was Francis Ram who held a state office.

The religious uncertainty of Tudor times turned into turmoil in the seventeenth century. The religious involvements of family members reveal clearly how individuals were caught up in this. William Ram's son Robert was rector at Copford for many years and had ten daughters of whom three married clerics. Elizabeth, his second eldest daughter, was nineteen when she married Israel Edwards in 1613. Her husband was vicar at East Mersea, near Colchester who could not have been a sympathiser of Parliament because he was removed in 1650, to be restored at the end of the Commonwealth in 1660.[35] In 1649 he made a sizeable purchase of land at Copford from his wife's brother John, where it is possible he and Elizabeth lived until he was restored to his East Mersea living, using the land as a source of livelihood. On the other hand Mary Ram a younger sister of Elizabeth married Nathaniel Carr at the age of twenty in 1617. He was a Parliamentary sympathiser who benefited from the clergy ejections of 1647. He moved to Ardleigh following the ejection of the existing incumbent in 1644, after being at Langenhoe since 1616. In 1655 he moved to Boxted, from where he himself was ejected by the Act of Uniformity in 1662.[36] He was a sympathiser to Presbyterian forms of Church government and Boxted had been a centre of radical Protestant causes for many years. Christopher Ram, a great uncle of his wife, had been vicar there in 1562. The third clerical marriage was of Sara, the youngest of Robert's daughters, to John Argor. He was born in Layer Breton, Essex, graduating from Queens College, Cambridge in 1623-24. He was Priest in Charge at Layer de la Haye from November 1632 until 1637. He then became Rector of Leigh, in 1639-40. He was part of the classis movement in Essex, signing the Essex testimony in 1648 and the Essex Watchmen's Watchword in February 1648-49, both of which were drawn up to support statements by London Clergy upholding Presbyterianism. He became Vicar of Braintree in 1657, a living to which he was presented by Robert, Earl of Warwick. He was ejected in 1662, but stayed on at Braintree as schoolmaster until the passing of the Five Mile Act, when he settled in Copford. Here he took out a license in 1672, being buried there in 1679.[37] Two of the three marriages of Robert Ram's daughters to clerics were clearly to men of Parliamentary and reform sympathies, but the other was to someone more traditional. Their stories show how divided families could be at that period. One wonders how the situation and the turmoils it produced were lived with, and also what would have happened to Robert Ram if he had been alive at this time.

XXII

Influence 3 – how individual and group formation occurs

Family influences

Historical studies of individual families are relatively new. Most work on non elite social groups has been based on statistical approaches, in which family reconstitution is used as part of wider demographic enquires about whole populations or communities. The earliest historical studies of the family focused on the aristocratic classes, which led to wider understandings about the family being overly based on information from one social strata. A brief review of this field of historical study has been made in chapter VI. Church and government institutions have been interested in the family as a unit from early times, mostly for the purpose of promoting their own interests in monitoring and controlling family life. Rosemary O'Day believes there has been tension between the way external agencies have viewed the household and how its members saw, and presumably still see, themselves. 'After all, the family was not simply a passive recipient of society's ideas, and it was within families that individuals defined themselves ... Families developed their own distinctive ethos which surrounded and influenced the development of individual identity'.[38]

How that process happened, and still happens, is not all that clear. It is only possible to glimpse at how people in Great Waltham lived their lives through the way general relationships were handled, often revealed in wills or other formal documents. Moreover, understanding the role of the family in forging identity is further complicated by lack of agreement that the family is central in forming individual identity, and it is certainly not the only influence. The recent study of twins in Minnesota, which is discussed elsewhere, shows that heredity and socialising from outside the family may play a more important part. If this is true today it is very likely it has always been the case. But without doubt the family plays an important part in forming identity during the early years of life. It probably had a bigger and more long lasting role in earlier times, when the influence of family was generally more potent than it is today, as the wider community was more or less confined to the small community in which the family lived.

The immediate concern here is how the family played a part in forging identity. Most of the discussion which follows is based on early modern times when wills were more detailed. However nothing has been found for later periods which suggests attitudes or practice changed, while there is no reason to think the characteristics of family life were very different in ancient times, for family structure as we know it dates from at least the Roman period.[39] Research across Europe shows the role of the family in forging identity is complex, for they have been organised in all sorts of ways to meet particular regional and local cultural requirements. The range of the variations discussed in Rosemary O'Day's book seems almost limitless. In the nineteenth century Frederick Le Play defined three basic family forms: *the patriarchal*, which was traditionalist and retained all the sons in a single household after marriage, *the stem*, which was similar although only one of the sons was selected as heir and the others were set up in separate households if married, and *la famille instable*, a form of household which was created on marriage and continued until the final death of the spouses when any inheritance was divided up.[40] The history of the Ram family in Great Waltham during the period from the early fourteenth century onwards does not fit neatly into any of these categories, which is also true for the families they mixed with.

Two things are quite clear about the Ram family. The linear nuclear family, that is one in which the husband, young children, and spouse, live in a house on their own, was the basic building block. This functioned on the 'lineage principle', where property was conserved, built up, passed on, and sometimes dissipated, from generation to generation, but in a variety of ways according to needs and fortunes of the family at any one time. The second thing that manifests itself forcefully is that inheritance around the nuclear family was designed to safeguard the future of all the family members, and was for their benefit. It served the family, so was not an institutional imposition. Rosemary O'Day writes that the lineage principle…'certainly pertained to property but it also governed family feeling, responsibility and relationships in a way that historians have not recognised'.[41]

There is a need now to extract from the Ram history, mainly with the aid of wills, how family life worked, particularly in regard to the ways it helped to develop a sense of identity. There is a very fine series of wills for Robert Ram's immediate family from his own death in 1576 until 1726. Indirectly these give important information about family values. They also set out in detail how land is to be distributed among heirs, particularly during the earlier years. This was because of the importance attached to sharing out the overall inheritance fairly. If there were no sons it was left to other relatives, sometimes including women, or it was sold and the proceeds distributed. Usually children benefited but other relatives could be included. These practices of themselves say a lot about identity, because they show how important land and its distribution was to the middling farmers at this period. There was less incentive for those who held land to move than people who were landless or held only a very small amount. It was through the land that the family sustained its basic identity and livelihood. The amount of detail in wills about the inheritance of land declines in the later eighteenth century, perhaps because the traditional copyhold system, in which land and property was left to heirs as though it was owned, had largely been superseded by the direct leasing of land from the landowners. The making of a will and what flowed from it had a powerful impact on the family group, and people's wills showed how they were both moulded by and also shaped family aims. The expression of fairness is a striking feature of many of the wills that involved passing on land and property. How Richard Ram provided for his five sons is a good example of this.[42] People also showed love for children and grandchildren, and a concern to provide for heirs in transparent ways. When Agnes Ram came to prepare her will in about 1581 she was very careful to involve all the key family members. Her son and a member of her own family were made executors, whilst her brother was made overseer.[43]

Although wills are very informative a note of caution has to be made about the extent they contain a total overview of inheritance. Rosemary O'Day states they were often only an adjunct to common law provision for wives, children and direct descendants. For example where there had been no marriage settlement containing a jointure, the widow would be entitled to a third of her husband's freehold lands during her life. Neither was it necessary to mention in wills property and goods that had been devised to other relatives before the death of the owner, or the existence of such an arrangement.[44] In medieval times the custom of widow's free bench was observed in Great Waltham, whereby a widow kept all her husband's land for her lifetime, but such practice had generally died out by early modern times, although widows sometimes kept some of their husband's land for their lifetime. As far as the Ram family wills at Great Waltham are concerned it is likely most of them cover all the property there was, for there are only one or two cases where it is obvious the will gives an incomplete picture. For example, in Robert Ram's will of 1576 Thomas, almost certainly the eldest or an older son, is not given any land, but he is described as a yeoman in his own will so he must have come by land other than through his father's will. Thomas lived outside Great Waltham at the time of his father's death and most likely obtained his land before that event. The fact that Thomas is made one of two overseers of his father's will shows his relatively small inheritance was not due to a broken relationship. How widows were provided for is not always clear. Sometimes quite precise directions are given, often by leaving a widow land with presumably a cottage, during her lifetime, or making sons responsible for looking after their mothers while they live. Sometimes it is possible to detect an arrangement that is never formally specified. When Joseph Ram died unmarried in 1614 at the young age of 20 or 21 he made a will that left all his land to his mother Dorris for her lifetime and then to his eldest brother John after her death.

Dorris was a widow at this time and her husband's will made no reference to her maintenance apart from receiving all the residual goods and chattels, so Joseph's bequest served to safeguard her economic situation in the later years of her life. She may have been living with Joseph when he died. In general terms What is clear from the wills as a whole is that they sought to meet particular family needs prevailing at the time they were written.

The immediate nuclear family was not the only point of focus in wills. There is some evidence that land and property was occasionally left to cousins. Circumstantial needs were the governing principle. Sharp distinctions are often drawn between family life in North West Europe, where the nuclear family was the norm, and Southern Europe, where more than one family unit might live in the same house. In Great Waltham in the late sixteenth and early seventeenth centuries there were often several nuclear families within the wider Ram family. The largest number seems to have existed around 1610 when at least eight can be identified. Although these nuclear families lived in separate houses, it could be asked what the difference is between a number of nuclear families all living close together and several nuclear families living in one house.

Little is known about the inter-relationships that occurred among family units all living close together, and it is doubtful whether it will ever be possible to document relationships. Common sense suggests there must have been social and other kinds of sharing, mixing, and support. There is the possibility that economic enterprise went on among them. The large numerical presence of the Ram family was not unique in Great Waltham, for in 1577 there were thirteen families with two or more resident individuals having separate land holdings, each of whom probably had families. The size of the Ram presence locally was even bigger if family members living in neighbouring villages are taken into account, which was equally true of some other families. For example John Ram I who lived at Brades Green in Great Waltham died at Nevendon in 1588, about fifteen miles away. He had a kinsman, Geoffrey Ram, who farmed there and died in 1584 with a family of young children. It is possible that John I had gone to help that family out and died there.

Even though the role of women in the family is difficult to discern enough information is available to build up a reasonable picture. When the elderly John Ram 1C died as a widower in 1568 he lived with his married daughter, so she was carrying out what we would call a caring role. Some women, especially during Tudor times left wills as widows, and in these it is possible to glimpse their attitudes and social standing. In their wills they appointed executors and overseers, just like the men. Usually the contents were more domestic than those of the men, often featuring personal bequests of goods and money to family members, although that was not always the case. In 1592 Rose, the widow of

John Ram 1B, was clearly active in husbandry for she left her animals, each one identified clearly, to different family members. Sometimes women took on more independent roles. Sabyan Ram was a widow in the middle part of the sixteenth century, who in 1563 personally held a sizeable holding of half a yard of freehold land. At a later date she lived in a cottage with a garden in the middle of Great Waltham village for which she paid 3d rent. The 1577 survey says she has this cottage 'for the term of her life' and that it shall then go to her daughter Margaret. Here is an example of independent retirement in the sixteenth century. Nearly all the women who held property in their own right were widows or unmarried. What is clear from family records is that women came into their own when special needs arose at any time, when they were clearly capable of taking over roles normally held by men. There are examples of women taking charge of farms if they were widowed or had sons who were minors when their husband died. It has been seen earlier how Agnes Ram took over her husband Robert's farm when he died in 1576 because Richard their son was a minor. Agnes and Richard initially held what had been Robert's holding in joint names. Agnes had the extremely valuable role of bringing Richard into his inheritance. The same phenomenon is to be found in nineteenth century Purleigh. When John 7B died at the age of forty six in 1852, his wife Mary is charged in his will to administer a trust set up to run his farming business at the height of the mid nineteenth century agricultural depression. She also had nine children to look after, six of whom were fifteen or under when he died. There is really very little difference in these situations between the role women play in sixteenth century Great Waltham and in nineteenth century Purleigh.

In the late Tudor and early Stuart period there are signs for the first time of individuals, including women, granting, purchasing, and selling property in their own right, particularly among family members who lived in or near London. The maternal grandmother of William Ram (d. 1612), a son of Francis Ram 1, left money to his widow and two young boys in her will of 1639, and also copyhold land which was to be held in trust for them until they reached the age of 21. When Edward Ram died in 1617, one of Francis 1's sons who lived in London, died at the age of 27 he left a house in Clapham, plus money, to his wife Joan, so she had property of her own to dispose of. William Ram, one of the children who was left land in 1639 by his grandmother, himself left houses, land, and buildings to his two daughters in 1712. There is one example of a woman leaving property in Colchester although not until the middle of the eighteenth century. Bridget, a sister of Nicholas Ram married someone called Warren and probably acquired some land through him. She died in 1747, apparently with no heirs, leaving a small farm to her nephew John Ram 5C.

Five men in the family are known to have had grandchildren during early modern times; Geoffrey Ram (d. 1530), John Ram IC, Robert Ram (d. 1576), Richard

Ram (d. 1611), and John Ram 3B. As life spans gradually increased more people lived long enough to know their grandchildren, who were mostly left small sums of money, bedding or items of furniture, sometimes to be given to them when they reached a specified age – usually eighteen, twenty one or twenty four. On a few occasions they were given animals – a sheep or a cow. Mostly no great sentiment is revealed, although mention has been made to the touching way gifts of furniture were left to his grandchildren by John Ram 3B. What is clear is that grandchildren were viewed as important members of the family network.

Something rather difficult for us to appreciate today is the degree that family life was closely knit in earlier times. It is evident from the preceding paragraphs that when death came to the leading family members, providing for spouses, children and grandchildren were their main considerations. Ongoing loving concern for children is shown in wills by the careful way land, property, and chattels were apportioned. This was not always manifested in the same way. In the sixteenth century they tended to get cash, feather beds or pewter plates whilst in the eighteenth centuries they got legacies or small incomes. Such care would have been strengthened by a number of factors that worked to hold families together. Until quite recent times mothers were often pregnant, children of varying ages were ever present, people died much younger in unpredictable circumstances, and family members lived much more on top of each other than they do today, both within individual households and among related nuclear family units. Communal sleeping was common in rural areas of England until the late seventeenth century.[45] Older children must often have been surrogate parents.[46] It was normal for farmers' sons to be drawn into the family enterprise as workers. This had two aspects. It helped to provide labour, but it also offered a sort of apprenticeship for the time when they would be farming in their own right.[47]

There are a few references to servants in Ram family households. Robert Ram had three when he died in 1576, one of whom was left ten shillings, twice as much as most of his grandchildren got. Whether all, or some of these were farm servants, who often stayed short times with individual farms, or personal servants is not clear. The latter were not simply employees in the sixteenth century, having a dependent relationship rather than a job, so they were effectively part of the family, which must have had an impact on family life. Servants may have been social equals or even family members.[48] The will of Francis Ram of Havering in 1617 says that a daughter of his nephew Robert of Colchester had once been a servant in his household.

The concern here is to bring out how family life affected identity, so what do the reflections made on family life contribute to this? In the kind of way children grew up in the world described in early modern times the family cannot but have influenced identity. For boys destined to become farmers, or girls who were to become farmers' wives the family provided their introduction to their world and their role. The growing up, the preparation, and the succession were almost seamless. But what sort of identity would the family in this cultural situation have helped to forge? It is likely influences pushed in two, somewhat contradictory directions. They no doubt acted as a force to uphold tradition and conformism, since the continuation of the family fortune depended on it. But, particularly in an age when education was limited, in which families were large and lived close together, they would also have provided a source of beliefs and ideas. The yardstick on individual ideas shows that the social group to which the Rams belonged was independent minded and assertive of its own interests. No doubt children picked up what people outside the family thought about all sorts of matters, but views expressed within their families must have been a significant influence. Children would have grown up hearing over and over again what the members of the family thought about various subjects.

Although the detailed circumstances and contexts vary, it is noticeable that the basic framework of family life continues unchanged, whether the scene is Great Waltham, Hornchurch, Colchester, or London. Some of Francis Ram's children were the first members of the family to transfer to an urban way of living in London but links were clearly retained with parents back in Hornchurch. No doubt it was a place of safety from the unhealthiness of London, and it was certainly a refuge in times of crisis. Elizabeth Ram, the only child of Edward died in Hornchurch in 1618 aged two, one year after her father died in London. One of the family who lived in Hornchurch must have been caring for Elizabeth, but it was not her grandparents for they were both dead by 1618. A rather similar, but even more tragic, circumstance is associated with the death in Hornchurch in 1625 of Francis aged five. He was the only surviving child of Benjamin Ram, who, along with his wife and another child all died of the Plague in London in 1623. As with baby Elizabeth care was provided for Francis within the extended family network. So, the nuclear family unit was set in a wider and extended network.

Once the family became divorced from the land the tradition of sons following fathers as farmers obviously ended. Sons had to find their own way, with or without the help of their fathers. It is very obvious that Francis Ram furthered his sons' interests through his own networks. It is not so obvious in Colchester but it almost certainly happened there too. There is evidence that Francis Ram's children who lived and worked in London were part of networks, often based on city churches, which mirrored the networks they sprang from in Havering. This involved the Ram, Greene, and Wright families. Effectively the networks that originated in Havering were extended into the London environment through the next generation. Similar spontaneous connections occurred among young family members who went to London in the nineteenth century. If this happened widely among families, and there no reason to believe it did not, it is a further indication of the importance of family in strengthening individual and community bonds.

One of the things that studying the Ram family over such a long time span has revealed is just how important various kinds of network have been in supporting, developing, and shaping the identity of individual and family life, certainly from the early sixteenth century. As has been seen at various points in the Ram story formative influences tended to develop around common interests, which could be work related or socially inspired. Networks included a mixture of family and wider social contacts, in which several different interests could be intertwined. It is possible that chance social meetings, reinforced by mutual attraction, were sometimes the originating sparks. An important question arises. Such networks are known to have existed among the elite, but partly because other social groups are less studied it is not clear how far they have been common in society at large. Some writers, like Leonora Davidoff and Catherine Hall, who have specialised in middle class eighteenth century families, stress the interest networks which characterised the time.[49] The impression is sometimes conveyed that these were a special feature of modern middle class entrepreneurial society, but the history of the Ram family shows conclusively they existed among the middling sort from at least early modern times.

In the late eighteenth and nineteenth centuries networks became loosened because community life was increasingly less locally focused. Although there was significant geographical scattering of the Ram family at that time family connections and identity with it were still retained. In some ways what happened in the nineteenth century is comparable with, though on a larger scale, the experiences of Francis Ram's family in Stuart times. If these happenings are at all typical the popular understanding that there has been much family breakdown in modern times because of dispersal is effectively questioned. The experiences of the Ram family affirms that the nature of family association changed rather than broke down. The paragraphs which follow on coming together in the group show how tenacious is the maintenance of traditional identities.[50]

Concern about property has always been of fundamental importance in helping to shape identity in the Ram family, and a story from Colchester covering the years from the mid eighteenth to the late nineteenth century illustrates this strikingly. It is about the importance in the family of a small farm of about fifty acres. The history of Stoke or Ram's Farm at Stoke by Nayland has already been told in detail.[51] The point that is important here is the enormous effort that was made to share rights in the farm as fairly as possible among the family, especially as the total rental value was only about £40. Admittedly when it formed part of a marriage settlement for James and his wife in 1826 it was of some worth, as it was when other spouses benefited from it in a similar way. But it has to be asked if the farm seemed more important to them than it really was. No other of their properties acquired the same importance, so did sentiment play a part, as the farm had originally become associated with the family in the seventeenth century. But the interest in it was more than nostalgic for all the rights of different family members were meticulously documented in deeds and wills. Perhaps it was thought to be a sort of security against hard times. It was not sold until after James died in 1870, getting on for a hundred years after his branch of the family had anything to do with farming. There do not appear to have been family divisions over the farm. Indeed it could be seen to have been something which helped to keep them together. Was their careful sharing of it a reflection of the importance they attached to proprietary property rights? The practice followed strongly resembled the inheritance customs of their farming forebears in Great Waltham – in which equal sharing rather than the primogeniture practices followed by the gentry was common. What does emerge without doubt from their attitude to the farm is their pride in property and the status it conveyed.

Dealing with people through citizenship

According to Mildred Campbell neighbourliness was strong in yeoman society, being grounded in hard-headedness, arbitrating in quarrels and participation in other local issues.[52] The spirit of good fellowship which neighbourliness bred permeated and helped to shape the most colourful and attractive features of social relationships. It pervaded the atmosphere of community gatherings'.[53] Neighbourliness offered opportunity to show the finest traits of character. 'A man could, and would, be forgiven much if he were known to be a good neighbour'.[54] The ways individuals deal with others, within and outside the family, forms an important constituent of identity. The story that emerges from this study of the Ram family in Great Waltham shows them able to influence their local community, through their general social position and the part they played in the running of the parish over a long period of time. It would seem likely that families like the Rams helped to sustain stability and traditional values, which were possibly, though not necessarily, conservative ones.

Although the Ram family made an important contribution to citizenship in Great Waltham, there is little evidence, apart from Francis Ram's involvement in sixteenth century Havering together with his role in the Essex magistracy, that this happened in other places where they lived. Their life in Colchester and London seems to have been more individualistic and private. Admittedly William Ram was Deputy Town Clerk of Colchester in the late sixteenth century, but his contribution was in the nature of professional work rather than public service. The only known references to public service as such in these two places are John Ram 4C's membership of Colchester's Common Council and the involvement of the richest of the Rams there, John 5C, as a member of the vestry at St Leonard's Church. Some sources suggest this pattern was not typical and that contributions to community life in urban areas were not very different to those at Great Waltham. It seems that in Elizabethan and Stuart Colchester numbers of people held offices, who were drawn from across the social spectrum. There was though a relationship between level of office held and status, with the wealthier tending to hold the more senior positions.[55] Peter Earle believes parish life was quite strong in late seventeenth century London. It was in fact much like that in villages. Better off people lived side by side with poorer ones. The vestry was open to all householders with about a quarter of them attending. Status was not accorded to individuals on the basis of wealth alone, e.g., the wealthy did not monopolise the best seats in church. Special recognition was given to people who were active in parish life regardless of their income. Lengthy residence was also needed to get a good seat, at least at All Hallows in Bread Street. So church seating plans reflected a sort of social hierarchy, which was based on a number of factors.[56] This pattern is not unlike the one that prevailed at Great Waltham.

The information about Ram family roles as good citizens raises an important issue. Why was their contribution in rural Great Waltham and Havering so much greater than in urban contexts? Was it simply a reflection of a general trend, especially from the later eighteenth century onwards, or was it peculiar to the family? This impression is possibly a false one for the Ram contributions may be better documented at Great Waltham and Havering than in London and Colchester. However, so little information has come to light about urban office holding by family members that it seems it really was at a much lower level in these places and in later times. Recently H R French has made an extremely detailed study of how local English communities were run in the seventeenth and early eighteenth centuries. He has examined three areas of England in Lancashire, Dorset and Essex. In broad terms his findings are very similar to those of this study. He found many local communities at that time were run by the local inhabitants, who were elected to various offices, much as in Great Waltham. In many of them the majority of people elected were what are often described as the 'best men' or 'chief inhabitants', although this group were not all that narrowly confined, certainly not just to the most wealthy. The 'chief inhabitants' were not generally self appointing cliques but selected because they were fit for office.[57] H R French has also provided some evidence that the pattern of public contribution found in the Ram family was not simply peculiar to that family. He has found that a bigger proportion of community members were office holders in smaller communities than larger ones. In Lyme Regis, quite a small town with a population of around 1300 in the late seventeenth century, but one of the largest in the area of Dorset he studied, had a 'much more extended (and unequal) social hierarchy' than other smaller parishes around it.[58]

The findings of H R French at Lyme Regis differ from Peter Earle's conclusions about community life in London at roughly the same period. What is not clear in either instance is the extent that there is a natural tendency in larger communities for local government to be less mutual. Perhaps there is an optimum community size beyond which levels of involvement naturally diminish. More will be said about this in Part 5. It does seem inevitable however that gradual centralisation of government followed by the reforms of the nineteenth century almost certainly had an important influence on a lessening of mutuality. The whole process resulted in the decay of the local autonomy that existed in earlier times. In the early sixteenth century Great Waltham had been a virtually self governing community, in which local people, especially the middling sort, played a key role. This autonomy was gradually eroded from the sixteenth century onwards by the growth of county administrative authority, and then in the 1830s the old system of local government was swept away.

The diminution of the Ram family involvements in public life is one of the most interesting findings to emerge from their story. If the proportion of the middling sort involved in office holding declined generally from the eighteenth century onwards it represents a really significant shift in the pattern of social participation. Most of the male Rams and their social equivalents all over the country first got a national democratic vote during the nineteenth century. We tend to think of this as an extension of democracy, but was it if at the same time real involvement in the democratic process was in marked decline? Perhaps proportionally more, or many more, people were actually involved in practical democratic structures in Elizabethan and Stuart times than was the case later, and certainly today. It is arguable that there was a decline in political involvements among ordinary people, as evidenced by the Ram family and their equivalents in both rural and urban situations. But much wider investigation of many local situations is required to see how far the experiences of the Ram family were typical.

Today we see citizenship as being public spirited, getting involved in good causes which interest us, taking a part in voluntary activities and voting in local and national elections, rather than holding elected public office. Indeed, as government has become increasingly centralised in the last two centuries there has been a drift towards elected office holding becoming professionalised. There is obviously unease about modern developments because public governance is perceived to be getting more remote from daily life, which government and other political authorities are much concerned about. One of the things that this study shows is how much citizenship has been affected by the decline of the small self sufficient local community. Whilst at national level in early modern times there was little involvement outside elites this was not so true in local contexts. it is ironic that we see our society as more democratic than in the past whereas in practical terms it may be less so, certainly as far as the middling sort are concerned.

Dealing with people through mirroring

Examples of the practice of mirroring, that is seeking personal assurance by bonding with others, can be found regularly in the family material. The part played by bonding in sustaining farming within the Ram family and other Great Waltham families from generation to generation is obvious. The break with the farming bond which happened in the lifetime of Benjamin 4 involved severe loss of image, status and income, so it is safe to assume it only happened under considerable pressure of some kind. Bonding of another type also occurred in the family of Francis Ram in late sixteenth and early seventeenth century Havering. One is aware of Francis seeking, through promoting the life interests of his children, to attain the kind of status and identity enjoyed by associates and working colleagues in the Greene, Wright, Cotton, and Atwood families. This kind of mirroring was rather different to that which went on in Great Waltham for it was governed by a desire to achieve new and raised social identities rather than to perpetuate existing ones. The mirroring exhibited by family members in Colchester and London was more akin to that found in Havering than Great Waltham.

In earlier times neighbourliness was, in a way, a mirroring process, for it involved developing self through others, and in this process identity was found and passed on. Neighbourliness still plays its part today, but the peer group at school and at work may have become more important as an aid to mirroring with the decline of local community.

Dealing with people through exchange

Exchange, i.e., giving and taking in social and work related life in ways which preserve individual identity, was something many of the male family members were required to be adept at because they had to establish a position and then to work at retaining it. A number of writers about the middling sort see this as an important feature of being 'middling'. This can be illustrated in a touching way through the correspondence quoted elsewhere between Nicholas Ram and the Ward family, from which he rented land. A very long term relationship lasted between them for over fifty years, that clearly included personal friendship. It contained some mutuality, but always within the boundaries created by their business relationship, in which Nicholas was the dependent partner.[59] At times exchange could be bound up with mirroring because what one person sought from another involved modelling themselves on others.

The complexity of family life and local landholding networks, meant exchange was important in all sorts of ways. Many of the middling sort held land in neighbouring villages as well as their main centre, with sub letting being quite widespread. Much land changed hands over the years, in which there must have been considerable economic and social calculation. The handling of all these situations would have required the possession of significant skills in dealing with people, and managing diversity. Most men had some land so its management was a dominant preoccupation for many. In this kind of world lots of people behaved as entrepreneurs, which too required skills in exercising exchange.

Exchange presupposes there exists a process of mutuality in which people give and take on a more or less equal basis. This is very like the assumptions than underlie fruitful citizenship. Yet just as citizenship based on mutuality declined so has the basis of exchange as it existed in early modern times, for it depended on a mutually integrated local community in which people knew each other as individuals. Modern society has become more depersonalised and individualism has grown stronger. Although exchange still exists has its weakening had an impact on group and social identity?

Dealing with people through the interaction of body and mind
Some elements included in this yardstick can be discerned in historical documents. Wills reveal attitudes to people through the choices made about what items are left to whom, and how family, friends, and more distant associates are viewed. These processes can tell us much about the dynamic of interpersonal relationships.

Dealing with people through management of diversity
Although Great Waltham in early modern times appears superficially to be a simpler kind of society than we have today there was still a lot of social diversity. Perhaps the fact that people lived so close together in overlapping worlds made the personal management of diversity more important and demanding than today. The ability to rub along with people and to socialise would have been a strong requirement. There was much less privacy than we take for granted, and living in such a self contained and self managing community would be a stressful experience for many people today. In London during the seventeenth century, in the only big city, life was beginning to be like the urban world that became typical of social living in the nineteenth century. In the big city the 'large group' of necessity worked in different ways than was the case in more traditional local communities. New focus points emerged – on job rather than way of life, and on the owning, or possession, of property not linked to land. Although farming in Great Waltham formed a continuum and remained the main way of life, it also changed over time as landholding practice was modified. Ironically life in Great Waltham became less diverse than it was in the sixteenth century because some of the entrepreneurial opportunities of that time diminished. Less people were involved in the leadership of the village community as farms became larger, the number of farmers became reduced, and the proportion of landless labourers increased.

There is evidence that notwithstanding these transformations earlier ways lived on in people's minds. Although the old copyhold system had virtually disappeared by the end of the eighteenth century the members of the Ram family who were large tenant farmers left the remains of existing leases to their children much like copyhold land had been left in the sixteenth century.

Through all this change and increasing diversity a continuum can be detected. Life did not fracture under the influence of change. The children who belonged to family alliances created by their parents in sixteenth century Havering extended these into London, which enabled them to retain group solidarity there. In the nineteenth century people still came together in groups, much as they had always done even though the immediate context changed. They still went to church and family life continued. Nor were all of the diverse alliances and networks in which people became involved wholly economic in function. The cultural circle of Francis and William Ram in the late sixteenth and early seventeenth centuries shows that socially creative intercourse was not confined to elites.

Marriage arrangements played a vital part in managing diversity and related uncertainty helping to reinforce networks generally. Agreements relating to marriages could be very formal. The jointure system used by the landed classes had two parts – the portion, brought by the girl, and a settlement, to provide for her maintenance if the husband died first. It had the advantage of being fixed in advance, but to business people it was not so attractive. It tied up capital, often in land, which brought a low return of about 5 per cent. An alternative was to promise to buy land on death or to leave an equivalent portion to be invested in a trust. Yet another way of achieving the same end was for the man to bind himself at marriage to leave his wife an agreed sum at his death. The second and third approaches were gambles in that they depended upon the man developing or holding on to a significant estate. The men who agreed to leave widows a fixed capital sum amounted to only 15 per cent of the total.[60] All these arrangements are discernible in the Ram family, particularly in the Colchester branch where the level of prosperity was possibly higher and the records are more complete.

Dealing with people through need for coming together within the group

In early modern times the closely interlocked nature of social life in Great Waltham, between peers and family, with fellow farmers, upward and downward economic relationships, and the locally complex nature of these relationships, illustrates clearly how people belonged to several kinds of groups. Participation in these of course needed to be managed. The records of Walthambury Manor Court show that tensions occurred which involved members of the Ram family from time to time. People obviously brought their own personal identity to such groups. The parish community at Great Waltham, probably not more than three hundred adults, was really what psychologists call a large group, and comparisons can be made with similar modern large groups, such as a hospital, school, church, or leisure club.

Respect in the community was a sign of ability to manage group relationships well. Many of the male members of the Ram family are recorded as being witnesses to grants and wills, and of being executors, supervisors and administrators of wills. Being asked 'to do things' is a tell tale sign of a particular kind of identity – being trusted, being respected and being competent. Coming together in the group was also important within the family. This has been illustrated by the way the Colchester Rams in the eighteenth and nineteenth centuries took such a corporate interest in Rams or Stoke Farm which figured prominently for nearly two hundred years in family inheritances.

The collective Ram family could also be considered a large group, but the degree to which contact existed between the separated branches – based in or near Great Waltham, Havering, Colchester, and London – is unclear. There is definite evidence that they knew of each other but direct relations were uneven and patchy in later periods, tending to happen at times of crisis. In the sixteenth and seventeenth centuries there is ample evidence that the sons of John Ram 1C, William of Colchester and Francis of Hornchurch and their families, were in close contact with each other. But there is no evidence of relationships between Francis Ram's family and the farmers in Great Waltham. There is also information about cross contact between the family branches in the nineteenth century. Baptisms occurred at St Luke's parish church Chelsea in the 1830s in both James Ram's family and a descendent of his uncle who went bankrupt in Colchester. When Benjamin 4 of Steeple, near Great Waltham got into difficulties during the agricultural depression of the 1850s he went to live and work in Ipswich from the mid 1850s onwards, where in 1858 he baptised a daughter named Jennie Maria at the parish church attended by James Ram and his family. It looks very much as though James Ram gave his farming cousins some support during this time.

The collective nature of family life included families related by marriage. Links which Robert Ram's family had in the sixteenth century is evidence of this. It is almost certain that memories of relationships between families related by marriage were possibly retained over long periods of time. In 1822 John Ram 6B's father in law, Thomas Boltwood died leaving half a yard of land called Eldersfield to John's eldest daughter, Sarah, who was twenty one at the time.[61] Now Eldersfield had been held by members of the Ram family in the sixteenth century and it may have been given to her as a coming of age gift by Thomas Boltwood with this knowledge in mind.

SECTION 2   A PICTURE OF IDENTITY

XXIII
Interpreting the data

How it is done
Having collected together the information about the Ram family and its contexts within *The Thread's* framework the picture obtained has to be interpreted. This is to be done by describing two profiles of identity. Profile 1 interprets that information in the traditional way of commentators, that is of fitting events together in a global rather 'top down' way, called here *looking for an ordered world*. Profile 2 brings out a quite different view which is based on how the identity of individuals and small groups might be expressed looking at the world from their own place in it, here called, *looking outwards from the local community*. It is important to hold these two start points in mind when reading the remainder of this chapter.

Both profiles will be informed by the considerable length of the Ram family story, which makes it possible to trace patterns of identity over an unusually long time period. The fact that the Ram story has been set in its context means the profiles can also relate to the wider world. There are limits to this however because of the Ram family's identification with the middling sort, and it cannot be assumed the findings presented here relate to all social groups.

Of course this exercise is a subjective one but it is done with respect for all the information known about the family and their contexts so it is not unrealistic. Moreover the validity of the approach can be tested by each reader for themselves. Do the contrasts between the analyses set out in Tables 18 and 19 increase your individual understanding of identity and meaning? Looking at identity in the way done here suggests that society is much richer and more complex than the hierarchical model alone takes account of. After all people live their lives with a strong personal and local focus, and who is to say that the hierarchical model is any more valid than the individual models of reality people create for themselves, or that are formed within the small groups they belong to.

The definitions of the yardsticks and related influences are the same as explained in chapter VIII. In each profile the influences can have three types of impact – strong, adaptive, or largely unrecognised. The first kind of impact requires little unpacking because its significance is readily apparent, but the others do. Adaptation can be institutional in form, e.g., local government adjustment to the growth of large cities, or the making of choices by individuals and groups, either to conform to or exploit change. 'Largely unrecognised' is the most complex aspect of the impact made by the influences. Without doubt this often happened in indirect, long term ways, that were not recognised by the people involved. One simple example is that no one discussed in the Ram story ever had an understanding about the part played by genetics in his her formation, because there was no knowledge of genetics, except perhaps at the very end. Another, more complex example is that the yardsticks relating to Influence 1 – general forces in society usually impacted over the long term in ways that were not immediately apparent to people. What is also clear is that the pattern of recognition or non recognition of influences differs in the two profiles – depending on the originating focus point.

Adaptation is shown to be an important element in identity. Even in Influence 1 of the first profile, where forces for change are strongest the actual source of change is predominantly economic impact, with the other yardsticks mainly providing accommodating institutional adjustment. In both profiles influence 2 is predominantly adaptive, being characterised by individual people or groups making choices, either accommodative or exploitative. Again in both profiles most of the yardsticks in Influence 3 are concerned with how individual people and groups fit themselves into a wider social framework.

Each profile shows how the three influences together define a cohesive and balanced social framework. They are quite different, but are complementary. Both of them are valid. What the analysis in this chapter highlights is that the hierarchical approach is not the only one possible, and that in isolation it provides an incomplete picture. Although the data used is drawn from the middling social group, how different would be the patterns shown in tables 19 and 20 if the Ram family was aristocratic or labouring in type. Would there in fact be much difference?

Two defining stories – Francis Ram and running Great Waltham. These are told to assist understanding of the characteristics of the two profiles. The first story provides an illustration of the view of identity dominant in profile 1. Francis Ram was the most establishment oriented member of the Ram family. Through administrative service to Sir Anthony Cooke he gradually took on several roles that would have led to him developing a 'top down' view of the world. Anthony Cooke owned several thousand acres of land, mostly but not wholly, in Essex, and was active in the very lively land market of his time. Francis Ram became his agent in around 1558, when quite young, which he continued to be for the Cooke family until the early years of the seventeenth century. He must have been very capable for Anthony Cooke nominated him for several roles in which he acted as Anthony's deputy. One was as Deputy Steward of Havering in Essex. This was a Liberty which had the administrative powers of a county including running its own courts of justice. Francis became one of the magistrates and effectively ran the local government of Havering for Anthony Cooke who was much involved with national government. In 1572 Anthony Cooke became *Custos Rotulorum* (keeper of the rolls) for Essex which was really the post of Clerk of the Peace for Essex. As was his right, he nominated Francis Ram to perform this task for him, a role he continued to hold for around the next thirty years. It meant he became the senior administrator for Essex local government at a time of considerable expansion beyond the specific administration of justice. He also became an Essex Magistrate. Through his initial association with Sir Anthony Cooke, who died in 1576, Francis Ram worked and mixed with many of the social elite in Essex. Looking at society from this position tends to foster an attitude of mind which makes the preservation of order paramount and sees individuals and groups as cogs in that process.

The second of these stories does the same for Profile 2. From the late Middle Ages right through the period of unreformed local government Great Waltham was run by the middling sort. There was a large group of middle sized holders of land until the eighteenth century which helped to ensure that involvement in parish government was shared fairly widely. The Ram family were among this group, and what we learn about its significant contribution to community life is typical of similar families in the parish. The reality of the social situation in Great Waltham suggests it was a community of sorts, in which, although there were gradations of influence according to social levels, probably the majority of men had some part to play, which of course influenced how identity was perceived. The openness of the community would have made people more open than they otherwise would have been.

XXIV

Two profiles of identity

Profile 1 – looking for an ordered world

Table 18 outlines a hierarchical view of identity that seeks to present an overview of society looking in from the outside. Three influences are at work in an inter-related way. Influence 1 brings and manages general change whilst influence 3 deals with how individual and group formation happens. This is essentially a force for social stability, which holds the change emanating from Influence 1 in check. Its importance is largely unrecognised in this view of identity. Influence 2, sits, as it were, in between the other two being the space in which social reality is generated – where individual people adapt to or exploit opportunities that arise in their lives. They do this in different ways in different generations, but always within the constraints of human genetic makeup. I believe that if I met John le Ram who lived in Great Waltham at the beginning of the fourteenth century we would essentially be able to understand and communicate with each other, although our way of speaking might be a bit different.

Table 18. Identity profile 1 – looking for an ordered world.

INFLUENCES AND THEIR YARDSTICKS	INFLUENCE DEFINITIONS	IMPACT IN THIS PROFILE		
		Influence 1	Influence 2	Influence 3
Influence 1 Frameworks: 1a. Economic. 1b. Demographic. 1c. Customary. 1d. Political. 1e. Legal.	General. Forces which generate change in society. In this profile. Agents of change.	Strong	Adaptive	Largely un-recognised
Influence 2 2a. Freedom of choice among the middling sort. 2b. Life chance. } Arbiters 2c. Wealth. } of 2d. Influence. } choice. 2e. Power. } 2f. Individual beliefs and values. 2g. Religious practice	General. How individuals and groups consciously express themselves – their hopes, individuality and ambitions. In this profile. Making individual choices in the midst of conflicting pressures.	Adaptive	Adaptive	Adaptive

Influence 3	General.			

3a. Family influences.
3b. Citizenship. }
3c. Mirroring. } Dealing
3d. Exchange. }
3e. Interaction of } with
  mind and body. }
3f. Management } people.
  of diversity. }
3g. Coming together}
  in the group.
	How individual and group formation occurs, either through socialisation or genetic inheritance.
	
	In this profile.
	Agent of individual and social cohesion.
		Largely un-recognised	Adaptive	Largely un-recognised

Explaining the impact of the individual yardsticks in profile 1.

The five yardsticks of Influence 1 cover aspects which generate visible change in nearly every area of life, and shape the corporate framework of society. Although individuals influence particular developments included in them, sometimes quite strikingly, this group of yardsticks has an identity or force of their own which individuals and groups find it difficult to control, but can manipulate. This is particularly true of the economy. From early modern times onwards it grew much more diverse which led to new occupations appearing to support the complexity. Farming became more commercial and less dominant. People who remained agriculturalists shared in the increased energy and wealth created by economic growth, but those of them who were not landowners had their identity as free and copyhold landholders changed radically to that of leasehold tenant. Population changes were entwined with patterns of economic growth or stagnation, whilst customary practices were modified by both economic and demographic developments. Legal practice simply adapted gradually to other changes. Political and administrative institutions altered slowly to cope with economic and demographic change but in complex ways, whilst the independence of local communities gradually gave way to centralising and bureaucratic influences. In all this change it is economic forces that appear to be the most dominant. In early modern times developments were particularly strong in London, but they were mirrored in a lesser way in other towns, including places like Colchester, and as time went by they happened throughout the country. In this change many of the Ram family carried on doing what they had always done gradually adapting to external forces. But a relatively small minority migrated from the traditional agrarian way of life into new occupations and environments, which extended possibilities for choice and personal autonomy in occupational, wealth and social terms. They were enabled to do this largely by the achievement of higher levels of education.

The yardsticks included in Influence 3 function primarily through the way people were formed, often in unconscious ways. Some of this happened in face to face peer relationships – mirroring, exchange, management of diversity and coming together in the group. This went on, and still does, in 'peer group' networking, by receiving and giving patronage, or exercising power and influence. Many examples have been given in the history of the Ram family of how net workings of various kinds supplemented each other and intertwined. Career and friendship groups tended to be the original focus, but they sometimes led to marriages. On several occasions they combined all of these elements. Such net workings are of great importance in providing social stability and can be found in all the generations of the family. In this view of identity the yardsticks of Influence 3 operate relatively unrecognised. However tension can be generated for individual people, especially in the areas of exchange and citizenship, by forces for change emanating from the yardsticks of influence 1.

The yardsticks of influence 2 are concerned with how individuals and groups define their own existences against the background of the other two. All the yardsticks involved relate to how individuals and groups express themselves, their hopes, individuality and ambitions, within a variety of constraints put upon them by the yardsticks that belong to influences 1 and 3. In the table influence 2 is deliberately placed between the others because this represents the position it occupies in the overall picture of identity.

The family has always had an important role in both influences 2 and 3. It is part of Influence 2 because it is an important focus for individual people coming together in the group, i.e., to cope with the turmoils of life. It is because of this that Government and Church have often sought to contain family life within legislative frameworks from the earliest times, as they fear it as a source of independence from themselves. The family has always had an ambiguous relationship with the institutions which represent the power holders in Influence 1. The family is part of Influence 3 because it helps to maintain social cohesion as a socialising agent and is the main mechanism by which genetic inheritance is passed on.

Profile 2 – looking outwards from the local community
In the first profile the identity of the Ram family has been viewed from the perspective of how it fits into the wider picture. This is the usual and hierarchically inspired approach in which the family, the group, and the individual appear as small cogs in a huge impersonal world. But this may not be the whole story. Another perspective might be as, or more real for people. A way of exploring this question, still using the same yardsticks and influences, is to envisage identity looking outward from the context of the experience of individuals and small groups. The definitions given to the three influences in this view are changed to reflect the new perspective.

Table 19. Identity profile 2 – looking outwards from the local community.

INFLUENCES AND THEIR YARDSTICKS	INFLUENCE DEFINITIONS	IMPACT IN THIS PROFILE		
		Influence 1	Influence 2	Influence 3
Influence 1 Frameworks: 1a. Economic. 1b. Demographic. 1c. Customary. 1d. Political. 1e. Legal.	General. Forces which generate change in society. In this profile. Being shaped by the broader world.	Largely un-recognised	Adaptive	Largely un-recognised
Influence 2 2a. Freedom of choice among the middling sort. 2b. Life chance. } Arbiters 2c. Wealth. } of 2d. Influence. } choice. 2e. Power. } 2f. Individual beliefs and values. 2g. Religious practice	General. How individuals and groups consciously express themselves – their hopes, individuality and ambitions. In this profile. Being shaped from within.	Adaptive	Adaptive	Adaptive
Influence 3 3a. Family influences. 3b. Citizenship. } 3c. Mirroring. }Dealing 3d. Exchange. } 3e. Interaction of } with mind and body. } 3f. Management } people. of diversity. } 3g. Coming together } in the group.	General. How individual and group formation occurs, either through socialisation or genetic inheritance. In this profile. Being shaped in and by the local community.	Largely un-recognised	Adaptive	Strong

Table 19 shows the outcome of looking at identity in this way, which produces a picture almost exactly opposite to that obtained in Profile 1. It raises questions about nature and complexity of identity. Over the last twenty years historians have given much greater recognition to the richness of life apart from the hierarchical model, particularly in terms of the local community and the family. This development has been reviewed in Part 2.[62] Moreover very recent studies of heredity along with discoveries in genetic science are raising questions about the validity of a simplistic understanding of social reality. But the hierarchical model remains dominant. How exactly is this alternative model different? In it the most important yardsticks become individual beliefs and values, family influences, mirroring, exchange, management of diversity and need for coming together in the group, all to be found in influences 2 or 3. All the yardsticks having a strong influence are those grounded in facilitating individual formation. The weight of influences 1 and 3 are reversed compared with Table 18. This is particularly true of economic frameworks, which from a hierarchical perspective appears a dominant influence, but which seen from the non-hierarchical situation is perceived to be more muted, except in times of crisis. In both tables influence 2 represents how individual people found their own identity among the pressures of influences 1 and 3. However, in the second profile there is an emphasis on self shaping rather than simply reacting to external circumstances.

Explaining the impact of the individual yardsticks in profile 2

Although from the perspective of profile 1 the economy appears to be the most powerful change agent, it is not likely that the Ram family, and many others like them, often appreciated this. Even though its cumulative impact was very great its influence was relatively gradual and long term, certainly over more than one generation, except at times of crisis. In the good times of the later sixteenth century and early seventeenth century the more senior members of the Ram family shared in the prosperity of the period, both as farmers and professional people. Their wills show quite clearly they were conscious of this prosperity for many of the domestic consumer items, like feather beds, bedsteads, pewter ware, and sheets which the middling sort of people could now buy are mentioned frequently and with pride. These members of the Ram family were among the more successful people in their communities and some of them were confident enough to have very large families, but it is likely they paid more attention to enjoying what they had than analysing what made it possible. This kind of impact was even truer of the other yardsticks in influence 1. All of them would have constituted a partially understood background to the more immediate focus points of daily life, to be found in influences 2 and 3.

Demographic trends provide a good example of a force for change operating in an unrecognised way. Looked at from a generalised and aggregated perspective the profile of English population development from the sixteenth century onwards is quite clear. The details of this have been discussed elsewhere. It is equally apparent from Appendix 2 that the aggregated demography of the Ram family has a very similar shape. These shapes and patterns are meaningful when looking from the general to the particular. But would family members have ever been aware of this? Would the same have been true of the vast majority of individual families? People in local places would only have known what happened to them and others in their immediate circle, whilst being only vaguely aware of what was happening in the widest sphere or because of catastrophic events. After all detailed information about population movements and statistics was not available in the nineteenth century and certainly not before.

Aspects of the law which influenced the family functioned in an even more background way. Although it provided the framework within which the family acquired and disposed of property and made contracts, practice in these areas always ran in advance of the written law. This was particularly true in regard to the copyhold system of land holding. By the mid sixteenth century it had become little different in practice from holding land freehold, but it was only gradually recognised in this way by the legal system, and then although copyhold became more or less obsolete during the eighteenth century it was not abolished until 1925. Because the legal system changed very slowly, mostly in reaction to wider economic and social forces, it was never more than a background influence.

Family involvement in the national political system was minimal until the nineteenth century, so it was always a background influence. In earlier times the only member of the family known to have had a vote was Nicholas Ram of Colchester, as a freeholder in the eighteenth century. Greater participation did not start until the better off male members of the family were enfranchised in the nineteenth century by the 1867 Parliamentary Reform Act. However, as will shortly be seen, they participated in local administrative life at far earlier periods in influential ways.

Established customary practices were obviously important in providing the general conventions of social practice and behaviour, which the Ram family conformed to like the vast majority of other people. But they changed only slowly, often under the influence of economic events. Perhaps the most significant development in customary practices was the growing desire, throughout the period covered by this book, to acquire and protect privacy. The desire for this increased during the middle ages and gathered pace in more modern times. The medieval pattern of a whole household living in a single room in a house had given way to having several rooms by the seventeenth century, a development that was not simply the product of technical improvements in amenities. It was a social trend, which some historians see as being closely associated with the emergence of the individual as a social entity.[63] The growth in the importance of privacy may have been one of the contributory causes to the decline of the local community, because people had a lower regard for community and were less willing to play an active part in sustaining it.

In the second profile Influence 2 is about making choices and appears as one of the most powerful of all influences when identity is looked at from the perspective of people looking outward from themselves. A central feature of this identity profile is that choice for the Ram family was more influenced by the yardsticks included in influences 2 and 3 than those in influence 1. Most immediate choices emanated from involvements family members had in practical living, working, and education, not general background influences. It is by such involvements that individual and group identity is formed and expressed. People would have perceived choices were more affected by what happened in their individual lives and local communities than by background forces. Nonetheless several forces, mostly derived from influence 1, served to modify the making of choices, here identified as the arbiters of choice – life chance, wealth, influence and power, and they could produce positive or negative outcomes. Influence 2 is derived from several sources in a complicated way. Some come from family, or peer group, and some are inherited. Although the 'nature' and 'nurture' controversy discussed elsewhere has clouded judgements for many years there is a growing view that both nature and nurture are involved in creating identity. It is possible that as understandings about the part genes play in forming individual identity become better understood the social sources of identity will be downgraded in importance.

One thing the Ram story shows without doubt is that levels of intensity about beliefs varied considerably among male members of a very small family. An example of this is the interest shown in religion. Most of the males were only concerned about it in a formal way, to the extent of having their children baptised and wanting to be buried in the local churchyard, yet for some it was much more important. One branch of the family descended from John Ram of Great Waltham (d. 1568), who was a fervent Protestant. His son William was like minded, and several of his children and grandchildren became Church of England clergymen. Several more of this branch took up the same career in the nineteenth century. But was their heightened interest in religion socially derived or inherited? The fact that the interest extended over such a long period of time with gaps suggests there might have been an hereditary element.

People expressed the choices they made almost wholly through the yardsticks concerned with the way we deal with people, which are part of influence 3 and include citizenship, camaraderie and friendship; mirroring – by which people learn how to bond with others by copying the behaviour of others into themselves; exchange, which facilitates sharing without losing; the interaction of body and mind and their impact on associates; and finally the management of diversity linked with coming together with associates to help survive emptiness, loneliness and confusion. It is a complex process in which personal identity is forged, when young and as an adult. These yardsticks were particularly important for the leading members of the Ram family, because of their independent occupational position.

Dealing with people is based in face to face experience and engenders powerful emotions. It is therefore of enormous importance in the immediate lives of individual people and the groups they are part of. Each individual and group has to work out for themselves how to deal with people, it being very important for individual and family success that this is achieved effectively. Influences 2 and 3 as expressed in the second profile are clearly more important for the Ram family in dealing with people than the impact of Influence 1 – being shaped by the broader world. Influence 3 was especially significant because the yardsticks associated with it provided the means for structuring daily living.

How the Ram family dealt with people was influenced by several kinds of involvements in the local community. It made a major contribution through employment of other people, neighbourly acts, and the purchase of services from tradesmen. This happened as a by product of their being farmers, some of them on a large scale. As farmers they also helped to shape and maintain the character of the farming environment. Moreover many of the family were of sufficient standing in the local community to perform supportive community related roles; acting as witnesses to legal documents, giving sureties for people when they needed them, and helping them when in need.

Along with other middling families the Rams dealt with people through holding offices of various kinds, a function that was not viewed in the same way in medieval and early modern times as it is now. Then, being appointed or elected to a public office or role was more closely associated with the social standing and perceived values of individuals, not simply declared personal interest and willingness to serve. People were elected to office because they were respected by their community, and in anticipation that they would implement in the role what they were perceived to stand for.

All these community involvements – office holding, job holding, being a good neighbour, contributing to the care of the rural environment, employing others, giving and receiving patronage – involved dealing with people in what today would be called networks. They were possibly most intense in Great Waltham because of the extremely local nature of community life. We tend to think today that networking is a modern phenomena, but it clearly is not. The networks of the Ram family and other middling families they were involved with were rich and varied, and they have been discussed in detail as the family story has been described.

Perhaps the most important social element in making choices and dealing with people among the middling sort was the way the men, certainly the most important of them, lived by self employment. Most were farmers, entrepreneurs of various kinds, or a combination of both. Some were professional people, working either in the Law or the Church. Practically the only known 'employee' in the Ram family was Francis Ram, as the agent and estate manager of Anthony Cooke in the sixteenth century. So skill in managing and husbanding resources was an essential requirement. The attention of the farming members of the family was focused on the land they farmed. They earned their living from it, apart from the letting of mostly small properties, and any other ventures they were involved in. Many of the family associated with Colchester became entrepreneurs with interests in a combination of farming, property dealing, and the running of business enterprises. They had to harbour their capital resources and entered into partnership with other similar people. The professionals had to build and maintain their careers, and through these, earn income.

The way of life of the middling sort depended on maintaining their independence, and to do this they had to be resourceful, adapt to change, and be tenacious and stubborn. Just hanging on must have been important at times. Some members of the family were ambitious and prepared to take risks. Many showed signs of protecting themselves by being involved in more than one economic activity. Sustaining independence involved complex relationships in which patronage was both sought and given. It is self evident in the story of the Ram family that the extent of the success men had in running farms and businesses was extremely dependent upon the goodwill of others. Relationships were fostered with people of all types, not just important local figures, particularly landowners. All these features of middling life show why influences 2 and 3 in the second profile are so important in shaping identity.

XXV
What changes and what stays the same?

In the overall pattern of identity revealed in this part of the book some things change and others stay the same. There are clearly forces that generate and institutionalise change right across society, and they are found in Influence 1. On the other hand there are other forces that are much more identifiable with individual people and small or large groups which, stay the same, or more or less the same. They are found in Influences 2 and 3. Things which change are by and large identifiable with influence 1 and those which stay the same with influence 3. But even things which change tend to do so more slowly than we tend to believe and there is much more continuity that we perhaps realise. This is an important matter which the Ram story throws light on again and again, which is now assessed by examining some ideas in a book by Jose Harris on British social history in the late nineteenth century and Edwardian era.[64]

One of the major cultural issues she discusses is 'Modernity'.[65] She sees many of the particular features of the nineteenth century, like imperial expansion, state intervention, class division, and the growth of cultural uniformity, as key features of 'modernity'. Even if these features are typical of the nineteenth century, how far are they also to be found in other periods? Empire is clearly identifiable with a period roughly equivalent to the nineteenth century because the scale and style of empire at that time did not exist in earlier periods. But the findings of this book suggest most of her other themes ought to be understood against a much longer timescale and that they almost certainly originated in earlier times.

Jose Harris' discussion of class, seen in relation to this book's context, epitomises the issues raised by this study of the Ram family about the extent that things are new or stay the same. What she writes about class is prefaced in a particular way, by the term 'emergence'.[66] This suggests that it is a nineteenth century phenomena, but several questions are raised. How far did class really 'emerge' in the nineteenth century, and how far were families class conscious in the way that class is often talked about, then and today? What did the middling nature of the Ram family mean to it in status and class terms?

They must have been aware of differences between the poor, the rich and the middling and where they fitted in, but the level of their class consciousness is far from clear, or how this affected understandings about identity. Nothing has ever been written down about these kinds of awareness in the Ram family and in interpreting what they might have thought from their known actions in the community we, in a class conscious age, have to be careful not to impose our own understandings. In class terms the Ram family almost certainly saw themselves in rather similar ways across the centuries, which implies the 'middling sort' and the 'middle class' are one and the same, and that this social group existed, at least from the sixteenth cemetery, as is suggested in an important book about the middling sort edited by Jonathan Barry and Christopher Brooks.[67] There is no clear cut evidence from family records that social difference lead to family members viewing class in the divisive way that became common in the ninetieth century under the influence of Karl Marx.

Moreover the findings of this book suggest that community based values have a wider and deeper influence in society at large than concerns about class and social hierarchy, certainly in earlier times. George Evans, writing in 1956 about the village of Blaxhall in Suffolk, was of the view that much has been lost by the demise of self sufficiency in village life. 'A community is not formed by a number of people living together in chance association. The old village was integrated, in spite of the inescapable tensions due to class divisions and a prolonged farming depression, because its inhabitants had to work together within the framework laid down by the necessities of the time'.[68] Jose Harris raises the importance of key cultural issues like these in the context of what she calls the 'Lost Domain'. She sees that certain cultural identities, perhaps of much importance, were lost in the political and administrative reforms of the nineteenth century.

Yet many to day would believe that class and social hierarchy issues are more important than community. We are hardly aware of the discontinuities and social upheaval caused by the centralising political and administrative reforms of the nineteenth century which are continuing today. There is no doubt that within the tension between influences 1 and 3 an overall cohesion in the functioning of society is created. But the top down way of looking at identity, followed by numbers of historians, takes little account of the impact made by yardsticks belonging to influence 3, and they do not appear in Jose Harris' list of important themes. Yet they play a significant part in forming our history and are important in terms of the way society is moulded. It is not possible to read what is said about the role of individual yardsticks in the two profiles of identity just discussed, without realising how the fabric of society is sustained by the interpersonal networking associated with influence 3. As a society we can encourage frameworks which help to sustain the natural social structures or introduce ones which help to weaken them. The contemporary importance of how we mould society is discussed in Part 5. The significant point that emerges from this section is that moulders of society should have a complete picture of it. In some ways the picture of identity presented, with its two profiles, is obvious but shapers of policy, commentators and writers often fail to take account of their shared existence and impact.

Two last questions remain. What weight might Jose Harris' general themes have in the Ram family's view of the world? Would they count much at all? It is likely that the most important themes for them, at any period in their history, are those outlined in Profile 2 – ones which looked outwards from themselves, and focused on the aspects of their lives that they perceived to affect them most directly and deeply. The same would almost certainly be true for many people of the middling sort and in other social groups too.

PART 5

THE MODERN WORLD
AND *THE THREAD*

SECTION 1
HOW PEOPLE SEE IDENTITY TODAY

XXVI
The dominant way of looking
at identity and related problems

The obsession with hierarchy

When the first status classifications were made in early modern times by people like William Harrison, Thomas Wilson and Gregory King, they presented society as a highly stratified hierarchy, in which gentility was pre-eminently important. First came gentlemen, then citizens and burgesses of towns and cities, then yeomen, and finally husbandmen, labourers, and servants. But in this pecking order there were a number of separate categories at the bottom, whilst the top one 'gentleman' included dukes, minor gentry, and some people who did not have titles at all, like William Ram.[1] Wrightson reviews these classifications in his book *English Society, 1580-1680*, and discusses the significance of stratification and status. He questions whether social distinction was really so clearly defined as the early status classifications make out, and also the extent they reflected the reality of how power was held. Wrightson believes modern research indicates that actual hierarchy and power was much more permeable and flexible than early status classifications suggest, and the story of the Ram family roughly supports his view. An extension of his questioning raises another, and related issue – how far were the castes of class set out by Karl Marx a social reality?

Although the meaning of the social groups described in the seventeenth century classifications have changed or disappeared the concepts that underpinned them are far from dead. The aristocracy may have got pushed off its pedestal but we still see society very much as a hierarchy with set pecking orders. Indeed recent reviews of social mobility suggest there is less chance for poor able individuals to be socially mobile than was the case fifty years ago.[2] Where there were gentlemen, citizens and burgesses of towns and cities, then yeomen, and finally husbandmen, labourers, and servants there are now professionals, managers – split into several levels – supervisors, technicians, clerks and workers. The top group of 'gentleman' , which really included everyone with a significant amount of wealth is now equally 'catch all' but the people in it are self made millionaires, rich personalities, and top flight footballers, rather than 'gentlemen'.

All these kinds of classification are based on wealth and related power. It is of course true that there has to be order in society and that there have to be people who do things and those who run them. Most of us like to have an ordered world partly because we feel more comfortable. Moreover people have a strong urge to preserve what they have. So, in one way or another, the hierarchical way of looking at identity is built into social consciousness and guides not just what we think about each other but how society is run.

What is noticeable from only a cursory look at the history of our country is that there have been progressive moves throughout it to limit the freedom of the powerful to do just what they want. There have equally been moves to contain the poor. Democracy has been institutionalised nationally and at local levels. There have always been councils of men who met to make decisions about how to run communities. The way Great Waltham was run, certainly from the sixteenth century to the nineteenth, and probably a lot earlier, shows that power in the local community was not always exercised by the richest people. But the hierarchical model is still dominant and some aspects of popular democracy are a social veneer. This book shows that the hierarchical model may be even more dominant now than in the past, brought about by the progressive centralisation of government over the last two hundred and fifty years. Even though there is some concern today about the breakdown of community, with a degree of acceptance that the rigidity and centralisation of our society is partly the cause of it, in reality, for one reason or another, no real alternative is contemplated. Most policy making today is based, consciously and unconsciously on the hierarchical model. We are trapped by it. Why is this so? It can only be because of the conservatism of those that 'have' – wealth, or property, or identity with the running of the state. it has to be remembered that the total number of people involved in running government nationally and locally is much bigger than it has ever been before and that all these people, the politicians as well as the bureaucrats, earn their livings by it, which reinforces the forces wanting to preserve the existing hierarchical framework. The social group that tends to resist change is not just the very rich. In some ways anyone who has property, capital or professional interest is part of it.

The danger of oversimplified models

Life is often more complicated than we like to think. Our notions of hierarchy and the importance of the social pyramid are almost certainly an oversimplification of social reality and identity. I am going to illustrate how social stereotypes can be misleading by recounting the debate that has gone on among historians about the social group that is often regarded as the bedrock of society – the middle class. The central feature of the debate is whether the middle class has always existed, or ever existed. We tend to think of middling people literally being in the middle between the rich and the poor, but there are many intermediary levels within this group, and the meaning of middling can also vary according to the immediate social focus. Shani d'Cruze, a researcher on Colchester in Essex, speaks of the middling sort in that town as being minor professionals, craftsmen, shopkeepers, yeomen and husbandmen, and she did not regard the elite professionals, merchants and big traders of that place as being middling.[3] This would place numbers of the Ram family in Colchester among the elite, even though in the context of England at large they are clearly no more than of the middle. In a book about London Peter Earle defines the middling sort in terms of seeking to turn over capital to make a profit on an expansionist basis. This defining element of 'middling' was important for Earle because he believed the small husbandman who scraped a living and had no hope of increasing his lot was just as much a capitalist, but he was not of the middling sort.[4]

Another book edited by Jonathan Barry and Christopher Brooks makes clear the term 'middling sort' has been used by many historians because of the uncertainty that the modern 'middle class' is the same as the middling sort of earlier times. They refer to a compact definition by Shani d'Cruze that conveys many of the important features of this social group. 'The middling sort has to work for their income, trading with profits of their hands, e.g., farmers, or with skills in business or the professions for which they had trained ...They were rarely employed by others ... The middling sort defined themselves in relation to households, which often formed the heart of a trading unit ... but also acted as the key unit for the reproduction and security of the family centred on the figure of the adult male householder'.[5] The work of such a household ensured its independence from poverty and thus laid the foundation for social, cultural and political independence. Perhaps the notion here of self sufficiency is a key to the identity and description of the middling sort.

But where do professional people fit in? At the upper end there has been much blurring from at least the sixteenth century. Did the members of the Ram family who became clergymen in the Church of England during the sixteenth and seventeenth centuries become 'gentrified'? They didn't turn over and make capital, but they had to work, and their status was generally of the middling sort. There was also the question of what constituted a gentleman. Increasingly as the seventeenth century went by it was anyone who had money and called themselves 'gent'. John Ram 5B left Great Waltham to become a cordwainer in eighteenth century Chelmsford and was called 'gent' in his will although his wealth and position were both quite moderate. Many younger sons of the gentry went either into the church or trade through apprenticeships. This encouraged the blurring of who was, and was not, a 'gentleman'.[6] Merchants, who in the seventeenth century tended to be looked down upon socially, had by the eighteenth century come to be seen, particularly in the second generation, as gentrified.[7] Their wealth made this status accessible to them. To add to the complexity it might be asked to what extent were members of the legal profession gentlemen? This profession grew particularly rapidly in the half century before the civil war, as a major by-product of the growth of the metropolis. Top flight barristers could get annual incomes of £3000-£4000, far higher than any except those of the very richest merchants, financiers and wholesalers. Yet becoming a barrister was a great gamble as only the small top group earned really large incomes. Moreover there was no extensive professional training required of barristers, since being called to the bar in the seventeenth and eighteenth centuries only involved becoming enrolled as a student for seven years and eating dinners in the hall of one's Inn for 12 terms. The financial cost of doing this though was high – simply living in the correct manner could cost £200 a year so the overall investment was between £1000 and £1500 – with no guarantee at the end of even a decent living. So most barristers came from a gentlemanly background.

Clearly people can be identified as being of the middling sort by their wealth as well as occupation, though measuring wealth is always difficult when looking back in time. Many of the criteria that can be used to do this change in character, cease to exist, or undergo a shift in their significance. Peter Earle says in the sixteenth and seventeenth centuries a person's status was measured by wealth and assets rather than income.[8] The richest middling people in London were merchants, wholesalers and shopkeepers. Merchants were seen as a group apart.[9] These comparisons are very crude and relate to London but they provide a yardstick for assessing the economic standing of people in other places. But wealth is not the only way to establish position in society. Other characteristics can be seen to be strongly associated with the 'middling sort' – they were significant 'community brokers and 'contributors to the articulation of major discourses, such as those connected to law and religion'.[10]

There is another problem about the use of the term middling. How is it bound up with notions of class? The aristocracy has been seen historically to occupy the social pinnacle, and even to be the source of entrepreneurialism by some writers. The allocation of dominance to this group was assisted in the sixteenth and seventeenth centuries by the growth of a national culture centred on London in which the aristocracy dominated national politics, the church and cultural fashion. Many historians have believed that other social groups sought to aspire to or ape this elite, an understanding that has become so dominant that much social momentum of early modern times – the Reformation, the civil war, and the growth of the state and political parties – has been seen to come from within the ruling elite, or splits in it, rather than under the pressure or with the involvement of the middle classes, or other lower social groups.[11] Historians who play down class involvements in social evolution empathise strongly with this approach. It has also produced a view of history based on a polarisation between those at the top and those at the bottom, much advocated by the historian E P Thompson.[12]

So, the traditional way of looking at social hierarchies squeezes out the middling sort. But Jonathan Barry and Christopher Brookes believe such a view 'ignores the largely urban world of association, where the particular values of the middling sort may be identified'.[13] They also believe this view draws distinctions between 'the people' and aristocratic dominance which may be false. A trend away from this position is now being supported by some historians who see difficulty in making clear differentiation between social groups, as between the 'popular' and the elite since the crowd can be divided and contain all sorts of separate identities. Jonathan Barry believes that the downgrading '... of the significance of the middling sort has appealed to those eager to put politics and religion, rather than social relations, at the heart of the agenda about political change, and to those for whom the significant conflicts in society lay between the top and the bottom'.[14]

This review of historians' perspectives on the middling sort shows practically any position can, and has, been taken about the middling sort as a social group. The concerns of historians may seem academic to many people, and they may be right, but the picture given here does show how complex social reality is. Of course hierarchy exists but we often present it in an oversimplified way. It follows that unreal social models can blind us to the realities of life, and that total reliance on them will likely lead to us organising our society around a myth rather reality.

The absence of a holistic understanding of identity
In Part 4 of this book *The Thread* was used to detect patterns of identity revealed by the contextual history of the Ram family. The conclusions were pulled together in chapter XXIV where two different profiles of identity were presented. The first one, *Looking for an Ordered World*, is essentially the hierarchical model we have just been discussing. In this profile the predominant forces are the broad brush economic, demographic, customary, political and legal influences, whilst elements of life emanating from the local scene and through individual people and small groups are effectively treated as cogs in the machine. This way of looking at identity results in an incomplete understanding of society, because it does not take proper account of the immediate reality of most people. If policy makers, politicians, and other people with power in Britain today draw wholly on this model there is significant danger that governmental, administrative and management practice will drive society apart rather than bring it together. Such practice is the opposite of holistic which can only flourish in situations where there

is true mutuality. The profound importance of this understanding should be abundantly clear from reading the earlier parts of this book. One of the basic problems about our society now is not the failure to recognise intellectually the importance of mutuality, but to make the changes that would encourage it to develop. It is easy for politicians to talk about reforming society in ways which reinforces community without realising the deep absence of mutuality, or how difficult it will be to create it. An example from my experience should help to make this fundamental point clear.

In February 1998 as part of my work involvements at that time I organised a weekend consultation in East London which had participants from Britain and Ireland and mainland Europe – from France, Holland and Germany. The contributors came from a variety of local community projects in these countries. The consultation was part of a much bigger process aimed at learning from the 'grass roots' about how community relationships could be more effective.[15] This particular meeting came about because people raised with me, as the organiser of the whole project, the fact that whilst our work was truly based in the grass roots the voices heard were nearly always of leaders and their helpers, and hardly ever those of the users of services – the clients or guests. At this consultation the main aim was to make presentations which included both local leaders and users, in which considerable efforts were made to give the users a real voice.

One of the six presentations was made by a night shelter in Newham, East London. Four people came to tell their story. One was an advocacy and advice worker, another was a committee member, whilst the other two were users of the night shelter who had volunteered to help tell the story. The personal story of one of the users is typical of stories this group told about other people who stayed in the night shelter. He was born in North London, being in his thirties in 1998. He had been in the Royal Navy for five years after which he served a further three years aboard HM ships as a civilian. In about 1990 he had gone to Spain, partly for employment and partly for family reasons. He came back to the UK in October 1996 in need of help and obtained a Job Seeker's Allowance. He came to the Newham night shelter which helped him to find accommodation in a local hostel. Two weeks later he was told that he was no longer entitled to social benefit. He therefore lost his room, causing the hostel which had accepted him in good faith to be out of pocket by two weeks' rent. The Job Centre told him that if he could stay for six months they might consider his claim again. He was one of three British citizens at the Newham night shelter at that time who were in this position. At the end of the winter he was helped to find and move into a room in a privately rented house. It was cheap and dirty but was one he was able to afford from income gained by leaflet delivery. On top of everything else, this man had some mental health problems which he refused to acknowledge. He therefore lost his room within ten days of moving in. At the time of the presentation he was homeless, having no income other than from casual work delivering leaflets door to door. The night shelter was very conscious of the problems people like him faced and was working at that time with Newham Community Drugs Team to find the resources to fund a resettlement worker who would give ongoing support to people in his position.

A really striking aspect of the Newham involvement in the consultation was the way the user volunteers reacted to the atmosphere of the meeting. One of them was so impressed that other people there really wanted to hear what they had to say, that he wrote an unsolicited account afterwards covering all the sessions with the discussion that took place and sent it to me. He was not a skilled writer so it must have involved him in considerable effort. I believe his effort was a product simply of his being taken seriously at our meeting. He was amazed that after the Newham group had finished their story, when it was lunch time, people were all talking about the presentation. 'Even when we stopped for lunch everybody was talking about the presentation we had done'. He was also struck by the lack of suspicion and defensiveness because he made a specific reference to how people sat together for breakfast on the first full day. 'The next day … we came down to breakfast and everybody sat at everybody else's tables, e.g., nobody sat in their own groups as if all the barriers between the different country's were left outside the door on Thursday night'. Clearly he was not used to being accepted as an equal like he was at the consultation.

The Newham group told their story in the form of play, described here in the account written by the volunteer user.

> We did our presentation about the night shelter and how we run it with all the same difficulties that we faced in the shelter every night from booking people in, to trouble with people that had a drink problem, to how we deal with people that used drugs plus the difficult problem of young males and females wanting to sleep together in the night shelter. After we had presented our presentation all the other groups and leaders came over and congratulated us on a job well done as they had no idea that there was so much work went into running a night shelter for the homeless.

The play consisted of two 'what if' cameos. They were both concerned with the application of rules. One of them was about a couple wanting shelter who were possibly under age. At that time if people were under 16 they were are not allowed to go to night shelter. The organisers were required to contact the police and the social services department, which then directed those concerned back to their families. In this situation the night shelter organisers had a dilemma because they wanted to keep people off the street but equally did not want to upset the authorities. How far do you follow the rules or work to achieve your main aims to support people? The second cameo was called *Disturbance in the night*. It raised questions about the point at which you call the police. When do you throw the offending people out? If the organisers bent the rules they needed to be sure of their ground. The Social Services Department had guidelines about how to act in these situations. But the main aim of the night shelter organisers was to welcome the young people, and excluding them did not do this. But if the rules are bent people should know this is happening on their behalf, and be given help in the longer run (next day) to sort things out. The organisers' view is that rules in this and other comparable situations should be made for the people not vice versa as often seems the case.

A number of issues were raised by the play about the way rules are applied. If you have rules why should you make any exceptions? There is a need to have a consistent approach to both rules and applicants. But how should rules be understood? When people come to night shelter they become part of it. When problems arise who should be involved in discussion about what should be done about them and how? Some people in the official world even question whether issues like these are important. The organisers of the Newham night shelter believed involvement of everyone brings greater positive results in the long run. This is a holistic view about how things should be done and an example of the basic importance of mutuality.

At the end of the day rules must be enforced in order to maintain order. But they only address symptoms, so if they are applied blindly little is done to resolve social problems related to homelessness or other situations. In the experience of the volunteer group which ran the night shelter reflection about remedying the underlying problems that caused the symptoms usually stayed in the volunteer group, rather than being taken seriously by people in the political and policy making arenas. MPs came and visited but did not know about the inner issues being raised, e.g., the way people in need are dealt with by authorities and rules. The organisers quoted the example of a home for old people that had been empty and boarded up for two years. It cost a lot to keep empty and could have accommodated 35 homeless people. In the view of the Newham group the costs were not the real reason it remained boarded up, which was more to do with neighbourhood pressures and related conflict in the local Council. Moreover the home could have been run as a voluntary scheme but there were problems about meeting regulations. The organisers said they needed publicity to generate action about situations like this. It was apparent to them that people in local government felt oppressed by national government about doing anything – partly because central government used places like Newham as dumping grounds. The question of the left hand not knowing what the right hand is doing was also apparent. The bureaucratic machine always seems very difficult to penetrate. People are treated very badly by it, just like numbers, and helpers are forced to represent them. It seemed the local government offices were glad when the summer came and the night shelter shut down.

The issues raised by the Newham presentation demonstrate very clearly how far our society is from being holistic and how mutuality is so lacking. At that time when homeless people went to seek jobs no allowance was made for their being homeless. In Newham it was almost impossible for a homeless person to get registered with a doctor. Rules of various kinds dominated the lives of homeless people, including what to provide for their needs and how to do it. There are many reporting, enforcing, and understanding rules, e.g., about how to live together in the night shelter, and terms and conditions in which benefits are paid. The fact has to be recognised that many homeless people are often treated very shabbily by employees in the police and local authorities. Some people may question the views expressed in the presentation, but that the people involved felt like this is irrefutable, and I know from wider experience that much of what they said is often true. Since 1998 events and relationships between the nightshelter and local government bodies in Newham have moved on in a creative way.[16]

But the story as told here contains many truths which reflect general and deeply ingrained features of our society way beyond Newham that will not be removed in the short term. The consultation as whole raised three groups of questions and concerns which are all very relevant to creating a truly holistic society. How do we help people to realise their own powers? How can the gaps which exist between people at the grass roots, policy makers and administrators be ameliorated? What can be done about the issue of fragmentation at grass roots? Who represents who in this scene? Are there any common themes? How can you tackle value issues in this situation?

XXVII
Other possibilities

Looking Outwards from the Local community

Looking for an Ordered World is not the only pattern of identity that is possible. Another, also described in chapter XXIV, has been called *Looking Outwards from the Local community*. It is not an alternative to the top down view for the two can, and do, co-exist. They have always done so, but the second one has always been subordinate and suppressed. It looks at the world from the perspective of ordinary people, set in their local communities, albeit mainly middling ones in this book because of the influence of the Ram family. *Looking Outwards from the Local community* is a profile of identity based in the world of everyday experience. This start point is almost certainly more real than the hierarchical model for most people. If we are to create a holistic society this model has to be taken as seriously as the one that is hierarchically based. *Looking Outwards from the Local community* expresses identity in a 'bottom up' way. It shows there are other focus points than ones which emanate from the powerful. It is a way of looking at identity which can encourage mutuality because it is based in how people relate together in local groups.

How conventional wisdom hides reality

Exactly how commonly held understandings of identity fail to mirror the real world requires further exploration. An example from this book might be helpful here. The story of the Ram family shows clearly how socially rich and varied their lives and relational networks have been over the centuries but because families like them often leave no records of their lives this part of general cultural life is under-recorded and under-appreciated. This reality often leads to the assumption that lives of people outside the elite are socially narrow. The Ram story tells us clearly that ordinary people, as well as the wealthy and powerful, have a rich world of their own. In the last twenty or thirty years historians have gone some way to correct this weakness but societal levels below the elite are still inadequately researched especially in rural areas. This book contributes to a deeper understanding that our world is not simply top down in its orientation.

Greater appreciation of the general richness of life in all social groups might encourage the elite to be rather more humble. Until modern times the humbler classes of people had to sort out their own lives, using the skills and qualities highlighted by *The Thread*, especially those highlighted in influences 2 and 3 of Profile 2.[17] Many people no doubt had difficulties and some failed to cope, but society went on nonetheless. So the majority must have coped reasonably well. Whilst it is obviously right to help the needy, many of our systems, as the story from the Newham night shelter shows, are superficial and do not address root causes. When do our welfare policies and practices become interference? When does support become nannying and big brotherish? If there is to be mutuality in society more respect needs to be shown for the abilities of ordinary people to cope, allied with greater resources being put into genuinely supporting them in open ended ways. Although there are obviously people who behave irresponsibly and require to be checked, this is almost certainly not how the majority conduct themselves. Giving support in ways which gives individual people respect and encourages their independence might prove to be a more cost efficient way of dealing with social problems than spending large amounts of money in bureaucratic ways which only addresses symptoms.

Another example of how conventional wisdom often hides reality concerns the relative place of men and women. Many older 'practice' books about social etiquette suggest there was an historical division between the roles of women and men and that during the eighteenth and nineteenth centuries this became more marked. Some historians support this idea. There is no doubt that in married situations legal frameworks gave men a dominant formal position throughout the period covered by this book, which has led to the assumption that all relationships between men and women fell into the same pattern. More recent studies take the view that the roles of women in general were not necessarily so circumscribed and subordinate as often thought.[18] In practice there may well have been sharing and mutuality in which women played a positive and creative role.[19] The story of the Ram family told in this book shows how men and women worked together, often quite reciprocally. Women could, apparently quite smoothly, assume leadership roles when required by the untimely death of spouses, which suggests they were normally involved in the management affairs of farms and land by their husbands. The Ram story also shows that there was little change in practice in the role of women between the sixteenth and nineteenth centuries. The only difference is that in later times arrangements relating to them tended to be more formally defined.

Helping to create a holistic society
We can never put the clock back in a nostalgic way to re-establish a lost culture, but if we have problems about cohesion in our society, as we have, it is

potentially fruitful to explore how the elements of social cohesion we appear to have lost can be re-invigorated. To do this we have to understand the basic social features we need to rediscover linked to exploration of how they can be made meaningful in our own social context. Of course the earlier world was very different, one in which most people lived in small rural communities. Sometimes these were dominated by a local elite family, but this did not always happen, as was the case at Great Waltham. If there were a significant number of self governing villages spread across the country this kind of community may well be the origin of the 'English spirit' described by Alan Macfarlane, as well as modern democracy, and individual freedom. What is sustaining these characteristics today? Great Waltham now has little self government, for most administration is either centralised or run from larger semi-local units. Is this development, generated by the growth of very large urban communities in the nineteenth century undermining the 'English spirit'? It might be contributing to our contemporary confusion about the issues of freedom, individuality and responsibility.

In the past it is highly likely that mutual respect was derived from living in holistic small, medium and large groups. Although some administrative change was inevitable to cope with enormous structural change in the nineteenth century, it may have been overdone so that 'the baby is thrown out with the bath water'. We may well now be in the position of needing to relearn the importance of the small holistic community, together with how its characteristics were generated. It is possible to shape administrative practice so that the strengths of the past are applied in modern ways. The lesson is that If we want to achieve a genuine level of respect today we have to run our society so it actually fosters the kinds of relationships found in the Great Waltham of earlier times.

SECTION 2
LEARNING FROM *THE THREAD*

XXVIII
The challenges

Maintaining continuity within change

In the course of reading all the papers, books, and documents used in writing this book one thing has impressed itself time and again; the relevance that so many of the issues and events of the past have to our own world. There is nothing new in the view that we can learn from history and Arnold Toynbee gave the notion great publicity.[20] But relatively few of us have enough detailed historical knowledge to do this, and nearly everyone is far more absorbed with our own world than that of the past. So we view and treat our own times as something unique, which means we have to relearn many of the lessons of life over and over again in each generation. Today we are restless people who are always seeking improvement on the way things are done, especially in business and government. We have a strong tendency to assume things can be done better, together with the belief that we have the answer. Sometimes good things happen as a result of our restlessness but we also spend much time experimenting with dead ends or simply going round in circles. If we really could learn from history we might be much more effective at shaping both our present and our future for the better.

How can *The Thread* help? The Ram family has been viewed over a very long period with the aid of this device – nearly seven hundred years, which has assisted the detection of patterns of various kinds. It has been observed that features in society appear at a particular time and then fade away to be replaced by others – for example the successive patterns in land holding between the sixteenth and nineteenth centuries. Many local communities have expanded greatly in modern times, which has affected their character and transformed the way they are run. In the big cities of the nineteenth century and today people are far less inter-dependent and community care has become systematised and largely depersonalised. Throughout many changes there does appear to have been cumulative trends in a number of ways, for example in the gradual growth of generally available education and community care. But one of the most striking developments to emerge from this study is the way many local communities, like Great Waltham, have lost responsibility for running themselves and become subject to external, and largely centralised, control.

It is noticeable that in all this change elements of continuity persist, although they tend to get adapted to fit with changed ways of living. Examples of this can be found in the Ram family. In the sixteenth century about half of Francis Ram's immediate family moved over two generations from Great Waltham, a small rural and traditional community, to London and became urbanised in a way that is surprisingly modern. The men had commercial or professional jobs and each nuclear family lived separately, often several miles away from the others. Although Francis Ram himself lived in Hornchurch in Essex, about fifteen miles from London, he was not separated socially from family members there, nor they from each other. The family network simply changed its shape and form compared to the more traditional one to be found in Great Waltham to fit the new situation. It had originated in Francis Ram's own working and social contacts in Essex with a number of families, and was replicated among the younger generation as some of the children from all the families moved on into London. Two inter-marriages between these families and the Ram family were part of this development. The same thing happened among family members in the nineteenth century. Another example of adapted continuity is how sharing in the village life of Great Waltham was a continuum, although its detailed expression changed through time. No doubt the shared running of that village among many of the villagers continues at the present time in a lessened form than in earlier days.

The general preponderance of continuity and gradual change that appears in the Ram story has several implications for understanding contemporary society. It is a warning that events, let us say, during the period of the sixteenth century are not necessarily as distinctive, or separate from, those which went before or followed after, as we might think. It is easy to underestimate the implications of such oversights. For example, the question of class and class conflict has become a subject of enormous debate over the past hundred and fifty years. Marx raised it to a great pitch, but with the collapse of the Russian Empire other issues are perhaps making class and class warfare seem less important than it was. Moreover the Ram family were a middling family before debate about class began, and it is not at all clear how this debate contributes anything to their own identity. If people are much the same across the generations and most change is only gradual we can learn from the experience of previous generations. It is also a sign that we should not make rapid and traumatic social change but build on what is already present.

One of the strongest features of continuity, albeit in changed ways, is the fact that life among the middling sort has always had its own social richness.

Networks and alliances of a social and recreational character are common among the Rams thorough the whole period, and are certainly not just a modern phenomena. Lawrence Stone indicates that the senior peerage, above the levels of the knights and gentry, were free from many of what he calls the burdens of local government. 'They did not sit on juries, could not be picked as sheriffs, and were not obliged to turn up at county musters'.[21] It is abundantly clear from information gathered about Great Waltham that from the late middle ages right through the period of unreformed local government it was run by the middling sort which without doubt involved making and running alliances of many types. Some sources of historical enquiry suggest that in times past only the aristocracy had leisure networks and that the peasants most definitely did not.[22] But if the middling sort did have them, why should not the poorer people also? All these networks provide avenues for creating and maintaining the values in our society that encourage basic respect, social concern and love for people. They are just as important to people today as they were in the sixteenth century, as no doubt are the relationships connected with the darker side of life – hates, jealousies and resentments. Bonding and patterns of exchange in large groups and nuclear families still provide the continuity in life. The trick of managing change is to marry it with the elements of continuity that form the basic fabric of human identity.

Dealing with disconnectedness

But even though there is underlying continuity our society it is afflicted with a deep awareness of its opposite. People have a deep disconnectedness from institutions of all kinds, and there is much rebellion and disaffection among young people. An example of this is how schools and now government is drawn into attempting to control delinquent behaviour by general legislation. This is being forced upon us by a breakdown of functioning values in local situations. But just as in the context of homelessness dealing with the problems is mostly confined to ameliorating the immediate symptoms. We seem unable to tackle deep underlying problems, often associated with the breakdown of value networks. Institutions appear unable to grapple with the deep hole in our society left by the breakdown of functioning values, largely because society as a whole does not know what to do about it. In this situation identity in our society is becoming increasingly fragile.

So, drawing on the village of Great Waltham, particularly thorough the Ram family, what principles of community formation in such places can be used to further modern day mutuality? The part of *The Thread* called *The way we deal with people* can help to find some answers to this question. Five yardsticks are involved, each covering aspects of person to person relationships: citizenship; mirroring (how we learning by copying others); exchange (sharing without losing); the interaction of body and mind with the group (managing emotions and feelings); management of diversity and coming together in the group. When people lived in small self contained communities they were thrust together in networks of relationships that must at times have become intense and difficult to handle. Exactly how community relationships functioned in past times is something we find difficult to understand in the more private and disconnected social frameworks of today. The stories that are regularly brought to us now on television screens from around the world, and in some ways form a major part of a lot of people's social interaction, did not exist until a surprisingly short time ago. News of national events took days or even weeks to reach local environments so the face to face relationships of the local community were the most real and important social involvement people had.

The yardstick called citizenship includes contributing to community life through such things as friendship and camaraderie as well as more formal participation in institutional and representative roles. In Great Waltham it has been seen that this meant being good neighbours as well as showing among other things, willingness to witness wills, helping out fellow farmers, acting as arbiters in quarrels or other sorts of arbitration situations, becoming involved in the governance of Great Waltham in a variety of ways, and in forging marriage alliances with other village families. There was genuine concern and affection in these involvements, The spirit of good fellowship which neighbourliness bred permeated and helped to shape the most colourful and attractive features of social relationships.. 'It pervaded the atmosphere of community gatherings'.[23] Neighbourliness offered opportunity to show the finest traits of character.[24]

How neighbourliness was expressed when members of the family moved away from Great Waltham into much larger more amorphous communities is much less clear, but as far as can be seen formal involvement in representative and governmental institutions stopped. Neighbourliness presumably continued in some form in urban situations but it could not have taken the form it did in Great Waltham. In Colchester Rams only contributed fleetingly to its intuitions and in London not at all. These experiences may or may not have been typical.

Mirroring is an important element of individual formation in the group, being a key to achieving successful social adjustment and acceptance. Through bonding with others each individual develops a sense of belonging. Direct evidence of how the Ram family achieved this is not available, but the way they exercised choice and developed citizenship involvements provides clues. Mirroring outside the family was probably more intense and direct in the environment of Great Waltham than it was in Colchester or London, because the local community was so much more self contained. In the towns the process inevitably became more indirect, caused by increased community size, and possibly higher levels of education which increased the range of individual choice.

Learning to be effective at exchange, or sharing without losing, was very important to a family like the Rams. This was especially true for men in running and managing their farms or taking on professional roles. Numerous examples can be found in the text of this book. But women in the family also had to possess this skill. One of the things that emerges from this study is the background but important role of women. Although married women could not have a formal status in business or ownership it is quite clear that when it was necessary, as when for example a husband died leaving a young son who was both unskilled and a minor, they managed affairs quite adequately. So girls must have been involved in learning the process of exchange as well as boys.

There is no direct information available about how family members learned to manage the interaction of body and mind within the group, that is to control their emotions and feelings. But their demeanour can be gleaned from their public conduct. One of the striking things about the Rams in Colchester is that although they had ceased to be yeoman farmers and become partially acculturated in an urban environment they retained significant identity with the definition of yeoman farmers offered by Mildred Campbell, and quoted elsewhere, as being ambitious, aggressive, small capitalists, without enough surplus to take great risks, but determined to take advantage of every opportunity for increasing profits.[25] They even continued in the late eighteenth century to give attention to the apportionment of small farms they owned, copyright or freehold, although the amounts of capital involved were quite small. This tendency continued In the nineteenth century among the upper middle class members of the family even though they were mainly occupied in professional occupations.

Dealing with diversity is not something that is peculiar to modern times. Being one's own master and running a business of some kind could be lonely and cause just as much strain in the past as it can now. Many diverse functions and relationships were involved. There is evidence that these pressures were contained by business being kept within the family or among a small band of well regarded associates in the form of partnerships. Before the nineteenth century this approach helped to overcome the intense riskiness of running a business enterprise when there was no form of limited liability. Efforts to limit risk were common among the Rams whether they were farmers, lawyers, or ran businesses of some kind. Throughout the period of this study it is also clear that the giving and receiving of patronage was very important in managing diversity. Neighbourliness and representative social involvements in part helped to fulfil the same function.

There was another less creative side to the question of managing diversity and that concerns the handling of failed relationships – if you like the dark side of managing diversity. Today newspapers and the media as a whole bring us bad news continually and we can believe, quite falsely, that there is nothing but violence, crime, social breakdown, and disharmony. Is this really the reality of what life is like and was like in earlier times? Some writers have found numerous disputes recorded in the church courts during early modern times, as was the case in a study of a village called Terling which is only a few miles from Great Waltham.[26] But equivalent records for Great Waltham do not appear to have survived, so other ways have to be used to assess this dark side. One of the striking understandings to emerge from the analysis of Great Waltham and members of the Ram family who lived there is the apparent lack of social breakdown. A few of the family members were taken to the manor court for minor offences, and one was branded. It is possible that difficulties and unpleasant experiences were suppressed. Although wills can hide relational difficulties, it is not easy to hide catastrophic breakdown in family relationships because rightful inheritances would be denied. There is only one example of this in the many Ram wills used and that was not connected with Great Waltham. Wills also indicate friendly relationship patterns with people outside the immediate family on a surprisingly large number of occasions, and there is no reason to believe this pattern was peculiar to the Ram family. So, the major impression obtained from this study is that communities in the past were not riddled with disharmony.

The picture given here of how middling families like the Rams adjusted to living in their communities is virtually a description of the middling sort itself, and in some respects it fits with Shani d'Cruze's definition of the middling sort quoted earlier.[27] But some characteristics identified here do not appear in her definition, especially the importance of citizenship and the fulfilling of public roles. The general pattern of socialising described above is probably part of the human makeup that dates back into the dim past. One of the reasons human beings came to have such large brains may be because their ancestors found the most efficient harvesting of tree borne fruit was by individuals foraging in small family groups within larger clan groups. Living in this way requires a lot of brain power and social skills. In a fascinating book Robin Dunbar, a researcher in this field has something to say about the origin and function of large groups among human beings. He has deduced, by research on the size of the human brain compared with other living animals, that hunter-gatherer humans formed groups of about 150.[28] If this argument is true it points out with great force how important groups of about this size are to human beings. If small to middle sized groups are favourable social environments for human beings it is important to encourage the completion of activities around such groups today. This is obviously difficult because of the many tendencies towards centralisation.

In this chapter ways of learning from *The Thread* have been discussed in the context of 'maintaining continuity within change', and 'dealing with disconnectedness', two key areas in relation to today's needs. A number of key qualities and skills connected with generating healthy community have been outlined based on historic society, especially of the sort to be found in places like Great Waltham. The point of doing this is to highlight their importance for our society today, and also to generate pointers to the areas of community support where current effort should be concentrated, of course in ways that are meaningful for us today. What might be done will be addressed in the next chapter.

XXIX

Facing up to the challenges

The role of the small community

The subject matter of this book inevitably relates to wider debates about economic and social change, some of which have generated controversy over the years. One that figures strongly concerns the nature of 'community', especially the characteristics of local communities. Quite recently N J G Pounds wrote a book called *A History of the English Parish*[29] and in chapter seven, called *The Parish and the Community,* he made a survey of the different interpretations made by historians about the nature of life in local communities in medieval and early modern times. He shows they are very mixed, and that they range from acknowledging the strength of self governing small human groups to giving prominence to bickering and division. He himself says 'In the village community there was always much to dispute and abundant occasion for friction and feuding.[30] But later on he allows that local communities could be more or less self governing. He quotes F M Stenton on the question as follows, '...it is impossible to ignore the varied evidence which reveals the village and not the manor as the essential form of rural organisation".[31] He also quotes Marjorie McIntosh, who writes of Havering in Essex, that the tenants '... enjoyed exceptional autonomy...' encumbered by little outside supervision apart from the workings of the criminal law.[32] It has been noted earlier how the very recent work of H R French on how local English communities were run in the seventeenth and early eighteenth centuries confirms this view. Eamon Duffey's recent book on Morebath has also provided a detailed picture of how highly community life was developed there during the late middle ages, and how inclusive social life was.[33] Morebath was a tiny village, but like Great Waltham, was run by the local villagers. Both sexes, people of different social levels, the young and the old, all played a part in a shared way. Various offices were filled on a regular basis which were not monopolised by the better off, and even allowed women to participate. Most community decisions were taken by consent with the majority of the village present. Moreover, until the Protestant reforms of the late 1530s suppressed the cult of the saints several such cults flourished. These provided a cultural as well as a spiritual focus, because money and other resources were required to support the reverence of each saint. The resources were raised within the local community in ways which drew on all social and age groups, including young men and girls.

It has been found out during the writing of this book that Great Waltham had a great deal of local autonomy, which almost certainly produced strong independence among the villagers. That such a characteristic was a strong feature of local communities in the past raises an issue of considerable importance, something written about by Alan Macfarlane in his book *The Origins of English Individualism*.[34] He was interested in how England came to develop a noticeable spirit of independence and creativity. He believed it was certainly in existence by early medieval times. He also believed this spirit played a fundamental part in the development of the first industrial revolution. Studying the Ram family in its contexts leads to conclusions about the existence of individual vitality that have much in sympathy with Macfarlane's thinking, but the understanding developed here is that this spirit was as important in the development of community life as individual qualities. The sort of local independence that can be discerned in Great Waltham had social and political aspects as well as personal ones.

We have seen how in 1956 George Evans, writing about Blaxhall in Suffolk in *Ask the Fellows who Cut the Hay*, believed the self sufficient village had much to offer to successful community life. He was of the view that the demise of self sufficiency in village life was a great loss, and that the essence on which such communities was based was the need inhabitants had to get on and work together within the given frameworks. He was also of the view that this capacity need not be lost. 'But it is within the power of the parish council to supply leadership to a village, a true leadership of ability and interest and not one solely of status and of wealth'.[35] It is possible, even today, to imagine how this might happen in small villages if they were given real powers and tasks to fulfil, but how it could happen in large urban and inner city environments is not so easy to imagine. The story of the Ram family has shown that as family members moved away from the small self contained community their role in community declined. They moved into larger communities where their privacy was much greater and there was almost certainly less mutuality. The discovery of H R French that local government in Lyme Regis, one of the biggest towns in Dorset, was less open than that in surrounding rural parishes has been noted earlier. This may indicate that mutuality in community life is easier to achieve in smaller contexts. It could also explain why the Ram family were less active in Colchester and London than in Great Waltham. It is possibly a finding of crucial importance in developing contemporary initiatives.

Generally speaking mutual sharing and exchange is most successful when all the parties involved in a shared inter-dependant situation have a real need to get something out of it. It is important to realise though that the actual benefits are not usually the same for everyone. Contemporary concern about respect and identity is probably part of a confused search for a form of mutual sharing and exchange that works in the society of our day. Is some alternative approach to the centralised running of society possible? How in our modern world could we try to create the benefits of smaller face to face communities? In searching for a useful contemporary framework of mutual exchange something known in psychiatric language as the large group has potential to help. In the 1940s S H Foulkes hit upon the idea of developing group therapy out of Freudian one to one analysis. This development has been discussed already.[36] In the form of therapy he practised small groups of patients engaged in self analysis with the help of a professional psychiatrist. But Foulkes also saw this principle could be applied to work groups. The testing ground was the Maudsley Hospital where all the participants in the hospital; patients, medical staff and administrators, joined together in an ongoing continuous process of self review in a mutually open way, so that the hospital might be better run. He called this process a 'large group'. His idea has been adapted to many different situations and is still used on a relatively small scale. The essential idea of it is that mutuality is facilitated by free exchange in a group of people where everyone has a stake and something to gain from co-operation together.

Many people today are members of large groups of different kinds, which can overlap in quite complex ways. The phenomena is not new, for, as has been seen, members of the Ram family have been involved in such groups in earlier times. But the problem today is that, as Richard Sennett writes, the large group of the past has been hijacked by the centralised state. How can the large group help in this situation? Many of us today work in hospitals, schools, offices, factories, universities, or belong to churches, clubs, societies, or similar bodies. They are all 'large groups' but in very few of them is there real effort to run them in a way that encourages mutuality. Most work related large groups are hierarchical, split into separate functioning sub units which at best have some inter-connection at the more senior levels, and are, in the public sector governed by rules and regulations drawn up by civil servants and politicians often remote from the operational scene. In voluntary associations there is a greater degree of mutuality in the way affairs are run but even in the Church and political parties, hierarchical practices exert a weighty influence. People of a hierarchical disposition may well be afraid of Foulkes' vision and say it cannot work, but even those who are prepared to think it has something to offer have to realise real fundamental change has to take place in the ways we do things to offer any chance of it making a real difference. Simply playing with words and ideas and then going on with the same old ways is not good enough.

The exact size that a large group should be is a critically important question. Nearly all apes and monkeys, our close relations, live in groups which vary in size. Dunbar believes the origins of apes living in large groups is partly connected with maximising food collection. Because it has more eyes and ears a group can be much more efficient at finding and gathering fruit from trees than an individual working alone, and it also aids protection from predators. But there are also social aspects to large groups among monkeys and apes. Much time is spent in grooming one another, far longer than is necessary for cleanliness purposes. A major theory of Dunbar's book is that grooming is a way of maintaining social connections among the group. Humans have developed language because human society began to function in large groups that were too big to be socially sustained by grooming. It would just take up too much time. Researchers in this area have evolved methods for identifying the optimum size of large group for different kinds of apes by measuring brain size. Put crudely they found the bigger the brain the bigger the group.

Researchers believe human beings have habitually lived in groups of about 150. Dunbar points to significant evidence that supports this understanding. It is a well established principle in sociology that human social groupings larger than 150-200 become increasingly hierarchical. In groups of this size it is difficult to sustain relationships on an informal basis, and sociologists have long recognised individuals possess limited acquaintanceship circles. Experiments have shown that most people know around 30 people who they feel able to ask favours of. Dunbar also points out that the basic fighting unit of armies, the company, ranges from around 130 to 230 men. His conclusion is that '...even in large scale societies, the extent of our social networks is not much greater than that typical of the hunter gather's world.... Psychologically speaking, we are Pleistocene hunter-gatherers locked into a twentieth-century political economy'.[37]

I have related these ideas to Great Waltham as it existed in early modern times. Although the precise population of the village and parish at that period is not known,[38] the adult male population (i.e., age 16 and over) has been estimated to have been around 120. If two further assumptions are made, one that about forty of this number were unmarried and secondly that family groups were on average 4.4 persons, the figure Gregory King calculated them to be in the seventeenth century, the total population of the parish would have been roughly between 350 and 400.[39] This figure is larger than 250, partly because Great Waltham has always been a very large parish. Even in Medieval times the ends or hamlets that grew up round the main settlement had their own constables and other local officials. Effectively Great Waltham functioned as a whole unit of just under 400 people within which there were several sub units. A reasonably accurate estimation can be made of the population sizes of these because the survey and rental of 1577 lists all the tenants within the ends where they lived. Sub unit populations have been calculated by assuming the percentage of tenancies in each end was a rough reflector of how population was distributed in the parish. Table 20 shows the resulting calculation. Here is an example of how a rural community in early modern times managed to maintain its large group identity.

It is an inescapable fact that our biology makes us much more efficient when we are part of large groups. An example of this is how we find it very difficult to make major decisions without meeting people even though modern technology makes this possible. Dunbar also points out other ways in which our basic biological programming causes tension with some of the features of modern industrial conurbations, especially the lack of a sense of community. Unhappiness and social problems are the outcome.[40]

Table 20. Population distribution within Great Waltham parish in 1577.

Location.	Resident tenants.	% of all tenancies. #		population size. #	
South End	23	(24.5)	22.5	(98)	90
Romfrey End	12	(13)	11.5	(52)	46
Fourth End	9	(10)	9	(40)	36
North End	12	(13)	11.5	(52)	46
Litley End	(21) 32	(23)	31	(92)	124
Not known	15	(16.5)	14.5	(66)	58
Totals	(92) 103	100.0	100.0	400	400

There is uncertainty about the actual number of tenancies in Litley End, so two calculations have been made, one based on a smaller and the other on a larger estimate.

This lesson from the past tells us that the large group can only work when it is fulfilling a real role. The danger in present day society is to play at creating large groups by decentralising functions whilst retaining overarching controls. The problem with this approach is that no real mutuality is present. In other words people do not feel they have real power and involvement. This only comes in situations where people are bound together around a common purpose, in which everyone gains and gives something tangible – in which there is mutual reciprocity – not just for the fun of it but because being involved makes them better off, makes life materially easier, or brings real benefits not otherwise obtainable. Seeing possibilities for such groups in our society is very difficult because we have spent several hundred years running the role of such groups down. But this does not mean we cannot reorganise the way we do things to give more room to such groups. The large group can be at the centre of social life.

The role of the family

Because this book has been focused around one family it has been possible to look closely at how both the nuclear family unit and the extended family contributes to the formation of identity. What has been found out about the Ram family shows that family cohesion and solidarity has been enormously important, not just for this one family but for all those that were part of their communities. These findings partly confirm and also extend existing understandings. Much initial research about families was focused on those belonging to the aristocracy and was motivated more by a desire to understand the economic operation of such families than to examine how their lives were lived for its own sake. But from this work there emerged a realisation that the heads of wealthy families have always been concerned for the well being of the whole family in apportioning inheritances, not just the main heir. 'The long term history of landowners' interaction with the common law would suggest that they have always been concerned for their families'.[41]

The fact that the nuclear family unit has survived for so long indicates it fulfils an important and useful social function. Most children are still brought up in one, and anyone who, as a grandparent, has observed relations between parent and young child within their own family, knows that these form powerful bonds. The linkage between grandparents and grandchildren assists the maintenance of family identity and its influence. Moreover every child inherits its genetic package through the family. Yet the importance of the family role has been questioned in modern research, some of which has emphasised the role of peers and the wider community group, and played down the importance of the family unit. There are certainly real pressures on the role of the family today. Many more people are living alone, the level of marriage is going down and the rate of divorce is increasing. Allegiance to the family may also be declining and it is associated in some circles with old fashioned and stuffy views about the way to live. The growth of individualism and the desire to be oneself is possibly a cause of negative attitudes about the family. The general reaction against institutions, which is so typical of today, may have contributed to the spread of negative views. Questioning of the family role may also be stimulated by difficult personal experiences of family life. But there are also many people who believe that the decline in shared values and respect is due to the weakening of family life, which of course suggests its importance should be raised.

If the family is important in helping to preserve identity, mutuality and respect, as seems likely, why does government legislate in ways that serves to weaken its influence rather than strengthen it? Dame Elizabeth Butler-Sloss, after retiring as President of the High Court's Family Division, highlighted the ambiguous attitude of government and society as a whole to the family. She has commented that the withdrawal of tax incentives for marriage is a discouragement to marry. 'It is a sad fact that a Government which has published excellent proposals on helping parents and children after breakdown of relationships, has done nothing practical to support married couples'.[42] Here is an example of the self deception and disconnectedness that affects how we deal with social issues. Richard Sennett's discussion about the negative impact of the bureaucratic system on welfare support applies equally to the family. Because of the disciplinary problems in schools and general rebellion among young people spawned by the weakening of shared values, the institutional authorities are increasingly being forced to take on the role of substitute parents, in a completely depersonalised way. Will we get to the point where children are brought up without any family life at all? One of the real problems with the present situation, which is recognised by very few people, is that institutional encroachment of parental authority has a circularity about it which only serves to make the whole problem worse. Can there ever be effective substitution of family by impersonalised institutions?

The role of the institutions

Two of the principle institutions in our society, government and faith communities, primarily the Christian Church, both have difficulties in relating to ordinary people today. There is clearly a pervasive suspicion of those who govern, and people are increasingly failing to attend local churches. In fact the Christian Church in Europe faces problems so severe that if things go on as they are there may be no Church after the passage of several more generations, except for a tiny rump of believers. So, within the natural framework of identity formation, how can institutions play a positive role?

Although politicians are acutely aware of their difficulties and are trying to do more to engage with people they often seem unable to make headway. One of the problems they have is their difficulty in escaping from the prevailing centralised system. But there is another even more complex reason for lack of progress, for politicians are trapped in the existing system by their own interest in retaining power. To generate more openness in society they will have to give up some of their power, perhaps a large amount of it. The issue of respect that has been a government focus point in the early years of the twenty first century can be used to illustrate the challenge. Richard Sennett wrote an article in *The Guardian* shortly after the opening Parliament in the Spring of 2005.[43] He saw the government of the day as having a crusade about respect. Tony Blair, when Prime Minister, always saw the weakening of morality in society as a major issue. In 2002 he spoke to the Women's Institute of the need to sustain '... respect for others, honour, self-discipline, duty, obligation, the essential decency of the British character'. Sennett believes that in Tony Blair's model of society respect is upheld by deference, which has today lost its cultural impact. Perhaps this is a good thing, but as deference has declined nothing has replaced it to underpin the fabric of our society. Sennett believes that the government makes things worse for itself by treating people with disdain when they do not agree with it. He cites Iraq as a major example but there could be numerous others. Indifference of this kind breeds indifference and disrespect in return. Sennett concludes by writing that politicians might 'restore their authority by learning better the manners of modesty', concluding with the charge that if government is really serious about strengthening respect it 'will have to embark on a sweeping transformation of the institutions of everyday life'. But is Richard Sennett trapped in the very ways he is criticising? How can any government simply make a sweeping transformation of everyday institutions by a grand gesture? Moreover, as this book shows, there is more to respect than deference.

In the government's tackling of these problems promotion of what have come to be called community values has a high priority. This includes giving new community related powers to the police, making hospitals accountable to local communities and possibly developing 'community councils'. Whilst the intent of such moves may be admirable there are significant difficulties about turning intent into reality. There are deep underlying reasons for this which politicians have little or no control over. True respect is grounded in a body of values which are generally accepted as a framework to live by. But we have already seen that people's understanding of values as a framework to live by is becoming increasingly fragmented and 'disconnected', which inevitably leads to further weakening. The value base is breaking down into a variety of egocentric variants held by groups and individuals, for example, 'New Age' or 'Women's Lib'. This fracturing is increased further still by the presence of other faith communities. As the value base becomes more varied the mix of moral views is increasing problems of understanding and communication. Even professionals and administrators, who ostensibly are working for the same community values, can be inhibited from actually working together because their own personal value bases do not match.

But problems are not only caused by the increasing range of moral viewpoints that are held. People also, as has always been true, have all sorts of self deceptions about other people, both as individuals and in groups. These mostly exist in semi- conscious or unconscious understandings, often based on stereotypes. In impersonal bureaucracies all such blind spots help to reinforce the remoteness of institutions.

This leads us back again to the key issue that true community requires there to be mutuality in relationships and shared activities, which involves listening to and understanding others, and giving as well as taking. It has been remarked already in this book that in reality there is little understanding or practice of such practices in the formal functioning of our society. If community values are to feature more strongly it will not happen just by saying they are important, or simply by legislating for them. We will also have actually to change the way we run society by allowing and encouraging much wider listening to and understanding of others, and giving as well as taking. I have on several occasions over the last ten years been involved in European community development projects, both local and international, some based in the Christian Church and others in secular contexts. This experience has developed an awareness of the really profound difficulties caused by ideological self deception among politicians, Church leaders and administrators, both public and Church based. The story about the Newham Night Shelter pinpoints these difficulties. People in government tend to say that the policies they form are morally neutral, but this is not the case. It is, for example, quite common for those 'in authority' to promote community values in principle, but be blind to the fact that the way they actually run government makes the achievement of such ideas almost impossible. If public forms of identity are to regain a greater degree of mutuality or respect two pre-requisites are essential, in both institutions and individuals. Firstly a willingness to engage in open-ended and truly level playing field dialogue. And secondly preparedness to act on the conclusions which emerge from that, even if it means giving up things and views which protect our self interest.

The other major institutions that are concerned about the role of values are the faith communities. The paragraphs that follow are addressed particularly to the Christian Church but to a lesser or greater extend they apply to other faiths as well. In Europe religious institutions as a whole have a similar problem to government about popular acceptability, but it does not entirely take the same form. The Christian religion has influenced European society profoundly for the last two thousand years, and has provided the moral framework on which respect as we know it is based. Today religion is playing less and less significance in a formal sense. People do not go to church and do not acknowledge Christian values as a guide to live by. Yet large numbers of people still say they believe in God. Moreover although religious values are not held in much regard there is also no alternative code of generally held values emerging. People seem simply to want to be free to pursue their own interests and ideas.

Historically the Church has adopted a didactic or teaching pose. It has seen itself as having a message for people which stresses the need to repent and turn to God for salvation. Such an approach clearly has authoritarian and hierarchical tendencies, and in the Middle Ages the Church stood side by side with secular powers, or competed with them, to maintain control of society.

The authority of this position has been crumbling gradually since the late Middle Ages, and although religious institutions, and this includes Protestant Churches as well as Catholic ones, have made efforts to come to terms with changing circumstances, the inner practices of those who govern the Church, in nearly every case the ordained priesthood or ministry, are still essentially didactic in their view and practice. Hardly any of them would however agree publicly with this picture of the Church. The trend that has been growing since early modern times in Europe for greater freedom and individuality, which has become an avalanche and in the last half century, is incompatible with the didactic approach of the Church. If the process continues and the Church does not change it will become increasingly marginalised, certainly in Europe.

The notion that all human beings live by an underlying body of values has been reinforced strongly by the material examined in the historical part of this book about the Ram family. Clearly, some of their values are learned as children or adults in the process of living with other people, and some are the product of genetic inheritance. Now these basic values owe nothing to Christianity, Islam or any other religion. They are simply part of basic humanity, of which an element, perhaps a large one, is genetically based. This does not mean higher religions have nothing of value to offer. Religious belief can help to nurture and preserve respect for values and deepen understandings about them. The fact that people have a natural and innate feeling for values is a challenge to all faith communities as well as an opportunity. But if they fail to convince people they can add anything meaningful to them support is bound to haemorrhage away, especially in times like today when people have much individual freedom.

As far as the Christian Church is concerned a new type of Church is required in Europe, one which is more inclusive and more firmly grounded in mutuality, one which is much more clearly modelled on that advocated by Roland Allan in his famous book on missionary methods.[44] The fact that the message of the book, written many years ago, is so relevant points to the lack of change in the Church. Allan attacked the builders of colonial Churches for failing to follow the basic missionary understandings of St Paul. Whereas he set up local independently run churches, they invariably established institutions with professionalised leadership and control, in which there was a minimal role for local people. Although easier said than done the Christian Church of today has to find a way of tapping into the concerns of ordinary people and helping them to make sense of daily life. The kind of large group envisaged by Foulkes has potential to be of practical help in doing this, because local churches are in fact large groups and are part of the wider larger local community group. Practices and processes are required which encourage mutuality within such groups. In some parts of the world the Base Christian Community has been a way of liberating energy for both lay people and clergy together, in one form in Latin America and in another in Africa. Such Christian groups are inclusively involved in working with the whole of the local community in practical ways. Something akin to this concept is probably needed here but we cannot just copy what has happened in Latin America and Africa. Two major changes of approach are required in Europe. Local churches need to become a much more integrated part of their own local communities through practical involvement and sharing. The other is closely related and involves creating a more inclusive way of exercising leadership. Such developments would present a message about holistic values that are earthed and practical. A sign of hope is that methods are developing in Europe at grass roots level which bring together clergy and lay people in such ways. The importance and origins of this work is discussed in more detail in Appendix 4.

What alternative is there to the hierarchical model?

In Chapter XXIV two profiles of identity are presented, both of which are real, but the top down hierarchical one is normally predominant. The other one, real though often unacknowledged, is more bottom up in orientation and looks at the world through the family and the large group in an inside out kind of way. This profile, which flags up the complexity of everyday life and its realities, has a lot to offer in dealing with the identity issues that perplex us today. One of the things it reveals is the variety and depth of personal networking which supports the maintenance of value based social cohesion.

The documenting of the Ram family has shown many examples of how this happens. A good one is William Ram and his botany circle in the sixteenth century. Various different interests merged through it, and were mutually reinforced. There were at least five – interest in botany, gardening, medicines, finding work and jobs, and the development of marriage bonds. This mutual reinforcement of different interests was not necessarily calculated, for it could have easily happened naturally as a result of a friendship network. This example shows how people have their own private sources of values, which are just as real today. We can easily relate to William Ram's botany circle, even though it existed nearly four hundred years ago. This is because it has something important to tell us about how people find meaning today.

The kind of bonding just described is an important root of mutuality in society and if there is a real desire to increase mutuality and meaningful respect the government could profitably support the growth of such bonding – simply through encouraging it to flourish. But in reality short term and immediate problems attract a much greater public focus and receive the vast proportion of public revenues. Such an emphasis in deploying resources does not help institutions to form creative relationships with the majority of ordinary people who are not problem cases. One of the major difficulties with supporting aspects of social life which help to form mutuality is the contemporary break-up of an agreed value base and the pressure it creates on policy making. Currently the recognition of individual rights and freedoms are given much more prominence than shared values which put being socially responsible first. The emphasis on individual rights and freedoms has increased the level of cynicism about government and institutions generally.

The European Union is particularly concerned about how remote it appears to people, and the same is true of the British Government. Politicians are so concerned about the widespread alienation from Government and formal public life that considerable efforts are now being made to restore some interest. It sometimes seems that modern forms of communication and the media crowd out the importance of broad based shared values. Perhaps the media are increasingly the source of our values. But how true is this? A recent report on the countryside, the first to focus on rural areas using the 2001 census figures, has made some interesting and relevant findings, which it says are surprising, itself an indication of the lack of understanding about how important traditional sources of values still are.[45] The report finds that 49 per cent of people living in the English countryside get their personal opinions about life in Britain today mainly from their families. In urban areas the figure is lower, especially in London, but it is still 38 per cent. Friends shape the opinions of those in the countryside more than television, and only 2 per cent say that advertising campaigns or community leaders had a significant effect on what they think. An even more recent report on general social attitudes comes to similar conclusions.[46] 79 per cent of respondents believed nearly everyone/ most people treated them with respect and consideration in daily life. One of the report's authors has commented, 'Informal social relationships continue to occupy a hugely important role in most people's lives ...'. These findings give support to the understanding that values are transmitted in traditional ways through personal circles and local culture. The enormous volume of public communication that takes place today, much of which is driven in ever faster ways by impersonal technology, obscures the underlying importance of traditional and more personal culture.

Right at the beginning of this book reference was made to Richard Sennett's book *Respect – the Formation of Character in an age of Inequality*, to help focus on the problems there are today about identity. The fact he wrote his book shows concern about decline in respect for broad based shared values remains alive. He regrets the lack in modern welfare systems of respect for those given benefits and the frequent inability of such schemes to help nurture feelings of self worth among them. The book is effectively a critique of the uncaring and selfish nature of our contemporary society, and makes a plea that care and respect for others is essential if our lives are to contain a sense of overall fulfilment. I have much identity with this perspective and believe we are diminished today by an excessive focus on individualism which neglects care for each other. This does not mean the thrust for individual freedoms is wrong, and there are many aspects about its development which are estimable, but our lives could be enriched if the emphasis on individualism was less dominant. Telling the story of the Ram family in association with *The Thread* is intended to help illumine our current cultural situation.

One thing is quite clear if the social problems we decry are to be resolved. Real change will have to be made in the way society is run. The hierarchical model has to become less dominant, which will be very difficult to achieve, because it is so strongly embedded in our culture. Breaking away from this model involves changing ourselves, not just wishing change through getting others to change. We often delude ourselves that it is others who have to change rather than ourselves, and it is particularly common among those who have power in the present system and have some controlling influence. Put bluntly, change will not happen unless people with power give some of it up. In so doing ordinary people could be allowed to play a richer and fuller part. Almost certainly this would make the administration of public services less costly and make them more humane and sensitive to individual and local needs.

New ways of doing things have to be invented. The large group has been discussed in this book as offering a way forward. One of its characteristics is that people involved in such a group are required to contribute personally, perhaps give something up, while in doing this they obtain a return for themselves which they would not otherwise get. Forms of large group which offer possibilities to generate greater mutuality can be found. They will need to deal with issues of real importance to people if their commitment and involvement is to be obtained. But with some imaginative thinking there must be many ways in which these principles could be worked out practical ways. For example, benefits of various kinds are paid out by specialist agencies that are segmentally unrelated to each other, and ineffectively co-ordinated. This even happens in relation to the provision of benefits in one age group, for example the elderly. Many efforts have been made to integrate the work of doctors, social services departments, and hospitals but with limited success. The basic reasons for failure is that they remain at root separately financed and administered services. There is no preordained reason why this should be so. Why could not the country be divided into suitable 'large groups' and all benefit services be administered through the agency of a single authoritative person or body, which had the freedom to do this working in a mutual way with local people, including the clients. Such 'large groups' should be small enough for everyone involved in each one to be known to each other. This would need to be a village, a district, or part of a town, but the area concerned should never be so large that the element of personal mutual contact in the delivery of services is lost. Those who are responsible for delivery need to be able to develop and maintain personal relationships with the local people, and should ideally live in that community. The providers may be democratically responsible to the local community.

Some services would have to remain on a scale larger than the large group, like core medical services and road maintenance, but many could be dealt with in a purely local way. Some people will say this would lead to iniquitous treatment and varying standards in different places. But this happens now and will never be entirely prevented. The great benefit of generalised localised application is that services can become personal and can also involve local people in their operation in meaningful and personalised ways.

How the present centralising of government came about is a fascinating story. Up until the end of the eighteenth century it was a gradual ad hoc process to provide more efficient services for the growing inter-linked national economy that was coalescing out of earlier independent regional and local economies. The requirement for more organised government to cope with rising population and the related growth of the poor was also growing. The Elizabethan poor law was one of the first real initiatives of central government, apart from tax collecting, dealing with military needs, and managing a judicial system. In the seventeenth century the county magistrates took on greater responsibility for co-ordinating and organising local services, effectively taking them over from the local manor. But by the end of the eighteenth century economic growth, industrialisation and unprecedented population growth led to more drastic, but still ad hoc centralisation. Even though the old manor and parish system was swept away in the 1830s there was no local government as we understand it. In the place of traditional local government a motley collection of water, sewage, gas, and road maintenance bodies appeared, all acting separately from one another, not to be replaced by more organised local government until quite late in that century. Nonetheless the centralisation of government that was established in the mid nineteenth century as a response to unprecedented demands continued and expanded. But many people opposed the growth of centralisation, for its merits were fiercely debated in the early ninetieth century. Nor was debate entirely between the old guard and the new. Many reflective people were very aware of the social merits that went with local autonomy.

The question now is whether centralisation has got out of hand, about which there is lively discussion. However, new ways of doing things will not work whilst the centralising attitudes revealed in the Newham Night shelter story persist. Changing them will require learning how to deliver services based on the vision of a mutual society. People currently find operating in this way very difficult because it is so alien to what normally happens, and little is done at present to help them do otherwise. The Churches are beginning to develop new enabling processes which have potential for great creativity, as exemplified in Appendix 4. One aspect of the process described there is the use of an open ended but structured working discipline which is sensitive to the local situation and is conducted in the spirit of 'a level playing field'. The second element is the encouragement of networking among similar groups and projects. The third, which some people see as the most important, is accompaniment in the longer term, over several years, by a person who is skilled at enabling small groups or projects and can help them achieve their objectives without telling them what to do. In the original research work involved in developing these processes mutually based story telling and listening was found to be enabling and uplifting. But Appendix 4 also shows the difficulties experienced in generating positive responses. There are at least three reasons for this: a general clinging to the past, a reluctance of people in formal leadership positions genuinely to share leadership with others, and a strong desire among some of the lay people to defer to traditional forms of leadership. These characteristics are readily paralleled in secular spheres.

The way of working described in Appendix 4 hardly exists in our society. Some of its aspects are used already, as in quality circles, but almost entirely within the framework of the hierarchical system, which throws considerable limits on what can be achieved. Used in the broader sense indicated here there is real possibility of enabling and empowering local 'large groups' of many sorts. The challenge lies in overcoming the difficulties faced in getting such approaches accepted in our culture.

APPENDICES

Family Time Line

Overview

Section 1 of the time line deals with the period from the early fourteenth century to the mid-sixteenth century. The nature of family information available for that period does not lend itself to drawing up a 'family tree', but it is possible to make a list of individuals, who lived in and around Great Waltham. This is derived from references in manor court rolls, deeds, or other official documents, and provides both proof of existence as well as background information. However some people may be referred to more than once.

The other sections pick up the story in a more connected way from then on, drawing on registrations of baptisms, marriages and deaths, wills and other public documents. Three nuclear Ram families lived in Great Waltham in the middle of the sixteenth century: those of Robert Ram (d. 1576), Thomas Ram (d. 1556), and John Ram (d. 1568). From them descended the three branches which continue throughout the book, and form the basis of the time line.

	Branch A Robert Ram (d. 1576)	Branch B Thomas Ram (d. 1556)	Branch C John Ram (d. 1568)
Time line section	2	3	4
Genealogical charts	A1-A2	B1-B6	C1-C11

The genealogical charts and the time line are inter-usable as shown in the above table.

Plus signs by numbers in the time line indicate the inclusion of further information about the person concerned, e.g., on page 369 there is a + sign by number 43 – Mildred Ram – and then on page 370 there is another reference to number 43 which concerns Mildred Ram's marriage.

Section 1

KNOWN RAM FAMILY MEMBERS BEFORE CHARTS BEGIN

The following list of Ram family members is based on Table 4, p. 110 and Table 5, p. 113 which contain full details.

John le Ram (mid 14C).
Thomas Ram (mid 14C).
John Ram (late 14C).
Valentine Ram (early 15C).
John Ram (early 15C).
Thomas Ram (early 15C).
Richard Ram (early 15C).
John Ram (mid 15C).
Thomas Ram (mid 15C).
William Ram (mid 15C).
Thomas Ram, sen. (late 15C).
William Ram sen. (early 16C).
Thomas Ram (early 16C).
Robert Ram (early 16C).
Robert Ram, jun. (early 16C).
John Ram, sen. (early 16C).
John Ram, jun. (early 16C).
Thomas Ram (mid 16C).
William Ram (mid 16C).
Robert Ram, jun. (mid 16C).
Thomas Ram (mid 16C).

Around 1530 there seem to be three family lines. This situation can be construed from references in the Great Waltham court rolls and Geoffrey Ram's will. The three lines are John, Geoffrey and Robert. How these link with the three nuclear families present in the 1560s, which are the chartable family starts, is not known. The first known nuclear family is that of Geoffrey Ram (d.1530) from details of his will – Geoffrey Ram and Jayne? plus their children, all alive in 1530.
John Ram, (b. abt. 1485).
Thomas Ram, (b. abt. 1490).
Geoffrey Ram, (b. abt. 1490).
Jayne? Ram, (b. abt. 1490).
William Ram, (b. abt. 1490).
This family lived in High Easter in 1530.

Sabi(y)an Ram, widow. (mid 16C).
Margaret Ram (late 16C).

Section 2

DESCENDANTS OF ROBERT RAM (d.1576)

SEE GENEALOGICAL CHARTS A1 - A2

First Generation

1. **ROBERT RAM**, held the following property in 1563: a ½ yard called ROTHES, + FLETCHERS + PURLEY (Total rent 14/2). In 1576 he was a Yeoman. In his will of 1576 he possessed 1 customary tenement (rented), 2 a piece of copyhold pasture, 3 another tenement (rented), 4 a customary tenement called ROTHES (½ yard), 5 a field called WISTOCKE, 6 (3 acres) and 7 a meadow. He leaves to son Thomas 1, 2 and 3 and to his wife and son Richard 4, 5, 6, and 7. At some point he married **Agnes Childe**. She and ROBERT RAM had the following children:

+2	Thomas Ram (d. 1611)
+3	Richard Ram (d. 1611)
+4	Agnes Ram (-)
+5	Jane Ram (-)
+6	Joan Ram (-)
+7	Elizabeth Ram (-)

Second Generation

2. At some point **Thomas Ram,** son of ROBERT RAM and Agnes Childe, married **Jayne**. Jayne and Thomas Ram had the following children:

8	Alice Ram (-)
9	Margery Ram (b. 1574)
10	John Ram (b. 1577)
11	Elizabeth Ram (-)

3. **Richard Ram,** son of ROBERT RAM and Agnes Childe. In his will of 1611 he left 1 to John, a customary messuage in Gt Waltham where I now dwell with all the copyhold and freehold belonging (rented out), 2 to Richard a messuage called LARKES in Broomfield and Chechnell, 3 to Robert a customary tenement called FLETCHERS + adjoining land (1 acre) + 3 acres of ROTHES ½ yard + freehold land called WISTOCK + other freehold by estimation 19? acres, 4 to Daniel a customary tenement, 5 to Joseph amessuage called MOTTE + 14 acres. At some point he married Dorris. Dorris and Richard Ram had the following children:

+12	John Ram (1577-1618)
13	Richard Ram (d. aft. 1611)
14	Robert Ram (-)

15	Dorris Ram (-)
16	Susan Ram (b. 1587)
17	Elizabeth Ram (b. 1587)
+18	DANIEL RAM (1588-1632)
+19	Sarah Ram (b. 1590)
20	Joseph Ram (1593-1614). *Joseph in his will of 1614 left to his mother Dorris MOTTE and 14 acres, and after her death to John.*

4. At some point **Agnes Ram**, daughter of ROBERT RAM and Agnes Childe, married Robert Shittlewithe.

5. At some point **Jane Ram**, daughter of ROBERT RAM and Agnes Childe, married xx Seriea. xx Seriea and Jane Ram had the following children:

| 21 | Joan Seriea (-) |

6. At some point **Joan Ram**, daughter of ROBERT RAM and Agnes Childe, married **Richard Ponde**. Richard Ponde and Joan Ram had the following children:

| 22 | Agnes Ponde (-) |

7. At some point **Elizabeth Ram**, daughter of ROBERT RAM and Agnes Childe, married **John Marshe**.

Third Generation

12. At some point **John Ram**, son of Richard Ram and Dorris, married **Unknown.**

Unknown and John Ram had the following children:

23	Richard Ram (b. 1604)
24	Dorris Ram (b. 1607)
25	Mary Ram (b. 1608)
26	Richard Ram (b. 1609)
27	Joseph Ram (b. 1613)
28	Sarah Ram (b. 1614)
29	Margery Ram (-)
30	Rachel Ram (-)
31	Elizabeth Ram (-)

18 **DANIEL RAM**, son of Richard Ram and Dorris, in will of 1632 left all lands and tenements in Gt Waltham to his wife Clemenc during her natural life on condition she pays Daniel and Richard 40/- a year after age 24. After death of Clemenc ROTHES to go to Daniel, MOWES? to Richard, and to John a yearnal or croft called EDCOMBES. At

some point he married Clemenc. Clemenc and DANIEL RAM had the following children:

+32	Daniel Ram (1617-1689)
33	Joseph Ram (-)
+34	Richard Ram (1618-1669)
35	Elizabeth Ram (b. 1622)
+36	John Ram (1625-1683)
37	Jane Ram (-)
+38	Mary Ram (b. 1631)

19. At some point **Sarah Ram**, daughter of Richard Ram and Dorris, married **Robert Everard**.

Fourth Generation

32. **Daniel Ram**, son of DANIEL RAM and Clemenc, left in will of 1689 all lands (customary, copy and freehold) to brother in law Wm Morrison, provided he sell them. Proceeds to be divided between his wife, sister Mary and brother Joseph. At some point he married Unknown. **Unknown** and Daniel Ram had the following children:

39	Elizabeth Ram (b. 1642)
40	Sarah Ram (b. 1647)
41	Joanna Ram (b. 1649)
42	Elizabeth Ram (b. 1656)

34. **Richard Ram**, son of DANIEL RAM and Clemenc, in will of 1669 left to Richard MOWES? (? acres) by will of deceased father Daniel, provided he pay 3? pounds to Joseph in a year of my death. At some point he married **Tamakin.**

Tamakin and Richard Ram had the following children:

+43	Mildred Ram (-)
44	Richard Ram (b. 1640)
45	John Ram (-)
+46	Joseph Ram (b. 1726)

36. **John Ram**, son of DANIEL RAM and Clemenc, left in will of 1683 to William the messuage and tenement now living in – 'houses, edifices, buildings, yards, gardens, orchards', on condition he pays stated legacies to the other children. Rest of goods to William. At some point he married Elizabeth. **Elizabeth** and John Ram had the following children:

47	John Ram (b. 1647)
48	Thomas Ram (b. 1650)
+49	William Ram (1656-1711)
50	Edward Ram (-)

+51   Daniel Ram (1659-1722)
52   Joseph Ram (-)

38. At some point **Mary Ram**, daughter of DANIEL RAM and Clemenc, married **William Marrion (Morrison?).**

Fifth Generation

43. At some point **Mildred Ram,** daughter of Richard Ram and Tamakin, married **John Tanner.**

46. **Joseph Ram,** son of Richard Ram and Tamakin, in will of 1726 left house to Mary, part divided for use of son Joseph, lands to daughter Mary to use and dispose of as she sees fit, but including maintenance of mother. At some point he married **Bathshua.** Bathshua and Joseph Ram had the following children:

53   Mary Ram (b. 1681)
+54   Joseph Ram (b. 1683)
55   Martha Ram (b. 1684)

49. **William Ram,** son of John Ram and Elizabeth, left no will. At some point he married **Mary.** At some point he married **Anne.**

Mary and William Ram had the following children:

56   Mary Ram (b. 1690)
57   William Ram (b. 1691)
58   Mary Ram (b. 1692)

Anne and William Ram had the following children:

59   Anne Ram (b. 1695)
60   William Ram (b. 1696)
61   Elizabeth Ram (b. 1699)

51. **Daniel Ram,** son of John Ram and Elizabeth, in will of 1722 left all lands to his wife for her lifetime and then to his brother Joseph. At some point he married **Ann.** Ann and Daniel Ram had the following children:

62   Elizabeth Ram (b. 1722)

Sixth Generation

54. At some point **Joseph Ram,** son of Joseph Ram and Bathshua, married **Jane Gardiner.** Jane Gardiner and Joseph Ram had the following children:

63   Joshua Ram (b. 1724)
64   Bethsheba Ram (1726-1731)

Section 3

DESCENDANTS OF THOMAS RAM (d.1556)

SEE GENEALOGICAL CHARTS B1 - B6

First Generation

1. **THOMAS RAM**, in will of 1556 beqeaths the use of his farm (not named) to William and John (sons) on condition they support his wife during her life. On wife's death home and lands to be sold, but if William and John want it they can buy. At some point he married **Unknown**. At some point he married **Margaret.**

Unknown and THOMAS RAM had the following children:

2	William Ram (-)
+3	Jane Ram (-)
4	Robert Ram (-)
5	Alice Ram (-)
6	Anne Ram (-)
+7	John Ram 1 (d. 1588)
+8	Thomas Ram (-)

Margaret and THOMAS RAM had the following children:

9	John Ram (Young) (-)
10	Thomas Ram (Young) (-)

Second Generation

3. At some point **Jane Ram**, daughter of THOMAS RAM and Unknown, married ? **Southbury.**

7. **John Ram 1B**, son of THOMAS RAM and Unknown, in will of 1588 leaves BRADES to his wife with 2 acres. + croft called YEDON with 2 acres + PONDON croft (4 acres) for her natural life (rent 3/4). Then to son Thomas if his wife pays Richard Ram £30 . He also gives freehold lands to his wife, to be split among the children after her death. In 1588 he was a Husbandman – about 10 acres. The £30 covers debt arising from a mortgage debt. At some point he married Rose. Rose and John Ram 1 had the following children:

+11	John Ram 2 (1566-1612)
12	Tho Ram (b. 1569)
13	Jane Ram (b. 1571)
14	Alice Ram (-)

15   Anne Ram (-)
+16   Thomas Ram (b. 1575)

8. At some point **Thomas Ram**, son of THOMAS RAM and Unknown, married **Unknown**. Unknown and Thomas Ram had the following children:

17   Margery Ram (b. 1566)
18   Ric Ram (b. 1571)

Third Generation

11. **John Ram 2B**, son of John Ram 1B and Rose, in will of 1612 was a weaver and had three sons: John, Thomas, and Richard, all under 26. Mentions 'the house I now dwell in' is called Purley Castle. At some point he married **Unknown**. Unknown and John Ram 2B had the following children:

+19   JOHN RAM 3B (1586-1667)
+20   Tho Ram (b. 1597)
21   Richard Ram (-)

16. In 1616 **Thomas Ram,** son of John Ram 1B and Rose, holds freehold ELMERS FIELD – 2 acres in South End. (Rent 12/-?). At some point he married **Ann**. Ann and Thomas Ram had the following children:

+22   Thomas Ram (b. 1595)

Fourth Generation

19. In 1616 **JOHN RAM** 3B, son of John Ram 2B and Unknown, holds ¼ yard called E Gates, and also in 1646. He lived in 1667 at Purleigh Castle, Great Waltham. In will of 1667 leaves tenement house and houses – wherein I now dwell called PURLEIGH CASTLE with grounds, appertenences , etc., to Richard. (Was most of the land already in Richard's hands – John was an old man). In 1667 he was retired – probably a yeoman. At some point he married **Maria Turner**. Maria Turner and JOHN RAM 3B had the following children:

+23   Mary Ram (b. 1615)
24   Johis Ram (b. 1616)
25   Johis Ram (b. 1618)
+26   Johis Ram (b. 1620)
+27   Clem Ram (b. 1623)
+28   Sara Ram (b. 1627)
29   Thomas Ram (b. 1631)
+30   Richard Ram (1634-1714)

20. At some point **Tho Ram**, son of John Ram 2B and Unknown, married **Unknown**. Unknown and Tho Ram had the following children:

31   Ric Ram (b. 1622)

22. At some point **Thomas Ram**, son of Thomas Ram and Ann, married **Anne.** Anne and Thomas Ram had the following children:

32	Edward Ram (b. 1620)
+33	Daniel Ram (b. 1622)
34	Jane Ram (b. 1628)
35	William Ram (b. 1631)

Fifth Generation

23. At some point **Mary Ram,** daughter of JOHN RAM 3B and Maria Turner, married xx **Gozlitt.**

26. **Johis Ram** was the son of JOHN RAM 3B and Maria Turner. Johis Ram had the following children:

| 36 | John Ram (b. 1647) |
| 37 | Thomas Ram (b. 1650) |

27. At some point **Clem Ram,** daughter of JOHN RAM 3B and Maria Turner, married **Unknown.**

28. At some point **Sara Ram,** daughter of JOHN RAM 3B and Maria Turner, married **Edwin Symonds.**

30. At some point **Richard Ram,** son of JOHN RAM 3B and Maria Turner, married **Ann.** At some point he married **Hannah Collyns.**

Ann and Richard Ram had the following children:

| 38 | John Ram (b. 1658) |

Hannah Collyns and Richard Ram had the following children:

39	Mary Ram (b. 1660)
40	Hannah Ram (b. bef. 1667)
41	John Ram (b. bef. 1667)
+42	Richard Ram (1668-1710)

33. At some point **Daniel Ram,** son of Thomas Ram and Anne, married **Elizabeth.** Elizabeth and Daniel Ram had the following children:

43	Samuel Ram (b. 1655)
44	Rebecca Ram (b. 1657)
45	Martha Ram (b. 1661)

Sixth Generation

42. At some point **Richard Ram**, son of Richard Ram and Hannah Collyns, married **Mary Stephens.** Mary Stephens and Richard Ram had the following children:

+46   JOHN RAM 4B (1688-1762)

Seventh Generation

46. **JOHN RAM 4B**, son of Richard Ram and Mary Stephens, in will of 1762 left his wife interest on £600 for her lifetime. All real estate left to eldest son Richard. (Was it divided up earlier – John was 74). At some point he married **Mary**. At some point he married **Rebecca Goodeve.**

Mary and JOHN RAM 4B had the following children:

47	Mary Ram (1710-1710)
48	John Ram (b. 1711)
49	Richard Ram (b. 1714)
50	Elizabeth Ram (b. 1714)
+51	Hannah Ram (b. 1715)

Rebecca Goodeve and JOHN RAM 4B had the following children:

+52	Richard Ram (1717-1781)
53	Ann Ram (1719-1719)
+54	Nathaniel Ram (b. 1720)
55	Elizabeth Ram (b. 1721)
+56	John Ram 5B (1723-1785)
+57	Rebecca Ram (b. 1724)
+58	William Ram (1725-1764)
+59	Daniel Ram (b. 1728)
+60	Benjamin Ram 1 (1729-1789)
61	Tamar Ram (b. 1731)

Eighth Generation

51. At some point **Hannah Ram**, daughter of JOHN RAM 4B and Mary, married **John Salisbury.**

52. **Richard Ram**, son of JOHN RAM 4B and Rebecca Goodeve, in 1781 left an almost Illegible will. Appears to leave monies and investments in a trust. One child Sarah Stagg is mentioned. No sons reached maturity. He was a Maltster in Chelmsford. At some point he married unknown. **unknown** and Richard Ram had the following children:

62	Mary Ram (b. 1751)
63	Tamar Ram (1753-1774)
+64	Sarah Ram (b. 1755)
65	John Ram (1756-1760)

54. At some point **Nathaniel Ram**, son of JOHN RAM 4B and Rebecca Goodeve, married **Mary Noaks or Doaks ?.**

56. **John Ram 5B**, son of JOHN RAM 4B and Rebecca Goodeve, in will of 1785 describes himself as Gentleman. No property mentioned, or a wife. Estate comes to £860 in legacies + residue. He was a Cordwainder in Chelmsford. At some point he married **Mary.** Mary and John Ram 5B had the following children:

66   John Ram (1744-1768)

57. At some point **Rebecca Ram**, daughter of JOHN RAM 4B and Rebecca Goodeve, married **Henry Gage.**

58. At some point **William Ram**, son of JOHN RAM 4B and Rebecca Goodeve, married **Elizabeth Blowers?.**

59. At some point **Daniel Ram**, son of JOHN RAM 4B and Rebecca Goodeve, married **Unknown.** Unknown and Daniel Ram had the following children:

67   Sarah Ram (-)
68   Benjamin Ram (-)

60. **Benjamin Ram 1**, son of JOHN RAM 4B and Rebecca Goodeve, in will of 1789 leaves to Benjamin and John 'the several leases and terms for years of and in my farms and lands which I shall die possessed of for the remainder of the terms. If they want to go their own way John can. But Benjamin 1 states if there is a division it will be by cash value rather than land division. At some point he married **Anne Nevil.**

Anne Nevil and Benjamin Ram 1 had the following children:

+69   BENJAMIN RAM 2 (1765-1825)
+70   JOHN RAM 6B (1768-1835)
+71   Ann Ram (-)

Ninth Generation

64. At some point **Sarah Ram**, daughter of Richard Ram and unknown, married **John Stagg.**

69. **BENJAMIN RAM 2**, son of Benjamin Ram 1 and Anne Nevil, in will of 1825 requests business to be kept on during his widow's lifetime. On her death, or remarriage, it is to be sold and the proceeds to be divided up. Eldest son Benjamin gets occupancy of all property at this point. But in 1851 Benjamin was a farm labourer near Chelmsford. In 1881

son William was occupying the family home. Benjamin 2 was a farmer in Roxwell, Newland Hall. At some point he married **Rosanna Stock**. Rosanna Stock and BENJAMIN RAM 2 had the following children:

72	Rosanna Ram (b. 1790)
73	Benjamin Ram (1792-d. bef. 1794)
+74	Mary Ram (b. 1793)
+75	Benjamin Ram 3 (b. 1795)
+76	William Ram 2 (1797-d. aft. 1881)

70. **JOHN RAM 6B**, son of Benjamin Ram 1 and Anne Nevil, was a farmer in Steeple at Steeple Grange. At some point he married **Abigail Boltwood**. At some point he married **Sarah**. Abigail must have come from the Boltwood family that held several farms in Great Waltham. See notes on typescript by H E Flight.

Abigail Boltwood and JOHN RAM 6B had the following children:

+77	Sarah Ram (b. 1800)
78	Abigail Ram (b. 1803). *She lived in 1881 at Prospect Place, Maldon St Peter, with Mary Ram and Susan Smith (nee Ram).*
79	Anne Ram (b. 1804)
+80	John Ram 7B (1806-1852)
+81	Anne Ram (b. 1808)
+82	Susan Ram (b. 1812)
83	Mary Ram (b. 1813)
84	Tamer Ram (b. 1813-)
+85	BENJAMIN RAM 4 (1814-1864)
86	Isaac Ram (b. 1815)
87	Joseph Ram (b. 1815)

71. At some point **Ann Ram**, daughter of Benjamin Ram 1 and Anne Nevil, married **James Marthams**. James Marthams lived at in Pleshey, Essex. He was a Shopkeeper.

Tenth Generation

74. At some point **Mary Ram**, daughter of BENJAMIN RAM 2 and Rosanna Stock, married **William Burr**.

75. In 1851 **Benjamin Ram 3**, son of BENJAMIN RAM 2 and Rosanna Stock, was an agricultural labourer at Rainsford End, Essex. At some point he married **Martha**. Martha and Benjamin Ram 3 had the following children:

88	Ellen Ram (b. 1841)
89	Selina Ram (b. 1843)

90   Janet Ram (b. 1844)
91   Benjamin Ram (b. 1847)
92   Fanny Ram (b. 1850)

76. **William Ram 2**, son of BENJAMIN RAM 2 and Rosanna Stock, was a farmer in Roxwell, Newland Hall. At some point he married **Mary Ann**. Mary Ann and William Ram 2 had the following children:

+93   Fanny Elizabeth Ram (b. 1824)
94   Jane Ram (b. 1826)

77. At some point **Sarah Ram**, daughter of JOHN RAM 6 and Abigail Boltwood, married John Chapman. **John Chapman** lived at in Danbury, Essex. He was in Farmer.

80. At some point **John Ram 7B**, son of JOHN RAM 6 and Abigail Boltwood, married **Mary Smith**. Mary Smith and John Ram 7B had the following children:

95   Mary Ram (b. 1832)
96   Emily Ram (b. 1834)
97   John Ram (b. 1836)
98   Agnes Ram (b. 1837)
+99   Elizabeth Ram (b. 1839)
100   Coswell Ram (b. 1841)
101   Walter Ram (b. 1841)
102   Alice Ram (b. 1844)
103   Arthur Ram (b. 1846)

81. At some point **Anne Ram**, daughter of JOHN RAM 6B and Abigail Boltwood, married **William Sewell**. William Sewell lived at Latchingdon, Essex. He was a farmer.

82. **Susan Ram**, daughter of JOHN RAM 6B and Abigail Boltwood, lived in 1881 at Prospect Place, Maldon St Peter, with Mary Ram and Abigail Ram. At some point she married **xx Smith**.

85. In 1841 **BENJAMIN RAM 4**, son of JOHN RAM 6B and Abigail Boltwood, was a farmer at Steeple, Essex. In 1851 he was still a farmer but lived at Chelmsford, Essex. In 1861 he was a Clerk at the Foundry in Ipswich, Suffolk. At some point he married **Mary Ann Young**. Mary Ann Young and BENJAMIN RAM 4 had the following children:

104   Mary Ann Ram (b. 1838)
+105   Benjamin Ram 5 (b. 1839)
+106   Thomas Ram (b. 1840)

+107	Charles Harry Ram (b. 1843)
108	John Ram (b. 1845)
109	Jane Ram (b. 1850)
110	Bertha Ram (b. 1853)
111	Jennie Maria Ram (b. 1858)

Eleventh Generation

93. At some point **Fanny Elizabeth Ram,** daughter of William Ram 2 and Mary Ann, married **Carr.**

99. At some point **Elizabeth Ram,** daughter of John Ram 7B and Mary Smith, married **Thomas Willett.** Thomas Willett and Elizabeth Ram had the following children:

| 112 | Mary Willett (b. 1868) |
| 113 | Henry G Willett (b. 1874) |

105. At some point **Benjamin Ram 5,** son of BENJAMIN RAM 4 and Mary Ann Young, married **Mary Ann.** Mary Ann and Benjamin Ram 5 had the following children:

114	Frederick M Ram (b. 1865)
115	Benjamin B Ram (b. 1867)
116	Joseph Richard Ram (b. 1872)
117	James A Ram (b. 1875)
118	William Edward Ram (b. 1879)

106. At some point **Thomas Ram,** son of BENJAMIN RAM 4 and Mary Ann Young, married **Annie.**

107. At some point **Charles Harry Ram,** son of BENJAMIN RAM 4 and Mary Ann Young, married **Susan.** At some point he married **Elizabeth Harris.**

Susan and Charles Harry Ram had the following children:

119	Charles Ram (b. 1865)
120	Thomas Benjamin Ram (b. 1867)
121	John Ram (b. 1869)
122	Susan Ram (b. 1873)
123	Lue Ram (-)

Elizabeth Harris and Charles Harry Ram had the following children:

124	Rose Ram (-)
+125	William Richard Ram (1877-1940)
126	Jane Ram (b. 1878)
127	Alice Ram (b. 1880)

128   Eadie Ram (-)

129   Lisa Ram (-)

130   Salt Lake City Ram (-)

Section 4a

FAMILY OF JOHN RAM (d.1568)

SEE GENEALOGICAL CHART C1

1. **JOHN RAM1C**, in will of 1568 in Leaves to William a tenement in Pleshey of free and copy hold land called HARRY'S + a parcel of copyhold land that was bought off John Pond. Also a parcel of copyhold land in Great Waltham of 4 acres. He also left to William a croft of free land (3 acres) in Great Waltham called LANGLER'S and a croft of copyhold land (3 acres) in High Easter called CxxxxLAND. Also 3 acres of copyhold land. He leaves to Francis a tenement in Pleshey (Gt Waltham?) called PADINGTON'S + garden ajoining called BARWYRE with rents due. In 1563 he held about 25 acres in 6 sites: 2 in Great Waltham (rent 4/-), 2 in Pleshey, 1 in High Easter, and PADINGTON'S. At some point he married **Unknown.** Unknown and JOHN RAM 1C had the following children:

2   Christopher Ram (d. 1572).*Christopher was a Cleric: Vicar of Boxted until 1563, Little Wendon until ? and then Bures in Suffolk until he died.*

3   Joan Ram (-)

4   WILLIAM RAM (d. 1602)

5   FRANCIS RAM (b. abt. 1536-1617)

This branch splits into two, through Francis (Section 4b) and William (Section 4c).

Section 4b

DESCENDANTS OF FRANCIS RAM (d. 1617)

SEE GENEALOGICAL CHARTS C2 - C3

First Generation

1. In 1580 **FRANCIS RAM** 1, son of JOHN RAM (d. 1568) and Unknown (-), held as a 'License' from the Cook family to Francis – Manor of LARKSTOCK and other lands in Gloucestershire worth £16 in 1579. In

his will of 1616 he bequeathed lands and tenements 'to the uses decided in an earlier indenture'. Only dealt with small legacies. Between 1558 and 1604 he was the Cooke family agent (started as bailiff to the Essex manors) and Deputy Steward of Havering. Became a' Gent' in his own right. At some point he married Ellen Foxe (Sope). Ellen Foxe (Sope) and **FRANCIS RAM** had the following children:

+2	Francis Ram 2(d. 1610)
3	John Ram (-1617). *John in his will of 1617 left house in Hornchurch to brother Benjamin. (This was let to a Mr Mason). May have left land to brother Benjamin. Left his father's arms to brother Samuel. Left several legacies, including 2 to servants.*
+4	William Ram (d. 1612)
+5	Anthony Ram (1582-1616)
+6	Samuel Ram (1583-1624)
7	Elizabeth Ram (1585-1586)
8	Nathaniel Ram (1588-1608)
+9	Edward Ram (1590-1617)
10	Joseph Ram (b. 1593)
+11	Benjamin Ram (1594-1623)

Second Generation

2. In 1603 **Francis Ram 2**, son of FRANCIS RAM 1 and Ellen Foxe (Sope), possessed lands transferred from Cooke family worth £460. In 1605 he was admitted to Grays Inn. At some point he married **Elizabeth Garrard.** Elizabeth Garrard and Francis Ram 2 had the following children:

+12	Elizabeth Ram (b. 1609)

4. At some point **William Ram,** son of FRANCIS RAM 1 and Ellen Foxe (Sope), married **Margaret Green.** In 1639 Christian Green (mother of Margaret) leaves £10 to grandchild Francis Ram of Hornchurch + £50 to Katherine Attwood his wife. Leaves copyhold lands in trust for children of Francis until they are 21. Margaret and William Ram had the following children:

+13	FRANCIS RAM 3 (1607-1644)
14	Daughter Ram (-)
15	Daughter Ram (-)
16	Daughter Ram (-)

5. **Anthony Ram,** son of FRANCIS RAM 1 and Ellen Foxe (Sope), in his will of 1616 leaves a number of smallish legacies to his family -His wife was born Bearblock – father William. Susan married Anthony as a widow. He was apprenticed to the Goldsmith's Company. Its records say he was presented by John Chalkhill in 1611, and apprenticed in 1614. He

presented a guilt cup and cover to the company in 1617. At some point he married **Susan Williamson (was born Berblock or Bearblock).** Married Anthony as a widow. She and Anthony Ram had the following children:

17   Susan(na) Ram (b. 1613)

6. **Samuel Ram,** son of FRANCIS RAM 1 and Ellen Foxe (Sope), in his will of 1624 left 3 farms to ? – Bin (en)trees in Dagenham, farms in Hornchurch, farm called Harrolds Wood, and farm called Bushe Elms. He was a farmer in Dagenham. At some point he married **Mary Bird.** Mary Bird and Samuel Ram had the following children:

18   Richard Ram (1618-1618)
19   Francis Ram (1619-1620)
20   Samuel Ram (1620-1625)
21   Elizabeth Ram (1623-1625)

9. **Edward Ram,** son of FRANCIS RAM 1 and Ellen Foxe (Sope), in his will of 1617 leaves to wife Joan house in Clapham + £385 (debts due). Leaves several other smallish legacies. In 1617 he was described in will as Gent. May have been a Goldsmith. At some point he married **Joan Bearblock (was Harlow).** Joan Bearblock was previously married to Mr Harlow and had 3 children. She and Edward Ram had the following children:

22   Francis Ram 4 (1614-1634). *In 1629 Francis was apprenticed to the Drapers' Company.*
23   Elizabeth Ram (1616-1618)

11. **Benjamin Ram,** son of FRANCIS RAM 1 and Ellen Foxe (Sope), in will of 1623 states he was a Goldsmith. In the Co. records – presented by Mr Bearblock in 1613, was apprenticed to him in 1615, and made free by redemption in 1616. He was admitted a freeman in 1616. At some point he married **Jane Harvey.** Jane Harvey and Benjamin Ram had the following children:

24   Francis Ram (b. bef. 1620-1625)
25   Frances Ram (1620-1625)
26   John Ram (1623-1623)

Third Generation

12. At some point **Elizabeth Ram,** daughter of Francis Ram and Elizabeth Garrard, may have married **Thomas Stevens.**

13. **FRANCIS RAM 3,** son of William Ram and Margaret Green, was a farmer. At some point he married **Elizabeth Willis.** At some point he married **Catherine Atwood.** Catherine Atwood and FRANCIS RAM 3 had the following children:

+27	Francis Ram 6 (1630-1683)
28	Catherine Ram (1631-1631)
+29	John Ram (d. 1713)
30	Stephen Ram (1634-1635). *Stephen twin of William.*
+31	William Ram (1634-1712)
32	Abigail Ram (1635-1638)
33	Samuel Ram (1637-1638)
34	Jane Ram (-)

Fourth Generation

27. At some point **Francis Ram 6,** son of FRANCIS RAM 3 and Catherine Atwood, married **Dorothy Spencer.**

29. **John Ram,** son of FRANCIS RAM 3 and Catherine Atwood, was unmarried. In 1639 he was given land by his grandmother Christian Green. In will of 1714 he was a Gent.

31. **William Ram,** son of FRANCIS RAM 3 and Catherine Atwood, was twin of Stephen. He went to school between 1648-1653 at Charterhouse. In 1639 he was granted lands by his grandmother Christian Greene. In 1651 he was apprenticed to Merchant Taylor's Company. Freeman in 1658. In his will of 1712 leaves house, buildings, and land called the BULL in Hornchurch to daughters Catherine and Jane. Leaves a property in Widford, bought off John Broom of Chelmsford, to Jane. No ref. to property in Broomfield where he lived. At some point he married **Penelope Freeman.** Penelope Freeman and William Ram had the following children:

35	Jane Ram (1667-1750)
36	John Ram (1669-1669)
+37	Amy Ram (b. 1670)
38	Penelope Ram (1672-1693)
39	Mary Ram (b. 1681)
40	Catherine Ram (d. aft. 1716)
41	Elizabeth Ram (d. 1716)

Fifth Generation

37. At some point **Amy Ram** married **James Porter.**

Section 4c

DESCENDANTS OF WILLIAM RAM (d.1602)

SEE GENEALOGICAL CHARTS C4 - C12

First Generation

1. **WILLIAM RAM** in 1551 matriculated pens. from Trinity Hall, Cambridge. He wrote a book published in 1606 – Ram's Little Dodeon, or a Brief Epitome of R Dodeon's New Herbal. He was an Attorney. Deputy Town Clerk of Colchester. At some point he married **Maryan**. Maryan and WILLIAM RAM had the following children:

+2	William Ram (d. 1620)
3	Richard Ram (-)
+4	ROBERT RAM (1564-1638)
+5	MARCELLUS RAM (b. 1571)
6	Martha Ram (b. 1572)
7	Rose Ram (1573-1573)
+8	Thomas Ram (b. 1575)
9	Wiston Ram (b. 1576)
10	Susanna Ram (b. 1577)
+11	Edmund Ram (b. 1579)
12	Francis Ram (-)
13	Susanna Ram (1581-1608)
+14	Elizabeth Ram (-)

Second Generation

2. **William Ram**, son of WILLIAM RAM and Maryan, lived at Romford, Essex. He was an Innkeeper and yeoman. At some point he married **Judith Nooth**. Judith Nooth and William Ram had the following children:

15	William Ram (b. 1588)
16	Susan Ram (b. 1591)
17	Thomas Ram (b. 1592)
18	Francis Ram (b. 1594)
19	Elizabeth Ram (1596-1596)
20	Elizabeth Ram (b. 1597)
21	Joan Ram (b. 1603)
+22	Anne Ram (b. 1605)
23	Margaret Ram (b. 1607)
24	Elizabeth Ram (b. 1609)
25	Edward Ram (b. 1612)

4. **ROBERT RAM**, son of WILLIAM RAM and Maryan, in his will of 1635 left small sums to poor in Copford and Birch. About £400 in family legacies. To son Robert advowson of Hockley Magna. To son Richard his house and lands £40 cheaper than to others. Book of Martyrs to daughter Sarah. To daughter Susan best English Bible 'lately bound in London'. 'The rest of my books to my sons Richard and Robert. Richard gained B A from Queens College, Cambridge in 1606, whilst Robert graduated from Jesus College in 1612. Robert, sen. gained B A Jesus College, Cambridge in 1583/4, B D 1595 and D D in 1602. He was a C of E Cleric. Rector of Copford and Gt Birch from ? to 1638. At some point he married **Elizabeth**. Elizabeth and ROBERT RAM had the following children:

26	Edward Ram (d. 1610)
+27	Richard Ram (-)
+28	Dorothy Ram (b. 1589)
29	Thomas Ram (b. 1590)
+30	John Ram (1591-bef. 1666)
+31	Robert Ram (1593-bef. 1675)
+32	Elizabeth Ram (b. 1594)
+33	Rebecca Ram (b. 1596)
+34	Mary Ram (b. 1597)
+35	Rachel Ram (b. 1598)
36	Charles Ram (b. 1600)
37	Anna Ram (b. 1602)
+38	Marthanna Ram (b. 1604)
39	Aquilla Ram (b. 1606)
+40	Susan Ram (b. 1607)
+41	Sara Ram (b. 1610)

5. At some point **MARCELLUS RAM**, son of WILLIAM RAM and Maryan, married **Ann Mannock**. Ann Mannock and MARCELLUS RAM had the following children:

+42	John Ram 2C (1598-bef. 1646)
43	Anna Ram (b. 1605)
44	Richard Ram (b. 1608)

8. At some point **Thomas Ram,** son of WILLIAM RAM and Maryan, married **Unknown**.

11. **Edmund Ram,** son of WILLIAM RAM and Maryan, in his will of 1620 left tenements, legacies, and goods to people including 'my nephew Robert's son of my brother Robert DD'. Leaves his house in Copford called FORDES in trust to pay to Margaret my wife the rents. By a codicil

leaves 47 acres bought in Copford to his wife. At some point he married **Margaret**. Margaret and Edmund Ram had the following children:

45   Martha Ram (-)

14. At some point **Elizabeth Ram**, daughter of WILLIAM RAM and Maryan, married ? **Bell**.

Third Generation

22. At some point **Anne Ram**, daughter of William Ram and Judith Nooth, married **William Mascall**.

27. **Richard Ram**, son of ROBERT RAM and Elizabeth, BA Queens College, Cambridge in 1607. He was in C of E cleric. Curate with father. Vicar of Gt Bentley, Essex, 1613-15. Rector of Peldon, Essex, 1615- 40. At some point he married **Alice?** Alice? and Richard Ram had the following children:

46   Robert Ram (b. 1630)
47   Ruben Ram (b. 1630)

28. At some point **Dorothy Ram**, daughter of ROBERT RAM and Elizabeth, married **John Goodwin**.

30. In 1649 **John Ram**, son of ROBERT RAM and Elizabeth, in ERO papers described as a 'gent'. In 1649 he was a party in an agreement for partition in Copford between Israel Edwards, and Edward and Charles Ram of London (deceased in 1659). In 1649 he possessed in the Manor of Copford a conveyance for £3500 from John Ram and W Kath to Israel Edwards of E. Mersea, Clerk, comprising various houses and land – all in Copford and Gt Birch. At some point he married Thomasin Mountjoy. **Thomasin Mountjoy** and John Ram had the following children:

48   John Ram (1639-bef. 1675)
49   A daughter Ram (Martha) (b. 1641). *In 1666 she receives annuity of £35 from Elizabeth Edwardes – aunt.*
50   Isabella Ram (b. 1642)

31. **Robert Ram**, son of ROBERT RAM and Elizabeth, gained B A Jesus College, Cambridge in 1612. He was ordained in 1622 in St James' Colchester. In 1622 he was a Clerk in holy orders. At some point he married **Joan Mountjoy**. Joan Mountjoy and Robert Ram had the following children:

51   Robert Ram (1621-1622)
52   Mary Ram (b. 1622)
53   Edmund Ram (1624-bef. 1675)
54   William Ram (b. 1677)

32. **Elizabeth Ram**, daughter of ROBERT RAM and Elizabeth, was a widow in 1666 when she made a grant to Martha, daughter of John Ram, deceased, of an annuity of £35 arising from tenant called Noaks in Copford. In 1666 she was involved in the Sale? to Hezekiah Haynes of a Copford house called DRETCHES and land. At some point she married **Israel Edwards**. In 1649 Israel Edwards was Vicar in E Mersea. In 1649 he possessed Mekes as a purchase of estate from John Ram.

33. At some point **Rebecca Ram**, daughter of ROBERT RAM and Elizabeth, married **Henry Shaw**.

34. At some point **Mary Ram**, daughter of ROBERT RAM and Elizabeth, married **Nathaniel Carr**. Nathaniel Carr was in Clerk in holy orders.

35. At some point **Rachel Ram**, daughter of ROBERT RAM and Elizabeth, married **Henry Goulding**.

38. At some point **Marthanna Ram**, daughter of ROBERT RAM and Elizabeth, married **William Willson**.

40. At some point **Susan Ram**, daughter of ROBERT RAM and Elizabeth, married **Thomas Nicholson**.

41. At some point **Sara Ram**, daughter of ROBERT RAM and Elizabeth, married **John Argor**. John Argor was in Clerk in holy orders.

42. In 1653 **John Ram 2C**, son of MARCELLUS RAM and Ann Mannock, was a weaver. See entry concerning son's marriage. At some point he married **Marie**. Marie and John Ram 2C had the following children:

    | +55 | John Ram 3C (1626-1666) |
    | 56 | Edward Ram (b. 1633). *Edward in 1646 was admitted to the Royal Grammar School at Colchester 21 September. In the register it says he is the only son of John Ram.* |

Fourth Generation

55. **John Ram 3C**, son of John Ram 2C and Marie, was married in April 1653. The marriage entry says he is son of John Ram, late of St Mary's, weaver. He was a merchant/farmer. At some point he married **Mary Place**. Mary Place and John Ram 3C had the following children:

    | +57 | John Ram 4C (1654-1713) |
    | +58 | WILLIAM RAM (b. aft. 1654-1732) |

Fifth Generation

57. In 1695 **John Ram 4C** son of John Ram 3C and Mary Place, was a merchant. 'At the request of the aldermen and some of the members of this corporation Mr John Ram was admitted and sworn a (something) burgess upon the payment of £15 (1695). In 1698 when he married a second time he was described as of St Nicholas ward, Colchester. In the same year he was elected to the common council of Colchester. In 1704 he had interests in Fingringhoe Manor and farms of Fingringhoe Hall and Wick. At some point he married **Unknown**. At some point he married **Elizabeth Goddard.**

58. **WILLIAM RAM**, son of John Ram 3C and Mary Place, was a yeoman. In 1697 he purchased Stoke Farm at Stoke by Nayland for £222. In 1732 his holding in Stoke Farm was conveyed from William Ram, Yeoman, of Wormingfold to Nicholas Ram of Stoke, Yeoman. At some point he married **Mary ?**. Mary ? and WILLIAM RAM had the following children:

59	William Ram (d. bef. 1716)
+60	John Ram (-)
+61	Francis Ram (d. 1750)
62	Audry Ram (-). *Audry lived at in London.*
+63	Mary Ram (-)
+64	Thomas Ram (d. 1776)
65	Katherine Ram (-)
+66	Bridget Ram (d. 1744)
67	James Ram (d. 1724)
68	Joseph Ram (d. 1748). *Joseph was a single man.*
+69	NICHOLAS RAM (d. 1788)
+70	William Ram (-)

Sixth Generation

60. **John Ram**, son of WILLIAM RAM and Mary ?, lived at in Eye, Suffolk. At some point he married **Margaret**. Margaret and John Ram had the following children:

71	John Ram (b. 1717)
72	John Ram (b. 1720)

61. **Francis Ram**, son of WILLIAM RAM and Mary ?, was nominated guardian of Nicholas in Stoke farm settlement of 1725. He was a farmer. In 1747 he took out a mortgage from John James on a property in Norrington St., Stoke by Nayland-Cocooks?. At some point he married **Mary ?**. Mary ? and Francis Ram had the following children:

73	Mary Ram (d. 1721)
+74	Mary Ram (b. 1722)
+75	Ann Ram (1724-1759)

63. At some point **Mary Ram**, daughter of WILLIAM RAM and Mary ?, married **Samuel Salmon.**

64. In 1698 **Thomas Ram**, son of WILLIAM RAM and Mary ?, was admitted into share of ownership of Stoke Farm. He was admitted to Colchester Grammar School 26 March 1709. He was a Surgeon (There is uncertainty about this. One source says he died in infancy).

66. At some point **Bridget Ram**, daughter of WILLIAM RAM and Mary ?, married ? **Warren.**

In 1744 Bridget Warren left money and land to the Ram family, almost certainly the daughter of William and Mary Ram.

69. **NICHOLAS RAM,** son of WILLIAM RAM and Mary ?, farmed at Monkwick Farm, Essex, from about 1735. New 21 yr lease taken up in 1753 (rent £112 plus rates and taxes) and extended to 1782. For further details see John Ram 5C. May well have had an earlier lease since 1732. In 1725 he was admitted into share of ownership of Stoke Farm as a minor and youngest brother and customary heir of James Ram. Guardianship granted to brother Francis. In 1732 he held Stoke Farm when it was conveyed from William Ram, Yeoman, of Wormingfold to Nicholas Ram of Stoke, Yeoman. In 1744 under Bridget Warren's will Nicholas was given land called 'Species' or 'Spencers' in Gt Bromley. In 1747 he was admitted with John Pearson to the Bromley title. In 1757 he was admitted to Raylins on surrender of John Pearson. In 1757 he held map of a farm called Porters in his estate. In 1758 he was party in an indenture with John Stubbins of Stoke (executors of Francis Ram deceased), and Richard Partridge re redemption of earlier mortgage. See Francis Ram. He is listed in the Essex County Poll Book of 1768 as a freeholder in Colchester. Calls himself Gentleman in his will. He almost certainly sub let. In 1781 he participated in a settlement between himself, father, Francis Ram, son, Elizabeth (D) Lay, and John Stubbin. Nicholas Ram conveys to John Stubbin, a farm called 'Fields' or 'Warriors' in Stoke to the use of Nich. In 1782 he leaves Bromley farm to James in will. In 1782 he leaves property 'wherin I now dwell' to son John in will with his wife having it during her lifetime. In 1782 he leaves to son James, farm, buildings, etc called 'The Tan? Office on the Old Hythe at Colchester. At some point he married **Abigail Sayer.** At some point he married Elizabeth Pearson. At some point he married **Mary Sollery.**

Abigail Sayer and NICHOLAS RAM had the following children:

76	Mary Ram (b. 1736)	
+77	JOHN RAM 5C (1739-1810)	
78	Bridget Ram (b. 1741)	

Elizabeth Pearson and NICHOLAS RAM had the following children:

+79	Jane Ram (1762-1812)	
+80	James Ram (1761-1798)	
+81	Sarah Ram (d. bef. 1782)	
+82	Francis Ram (d. 1782)	

70. In 1744 **William Ram**, son of WILLIAM RAM and Mary ?, was a farmer at Fingringhoe, Essex. At some point he married Jane Cocks. At some point he married **Elizabeth Blowers.**

Jane Cocks and William Ram had the following children:

83	Jane Ram (b. 1745)

Seventh Generation

74. At some point **Mary Ram**, daughter of Francis Ram and Mary ?, married **Nathaniel Goodrich.**

75. At some point **Ann Ram**, daughter of Francis Ram and Mary ?, married **John Stubbin(g).** In 1781 John Stubbin(g) was involved in Stoke Farm settlement – son of this John Stubbin?

77. **JOHN RAM 5C**, son of NICHOLAS RAM and Abigail Sayer, was a merchant. Calls himself Gentleman in will. Listed in 1793 Directory as Merchant. In 1744 land under the will of Bridget Warren of Gt Bromley was left there to John Ram, farmer, as a tenant in common with William Pearson, son of John Pearson, of Berechurch. In 1780 he paid land tax on Sheldrick's Farm (owned by Ralph Ward?). Presumably this was leased. In 1782 he held under will of Nicholas the property 'wherin I (Nicholas) now dwell'. John leased Monkwick Farm from 1780 to1795 (110 acres at £150). Also leased Lordswood (65 acres). In 1792 John Ram gave up his leases to James Ram, who had them for 11 years. In 1793 he held a copyhold farm at Battlewick, called Peacock's Garden – 40 or 60 acres, 31.75 acres around Colchester, Middle Mill, 10 houses in Colchester. At some point he married **Hannah King.** Hannah King and JOHN RAM 5C had the following children:

+84	Hannah Ram (1772-1793)	
85	Mary Ram (b. 1775)	
+86	John Ram 6C (1776-bef. 1810)	
87	Mary Ram (b. 1777)	
+88	Nicholas Ram (d. 1816)	
89	Jane Ram (-)	
90	William Ram (1785-1798)	
91	James Ram (1787-1804)	

79. At some point **Jane Ram**, daughter of NICHOLAS RAM and Elizabeth Pearson, married **John Bawtree 2**. John Bawtree 2, son of John Bawtree 1 (d. 1773) and Sarah Pearson (d. 1782), was the brother of Elizabeth Sarah Bawtree (1771-1857) who married Ralph Adye (d. 1804). She came from Wivenhoe. Their daughter Elizabeth Jane Adye married James Ram the legal writer. He was a Banker in about 1797, becoming a partner in the Colchester and Essex Bank. The family involvement continued until 1891 when the bank was taken over by Gurney's. He founded the Essex Equitable Insurance Society. He and Jane Ram had the following children:

92	Elizabeth Jane Bawtree (-)
+93	John Bawtree (-)
+94	Sarah Bawtree (-)
+95	Ann Bawtree (-)

80. **James Ram**, son of NICHOLAS RAM and Elizabeth Pearson, was a farmer. In will says he is a Gentleman. Listed in 1793 Directory as farmer. In a marriage settlement of 1791 James and his wife covenated 'Spencers' and 'Raylins' to each other for their lifetimes. In 1798 his will does not affect the property. A plan of the farm says it is 26 acres. At some point he married **Jane Meades**. Jane Meades lived in 1810 at East Doneyland. In her will of 1810 she leaves her estate at Great Bromley to daughter Jane. She and James Ram had the following children:

96	Jane Ram (1792-1812)
+97	JAMES RAM (1793-1870)
98	John Ram (1793-1793)

81. At some point **Sarah Ram**, daughter of NICHOLAS RAM and Elizabeth Pearson, married **John Pearson**. John Pearson was a Farmer. Alive in 1782 – executor of his sister's will. Nicholas Ram and John Pearson were admitted to a Bromley title. John Pearson withdrew in 1757. Is this the same title as involved John Ram and William Pearson. Is probably different?

82. In 1782 **Francis Ram**, son of NICHOLAS RAM and Elizabeth Pearson, was a merchant. His will of 1782 does not include Stoke Farm. After death of his father (1788) the property passed to Francis' wife, Elizabeth, for life. At some point he married **Elizabeth Lay**. Elizabeth Lay married again before 1788 – Harrington. She and Francis Ram had the following children:

| 99 | Joan Ram (-) |

Eighth Generation

84. At some point **Hannah Ram**, daughter of JOHN RAM 4 and Hannah King, married **William Keymer**.

86. In 1793 **John Ram** 6C, son of JOHN RAM 5C and Hannah King, held under his father's will a house, 27.5 acres in Colchester and copyhold farm at Battleswick 40 or 60 acres. He lived in 1806 at Fingringhoe, Essex. He had rented a mill off Joseph green in Colchester for 3 years in 1796. (Parish records). He was a farmer. At some point he married **Martha Brown.** Martha Brown and John Ram 6C had the following children:

100	Martha Ram (b. 1794)
101	Harriet Ram (1795-1811)
102	Robert Ram (b. 1796)
+103	JOHN RAM 7C (b. 1798)
+104	Joseph Ram (b. 1800)
105	William Ram (b. 1802)
106	Hannah Ram (b. 1803)
107	Bridget Ram (b. 1806)
108	Susannah Ram (b. 1806)

88. **Nicholas Ram**, son of JOHN RAM 5C and Hannah King, inherited from father Middle Mill, 4.5 acres in Colchester, 10 houses in Colchester. In 1816 he leaves all messuages, lands, tenements and heridiments to his wife Mary. At some point he married **Mary.**

93. **John Bawtree** 3, son of John Bawtree 2 and Jane Ram, lived in 1857 at Abberton. At some point he married **Helen Inglis**. Alive in 1871. Helen Inglis and John Bawtree 3 had the following children:

109	John Bawtree (-)
+110	Sister (-)

94. At some point **Sarah Bawtree**, daughter of John Bawtree 2 and Jane Ram, married ? **Baroker.**

95. At some point **Ann Bawtree**, daughter of John Bawtree 2 and Jane Ram, married **T J Turner.**

97. **JAMES RAM,** son of James Ram and Jane Meades, lived in London until about 1838, then Ipswich. He wrote at least 6 books on legal subjects. In DNB. 'As a legal author Ram obtained a well founded reputation for painstaking research, methodical arrangement, and lucidity of style'. In 1814 he was admitted to the Bromley property. He obtained in 1817 a B A from Pembroke College, Cambridge. Admitted at the Inner Temple 1813. Called to the Bar 1823. He was a conveyancer and legal author. In his marriage settlement of 1826 he covenants the Bromley farm to the joint uses of him and his wife for their lives, and to his heirs. Also to pay £200 a year to her out of his personal estate. In 1833 he was admitted to

Stoke Farm title, passed to him through brother Francis. Still held it at his death in 1870. In 1843 he made a lease of 'Spencers' and 'Raylins' to George Sargent for 7 yrs. With rent of £42. In 1849 he made a further lease to same person with a rent £43. 50, which was renewed in 1856 with a new rent of £45. At some point he married **Elizabeth Jane Adye**. Elizabeth Jane Adye and JAMES RAM had the following children:

+111	James Ram (b. 1828)
+112	Stephen A S Ram (b. 1831)
113	Jane Ram (1832-1905)
114	Mary Ram (1837-1864)
+115	Willett Ram (1839-1921)
+116	Edward Ram (b. 1843)
+117	Ralph Adye Ram (b. 1845)

Ninth Generation

103. At some point **JOHN RAM 7C**, son of John Ram 6C and Martha Brown, married **Ann**. Ann and JOHN RAM 7C had the following children:

119	William Ram (b. 1824)
+120	John H Ram (b. 1830)
121	Caroline Ram (b. 1828)
122	William B Ram (b. 1830)
123	George Ram (b. 1837)

104. **Joseph Ram**, son of John Ram 6C and Martha Brown, in 1819 became a poor rate charge on Layer de la Haye (Parish records). In 1819 he was a husbandman. In 1821 he was a shepherd. In 1822 he was a husbandman. In 1824 he was a shepherd. At some point he married **Susannah**. Susannah and Joseph Ram had the following children:

124	Susannah Ram (b. 1819)
125	Hannah Ram (b. 1821)
126	Elizabeth Ram (b. 1822)
127	Sarah Ram (b. 1824)

110. At some point **Sister**, daughter of John Bawtree 3 and Helen Inglis, married **Charles Hawkins**.

111. **James Ram**, son of JAMES RAM and Elizabeth Jane Adye, lived at Norwood. He was admitted to Pembroke College, Cambridge and matriculated 1847. Did not graduate. He was a Private Tutor – and author of *The Philosophy of War*. At some point he married **Charlotte Gurner**. Charlotte Gurner and James Ram had the following children:

| 128 | Charlotte Adye Ram (b. 1853) |

<table>
<tr><td>129</td><td>Jane Adye Ram (b. 1854). *Jane lived between 1890-1900 in Norwood and London. She was a sculptor but also exhibited a few flower and figurative paintings at the Royal Academy and Society of British Artists, London.*</td></tr>
<tr><td>+130</td><td>Edward A Ram (b. 1859)</td></tr>
</table>

112. **Stephen A S Ram,** son of JAMES RAM and Elizabeth Jane Adye, lived in Oakley Square. His photo is in a book about the Ram family in Colchester at British Library. He was in soliciter. At some point he married **Susan Amelia Scott.** Susan Amelia Scott and Stephen A S Ram had the following children:

+131	Gilbert Scott Ram (1865-1938)
+132	Stephen Adye Scott Ram (b. 1867)
133	Melville L Ram (1868-1880)
+134	John Adye Scott Ram (1869-1939)
135	Margaret E Ram (b. 1870). *Margaret and Susan E were twins.*
136	Susan E Ram (b. 1870).
+137	Arthur Scott Ram (b. 1872)
+138	Percival Ram (b. 1873)
139	Helen Mary Scott Ram (b. 1877)
140	Euphemia Jane Scott Ram (1880-1887)
+141	Henry Bernard Scott Ram (b. 1885)
+142	Humphrey Scott Ram (-)

115. At some point **Willett Ram,** son of JAMES RAM and Elizabeth Jane Adye, married **Lucy Annie Gill.** Lucy Annie Gill and Willett Ram had the following children:

+143	Willett Ram (1875-1921)
+144	Lucy Frances Ram (b. 1876)
+145	Francis Robert Ram (b. 1877)
+146	Earnest Arthur Ram (b. 1879)
147	Henry Arthur Ram (1879-1879)
+148	Mary Constance Ram (b. 1880)
+149	Frances Alice Ram (b. 1882)
+150	Emma Mary Ram (1885-1934)

116. **Edward Ram,** son of JAMES RAM and Elizabeth Jane Adye, in 1865 obtained B A London – 1st. He wrote a book in 1888 on *Leading Events in the Church of England.* He was a C of E cleric. Vicar of St John Timberhill, Norwich – 1871 -. At some point he married **Virginia Noverre.**

117. **Ralph Adye Ram,** son of JAMES RAM and Elizabeth Jane Adye, was educated about 1862 in Corpus Christie College, Cambridge. Two Irish Rams were

there about the same time – Abel John and Robert Digby. The latter was a contemporary. Ralph was a C of E cleric. Headmaster of Holbeach Grammar School, 1877-91. At some point he married **Annie Davies Johnstone**. Annie Davies Johnstone and Ralph Adye Ram had the following children:

151	Mary Dorothea Ram (b. 1878)
152	Phyllis Ram (b. 1880)
153	Elizabeth Adye Ram (-)

Tenth Generation

120. At some point **John H Ram**, son of JOHN RAM 7C and Ann, married **Unknown**. Unknown and John H Ram had the following children:

+156	John Henry Ram (b. 1855)
157	Walter Ram (b. 1857)
+158	Arthur Ram (b. 1855)
159	Louisa Ram (b. 1862)
160	Elizabeth Ram (b. 1866)
161	Alice Ram (b. 1869)
162	Sidney Ram (b. 1872)

130. **Edward A Ram**, son of James Ram and Charlotte Gurner, lived in Hong Kong. He was an FRIBA. He was in Architect. Trained in London. Practised in Hong Kong. At some point he married **Mabel Topham**. Mabel Topham and Edward A Ram had the following children:

| +163 | Joyce Adye Ram (-) |
| +164 | Elizabeth Adye Ram (-) |

131. At some point **Gilbert Scott Ram**, son of Stephen A S Ram and Susan Amelia Scott, married **Ada Findlater**.

132. **Stephen Adye Scott Ram**, son of Stephen A S Ram and Susan Amelia Scott, was ordained a Clerk in holy orders. He went to school at Charterhouse and then to St John's College, Cambridge. 1st class – 3rd div. in classics 1882. MA 1890. He was in various livings in the North of England. Vicar of St Mary's Lowgate in Hull from 1899-1926. Canon and Prebendary of York Minster 1926. At some point he married **Margaret King**. Margaret King and Stephen Adye Scott Ram had the following children:

165	Stephen Melville Ram (-)
166	Percival John Ram (-)
167	Euphemia May Ram (-)
168	Herbert Ram (-)

134. **John Adye Scott Ram**, son of Stephen A S Ram and Susan Amelia Scott, lived at 131, Clarence Gate Gardens, London, N W. He was educated at

Felsted School. Matriculated Non Coll 1887. Admitted solicitor 1895. Practised at 23 Red Lion Square (Messrs Bridges, Sawtell and Co). At some point he married **Bertha Graves**. Bertha Graves and John Adye Scott Ram had the following children:

169   Murial Susan Ram (b. 1910)

137. At some point **Arthur Scott Ram**, son of Stephen A S Ram and Susan Amelia Scott, married **Kate Ancaster.** Kate Ancaster and Arthur Scott Ram had the following children:

+170   Edith Marjory Ram (b. 1906)
171   Kathleen Marion Ram (b. 1909)
172   Helen Ada Scott Ram (b. 1913)

138. At some point **Percival Ram**, son of Stephen A S Ram and Susan Amelia Scott, married **Marion Blake**. Marion Blake and Percival Ram had the following children:

+173   Doris Ram (b. 1908)

141. At some point **Henry Bernard Scott Ram,** son of Stephen A S Ram and Susan Amelia Scott, married **Mary Tipping.** Mary Tipping and Henry Bernard Scott Ram had the following children:

174   Patricia Scott Ram (b. 1922)

142. At some point **Humphrey Scott Ram,** son of Stephen A S Ram and Susan Amelia Scott, married **Elizabeth Wilson.**

143. At some point **Willett Ram**, son of Willett Ram and Lucy Annie Gill, married **Ethel Blackstone**. At some point he married **Annie Mary Smith.** Ethel Blackstone and Willett Ram had the following children:

+175   William Francis Willett Ram (b. 1907)
176   Elizabeth Lucy Willett Ram (b. 1909)

144. At some point **Lucy Frances Ram,** daughter of Willett Ram and Lucy Annie Gill, married **Joseph David Dallin Paul.**

145. At some point **Francis Robert Ram,** son of Willett Ram and Lucy Annie Gill, married **Dora Bellas Thompson.**

146. **Earnest Arthur Ram,** son of Willett Ram and Lucy Annie Gill, was educated at Brighton College. Admitted to Pembroke College, Cambridge 1897. Admitted solicitor 1903. Practised in London. At some point he married **Marianne Upcher.** Marianne Upcher and Earnest Arthur Ram had the following children:

177   Beryl Ram (-)

148. At some point **Mary Constance Ram,** daughter of Willett Ram and Lucy Annie Gill, married **Robert Bland.**

149. At some point **Frances Alice Ram,** daughter of Willett Ram and Lucy Annie Gill, married **Revd Thomas Gaunt.**

150. At some point **Emma Mary Ram,** daughter of Willett Ram and Lucy Annie Gill, married **Edward Stokes.**

Eleventh Generation

156. At some point **John Henry Ram,** son of John H Ram and Unknown, married **Emily.** Emily and John Henry Ram had the following children:
     178   John Henry Ram (b. 1881)

158. At some point **Arthur Ram,** son of John H Ram and Unknown, married **Nellie.** Nellie and Arthur Ram had the following children:
     179   Reginald Ram (-)
     +180   Reginald Ram (b. 1884)

163. At some point **Joyce Adye Ram,** daughter of Edward A Ram and Mabel Topham, married **Geoffrey Miskin.**

164. At some point **Elizabeth Adye Ram,** daughter of Edward A Ram and Mabel Topham, married **D J Alfree.**

170. At some point **Edith Marjory Ram,** daughter of Arthur Scott Ram and Kate Ancaster, married **Hugh Currie.**

173. At some point **Doris Ram,** daughter of Percival Ram and Marion Blake, married **S L Spencer.**

175. At some point **William Francis Willett Ram,** son of Willett Ram and Ethel Blackstone, married **Kate Margaret Marshall.** Kate Margaret Marshall and William Francis Willett Ram had the following children:
     181   Kate Frances Ram (b. 1937)
     182   Carole Ram (b. 1940)

Twelfth Generation

180. At some point **Reginald Ram** son of Arthur Ram and Nellie married **unknown.** Reginald Ram and **unknown** had the following children:
     183   Violet Ram (b. 1886)

The demography of the Ram family of Great Waltham, Colchester, Hornchurch and London, 1575-1901

Part A: distribution of male family members. Part B: approximate numbers alive at 25 year intervals.

Explanation of place name abbreviations.
Great Waltham area. GW & R= Great Waltham and Roxwell, Ch = Chelmsford, Pu & S = Purleigh and Steeple.
Colchester area. Cl, B & P = Colchester, Berechurch and Peldon, Cp = Copford, and SN = Stoke by Nayland.
Hornchurch area. R = Romford, H = Hornchurch, Br = Broomfield, and SR = Stanford Rivers.
Ipswich area. I = Ipswich, N = Norwich, H = Hull, Ho = Holbeach, and Ha = Halesworth.
London area = L. (This area includes Middlesex and the inner parts of Essex, Kent, and Surrey).

Part A. Distribution of males alive in snapshot years.

> The numbers show males living at each time point. The unbracketed ones are where they were born and bracketed ones [ ] where they lived their adult life. Place names are given in full below the headings.

Date	Great Waltham area		Colchester area				Hornchurch area				Ipswich area				London area	Other	Totals
	GW/R	Ch	Pu/S	Cl/B/P	Cp	SN	R	H	Br	SR	I	N	H	Ha			
1575	8[6]			4[3]	0[1]		0[1]	0[1]									12
1600	11[9]			5[4]	4[5]		0[1]	10[9]									28
1625	5[5]			4[2]	2[3]			4[3]							1[2]		16
1650	6[6]			1[1]	4[4]	0[1]		0[1]		3{1}							14
1675	7[7]			0[2]	1[0]	2[1]				3[2]					0[1]		13
1700	6[6]			0[1]		4[4]				3{1}							13
1725	5[2]	0{3}		0[1]		5[4]			0[1]								10
1750	5[2]	1{4}		1[3]		3[1]											10
1775	5[3]	0{2}		3[5]		2[0]											10
1800	4[4]			7[7]													11
1825	3[2]		2[3]	3[1]											0[2]		08
1850	2[1]	0[6]	9[4]	2[0]							3[4]				3[4]		19
1875	1[1]		6[1]								3[0]	0[1]	0[1]	0[1]	15[20]	0[1]	25
1900			4[0]								3[0]	0[1]	3[4]	3[4]	26[28]	0[2]	39

Part B. Number of males alive in snapshot years.

Year	1575	1600	1625	1650	1675	1700	1725	1750	1775	1800	1825	1850	1875	1900
Total males.	12	28	16	14	13	13	10	10	10	11	08	19	25	39
Aged 21+.	07	10	09	08	10	09	06	08	08	03	06	07	13	22
Aged 21-	05	18	07	06	03	04	04	02	02	08	02	12	12	17

Ram, Pearson, Bawtree and Adye family networks in Colchester, 1750-1880

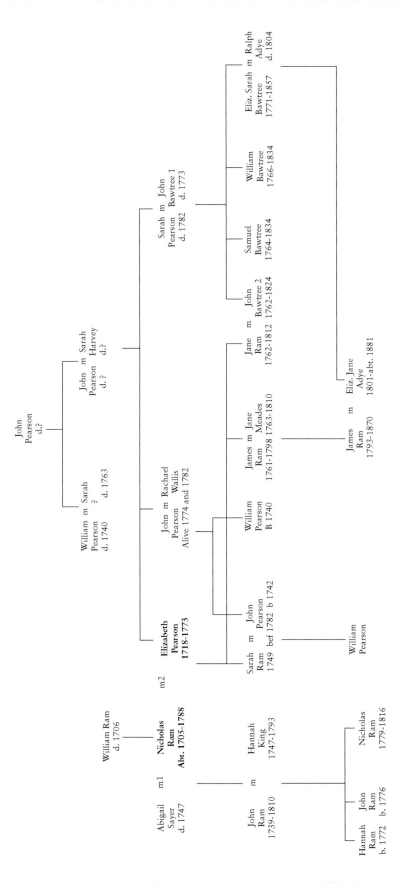

Building Bridges Of Hope Process

This appendix has been included as an example of how mutuality can be supported in our contemporary society. The process outlined is essentially an enabling device to facilitate mutual ways of working. It has been applied mainly in church contexts but can be used in and adapted to any situations where people, perhaps of different backgrounds, are trying to work together in a common cause.

The process outlined here is used by the Association of Building Bridges Churches. It grew out of an in depth investigation of mission and church life in our society run by the Churches' Commission on Mission, part of Churches Together in Britain and Ireland (CTBI). One stage of it involved visiting at regular intervals for three years some 40 local churches from a wide spectrum of traditions across Britain and Ireland. Through that initiative the value of working with small groups in open ended ways with the support of an accompanier and the sharing of stories became apparent. It is this open ended, non hierarchical sharing emphasis, possibly unique to this process, that is so important for the achievement of mutuality.

Broadly, the process has three aspects (1) team discussion around a number of key questions over a period of about three years (2) assistance of an outside accompanier, who is an enabler, not a consultant, and (3) networking with other places on a similar journey.

Where the process has been used it has almost always led to a strengthening of vision, morale and relationships, but there are difficulties. A lot of local Christian communities back away from the bottom up / open ended approach of the process because it can challenge existing structures, power holding, and practice. Such blockages to mutuality are to be found throughout community life, not just in churches and badly need clearing away.

At the time this book was published the Association of Building Bridges Churches is involved with several other Church related organisations in exploring what can be done to clear the blockages. Part of this has involved a small group reflecting on some questions against the background of a number of stories from the experience of the Association. These were some of the questions with church references removed. They may be able to contribute to unlocking problems in other areas of life.

q What do the eight stories show about doing things in new ways and using new language (discourse)?

q What do you miss in the stories and why?

q What indications are there in the stories of signs of future community life, or a new stage emerging in the life of the community?

q What are the obstacles to future community life coming from the stories?

q What can be done about these obstacles?

This appendix is the personal contribution.

Dr R W Ram.
November 2009.

SELECT BIBLIOGRAPHY

Primary sources

A selection of the more important ones is included below. Full coverage is in the end notes.

General

Census of England and Wales, 1841, 1851, 1861, 1871, 1881, 1891, and 1901.

Church of Jesus Christ of Latter-Day Saints, *1881 British Census and National Index*.

Church of Jesus Christ of Latter-Day Saints, *International Genealogical Index* (IGI). Ram entries for Essex, Suffolk, Cambridgeshire, Norfolk and London.

Dictionary of National Biography. Entries on Stephen Adye (d. 1794) which mentions several other members of his family discussed in this book, Richard Preston, (1768-1850), James Ram, (1793-1870), Thomas Ram (1564-1634) and Ralph Willett (1719-1795).

Churches Together in Britian and Ireland, Churches commission on Mission, *Findings on Local Churches Initial Report*, 2000, and Values Sharing Central Working Group, *A Summary of our Discoveries and Findings*, 1998.

Guildhall Library Ordination Register, 9535/2. See also Clergy of the Church of England Database (CCEd).

ONS, see especially Labour Force Survey – employment status by occupation.

Registers of baptisms, marriages and deaths for the following parishes up to 1900. In Essex: Great Waltham, Colchester (various), Purleigh and Steeple, and in Suffolk for Stoke by Nayland and Ipswich (various). Copies of all these registers are available in the ERO or SRO.

Solicitor's Journal, B L, 7611aaa.

VCH of Essex.

VCH of Middlesex.

VCH of Warwickshire.

Venn J A, *Alumni Cantabrigienses*, 1924.

Local

British Library

Essex Manorial Rental, 1328, B L, Cotton Charter.XIII.5.

Lease from John Hall of Pleshey, John Alfrith, Jun., and Thomas Ram of Great Waltham to William Skynner of Chelmsford, Thomas Aleyne of Pleshey and Roger Bright of the same tenement, B L, Add. Charter 18120

Lease from Margaret Everard, relict of John Skinner, late of Pleshey, John Alfrith, and John Clerk to John Cowper (alias Driver) of Great Waltham, John Glascok, Sen., William Ram and others of the same tenement. B L, Add. Charter18122.

Account of the lands held by the Cooke family in 1580 made by Anne Cooke, the widow of Richard, B L, Lansdown 30, no. 82. It is printed in full at the back of McKintosh, *The Cooke family of Gidea Hall Essex – see separate entry*.

Photograph of Stephen Adye Ram, in Mr Malden, *The Ram family in Colchester*, B L, Add. 38617.

Essex Record Office.

Walthambury Manor court rolls from 1250 in series TA 819/1/2/3, D/DTu/242-252, and D/DHh/M151-174, especially D/DHh M151 for lists of the 'head men'.

Abstract of Walthambury Manor, Great Waltham court rolls, 1769-1823, D/DHh/M174.

Surveys of Great Waltham: 1563, D/Dtu/254, 1577, D/Dge/M273, 1583, D/Dge/M274, 1616, D/Dtu255, and 1622, D/DB M142.

Survey of Lands of Manor of Walthambury Manor, Great Waltham, 1643, T/M 514 and *A true plan or Demonstration of all and singular Desmesne Landes beelonging to the Mannor of Waltham Burie situate in the Parish of Much Waltham* TM 514/1,also 1643.

The Wright Family of Kelvedon Hatch, n. d., T/G 134 and Pamphlet Box 136.

Manuscript copy of Visitation of Essex between 1613 and 1617, made in 1634, 1670 or later, with additions, D/DQs/43.

Rent receipt book for Langley Estate 1748-97, at least from October 3 1761 until February 1765, D/Dtu/287.

Account book of Samuel Tufnell 1725-30, D/Dtu/277.

Valuation of Steeple Grange, the property of Samuel Tufnell Esq situate in Steeple and Nayland, October 1810, D/DopF7.

Bamford,A B, Miscellaneous genealogical papers relating to the Ram(me) family pedigree and abstracts of wills, m.s., 1910, T/G 23/29 and T/G 23/37.

J B Butt, *Biographical Dictionary*, 2 vols., unpublished manuscript, n.d., Acc. C905 Box 13.

Court Rolls of the Borough of Colchester, vol. 1, 1310-1352, vol. 2, 1353-1367 and vol. 3, 1372-1379, E/COL.

Oath Book or Red Parchment Book of Colchester, E/COL.

Colchester *Collectors of the Poor Book, 1581-1595*, Accession C1 (part).

Report on the Records of the Borough of Colchester – calendar of the Court rolls of the Borough of Colchester with lists of Bailiffs and Mayors, 1865, E/COL.

Colchester Trade Directory 1793, D/DHt/t 72/111.

A *Plan of Monkwick and other Lands the Property of Ralph Ward, Esq.*,1806, D/DU 507/31.

Suffolk Record Office.

Tendring Hall Estate title deeds, relating to the estate of Sir Richard Williams, see especially HA/108/2/3.

Manorial records for the Manor of Stoke next Nayland with Shardlowes and Withermarsh. Steward's papers – a bundle with correspondence concerning the Ram family, HA 108/1/14/24.

Norfolk Record Office.

Additional parish records of Norwich, St John Timberhill, *Papers of Father Edward Ram, 1879-1917*, PD74/.

Indexed abstracts of wills.

F G Emmison produced a compendium of all the wills held at the ERO, *Wills at Chelmsford*, three vols., 1958. He also abstracted and edited twelve volumes of Essex wills, called *Wills of the County of Essex (England), published by the* Genealogical Society, Washington DC, in which there are very detailed cross referenced indexes. For details about the volumes and their usage in this book see the wills section which follows.

Wills

Unless stated all the will references below are in the ERO.

Ram wills at Chelmsford.

These are taken from Emmison F G ed., *Wills at Chelmsford*, three vols., 1958.

Some of the dates given are of deaths not the date the will was made.

1530	Ram Geoffrey, High Easter	15 BW 31
1557	Rame, Robert, Great Waltham	208 EW 3
1557	Ram Thomas, Great Waltham	209 EW 3
1558	Rame John, sen., Great Waltham	41 ER 8
1576	Ramme Robert, Great Waltham	161 ER 13

1582	Ram Ramme, Agnes, widow 263 ER 14
1584	Ram Geoffrey, Nevendon 258 BW 31
1588	Rame John, Nevendon 4 BW 32
1593	Ram Rose, widow, Great Waltham 55 ER 17
1611	Ram Thomas, Great Waltham 102 EW 14
1614	Rame Joseph, Great Waltham 60 EW 15
1617	Rame Francis, Hornchurch 52 EW 16
1618	John Rame, Hornchurch 132 EW 16
1618	Ram William, Romford 169 EW 16
1621	Ram Joan, widow, Romford 30 EW 17
1632	Ram Daniel, Great Waltham 156 EW 19
1641	Ram Elizabeth, spinster 108 ER 20
1667	Ram John, Great Waltham 187 ER 21
1670	Ram Richard, Great Waltham 171 ER 22
1685	Ram John, Great Waltham 255 ER 24
1689	Ramme Richard, Great Waltham 210 ER 25
1695	Ram Anne, Great Waltham 243 ER 26
1713	Ram William, Gent., Broomfield 307 BR 16
1723	Ram Daniel, Great Waltham 148 ER 31
1727	Ram Joseph, Great Waltham 244 ER 31
1747	Warren Bridget, Great Bromley 259 CR 15
1763	Ram John, Great Waltham 204 ER 34
1780	Ram Richard, Chelmsford 175 BR 27
1782	Ram Francis, Colchester 153 CR 18
1785	Ram John, Chelmsford 525 BR 27
1789	Ram Benjamin, Great Waltham 137 ER
1810	Ram Jane, widow, London 553 CR 19
1810	Ram John, Colchester 342 BR 30
1816	Ram Nicholas, Colchester 689 CR 19
1825	Ram Banjamin, Roxwell 62 WR 3
1834	Ram John, Steeple 46 BR 34
1852	Ram John, Purleigh 77 ER 37

Ram wills: Prerogative Court of Canterbury

1568	Ram John, Great Waltham/Pleshey 11 Babington
1611	Ram Richard, Great Waltham 28 Fenner
1616	Ram Anthony, London 94 Cope
1617?	Ram Francis, Hornchurch 32 Weldon
1617	Edward Ram, 7 Weldon
1624	Ram Samuel, Hornchurch 90 Byrde
1625	Ram Benjamin, London 88 Clerke
1625	Ram Jane, London 82 Clerke
1627	Ram Joan, London 77 Skynner
1628?	Ram Edmund, Colchester 24 Barrington
1636	Ram Francis, London 109 Pile
1798	Ram James, Colchester Prob 11/1319
1870	Ram James, Ipswich Copy in SRO HA 108/2/89

Other Ram wills

1635	Ram Robert (d. 1639) Bishop of London 364 Allen
1877	Ram Abigail (d. 1883) D/DCf/F523

Other wills in which members of the Ram family are mentioned

These are to be found in Emmison F G, ed., Archdeaconry Courts of Essex, Colchester, and Middlesex – vol. 1 1558-1565 (1982), vol. 2 1565-1571 (1983), vol 3 1571-1577

(1986), vol. 4 1577-1584 (1987), vol. 5 1583-1592 (1989), vol. 6 1591-1597 (1991), and vol. 7 1597-1603 (1990)

Vol. 1 1558-1565.

1557/8   THOMAS EVERARDE. Robert Ram a witness.

1558   THOMAS OODHAM (WOODHAM). Robert Ram a witness.

1559   AGNES WOODHAM. Robert Ram a witness.

Vol. 2 1565-1571.

1562   RICHARD HORSPIT of Great Horkesley. Christopher Ram a witness.

1565   MARGARET HOYE of Wormingford. Christopher Ram clerk (vicar of Boxted) a witness.

1565/6   THOMAS PACKE of Colchester. William Ram a witness.

1570   RICHARD FAKENER of Mucking. William Rames a witness.

Vol. 3 1571-1577.

1556   WILLIAM SOR[R]ELL of Great Leighs. Robert Ram a witness.

1572   JOHN ARWAKER THE ELDER. He leaves 2 bushells of wheat at Christmas and 2 at Easter for bread to be baked for the poor – 'to be delivered by John my son 'for ever'. He leaves to his godsons, John Billyreca and John Ram 'my best coat to the intent that they shall yearly see the bread delivered'. Robert Ram was a witness. Inventory £84 '4' 4. (One of the larger ones).

1574   HUMPHREY HORSNAILE. Robert Ram is overseer.

1575   GEORGE MALLE (Mawle in margin) of Hornchurch. Substantial yeoman will. 'I have appointed my loving friend Mr Francis Ram overseer'. He received 20s for his pains. 'Once a year when my executors and overseers shall assemble for taking the account (furthering settlement?) they shall have a competent dinner and each of my overseers 20d a piece for their pains'.

1575   WILLIAM UPHAVERING of Hornchurch, yeoman. My loving friend Francis Ram was one of 4 supervisors, and he was given 5s – the others got 3s 4d.

1576/7   JOHN BETTE of Hornchurch. Rented a tenement from Francis Ram. Made 'Mr Francis Ram my landlord' one of three overeers.

1576   PETER CLOISE ALIAS JENKIN, of Colchester. William Ram a witness.

Vol. 4 1577-1584.

1577   THOMAS DOBIDEWE of Thaxted, shoemaker. Francis Ram a witness.

1578   JOHN BRIGHT of Romford, innholder and yeoman. Francis Ram a witness.

1579   JOHN STORYE ALIAS BEALLE of Colchester, cooper. William Ram a witness and 'writer hereof'.

1582   'MARSCELIN' OWTRED of London. Very long religious preamble. He was owed an annuity of £10 a year for 14 years by a cousin and sells it to highest bidder. If Francis Ram pays £80 he can have it. Nominates his 'friend Mr Francis Ram, overseer.

1582/3   ROBERT BROOKES of Hare street in Hornchurch, Yeoman. Edward Ram A Witness.

n.d.   JOHN GREENE of Romford, yeoman. Francis Rame, gentleman, a witness.

Vol. 5 1584-91.

1586   HENRY BARNARD of Great Waltham, yeoman. Inventory £250 7/9. Very large. Richard Ram appointed supervisor, and he was also a witness.

1583/4   NICHOLAS COTTON of Romford, yeoman. To my loving friends Mr William Ram and Marion his wife 'each 20/- towards making rings to be worn in remembrance of me'. ALSO 30/- to Helen wife of Francis Ram, gent. for the same purpose. 'My loving friend' Francis Ram was made overseer, who was also one of the witnesses.

1590   JOHN STEVEN of Hornchurch, yeoman. Francis Ram a witness.

1582/3   LAWRENCE PORTER, of Chignall Smealey, yeoman. Leaves 10/- to John Ram of Chignall Smealey.

1586   JOAN WORTHINGTON, maiden, of Hornchurch. Left goods (quite a lot!) to William Ram her servant, plus 10/-. 'the rest of my goods to William Ram, desiring him to see me buried'.

1590   JOHN CLARKE of Romford, Butcher. William Ram a witness.

n.d.   WILLIAM RAM of Broomfield. Nominated John Ram of Great Waltham as one of two executors.

Vol. 6 1591-97.

1590   AGNES MALL, widow of Romford. Loving friend, Francis Ram, gentleman one of two overseers.

1592/3 THOMAS UPHAVERINGE of Havering Well in Hornchurch, yeoman. William Ram a witness.

1592   WILLIAM LAMBERT, vicar of Hornchurch. Francis Ram was one of two overseers. Also a witness.

1593   THOMAS LATHAM of Langtons in Hornchurch, esquire. Obviously very wealthy. Lots of lands in Essex, which are to be sold by Francis Ram and his brother in law. – each gets 66/8d. Francis Ram a witness.

1593   JOAN ADAMS of Hornchurch, widow. Bequests of rings to Francis and John, sons of Francis Ram, gent. Francis Ram, gent, and Francis Ram the younger are appointed 2 of three overseers. Francis and William Ram witnesses.

1593   ROBERT FABUTE of Upminster, tailor. Leaves two houses and lands in Hornchurch 'in the tenure of Francis Ram, gent' and two other people to relatives.

1593   MARGARET SHONCKE of Hornchurch, widow. William Ram a witness.

1593   WILLIAM BETT of Romford, fletcher. William Ram a witness.

1594/5 GEOFFRY HUMPHREY of Upminster, yeoman. William Ram a witness.

1594   GEOFFRY TYMAN of Hornchurch, husbandman. Eleen Ram a witness.

1594/5 WILLIAM PENNANT of Hornchurch, esquire. Francis Ram is a witness.

1594/5 RALPH WATSON of Hornchurch, bricklayer. 'To Agnes Brown, servant to Francis Ram gentleman, the bedstade in my palour after my wife's decease'. William Ram a witness.

1595   ELIZABETH BRIGHT of Romford, widow. 'To Master Francis Ram, for his good advice and friendship bestowed on me 40/-, I long bow and I sheaf of arrrows. To his wife two gold angels. To his eight children 10/;- a piece. To Francis his eldest son 20/- in gold'. Catherine Ram, her god daughter, gets 10/-. Her loving friend Francis Ram is executor.

1595   JOHN BUSHE of Hornchurch, yeoman. William Ram a Witness.

1595   WILLIAM HARE of Hornchurch, yeoman. William Ram a witness.

1596   SUSAN HOWNELL of Kelvedon, spinster. Alice Ram a witness.

Vol. 7 1597-1603.

1599   RICHARD AYLETT of Doddinghurst, yeoman. A long will and obviously well off. He lives at a place called Fletchers – which the Rams were associated with earlier. 'To my wife my messuage and land called Halls and Coles in High Easter in the occupation of Robert Ram for 8 years from Michaelmas 1602 until Richard be gone out of his years of apprenticeship for eight years from thence next ensuing; after the eight years Richard (Aylett's son) shall have Halls and Coles; for default of issue successively to Thomas son of Thomas, to Elizabeth Aylett my daughter, and to Edward Lambe my sister's son'.

1599/0 JOHN HARMER of Romford, baker. William Ram witness.

1600   GEORGE STREIGHTE of Wethersfield, husbansdman. Overseeers are brother and Richard Ram of Great Waltham.

1600   THOMAS DYER of Rettendon, yeoman. Thomas Ram witness.

1600   JOHN BROWNE of Dagenham, blacksmith. William Ram witness.

1602   LETTICE MULBERE of West Bergholt?. William Ram a witness.

These wills are to be found in Emission F G, ed., The Bishop of London's Commissary Court – vol. 8 1558-1569 (1993), vol. 9 1569-1578 (1994), vol. 10 1578-1588 (1995), vol. 11 1587-1599 (1998), and vol. 12 1596-1603 (2000).

Vol. 8 1558 -1569.

1558   ROBERT WYER of Little Waltham. Robert Ramme a witness.

1559   JOHN MARTEN (ALIAS WYGNALL) of Great Waltham. Robert Ramm my friend overseer and also a witness.

1561/2   ROBERT MARSHE of Felsted. To Elizabeth and Agnes Marshe his daughters he leaves £40 each, '£40 whereof shall remain in the hands of my loving friend Robert Ramme of Great Waltham to the use of Elizabeth' The other daughter is looked after by someone else of Braintree in the same way. 'Elizabeth shall be brouhght up under the governance of Robert Ramme'. Robert Ramme and the man fron Braintree were appointed executors. Thomas Childe the elder, a loving friend, is appointed supervisior.

1562   JOHN SMETH of Great Waltham. Witnesses are Robert and Thomas Ram.

1565   MARGARET CHALLKE of Little Waltham. Robert Ramme one of 2 executors – each paid ¾d.

1566   GEOFFREY CROWE of Great Waltham, carpenter. Robert Ram a witness.

1566   WILLIAM PIGOTE THE ELDER, smith of Colchester. William Ram a witness.

1568   WILLIAM KECHYN of Great Baddow. Lagacies of 6d to Francis Ram the yoinger and 6d to his sister Thomasine.

1569   WILLIAM DRANE of Stebbing, husbandman. Geoffrey Ram a witness.

Vol. 9 1569 -1578.

1570   JOHN WALDEN of East Mersea, yeoman. William Ram is the writer and also a witness.

1570   WILLIAM EVERARD of Great Waltham, yeoman. Makes loving cousin Richard Everarde of Walthambury an overseer and witness. Robert Ramme also a witness.

1570/1   MAUD HULKE of Great Baddow, widow. To Mary Rame I cupboard. To Ellen Rame 3 sheets that shall lie on me at the day of my burial. To Francis Rame's 2 children, Frances and Joan, 12d each. Francis Rame, her son in law shares residue with one other and he is also an executor.

1574   ROBERT UMFREY of Stock. To George Rame 2 Kine and 4 sheep at 18. If John Rame died before 18, Dorothy Rame, his sister, shall have the cow and 4 sheep and Richard (Umfrey?) The other cow. Geoffrey Rame is supervisor. Robert Umfrey's wife was called Alice (could she be a Ram?)

1576/7   JOAN ARWACRE of High Easter, widow. To William Ramme my eldest son 1 of my best beasts, 6 sheep, and all corn and other fruit growing at my decease in Byrdes Croft in Leaden Roothing. Also 20sh. To John Arwacre my second son my best horse.

Vol. 10 1578 -1588.

1579   RICHARD DRANE of Great Leighs, yeoman. Leaves 2¾ to his mother in law ? Rame. To Michael his brother 'my tenements and lands in Great Waltham and Broomfield called Fanners and Blatches with Cockes Croft which came to me by the marriage of my wife ...' He also leaves a 'manor' called Fulbourns (now Fulbourne farm).

1582   WILLIAM ALMON of West Hanningfield, husbandman. Thomas Ram is overseer and a witness.

1583   JOHN STANTON of West Hanningfield, labourer. Thomas Rame of West Hanningfield an overseer.

1584   JOAN POTTER of Billericay, widow. To John Rame my brother 30sh, to Elizabeth Sturgine my sister's daughter 6/8. To Thomas Rame, my brother, my sister Rose Rame, my brother Francis Rame, and my sister Goodin each 6/8. To my brother's son the son of William Rame 6/8 at 21.

1584   AGNES MAUGHT of Great Baddow, widow. Her daughter Joan is a child of Richard Hulck. Mary Rame gets a piece of pewter 'of the middle sort'.

1584/5   GEOFFREY CUCKOK of Colchester, baker. William Ram, notary public, a witness.

1587   ROBERT HUMPHREY of South Hanningfield, husbandman. Leaves Thomas Rame of West Hanningfield 5/-. Thomas Rame was a witness.

1587   MARGARAET FLUD of Colchester, widow. To my 'gossyppe' (godfather) William Ram 40sh and his child my godchild 40sh. To mistress Rose wife of my loving friend George Sayer my messauage wherein I dwell near the head Gate of Colchester with the yards and gardens, on condition she pay £10 towards my debts.

Vol. 11 1587-1599.

1590   AMBROSE STOCKE of Stebbing, bachelor. Witnesses Margaret and Geoffrey Ram.

1591/2   JOHN BRIANT of Copford. Robert Ram witness.

n.d.   THOMAS BIRGIN of Copford, hubandman. Robert Ram witness.

1592   ROBERT CAMOCKE of Copford, labourer. Witness, Robert Ram clerk rector.

1592/3   RALPH BELL of Colchester, yeoman. Witness, William Ram notary public.

1592   WILLIAM HEARD of Rainham, yeoman. Witness William Ram.

Vol. 12 1596 -1603.

1597   THOMAS GILBERT of West Hanningfield, husbandman. Margery Ram a witness.

1597   ABRAHAM FOKES of Peldon, yeoman. William Ram, notary public a witness. Probably wrote it – his style.

Wills of connected people

1527	Childe John, Sen	Great Waltham	266 BW 8
1529	Childe John	Great Waltham	47 ER 4
1552	Childe Thomas, sen.	Great Waltham	129 ER 7
1558	Child (Chyllde) Joan, widow	Great Waltham	273 BW 8
1569	Freman William	Broomfield	161 BW 14

1576   THOMAS GRIGGELL ALIAS GRIGGS. Styled yeoman. This is a substantial will. In it he leaves some money to fund a family member at Cambridge University. The person concerned was William Sorrell, brother of Thomas Sorrell, the son of his wife (presumably by a previous marriage). The bequest was of several tenements and land in Great Waltham to my wife and Thomas Sorrell on condition that they pay William an annuity of 40s for six years '...so that William do remain a student at the University of Cambridge during the six years'. He also left to William £10 within 1 month after he shall commence Bachelor of Art'. He was admitted sizar aged 23 at Caius College in 1571 and matriculated in 1571 – presumably he did not stay on to graduate. His school is given as Bury. A Robert Sorrell matriculated sizar from Magdalene College in 1597 and graduated BA in 1600-1.

| 1583 | Childe Thomas, yeoman | Great Waltham | 252 ER 14 |

Brother of Agnes wife of Robert Ram.

| 1583/4 | Nicholas Cotton | Hornchurch | 46 ER 15 |

See also Emmison F G, ed., Archdeaconry Courts of Essex, Colchester, and Middlesex – vol. 5 1583-1592 (1989), vol. 6 1591-1597.

1587	Child Thomas, sen. tailor	Great Waltham	119 ER 15'
1592	Childe John, yeoman	Great Waltham	41 ER 17
1592	Turner John	Great Waltham	72 ER 17
1600	Attwoode William, gent.	Stanford Rivers	295 ER 17
1604	Freman Richard, gent.	Broomfield	83 BW 15

Related to Penelope Freeman wife of William Ram who lived in Broomfield?

1625	Mountjoy Alan, gent	Copford	125 BW 46
1639	Mannock William	St Osyth	167 BW 55
1639	Mannock William, gent.	St Osyth	167 BW 55

1665	Child Elizabeth, widow		Great Waltham	126ER 21
1668	Turner Christopher, h'sb'dm'n		Great Waltham	94 ER 24
1710	Goddard John	Colchester	117 BR 16	
1710	Sayer John	Colchester	147 BR 16	
1726/7	Bayles Thomas	Colchester	in Butt dictionary	

Grocer. Directs sale of extensive property, the proceeds of which to be held in trust for the benefit of his three sons, sister Pepper, and five daughters.

1727/8	Bayles II Thomas	Colchester	in Butt dictionary	
1733	Sayer John	Colchester	123 BR 21	
1740	Pearson William, yeoman	Layer de la Haye	61 CR 15	
1744	Warren Bridget (d. 1747)	259 CR 15		
1763	Pearson Sarah, widow	Layer de la Haye	359 CR 16	
1773	Bawtree John	Wivenhoe	D/DEl T229	
1775	Bayles III Thomas	Colchester	in Butt dictionary	

Son of Thomas Bayles II. An attorney

1782	Bawtree Jane	Wivenhoe	D/DEl T229	
1782	Bawtree Sarah	Wivenhoe	D/DEl T229	
1790	King John	Colchester	as above F1/2	
1794	King John	Colchester	D/DCm F1/1	
1810	Ram Jane	East Doneyland	D/DEl T229	

Living at the time of her death in Bishopsgate Street, London.

Other

Ascinder G E, essay references to Mills, Batter and Co, Colchester and Essex Bank, and *List of Records of Mills, Batter and Co Bank 1884-91* in the Gurney papers (A18A) now part of the historical records of Barclays Bank.

Butt J B, *The Drinks Trade*, unpublished essay in the Biographical Dictionary papers.

Cockburn J S, ed., *Calendar of Assize Records, Essex Indictments, Elizabeth I*, 1978, and *Essex Indictments, James I*, 1982.

Essex Archaeological Society, *Feet of Fines for Essex*, vol. VI, 1581-1603, no. 11, 1964.

Essex Society for Family History, *Monumental Inscriptions at St Andrews Church Abberton.*

Foster Joseph, ed., *Marriage Licences, London 1521-1869*, 1887.

Foster Joseph, ed., *The Register of Admissions to Gray's Inn, 1521-1889*, 1889.

Harleian Society, *Visitations of Essex, Pt. 1*, vol. 13, 1878, B L, HLX 929.341.

Harleian Society, *Visitations of Essex, Pt. 2*, vol. 14, 1879, B L, HLX 929.341.

Harleian Society (visitation section) *Middlesex Pedigrees* lxv, 19.

Heal A, *The London Goldsmiths, 1200-1800*, 1972.

Metcalfe Walter, *Visitations of Essex, Miscellaneous Essex Pedigrees from various Harleian Manuscripts*, 1878.

Ram Francis, coat of arms granted in 1793, see College of Arms, MS. Miscellaneous Grants 1, f. 121, The grant was made by Robert Cooke Clarenceux King of Arms, and is recorded in B L, Harley 1359, f.103, and Queen's College Oxford, Oxford MS 146 Fol. 471.

Ram James, (d. 1870) related records of the Inner Temple. This information has been accessed and provided by Dr Clare Rider, the Archivist.

Ram Willett and Francis, *The Ram Family*, 1940. There are copies in the B L and the ERO.

Reaney P H and Fitch Marc, eds., *Feet of Fines for Essex*, vol IV, 1423-1527, 1964.

Round J H ed., *Register of the scholars admitted to Colchester School 1637-1740*, 1897.

Spence Craig, *London in the 1690s, A Social Atlas*, 2000, pp. 51, 70, 107 and 108.

Suffolk Family History Society, *Suffolk 1851 Census Index*, vol. 14: part 5, p. 27.

Suffolk Family History Society, Suffolk Burial Index CD.

The King's Own Regimental Calendar, 1897.

Ward Jennifer, ed., The Lay Subsidy of 1327, printed in, *The Medieval Essex Community, The Lay Subsidy of 1327*, Essex Historical Documents: 1, 1983.

Secondary sources

Reports

H M Countryside Agency, *On the State of the Countryside*, 2003.

The Panel on Fair Access to the Professions, *Unleashing Aspirations – The Final Report*, July 2009.

British Social Attitudes Survey, *25th Annual Report*, as reviewed in *The Times*, 28 January, 2009.

Theses

Crowley D A, '*Frankpledge and Leet Jurisdiction In Late-Medieval Essex*', Sheffield University Ph D thesis, 1971.

D'Cruze Shani, *The Middling Sort in Provincial England – Politics and Social Relations in Colchester 1730-1800*, University of Essex Ph D thesis, 1990.

Hull Felix, *Agriculture and Rural Society in Essex, 1560-1640*, London University Ph D thesis, 1950.

McIntosh M K, *The Cooke Family of Gidea Hall, Essex 1460-1661*, Harvard University Ph D thesis, 1967.

Poos L R, *Population and Mortality in two Essex communities, Great Waltham and High Easter, 1327-1389*, pt. 1 of a University of Cambridge Ph D, 1979.

Poos L R, *Population and Resources in Two Fourteenth Century Essex Communities, Great Waltham and High Easter, 1327-1389*, pt. 2 of a Cambridge University Ph D, 1983.

Ram R W, *The Social Evolution of Five Dissenting Communities in Birmingham, 1750-1870*, Birmingham University Ph D thesis, 1972.

Articles

Arkel Tom, *Identifying regional variations from the hearth tax*, The Local Historian, vol. 33, no. 3, August 2003.

Butt J B, *Dirty, Dirty Work, The brief history of Colchester politics, 1784-1790*, an unpublished typescript article in the Biographical Dictionary papers.

Clark Revd Andrew, *Great Waltham Five Centuries Ago*, Essex Review, January 1904, no. 49 vol. XIII. His article was continued in July 1904, no. 51. vol XIII, and October 1904, no. 52. vol XIII.

Clark Revd Andrew, *The History of Rectory Manor, Great Waltham*, Essex Review, April,1917, no. 102, vol XXVI.

Habakkuk H J, *Marriage settlements in the Eighteenth Century*, Transactions of the Royal Historical Society, 4th series 32, 1950.

Hunter John, *Field Systems in Essex*, The Essex Society for Archaeology and History, Occasional Papers, New Series, No.1.

McIntosh M K, *The Fall of a Tudor gentle Family: The Cookes of Gidea Hall, Essex, 1579-1629*. Reprint from The Huntingdon Library Quarterly, vol XLI, number 04, August 1978.

Persaud Raj, *The Animal Urge*, Financial Times Magazine, August 28 2004, Issue no 70.

Raimes A L, *The Family of Reynes of Wherstead in Suffolk*', Proceedings of the Suffolk Institute Archaeology, xxiii, pt 2.

Ram R W, *Agrarian Change and its impact, 1650-1850; the experience of a farming family in central Essex*, The Local Historian, vol. 37, No 1, February 2007.

Rimmington G T, *Edwardian Clerical Incumbents in Leicestershire*, The Local Historian, vol. 35, no.1, Febuary, 2005.

Storck Lauren E, '*Reality*' or '*Illusion*'? *Five things of Interest about Social Class as a Large Group*, in special edition of *Group Analysis*, the journal of Group Analytic Psychotherapy, *A Group Analysis of Class, Status Groups and Inequality*, volume 35, number 3, September 2002.

Sykes Brian and Irven Catherine, *Surnames and the Y Chromosome*, 2000.

The Guardian, 4 May 2004. See an article about the history of The Queen's Lancashire Regiment on p. 5.

Waddell John, ed., *Roxwell Revealed, An anthology of village history*, 1993.

Winston Robert, *Why do we Believe in God?* The Guardian Supplement, 13 October 2005.

Books

General

Adamson John, *The Noble Revolt, The Overthrow of Charles I*, 2007.

Adye Major S P, *Punishments and Rewards*, 1778, 1797 and 1800.

Adye Major R W, *The Pocket Gunner*, 1798.

Allen Roland, *Missionary Methods, St Paul's or Ours?* 1993.

Anderson M, ed., *British Population History, from the Black Death to the present day*, 1996.

Barry Jonathan and Brooks Christopher, ed., *'The Middling Sort of People: Culture, Society and Politics in England, 1550-1800'*, 1994,

Braddick Michael, *State formation in Early Modern England, 1550-1700*, 2000.

Brenner Robert, *Merchants and Revolution: Commercial Change, Political Conflict and London's Overseas Traders*, 1993.

Britten J and Boulger G S, *A Biographical Index of British and Irish Botanists*, 1893.

Burke J and J B, *Genealogical and Heraldic History of the Extinct and Dormant Baronetcies of England, Ireland and Scotland*, 1894.

Campbell Mildred, *The English Yeoman Under Elizabeth and the Early Stuarts*, 1960.

Corfield P J and Harte N B, ed., *London and the English Economy, 1500-1700*, 1990.

Daunton M J, *Progress and Poverty, an Economic and Social History of Britain, 1700-1850*, 1995.

Davidoff L and Hall C, *Family Fortunes, Men and women of the English middle class, 1780- 1850*, 1987.

Dunn Alastair, *The Great Rising of 1381, The Peasants' Revolt and England's failed Revolution*, 2002.

Duffey E, *The Stripping of the Altars, Traditional Religion in England 1400-1580*, 2005.

Dunbar Robin, *Gossip and the Evolution of Human Language*, 2004.

Dyer Christopher, *Everyday Life in Medieval England*, 2000.

Earle Peter, *The Making of the English Middle Class – Business Society and Family Life in London, 1660-1730*, 1989.

Eastwood David, *Governing Rural England, Tradition and transformation in Local Government 1780-1840*, 1994.

Ellis Hamilton, *British Railway History, 1830-1876*, 1960.

Evans G E, *Ask the Fellows who Cut the Hay*, 1969.

Foulkes S H, *Group Analytic Psychotherapy – Methods and Principles*, 1991.

French H R, *The Middle Sort of People in Provincial England, 1600-1750*, 2008.

Gerard John, *The Herball...or General History of Plants*, enlarged and amended by Thomas Johnson, 1633.

Glasscock R E, ed., *The Lay Subsidy of 1334*, 1975.

Griffiths P, Fox A, and Hindle S, ed., *The Experience of Authority in Modern England*, 1996, essay by Keith Wrightson on 'The Politics of the Parish in Early Modern England'.

Harris Jose, The Penguin Social History of Britain, *Private Lives, Public Spirit: Britian 1870-1914*, 1994.

Hey David, ed., *The History of Myddle*, by Richard Gough, 1981.

Hey David, *The Oxford Guide to Family History*, 1993.

Hey David, *Family Names and Family History*, 2000.

Holdsworth Sir William, *A History of the English Law*, 1938.

Hollingsworth T H, *Historical Demography*, 1969.

Houlbrooke R A, *English Family*, 1984.

Houlbrooke R A, *Death, Religion, and the family in England, 1480-1750*, 1998.

Hulme M and Barrow E ed., *Climates of the British Isles, present past and future*, 1997.

Jeffers R H, *The Friends of John Gerard (1545-1612) Surgeon and Botanist*, 1967.

Jones Dan, *Summer of Blood, The Peasants' Revolt of 1381*, 2009.

Jurkowski M and Smith C L, *Lay Taxes in England and Wales, 1188-1688*, 1998.

Keates-Rohan K S B, *Domesday People*, 1999.

Keith-Lucas Bryan, *The Unreformed Local Government System*, 1980.

Lazlett Peter, *The World we Have Lost*, 1965.

Lyte H, '*A New Herball or Historie of Plants*', 1578.

Macfarlane Alan, *The Origins of English Individualism*, 1978.

Macfarlane Alan, *Marriage and Love*, 1986.

Ed R B McKerrow, A Dictionary of Printers and Booksellers in England, Scotland and Ireland, and of Foreign Printers of English Books, 1557-1640, 1910.

Morrison Blake, *Things my mother never told me*, 2003.

O'Day Rosemary, *The family and Family relationships, 1500-1900*.

Pearl Valerie, *London and the Outbreak of the Puritan Revolution, City Government and National Politics 1625-43*, 1961.

Philippe Aries and George Duby, ed., *A History of Private Life, vol. 2, Revelations of the Medieval World*, 1988.

Pomery Chris, *DNA and Family History*, 2004.

Pounds N J G, *A History of the English Parish*, 2000.

Ram Edward, *Leading Events in the History of the Church of England*, 1888.

Ram James, *The Science of Legal Judgement: a Treatise designed to show the Materials whereof, and the Process by which, the Courts of Westminster Hall construct their Judgements, etc.*, 1822.

Ram James, *A Treatise on Facts as Subjects of Enquiry by a Jury*, 1851.

Ram James jun., *Notes upon The General Examination at the Royal Military College of Sandhurst, of Candidates for Direct Commissions in the Army*, 1855.

Ram James jun., *The Philosophy of War*, 1878.

Ram William, *Ram's Little Dodeon. A briefe Epitome of the new Herbal, or History of Plants*, 1606. See BL 987.e.19 for this book.

Razi Zvi and Smith Richard, ed., *Medieval Society and the Manor Court*, 1996.

Renfrew C, *Prehistory – The Making of the Human Mind*, 2007.

Ridley Matt, *Genome – The Autobiography of a Species in 23 Chapters*, 1999.

Round J H, *Geoffrey de Mandeville*, 1892.

Ruvigny and Raineval Marquis of, *The Blood Royal of Britain*, 1904.

Sanders I J, *English Baronies – A Study of their Origin and Descent 1086-1327*, 1960.

Scott George Gilbert, *Personal and Professional Recollections*, Ed. Gavin Stamp, 1995.

Sennett Richard, *Respect. The Formation of Character in an Age of Inequality*, 2003.

Shoemaker R B, *Gender in English Society, 1650-1850*, 1998.

Simpson A W B, *An Introduction to the History of Land Law*, 1961.

Simpson A W B, Biographical Dictionary of the Common Law, 1984.

Smith-Bannister Scott, *Names and naming patterns in England 1538-1700*, 1997.

Spring Eileen, *Law, Land and Family, Aristocratic Inheritance in England, 1300 to 1800*.

Spufford Margaret, *Contrasting Communities, English Villagers in the Sixteenth and Seventeenth Centuries*, 2000.

Stone Lawrence, *Family, Sex, and Marriage*, 1977.

Stone Lawrence, *The Crisis of the Aristocracy, 1558-1641*, abridged edition, 1967.

Thirsk Joan, gen. ed., *The Agrarian History of England and Wales*. W A Armstrong, *Wages and Incomes*, chapter 7 in G E Mingay, *The Agrarian History of England and Wales*, vol. 6, 1989. Also, vol. iv, *The Malting Industry*, 1967.

Toynbee Arnold, *A Study of History*, 1961.

Trevelyan G M, *English Social History, A Survey of Six Centuries, Chaucer to Queen Victoria*, 1944.

Uglow Jenny, *The Lunar Men, the friends who made the future, 1730-1810*, 2002.

Wright William, *Born That Way. Genes, Behaviour, Personality*, 1999.
Wrightson K, *English Society 1580-1680*, 1982.
Wrightson Keith, *English Society, 1580-1680*, 2003.
Wrigley E A, ed., *An Introduction to English Historical Demography*, 1966.
Wrigley E A, ed., *Identifying People in the Past*, 1973.
Wrigley E A and Schofield R S, *The Population History of England, 1541-1871*, 1981.
Yates W N, *Anglican Ritualism in Victorian Britain*, 2000.

Local
Boutflower D S, *The Boutflower Book A History of an English Middle Class Family from 1303-1930*, 1930.
Brown A F J, *Prosperity and Poverty, Rural Essex, 1700-1815*, 1996.
Brown A F J, *Meagre Harvest, The Essex Farm workers' Stuggle against Poverty, 1750-1914*, 1990.
Carter Douglas, *1000 years of Boxted History, Part 1, St Peter's Church*, (n.d.).
Drew Bernard, The Fire Office – The Essex and Suffolk Equitable Insurance Society Ltd., 1802-1952, 1952.
Duffey Eamon, The Voices of Morbath, Reformation and Rebellion in an English Village, 2003.
Flight H E, *Economic and Social Conditions in Great Waltham in the Later Georgian Period*, n.d.
Francis Steer, *Samuel Tufnell of Langleys*, 1960.
Gant Leonard H, *History of Berechurch in the County of Essex*, n.d.
Grace D R and Phillips D C, *Ransomes of Ipswich – A History of the Firm and a Guide to its records*, 1975.
Hussey Stephen and Swash Laura, Studies in Essex History, No. 5, *Horrid Lights, 19th-Century Incediarism in Essex*, 1994.
Martin Geoffrey, *Story of Colchester from Roman Times to the Present Day*, 1959.
Martins Susanna, *Farmers, Landlords and Landscapes, Rural Britain, 1720 to 1870*.
McIntosh M K, *A Community Transformed, the Manor and Liberty of Havering, 1500-1620*, 1991.
McLean Michael and Upjohn Sheila, *St John Timberhill Norwich*, 1982, with revisions by John Mountney in 1989.
Morant Philip *The History and Antiquities of the County of Essex*, vol. I, 1766 and vol II, 1768.
Newby J W, *The Patrick Stead Hospital*, 1964.
Penfold J B, *The History of the Esex County Hospital, Colchester, 1820-1948*, 1984.
Perfect C T, *Ye Olde Village of Hornchurch*, 1917.
Phillips R P and Bazett R, *Ages in the Making, A History of Two Essex Villages*, 1973.
Picard L, *Elizabeth's London, Everyday Life in Elizabethan London*, 2003.
Poos L R, *A Rural society after the Black Death, Essex, 1350-1525*, 1991.
Samaha Joel, *Law and Order in Historical Perspective. The Case of Elizabethan Essex*, 1974.
Shrimpton Colin, *The Landed society and the Farming community of Essex in the Late Eighteenth and early Nineteenth centuries*, 1977.
Silvester J, *An Elizabethan vicar of Great Clacton. John Markaunt and his famous hymn*, 1922.
Smith Harold, *The Ecclesiastical History of Essex under the Long Parliament and the Commonwealth*, n.d.
Smith R D, *The Middling Sort and the Politics of Social Reformation, Colchester, 1570-1640*, 2004.
Tuffnell E B, *The Family of Tuffnell*, 1924.
Twining Stephen, *The House of Twining, 1706-1956*, 1956.
Vaisey D ed., *The Diary of a Village Shopkeeper, 1754-1765*, 1998.
Wright A J, *St Michael and All Angels, Copford*, 1993.

Wrightson Keith and Levine David, *Poverty and Piety in an English Village, Terling, 1525-1700*, 1995.

Young Arthur, *General View of the Agriculture of the County of Essex*, vol. 1, 1807.

ABBREVIATIONS AND END NOTES

Generally used abbreviations

B L   British Library
C C Ed   Clergy of the Church of England Data Base
D N B   *Dictionary of National Biography*
E R O   Essex Record Office
I G I   Church of Jesus Christ of Latter-Day Saints, *International Genealogical Index*
N R O   Norfolk Record Office
O N S   Office of National Statistics
P C C   Prerogative Court of Canterbury
S R O   Suffolk Record Office
V C H   Victoria County History

End notes

When more extended discussion on a topic occurs elsewhere in the book cross references are provided. Sometimes there is a chapter reference or on other occasions page numbers alone. Such references are introduced by the phrase 'see internal reference' followed by the chapter or page number.

Part 1. Themes and inspirations

Notes to pp. 19-29

1   Richard Sennett, *Respect. The Formation of Character in an Age of Inequality*, 2003.
2   Ibid., p. 177.
3   Ibid., p. 263.
4   Ibid., p. 225.
5   G M Trevelyan, *English Social History, A Survey of Six Centuries, Chaucer to Queen Victoria*, 1944.
6   S H Foulkes, *Group Analytic Psychotherapy – Methods and Principles*, 1991. The approach he developed is currently promoted and practised by The Group Analytic Society.
7   *New Oxford Dictionary of English*, Second edition, revised, 2005.
8   See internal reference chart B6 on p. 240.
9   It is now necessary to consult the General Register Office or the National Archives.
10 General Register Office. Registration of the birth of Charles Harry Ram in the Registration District of Maldon in the County of Essex on April 2 1843.
11 General Register Office. Registration of the birth of William Richard Ram, son of Charles Henry Ram in the Registration District of Kingston on Thames in the County Of Surrey on July 7 1876.
12 ERO, D/P384/1/4. Register of baptisms at Steeple: Benjamin, 1839; Thomas, 1840; and Charles Harry, 1843.
13 ERO, D/P197/1/11. Register of baptisms at Purleigh, 1814.
14 ERO, D/ABR 34/46. Will of John Ram (1768-1835).
15 D S Boutflower, *The Boutflower Book A History of an English Middle Class Family from 1303-1930*, Newcastle upon Tyne, 1930, p. 11.
16 Suffolk Family History Society, *Suffolk 1851 Census Index*, vol. 14: part 5, p. 27.
17 Suffolk Family History Society, Suffolk Burial Index CD.
18 C Pomery, *DNA and Family History*, 2004, p.3.

[19] *Essex Manorial Rental*, 1328, B L, Cotton Charter.XIII.5.

[20] *Ram's Little Dodeon. A briefe Epitome of the new Herbal, or History of Plants*, 1606, B L, 987.e.19.

[21] James Ram, *The Science of Legal Judgement: a Treatise designed to show the Materials whereof, and the Process by which, the Courts of Westminster Hall construct their Judgements ...*, 1822.

[22] K S B Keates-Rohan, *Domesday People*, 1999, p. 35.

[23] I J Sanders, *English Baronies – A Study of their Origin and Descent 1086-1327*, 1960, p. vi.

[24] A L Raimes Proceedings of the Suffolk Institute Archaeology, xxiii, pt 2, *The Family of Reynes of Wherstead in Suffolk*' and J H Round, *Geoffrey de Mandeville*, 1892, pp. 399-404.
See a line of descent in Sanders, pp. 139-40.

[25] See internal reference p.88

[26] Willett and Francis Ram, *The Ram Family*, 1940. B L, 9906.r.10.

[27] *Dictionary of National Biography*.

[28] Marquis of Ruvigny and Raineval, *The Blood Royal of Britain*, 1904, tables xvii, xv, xiv, pp. 13, 14 and 15. The line of descent is as follows. Admiral Sir Montague Stopford (1798-1864), Lady Mary Scott-Montague (wife of James George, 3rd Earl of Courtown), Lady Elizabeth Montague (wife of the 3rd Duke of Buccleuch), George 4th Earl of Cardigan and 1st Duke of Montague, Lady Elizabeth Bruce, Lady Elizabeth Seymour, William Duke of Somerset (1588-1660), Edward Lord Beauchamp, Lady Catherine Grey (sister of Lady Jane Grey), Lady Francis Brandon, Henry Grey, 3rd Marquis of Dorset and Duke of Suffolk (1510-1554), Mary Tudor.

Part 2. Unpacking identity

[1] H R French, *The Middle Sort of People in Provincial England, 1600-1750*, 2008, pp.1-29.

[2] See chapter VIII for an explanation of the approach and Part 4 for an outline of findings.

[3] French, pp. 12-17.

[4] For a detailed discussion about these issues see internal references in chapters XXIII - XXV.

[5] The issue of freedom to make choices, and how the kinds of choices available to people may vary across historical time, see internal references in chapter XXI, especially in the paragraphs on *Freedom of choice among the middling sort*.

[6] Ed. Philippe Aries and George Duby, *A History of Private Life, vol. II, Revelations of the Medieval World*, 1988.

[7] See internal references in chapters XXVIII and XXIX , especially the paragraphs on *The role of the small community* on pp. 348-52

[8] Alan Macfarlane, *The Origins of English Individualism*, 1978.

[9] Ibid., p.123.

[10] Dan Jones, *Summer of Blood, The Peasants' Revolt of 1381*, 2009, pp. 50-51 and 211.

[11] See internal reference in chapter XXII for more detail, especially the paragraphs on *Family Influences*, pp. 297-305.

[12] Christian Greene is one example. She died in 1639, leaving money and land for the benefit of young grandchildren and their early-widowed mother. See internal reference on p. 193. Another example is Rose Ram who left her farm animals – ewes, lambs, bullocks and cows – to her daughters and each animal was specifically identified with a particular legacy. See internal reference on p. 73 for details.

[13] In 1576 Robert Ram left most of his holdings jointly to his widow Agnes and young son Richard, see internal reference on p. 124. Daniel Ram left his holdings in 1632 to his

widow Clemence for her lifetime, after which they went to his sons, see internal reference p. 127. Much later, in 1835, John Ram left his farming business to be run by a trust which included his daughter Abigail, see internal reference pp. 162-63.

[14] For examples see internal references: Robert Ram p. 134, Francis Ram, pp. 178-80 and his brother William, pp. 205-10 especially the story about his botany circle on p. 209. For later examples on the Colchester Rams, see the paragraphs on *Family networks in the eighteenth and nineteenth centuries*, pp. 226-32, and the paragraph on the *Purleigh relations*, pp. 245-46.

[15] The Walpole family picture at Mannington Hall, Norfolk includes Horatio Nelson and numerous relatives, some of whom were of assistance in the development of his career.

[16] R W Ram, *The Social Evolution of Five Dissenting Communities in Birmingham, 1750-1870*, Birmingham University Ph D thesis, 1972, especially chapter Four, Social Mobility, pp. 97-137.

[17] See internal reference Part 3, Section 4, Life without land, pp. 236-64.

[18] K Wrightson, *English Society 1580-1680*, 1982, pp. 52-58.

[19] H M Countryside Agency, *On the State of the Countryside*, 2003. For more details see internal reference p. 359.

[20] Rosemary O'Day, *The family and Family relationships, 1500-1900*, p. 217.

[21] Ibid., p.217.

[22] William Wright, *Born That Way. Genes, Behaviour, Personality*, 1999.

[23] Ibid., p. 62.

[24] Ibid., p. 40

[25] Ibid., p. 57.

[26] Ibid., p. 49-50.

[27] Ibid., p. 16.

[28] Ibid., pp. 85-98.

[29] Ibid., pp. 99-108.

[30] Matt Ridley, *Genome – The Autobiography of a Species in 23 Chapters*, 1999.

[31] Ibid., p.120. Quoted from W D Hamilton *Narrow Roads of Gene land*, vol. 1, 1995.

[32] C Renfrew, *Prehistory – The Making of the Human Mind*, 2007. For a summary of his argument see pp. 128-29.

[33] See internal reference, Part 4, especially chapters xxi and xxii, and Part 5, chapter xxviii the paragraphs on *Dealing with disconnectedness* on pp. 343-47.

[34] Robert Winston, *Why do we Believe in God?* The Guardian Supplement, 13 October 2005, p.16.

[35] For the detailed story see internal reference, the paragraphs on *A father's influence*, pp. 168-71.

[36] See E Duffey, *The Stripping of the Altars, Traditional Religion in England 1400-1580*, 2005.

[37] See internal reference, the paragraphs on *Religious Practice*, pp. 294-96.

[38] George Gilbert Scott, *Personal and Professional Recollections*, Ed. Gavin Stamp, 1995, pp. 4-23, especially 11-14.

[39] Raj Persaud, *The Animal Urge*, Financial Times Magazine, August 28 2004, Issue no 70, p. 23.

[40] Michael Braddick, *State formation in Early Modern England, 1550-1700*, 2000.

[41] See particularly, Peter Lazlett, *The World we Have Lost*, 1965, T H Hollingsworth, *Historical Demography*, 1969, and Ed. E A Wrigley, *An Introduction to English Historical Demography*, 1966.

[42] Ed. David Hey, *The History of Myddle*, by Richard Gough, 1981.

[43] For example see David Hey, firstly *The Oxford Guide to Family History*, 1993, and secondly, *Family Names and Family History*, 2000.

[44] M K McIntosh, *A Community Transformed, the Manor and Liberty of Havering, 1500-1620*, 1991.

[45] Keith Wrightson and David Levine, *Poverty and Piety in an English Village, Terling, 1525-1700,* 1995.

[46] L R Poos, *Population and Mortality in two Essex communities, Great Waltham and High Easter, 1327-1389,* pt. 1 of a University of Cambridge Ph D thesis, 1979, L R Poos, *Population and Resources in Two Fourteenth Century Essex Communities, Great Waltham and High Easter, 1327-1389,* pt. 2 of a Cambridge University Ph D, thesis, 1983, and L R Poos, *A rural society after the Black Death, Essex, 1350- 1525,* 1991.

[47] Keith Wrightson, *English Society, 1580-1680,* 2003.

[48] Ed. P Griffiths, A Fox, and S Hindle, *The Experience of Authority in Modern England,* 1996, essay by Keith Wrightson on 'The Politics of the Parish in Early Modern England', p. 36.

[49] Macfarlane, *The Origins of English Individualism,* p. 86.

[50] For full details on Francis Ram see below chapter XIV, *Francis Ram and his Family in Havering and London, 1550-1700.*

[51] M K McIntosh, *The Cooke Family of Gidea Hall, Essex 1460-1661,* Harvard University Ph D thesis, 1967, pp. 7-8.

[52] McIntosh, *A Community Transformed,* p. 34.

[53] H J Habakkuk, *Marriage settlements in the Eighteenth Century,* Transactions of the Royal Historical Society, 4th series 32 (1950), pp. 15-30.

[54] R A Houlbrooke, *English Family,* 1984.

[55] Alan Macfarlane, *Marriage and Love,* 1986.

[56] Lawrence Stone, *Family, Sex, and Marriage,* 1977.

[57] R A Houlbrooke, *Death, Religion, and the family in England, 1480-1750,* 1998, p. 2.

[58] L Davidoff and C Hall, *Family Fortunes, Men and women of the English middle class, 1780- 1850,* 1987.

[59] Eileen Spring, *Law Land and Family, Aristocratic Inheritance in England, 1300 to 1800,* p.149 following.

[60] Ibid., p. 158.

[61] Ibid., p. 155.

[62] Wrightson, pp. 74-129.

[63] O'Day, p. xvii.

[64] The summary of views which follows is based on the Introduction of Ed. Jonathan Barry and Christopher Brooks, 'The Middling Sort of People: Culture, Society and Politics in England, 1550-1800', 1994, especially pp. 1-17.

[65] Ibid., p. 6.

[66] Ibid., p. 7.

[67] Ibid., p. 3.

[68] Ibid., p. 7.

[69] Ibid., p. 5.

[70] Macfarlane, *The Origins of English Individualism,* especially chapters 7 and 8.

[71] H R French, pp. 143-44.

[72] Ed. D Vaisey, *The Diary of a Village Shopkeeper, 1754-1765,* 1998.

[73] Bryan Sykes and Catherine Irven, *Surnames and the Y Chromosome,* 2000.

[74] Chris Pomery, *DNA and Family History,* 2004, especially pp. 50-96.

[75] Blake Morrison, *Things my mother never told me,* 2003, p. 76.

[76] See internal reference, pp. 76-77.

[77] McIntosh, *The Cooke Family of Gidea Hall, Essex 1460-1661,* p. 7.

[78] Church of Jesus Christ of Latter-Day Saints, *International Genealogical Index* (IGI).

[79] Church of Jesus Christ of Latter-Day Saints, *1881 British Census and National Index.*

[80] See bibliography for a detailed list.

[81] R P Phillips and R Bazett, *Ages in the Making, A History of Two Essex Villages,* 1973, p. 71.

[82] David Hey, *Family Names and family History,* 2000, p.160.

Notes to pp. 68-81

[83] Phillips and Bazett, p. 72 and Mormon Index.

[84] See internal reference, pp. 365-66.

[85] The Great Waltham problem is discussed at internal reference on pp. 132-33 and that concerning the Colchester branch in the paragraphs on *Difficulties in the seventeenth century*, on pp. 215-16.

[86] Scott Smith-Bannister, *Names and naming patterns in England 1538-1700*, 1997.

[87] Ibid., p. 83.

[88] Ibid., p. 83.

[89] Ibid., p. 88.

[90] Ibid., p. 88.

[91] Ibid., p. 90.

[92] Ibid., p. 94.

[93] Ibid., p. 139.

[94] Ibid., p. 159.

[95] Ibid., p. 59.

[96] Ibid., p. 62.

[97] Ibid., p. 65.

[98] Her mother married Major Ralph Adye the brother of Major General Stephen Adye (1772-1838), one of whose sons was General Sir John Millar Adye (1819-1900), whilst a son of his, John Adye (b. 1857), became a Major General. All of them were officers in the Royal Artillery.

[99] McIntosh, *A Community Transformed*, p. 82, quoting ERO D/AED4, fols. 164v – 165r.

[100] Will of Rose Ram, ERO 55 ER 17.

[101] R W Ram, *Agrarian Change and its impact, 1650-1850; the experience of a farming family in central Essex*, The Local Historian, vol. 37, No 1, February 2007.

[102] G E Evans, Ask *the Fellows who Cut the Hay*, 1969, pp. 240-43.

[103] Ibid., p. 243.

[104] Ibid., p. 243.

[105] ERO, D/Dop F7.

[106] Ed F G Emmison, *Wills at Chelmsford,* three vols., 1958. This is a compendium of many of the wills held in the Essex Record Office. He also abstracted and edited twelve volumes of Essex wills, called *Wills of the County of Essex (England)*, with which there are very detailed cross referenced indexes. The wills in volumes 1 to 7 appear in the Archdeaconry Courts of Essex, Colchester, and Middlesex – vol. 1 1558-1565 (1982), vol. 2 1565-1571 (1983), vol. 3 1571-1577 (1986), vol. 4 1577-1584 (1987), vol. 5 1583-1592 (1989), vol. 6 1591-1597 (1991), and vol. 7 1597-1603 (1990). The wills in volumes 8 to 12 appear in the Bishop of London's Commissary Court – vol. 8 1558-1569 (1993), vol. 9 1569-1578 (1994), vol. 10 1578-1588 (1995), vol. 11 1587- 1599 (1998), and vol. 12 1596-1603 (2000).

[107] McIntosh, *A Community Transformed*, pp. 49, 141-3, and 423-4.

[108] F G Emmison, *Essex Wills: The Archdeaconry Courts, 1583-1592*, 1989, p. 22.

[109] See internal reference, pp. 122-28.

[110] See R D Smith, *The Middling Sort and the Politics of Social Reformation, Colchester, 1570-1640*, 2004, pp. 87-92 for a discussion about wills.

[111] McIntosh, *A Community Transformed*, footnote 53 on page 188.

[112] R D Smith, p. 230.

[113] Especially the paragraphs on *How Identity is formed*, pp. 33-36.

[114] W Wright, *Born That Way*, 1999, p. 5.

[115] See internal reference, chapter XXIX especially the paragraphs on *The role of the small community*, pp. 348-52.

[116] Matt Ridley, *Genome*, 1999.

[117] S H Foulkes, *Group Analytic Psychotherapy*, pp. 3-9.

[118] Special edition of *Group Analysis*, the journal of Group Analytic Psychotherapy, *A*

Analysis of Class, Status Groups and Inequality, volume 35, number 3, September 2002.

[119] Ibid., Lauren E Storck, *'Reality' or 'Illusion'? Five things of Interest about Social Class as a Large Group'*, pp. 351-365.

Part 3. The Ram story

[1] See the following internal references: for Great Waltham see pp. 92-94; for later moves around Great Waltham see paragraphs on *A picture of the Ram family in modern times*, pp. 153-166; for Havering see paragraphs on *Francis Ram's world*, pp. 171-74; for sixteenth century Colchester see pp. 204-206; for Copford and other places near Colchester see pp. 212-13, 216-19, and 224-26. Migrations to London are described on pp. 88-90.

[2] See internal reference, p. 252 for details.

[3] 120 Ordnance Survey, Explorer sheet 196, edn. A revised 1998, grid ref. 004362.

[4] John Hunter, *Field Systems in Essex*, The Essex Society for Archaeology and History, Occasional Papers, New Series, No.1, p. 4.

[5] Hunter, p. 9.

[6] H E Flight, *Economic and Social Conditions in Great Waltham in the Later Georgian Period*, n.d., p. 2. ERO, T/Z 13/110.

[7] ERO, DTu/254.

[8] Poos, *Population and Resources in Two Fourteenth Century Essex Communities*, pt. 2, p. 20.

[9] ERO, T/M 514 and 514/1.

[10] ERO, D/P 121/11/14.

[11] Essex Manorial Rental 1328, B L, Cotton Ch.XIII.5, and The Lay Subsidy of 1327, printed in Ed. Jennifer Ward, *The Medieval Essex Community, The Lay Subsidy of 1327*, Essex Historical Documents: 1, 1983.

[12] Information about the lay subsidies is taken from Ed. R E Glasscock, *The Lay Subsidy of 1334*, 1975, and from Ed. Jennifer Ward, *The Medieval Essex Community, The Lay Subsidy of 1327*.

[13] Poos, *Population and Mortality in two Essex communities, pt. 1*, figure 1 on p. 22, and pp. 53-61.

[14] Ibid., p. 55.

[15] Thanks are due to Janet Gyford for making this translation.

[16] Hunter, p. 7.

[17] Ibid., p. 80.

[18] Revd Andrew Clark, *Great Waltham Five Centuries Ago*, Essex Review, January 1904, no. 49 vol. XIII, pp. 75-6. His article was continued in July 1904, no. 51. vol XIII, pp. 129-49 and October 1904, no. 52. vol XIII, pp. 193-214.

[19] Ibid., p. 78.

[20] Ibid., p. 56.

[21] L R Poos, *A rural society after the Black Death, Essex, 1350-1525*, p. 45.

[22] Ibid., p.57.

[23] Phillips and Bazett, *Ages in the Making*, p. 10.

[24] Hull found the size of yardlands to vary – from about 16 acres in Barking to 40 in Great Waltham, and something nearer 80 at Felsted. See Felix Hull, *Agriculture and Rural Society in Essex, 1560-1640*, London University Ph D thesis, 1950, p. 362 and p. 364. ERO, T/256/1/4. See also ERO, D/Tu 254 and D/DCw M158.

[25] Clark p. 76.

[26] Mildred Campbell, *The English Yeoman Under Elizabeth and the Early Stuarts*, 1960, p.108.

[27] A W B Simpson, *An Introduction to the History of Land Law*, 1961, pp. 157-200.

Notes to pp. 102-115

[28] Poos, *A rural society after the Black Death*, pts. 1 and 2; Clark, *Great Waltham Five Centuries Ago*; Ed. Zvi Razi and Richard Smith, *Medieval Society and the Manor Court*, 1996.

[29] Phillips and Bazett, pp. 14-18.

[30] Christopher Dyer, *Everyday Life in Medieval England*, 2000, pp. 1-11.

[31] Poos, *Population and Resources in Two Fourteenth-Century Essex Communities*, pt. 2, pp. 65-88.

[32] Phillips and Bazett, p. 40.

[33] Poos, *Population and Resources in Two Fourteenth-Century Essex Communities*, pt. 1, pp. 10-11.

[34] M Jurkowski and C L Smith, *Lay Taxes in England and Wales, 1188-1688*, 1998, pp. 137-139.

[35] ERO, E179/108/151.

[36] K Wrightson and D Levine, *Poverty and Piety in an English Village, 1525-1700*, 2001, pp. 33-34.

[37] Francis Steer, *Samuel Tufnell of Langleys*, 1960, p. 23. See also J and J B Burke, *Genealogical and Heraldic History of the Extinct and Dormant Baronetcies of England, Ireland and Scotland*, 1894, pp. 189-90.

[38] Clark, pp. 1-19.

[39] Poos, *Population and Mortality in Two Fourteenth-Century Essex Communities*, pt. 1, table 3.1 p. 55.

[40] Ibid., Appendix B, p. 309.

[41] See internal references, chapter XII (especially the paragraphs on *The Tudor and Stuart surveys*, pp. 115-19 and Power and status in the community II, pp. 134-39) and chapter XIII, (especially the paragraphs on the 1805 survey, pp. 147-49, and Power and status in the community III, pp. 152-53).

[42] Campbell, pp. 317-320.

[43] D A Crowley, 'Frankpledge and Leet Jurisdiction In Late-Medieval Essex', Sheffield University Ph D thesis 1971, p. 240.

[44] Campbell, pp. 317-20 and p. 321.

[45] Ibid., pp. 84-86.

[46] Bryan Keith-Lucas, *The Unreformed Local Government System*, 1980, p. 84.

[47] Clark, April 1904, no. 50, vol. XIII, p. 71.

[48] See bibliography for a complete list of wills.

[49] Lease from John Hall of Pleshey, John Alfrith, Jun., and Thomas Ram of Great Waltham to William Skynner of Chelmsford, Thomas Aleyne of Pleshey and Roger Bright of the same tenement, B L, Add. Charter 18120.

[50] Lease from Margaret Everard, relict of John Skinner, late of Pleshey, John Alfrith, and John Clerk to John Cowper (alias Driver) of Great Waltham, John Glascok, Sen., William Ram and others of the same tenement, B L, Add. Charter 18122.

[51] Ed. P H Reaney and Marc Fitch, *Feet of Fines for Essex*, 1964, vol. IV, 1423-1527, p. 124.

[52] *Feet of Fines for Essex*, vol. IV, 1423-1527, p. 178.

[53] For more details see internal reference p. 153.

[54] Phillips and Bazett, p. 57.

[55] Campbell, p. 61.

[56] Ibid., p. 102.

[57] ERO, D/D/Tu/63.

[58] ERO, D/DTu/64 (1433), D/DTu/69 (1441), D/DTu/70 (1442).

[59] Poos, *A rural society after the Black Death*, pp. 250-62.

[60] M K McIntosh, *A Community Transformed*, p. 108.

[61] Hull, *Agriculture and Rural Society in Essex, 1560-1640*.

[62] The ERO references for these surveys are: 1563 D/Dtu/254, 1577 D/Dge/M273, 1583 D/Dge/M274, 1616 D/Dtu255, and 1622 D/DB M142.

Notes to pp. 115-131

[63] Ed. P Griffiths, A Fox and S Hindle,*The Experience of Authority in Early Modern England,* 1996, p. 106.

[64] ERO, D/Dge/M273.

[65] Hull, pp. 313-34.

[66] See internal reference, the paragraphs on *A picture of the Ram family in early modern times,* pp. 140-42.

[67] Langleys was acquired by the Everarde family in the early sixteenth century through marriage settlements. It was quite small. The manor was sold to Samuel Tufnell in 1711. Walthambury Manor itself was bought by Richard Rich at the time of the dissolution of the monasteries, along with Chatham Hall nearby, where he lived, and much other land in Essex. This manor remained linked to the Rich family until 1701 when it was bought by Herman Olmius a Dutch merchant. See Philip Morant *The History and Antiquities of the County of Essex,* 1763-68, vol II, p. 82. When Morant wrote his book the Olmius family still owned Walthambury Manor. Phillips and Bazett state in *Ages in the Making* that Walthambury Manor was later bought by the Tufnells, but no date is provided. See p.90. An agreement was made in 1780 between J J Tufnell and Drigue Billers, Lord Waltham, for the sale of the manor (ERO, D/DU1115/14) and there are further related documents in D/DU1115/15-18.

[68] Campbell, p. 100.

[69] Hull, *Agriculture and Rural Society in Essex, 1560-1640.*

[70] Ibid., p. 369.

[71] Ibid., table p. 367.

[72] Ibid., table on p. 326.

[73] Ibid., p. 333.

[74] Wrightson and Levine, p. 20.

[75] Ibid., p. 20.

[76] Hull, p. 313.

[77] Wrightson and Levine, p. 26.

[78] See internal reference chapter XI, especially the paragraphs on *The lay subsidy of 1523-1526,* pp. 104-05.

[79] M K McIntosh, *A Community Transformed,* p. 117.

[80] Ibid., p.117.

[81] Ibid., p. 183.

[82] See Chart C1 on p. 169.

[83] Ralph Houlbrooke, *Death, Religion, and the family in England, 1480-1750,* p. 119.

[84] McIntosh, *A Community Transformed,* pp. 59-59.

[85] Campbell, p. 213.

[86] Poos, *Population and mortaility in two Essex communities,* pt 1, p. 49.

[87] J and J B Burke, *Genealogical and Heraldic History of the Extinct and Dormant Baronetcies,* p. 190.

[88] See Davidoff and Hall, *Family Fortunes,* chapter 4 of part two, especially the section on *Land and capital,* pp. 205-07, for a short summary of attitudes and practice about inheritance in different social groups.

[89] See internal reference, p. 151.

[90] Wrightson and Levine, pp. 30-31.

[91] In the village survey of 1583 these lands are shown to be held by Richard Ram, so one wonders what Rose got out of this bequest!

[92] This may have been a roadside verge, which was the only form of waste in nearby High Easter in 1569, see Hull vol. 2, note 1, p. 389.

[93] Campbell, p. 91.

[94] Ibid, p. 157.

[95] Will of John Ram, (d. 1667), ERO 187 ER 21.

[96] Circumstantial evidence suggests this was the case, but there was another John alive in 1616.

Notes to pp. 132-145

[97] Emmison, *Essex wills, The Commissary Court, 1558-59*, will of Robert Marshe, (534), pp. 114-15.

[98] Poos, *A rural society after the Black Death*, p. 45.

[99] Hull, p. 276-280.

[100] Campbell, p. 74.

[101] Ibid., p. 75.

[102] David Eastwood, *Governing Rural England, Tradition and transformation in Local Government 1780-1840*, 1994, p. 153.

[103] Phillips and Bazett, p. 61.

[104] ERO, D/DTu/254.

[105] Hull, p. 346.

[106] Ibid., p. p353.

[107] Ibid., p. 333.

[108] Ibid., pp. 313-34 and 317-26.

[109] Ibid., pp. 326-336.

[110] Wrightson and Levine, p. 26.

[111] F G Emmison, *Wills of the County of Essex*.

[112] Ed. F G Emmison, *Feet of Fines for Essex*, vol VI, 1581-1603, 1993, p. 111.

[113] Ibid., vol. VI, p. 122.

[114] Ibid., vol. VI, p. 149.

[115] See will of Geoffrey Ram (d.1584), ERO, 258 BW 31.

[116] Campbell, p. 102.

[117] Gen. ed. Joan Thirsk, *The Agrarian History of England and Wales*, vol iv, chapter ix, Peter Bowden, *Agricultural prices, farm profits and rents*, table 25 on p. 653.

[118] Bowden, p. 610-11.

[119] Peter Earle, The Making of the English Middle Class, Business Society and Family Life in London, 1660-1730, 1989, p. 11.

[120] Bowden, pp. 653-7.

[121] Ibid., p. 594.

[122] Ibid., pp. 598-600.

[123] Ibid., p. 593.

[124] Ibid., p. 635-38.

[125] Ibid., p. 609.

[126] Campbell, p. 104.

[127] The years between the mid seventeenth and eighteenth centuries are sometimes known as the Little Ice Age and the period between 1650 and 1700 were especially cold. This fact may have influenced the farming decline. See ed., M Hulme and E Barrow, *Climates of the British Isles, present past and future*, 1997, pp. 173-196.

[128] ERO, TA 169/3.

[129] ERO, Q/RTh 5.

[131] Margaret Spufford, *Contrasting Communities, English Villagers in the Sixteenth and Seventeenth Centuries*, 2000, pp. 39 and 40.

[132] Ibid., p. 41.

[133] Tom Arkell, The Local Historian, *Identifying regional variations from the hearth tax*, vol. 33, no. 3, August 2003, p. 165.

[134] See internal reference p.108 for discussion about the role of Constable.

[135] Campbell, p. 340-41.

[136] Ibid., p. 347.

[137] Ibid., p. 353.

[138] See internal reference, XIII, the paragraphs on *Power and status in the community III*, pp. 152-53.

[139] F G Emmison, *Wills of the County of Essex*, Archdeaconry Court, 1597-1603, will of Richard Aylett.

Notes to pp. 147-159

[140] ERO, D/P 121/11/14.

[141] ERO, Q/RZ2.

[142] ERO, T/Z 13/110. H E Flight, *Economic and Social Conditions in Great Waltham in the Later Georgian Period*, n.d., p. 3.

[143] Flight, p.3.

[144] Census of England and Wales, vol. 2, 1891, p. 295.

[145] Ibid., p. 6.

[146] Wrightson and Levine, p. 35.

[147] See internal reference chapter XII, the paragraphs on, *Comparisons with other research*, pp. 119-21.

[148] Bowden, p. 674.

[149] Ibid., p. 685.

[150] Ibid., p.689.

[151] Ibid., p. 682-1.

[152] Ibid., p. 659.

[153] M J Daunton, *Progress and Poverty, an Economic and Social History of Britain, 1700-1850*, 1995, p. 75.

[154] Flight, p. 2.

[155] ERO., T/M 514, *Survey of Lands of Manor of Walthambury Manor, Great Waltham*, 1643, and T/M 514/1, *A true plan or Demonstration of all and singular Desmesne Landes beelonging to the Mannor of Waltham Burie situate in the Parish of Much Waltham....also 1643*.

[156] A F J Brown, *Meagre Harvest, The Essex Farm workers' Struggle against Poverty, 1750-1914*, 1990, pp. 2-3.

[157] Stephen Hussey and Laura Swash, Studies in Essex History, No. 5, *Horrid Lights, 19th-Century Incediarism in Essex*, 1994, p.15.

[158] Ibid., pp. 8-13.

[159] Ibid., pp. 15-18.

[160] Ibid., p. iii.

[161] Colin Shrimpton, *The Landed society and the Farming community of Essex in the Late Eighteenth and early Nineteenth centuries*, 1977, p. 247.

[162] Ibid., p. 19.

[163] Hull., p. 338.

[164] ERO, D/Dtu 254.

[165] ERO, D/DHh/M173 mentions these names in the years noted.

[166] ERO, D/P 121/11/3.

[167] ERO, D/P 121/8.

[168] ERO, D/AEP 35/137.

[169] ERO, Q/RPI 190.

[170] Essex Review, April,1917 (No. 102, vol. XXVI), pp. 71-76.

[171] ERO, D/p 121/1/5.

[172] ERO, D/APW/R3.

[173] Ed. John Waddell, *Roxwell Revealed, An anthology of village history*, 1993, pp. 23-31.

[174] ERO, D/CT 301.

[175] 1881 Census.

[176] 1851 Census.

[177] ERO, D/DopF7, Valuation of Steeple Grange, the property of Samuel Tufnell Esq situate in Steeple and Nayland, October 1810.

[178] Arthur Young, *General View of the Agriculture of the County of Essex*, vol. 1, 1807, pp. 58-60, and, p. 67 foll.

[179] Ibid., pp. 77-79.

180 Shrimpton, p. 249.
181 Ibid., p. 251.
Notes to pp. 159-173

182 Young, *General View*, p. 251.
183 W A Armstrong, *Wages and Incomes*, chapter 7 in G E Mingay, *The Agrarian History of England and Wales*, vol. 6, 1989, p. 704.
184 Young, *General View*, pp. 97-100.
185 Shrimpton, p. 273.
186 Shrimpton, p. 265.
187 ERO, DDOp F7.
188 Shrimpton, pp. 289-90.
189 Ibid., p. 300.
190 A F J Brown, *Prosperity and Poverty, Rural Essex, 1700-1815*, 1996, p. 24.
191 Susanna Martins, *Farmers, Landlords and Landscapes, Rural Britain, 1720 to 1870*, p. 135.
192 Ibid., p. 21 and *Essex Standard*, 17 July, 1874.
193 Shrimpton, p. 323.
194 ERO, D/AER 34/204.
195 ERO, D/DHh/M174.
196 ERO, D/ABR27/175.
197 See *The Agrarian History of England and Wales*, gen. ed., Joan Thirsk, volume iv, *the Malting Industry*, pp. 501-519, especially the tables on pp. 502 and 503.
198 ERO, D/ABR27/525.
199 ERO, D/Dtu/287, *Rent receipt book for Langley Estate 1748-97*, at least from October 3 1761 until February 1765.
200 Will of John Ram 6 (d. 1835), ERO, 46 BR 34.
201 ERO, D/Dtu/277, Account book of Samuel Tufnell 1725-30.
202 ERO, D/Dtu/287, This starts with accounts paid.
203 Ibid.
204 Much of the information in this paragraph is drawn from Martins, chapters 6 and 7.
205 Will of Abigail Ram (d. 1883), ERO, D/DCf/F523.
206 *Abstract of court rolls, 1769-1823*, ERO, D/DHh/M174.
207 ERO, D/P 121/12/2.
208 Flight, p. 8.
209 Flight, pp. 4 and 8.
210 This survey of family members and related individuals living around Great Waltham in 1881 has been obtained from the 1881 Census.
211 ERO, D/DCF T98.
212 ERO, D/AER 37/77.
213 The grant was made by Robert Cooke Clarenceux King of Arms, and is recorded in B L, Harley 1359, f.103, as well as Queen's College Oxford, Oxford MS 146 Fol. 471. See *The Ram Family*, p.33.
214 Will of John Ram (d. 1618), ERO, D/AEW 16/132.
215 B L, Harley. 1422, fol. 56 and Add 14295, fol. 25b.
216 The drawing of the arms is from College of Arms MS. Miscellaneous Grants 1, f. 121.
217 See internal reference p. 170 and will of John Rayne of Pleacy, PCC 11 Babington.
218 For details, see internal reference, p. 181.
219 See internal reference chapter XV, the paragraphs on *William Ram (Abt 1535-1602)*, especially pp. 205-06.
220 Douglas Carter, *1000 years of Boxted History, Part 1, St Peter's Church*, (n.d.), pp. 6- 7.
221 Ibid., pp. 12-13.
222 R D Smith, *The Middling Sort and the Politics of Social Reformation, Colchester, 1570-1640*, 2004, pp. 97-100, and especially p.99.
223 M K McIntosh, *A Community Transformed*, p. 141.

[224] Ibid., p. 6-7.

[225] Ibid., p.13.

Notes to pp. 173-182

[226] Will of Francis Ram, (d. 1617) PCC 32 Weldon.

[227] Ibid.

[228] See *Cotton and Dalton families*, ERO, T/G 23/7.

[229] Walter Metcalfe, *Visitations of Essex, Miscellaneous Essex Pedigrees from various Harleian Manuscripts*, 1878, vol. XIII, p. 319.

[230] F G Emmison, The Archdeaconry Courts, vol. 5, 1583-1592, 1989, p. 22.

[231] McIntosh, *A Community Transformed*, pp. 141-42.

[232] Ibid., p. 388.

[233] According to Walter Metcalfe, *Visitations of Essex*, p. 532, the first grant of arms to the family was made to Middle John in 1590. The identification of his father as 'Sir' John Wright may therefore be incorrect.

[234] ERO, T/G 134 and ERO Pamphlet Box 136, *The Wright Family of Kelvedon Hatch*, n. d.

[235] McIntosh, *A Community Transformed*, p. 316.

[236] McIntosh, *The Cooke Family of Gidea Hall Essex, 1460-1661*, Ph D thesis, Harvard University, 1967, p. 250.

[237] Ibid., p. 250.

[238] ERO, Q/SR 39/9 and 10. This document states – 'Memorandum at this Session Sir Anthony Cooke became Custos Rotulorum and Mr Francis Rame Clerk of the Peace'.

[239] McIntosh, *The Cooke family of Gidea Hall*, p. 250.

[240] ERO, Q/SR177/55-59.

[241] Joel Samaha, *Law and Order in Historical Perspective. The Case of Elizabethan Essex*, 1974.

[242] McIntosh, *A Community Transformed*, p. 342.

[243] ERO, Q/SR183/81.

[244] Ed. J S Cockburn, *Calendar of Assize Records, Essex Indictments, Elizabeth I*, 1978, and *Essex Indictments, James I*, 1982.

[245] The account was made by Anne Cooke, the widow of Richard. It is in B L, Lansdown 30, no. 82, and is printed in full at the back of McKintosh, *The Cooke family of Gidea Hall Essex*.

[246] McIntosh, The Cooke family of Gidea Hall Essex, p. 293.

[247] McIntosh, *A community Transformed*, p. 353.

[248] Ibid., p. 353. The general information provided here about Sir Anthony Cooke is based on McIntosh, *A Community Transformed*, pp. 352-53.

[249] Information about Richard, Young Sir Anthony and Edward Cooke is drawn from McIntosh, *The Cooke Family of Gidea Hall*, pp. 116-169.

[250] McIntosh, T*he Fall of a Tudor Gentle Family*, p. 293.

[251] McIntosh, *A Community Transformed*, p.142.

[252] In the VCH of Warwickshire there is mention of Lark Stoke manor which is in Ilmington, Warwickshire, ref. C.P. 25(1)/292/69/221, printed in *Warwickshire Feet of Fines*, iii (Dugdale Society xviii), p. 159.

[253] McIntosh, The Cooke family of Gidea Hall Essex, p. 207. The source of this information is PRO C 54/661 or 655.

[254] F J Fisher (Ed. P J Corfield and NB Harte) *London and the English Economy, 1500-1700*, 1990, pp.82-83.

[255] Essex Archaeological Society, *Feet of Fines for Essex*,1964, vol. VI, 1581-1603, no. 11, p. 35.

[256] Ibid., no. 6, p. 37.

[257] Metcalfe, *Visitations of Essex*, p. 338.

[258] McIntosh, *A Community Transformed*, p. 399.

[259] Will of Francis Ram, (d. 1617).

[260] McIntosh, *A Community Transformed*, p. 143.

261 Valerie Pearl, *London and the Outbreak of the Puritan Revolution, City Government and National Politics 1625-43*, 1961, p. 331.

Notes to pp. 182-192

262 Emmison, *Wills of the County of Essex*, vol. 4, 1577-84.

263 McIntosh, *A Community Transformed*, p. 182.

264 Ibid., p. 211.

265 The account that follows about Havering affairs into the 1640s is based on McIntosh, *A Community Transformed*, pp. 370-401.

266 See McIntosh, *A Community Transformed*, p. 382, n. 59. It has not been possible to establish exactly the relationships of the Hornchurch Harveys with Sir Simon Harvey.

267 Ed. Joseph Foster, *Marriage Licences, London 1521-1869*, 1887.

268 McIntosh, *The Cooke family of Gidea Hall*, p. 92.

269 C T Perfect, *Ye Olde Village of Hornchurch*, 1917, p. 40.

270 VCH of Essex, vol. 7, p. 54.

271 Emmison, *Essex Wills, The Commissiary Court, 1569-1578*, p. 91.

272 Emmison, *Essex Wills, The Archdeaconry Courts, 1571-1577*, p. 183-86.

273 McIntosh, *A Community Transformed*, p. 264.

274 Emmison, Wills of the County of Essex, The Archdeaconry Courts, 1591-97, p. 75.

275 McIntosh, *A Community Transformed*, p. 347-48.

276 Emmison, *Wills of the County of Essex*, vol. 3, 1571-77, (1986).

277 See internal reference, p. 73.

278 Emmison, Essex Wills, The Archdeaconry Courts, 1583-92, p. 63.

279 Will of Francis Ram (d. 1617).

280 ERO, D/AEW 16/132.

281 Emmison, *Wills of the County of Essex, vol. 5, 1583-92, (1989)*.

282 Craig Spence, *London in the 1690s, A Social Atlas*, 2000, pp. 51, 70, 107 and 108.

283 Ed Joseph Foster, *The Register of Admissions to Gray's Inn, 1521-1889*, 1889.

284 McIntosh *The Cooke family of Gidea Hall*, Appendix G, Young Anthony Cooke's sale of land, p. 351.

285 *Harleian Society (visitation section) Middlesex Pedigrees* lxv, 19. William Gerard, of Flamberds married Dorothy daughter of John Ratcliff of Langley, and dying 1583 was succeeded by his son, Gilbert Gerard who was created a baronet in 1620 and represented Middlesex in Parliament. William was descended from the second son of James Gerard, himself second son of William Gerard of Ince, in Lancashire, by Elizabeth his wife, daughter of Sir John Biron, who married Margaret, daughter of John Holcroft and had two sons, Gilbert Gerard, a distinguished lawyer and Master of the Rolls in the reign of Elizabeth who founded line of Gerards of Bromley, earls of Macclesfield, and William Gerard of Flamberds.

286 VCH of Middlesex, vol. 4, pp. 209-11.

287 See internal reference, pp. 207-10.

288 Will of John Ram, (d. 1627), ERO, D/AEW/6/132.

289 Ibid.

290 *London Marriage Licences, 1520-1610*, p. 325.

291 Peter Earle, The Making of the English Middle Class - Business Society and Family Life in London, 1660-1730, 1989, p. 251.

292 A Heal, *The London Goldsmiths, 1200-1800*, 1972. This book contains an alphabetical list of goldsmiths with biographical details, from where the information about Anthony, and that which follows on his brother Benjamin and the Bearblock family has been obtained.

293 Will of Samuel Ram, (d. 1624), PCC 90 Byrde.

294 Will of Edward Ram, (d. 1617), PCC 109 Pile.

295 Will of Joan Ram, (d. 1627), PCC 77 Skynner.

296 Will of Francis Ram, (d. 1634), probate 24.11.1636.

297 Wllett and F R Ram, *The Ram Family*, pp. 105-106.

298 Will of Benjamin Ram, (d. 1625), PCC 88 Clarke.
299 Will of Jane Ram, (d. 1625), PCC 82 Clerke.
Notes to pp. 192-202

300 ERO, D/Dmy/15M50/240. Item 72 reads, 'A note from Mr Rame for paying alienation for Marks' and Item 73 'Mr Rame's line/fee? about a writ of error brought by Mr Roche'. Item 75 speaks about the relief and surender of Marks unto me.
301 McIntosh, *A Community Transformed*, note on p. 372.
302 ERO, D/D My/15M50/296/8 and 13.
303 ERO, D/DQs/43. *Manuscript Visitation of Essex*, 1614, 1643, with additions.
304 Ed. Michael Anderson, *British Population History*, 1996, Chapter 3, R A Houston, *The Population History of Britain and Ireland, 1500-1750*, p.118.
305 McIntosh, A Community Transformed, p.11.
306 Ibid., p.14.
307 L Picard, *Elizabeth's London, Everyday Life in Elizabethan London*, 2003, p.89.
308 Ibid., p.89.
309 Will of William Ram (d. 1713), ERO, 307 BR 16.
310 ERO, D/ABR 30/342.
311 ERO, Acc. C905 Box 13, unpublished manuscript, J B Butt, *Biographical Dictionary*, vol. 2, p. 152 and the *Ipswich Journal* 15.10.1791 and 22.10.1791.
312 Butt, *Biographical Dictionary*, vol 2, p. 151.
313 Ibid., p. 144.
314 Ibid., p.152.
315 Ibid., p. 151.
316 Ordnance Survey 25 inch map, new series 37/3, 1923 edn.
317 *Ipswich Journal*, 09.01.1796.
318 Butt, vol. 2, p. 152.
319 *Ipswich Journal*, 09.01.1796.
320 Robert Tabor (1736-1818) was a leading Hythe Merchant and the third of four generations of the family to be significant Colchester merchants. He was active in the Harbour Commissioners and in Lion Walk Chapel. He was something of a radical in politics. See John Butt, *Biographical Index*, vol. 2, p. 163.
321 Butt, vol 2, p.152.
322 *Ipswich Journal*, 9.1.1796.
323 ERO, P/Lw R20, states this in a biographical note connected to the claim his son Joseph made in 1819 to become a poor rate charge on Layer de la Haye. See Butt for information about Joseph Green. He was propritor of the Lime Kiln at the Hythe and was also a merchant and owner of property. In 1776 he was worth over a £1000 for insurance purposes.
324 *Ipswich Journal*, 04.11.1809 and *Colchester Chronicle*, 27.10.1809.
325 J B Butt, *Dirty, Dirty Work, The brief history of Colchester politics, 1784-1790*, pp. 20-21, an unpublished typescript article in the Biographical Dictionary papers.
326 Will of John King, ERO, D/Dcm F/1/4.
327 Daunton, *Progress and Poverty*, p. 249. The observations about eighteenth century bankruptcy are based on pp 238-252 of this book.
328 Ibid., p. 249.
329 *Ipswich Journal*, 1.11.1794.
330 See biographical note in Joseph Ram's claim of 1819 to be poor rate charge on Layer de la Haye.
331 The VCH of Essex, volume 9, *The Borough of Colchester*, 1994, is the most valuable source. Other books are of relevance at particular points, for example, R D Smith, *The Middling Sort and the Politics of Social Reformation*, provides good background on the period when William Ram (d. 1602) was active.
332 ERO, E/COL, *Court Rolls of the Borough of Colchester*, vol 3, 1372-1379, pp. 146, 159, 169, 175, 179, 188, 202.

333 Ibid., vol 1, 1310-1352, p. 224.

334 Ibid., vol 2, 1353-1367, pp. 36, 48, 49, 67, 93, 96, 105, 114, 116, 119, 122, 127.
Notes to pp. 202-210

335 A person could become a free burgess by birthright, purchase, or grant and they could vote at annual elections. In 1619 there were about 450 of them. See R D Smith, footnote 97 on page 32.

336 Will of Joan Potter, (d. 1584), ERO, D/ABW 29/74.

337 See above p.141.

338 JA Venn, *Alumni Cantabrigienses*, CUP, 1924, pt. 1, 1751, vol. 3.

339 ERO, E/COL, The *Oath Book or Red Parchment Book of Colchester,* p. 180.

340 ERO, TA428/1/8.

341 ERO, D/B 5 R7, Minutes of Assemblies, folios 235r-287r, 2 August-29 October, 1576.

342 Ed. J S Cockburn, Calendar of Assize Records, Essex Indictments, Elizabeth I, 1978, No. 1319.

343 Ibid., Nos. 928 and 929.

344 Grant of lands from William Ram to Nicholas Eve of High Easter, 1587, B L, Add. Charter,18131.

345 ERO, *Collectors of the Poor Book, 1581-1595*, Accession C1 (part).

346 R D Smith, p. 28. There was a steady increase of population during the sixteenth century. In 1524-25 it was about 3500 and by the 1570s about 4500. In the 1620s it had reached 11,000, but fell slightly as the century progressed. In the sixteenth and seventeeth centuries Colchester was the tenth biggest town in England, although it fell in status during the eighteeth century.

347 VCH of Essex, vol. 9, p. 97. See also R D Smith.

348 Will transcriptions ERO, T/A 48/3 and D/DCm F1/97-196. William Ram figures in a small number of this large bundle of transcripts, largely of wills made by leading Colchester citizens contemporary with him.

349 R D Smith, footnote 96 on p. 32.

350 R D Smith, footnote 114 on p. 35.

351 Ibid., footnote 114 on p. 35.

352 ERO, E/COL, *Report on the Records of the Borough of Colchester – calendar of the Court rolls of the Borough of Colchester with lists of Bailiffs and Mayors,* 1865, p. 66.

353 Ibid.

354 Ibid., Number 309.

355 J Silvester, *An Elizabethan vicar of Great Clacton. John Markaunt and his famous hymn,* 1922. See also ERO, EA S.

356 VCH of Essex, vol 9, p.130.

357 Ibid., p. 130.

358 R D Smith, pp. 93-96 and 111-143.

359 Ed. R B McKerrow, *A Dictionary of Printers and Booksellers in England, Scotland and Ireland, and of Foreign Printers of English Books, 1557-1640,* 1910, p. 254. Simon Stafford was a draper and printer in London from 1596- 1626. He served an apprentiship with Christopher Barker, the Queen's printer. He was a member of the Drapers' Company and also of the Stationers' Company.

360 J Britten and G S Boulger, *A Biographical Index of British and Irish Botanists,* 1893, p.140. This book mentions that William Ram wrote '*Little Dodeon*' in 1606, calling it an epitome of Lyte's Herball. The source of this information is given as John Gerard, *The Herball...or General History of Plants,* enlarged and amended by Thomas Johnson, 1633, p. 278 following.

361 William Ram, *Little Dodeon*, p.176.

362 H Lyte, '*A New Herball or Historie of Plants*', 1578, pp. 2-4.

363 R H Jeffers, *The Friends of John Gerard (1545-1612) Surgeon and Botanist,* 1967.

364 Ibid., p. 52.

365 Ibid., p. 54.

366 See above, pp. 150-51.

367 Robert is mentioned in the paragraph after the reference to Thomas in a way which suggests they are the same person, Jeffers, p. 52.
Notes to pp. 210-223

368 Jeffers, p. 18.

369 Ibid., p. 23.

370 See above p. 151, footnote 284.

371 Jeffers, p. 20.

372 Ibid., p. 36.

373 See above, p. 157 and pp. 161-62.

374 *Allumi Cantabrigienses*, pt 1, 1751, vol. 3.

375 Guildhall Library Ordination Register, 9535/2. See also Clergy of the Church of England Database (CCEd), ordination record ID172082. This record stated Robert was ordained at the age of 34 but other information about the family and his education suggests it was much more likely to be 24.

376 A J Wright, *St Michael and All Angels, Copford*, 1993, p. 2.

377 Harold Smith, *The Ecclesiastical History of Essex under the Long Parliament and the Commonwealth*, n.d., p. 233 foll.

378 VCH of Essex, vol 10, p. 150.

379 Harold Smith, p. 38.

380 Will of Robert Ram, (d. 1638), Bishop of London 364 Allen.

381 VCH of Essex, vol 10, p. 143.

382 *Allumi Cantabrigienses*, pt 1, 1751, vol. 3.

383 See internal reference, p. 296.

384 ERO, D/DU 161/407. There were six lots which included six houses with land amounting to about 40 acres.

385 ERO, D/DU 161/431.

386 Will of Edmund Ram, (d. 1625?), PCC 24 Barrington.

387 ERO, Q/SR 221/55.

388 Ed. J H Round, *Register of the scholars admitted to Colchester School 1637- 1740*, 1897, Thanks are due to David Tomlinson for drawing my attention to this register.

389 *The Ram Family*, pp. 35-36.

390 The *Oath Book or Red Parchment Book of Colchester*, p. 248.

391 Philip Morant, *History of Essex*, vol I, 1766, p. 215.

392 ERO, D/DU 207/40-43.

393 ERO, D/DC/33/3 and 4.

394 Harleian Society, *Visitations of Essex, Pt. 2*, vol. 14, 1879, p. 638, B L, HLX 929.341.

395 Ordnance Survey, Explorer series, sheet 196.

396 SRO Ipswich, HA 108/2/89.

397 SRO Ipswich, HA 108/2/3.

398 SRO Ipswich, HA 108/2/89.

399 Tendring Hall Estate title deeds, relating to the estate of Sir Richard Williams, especially SRO HA/108/2/3.

400 Will of Bridget Warren, (d. 1747), ERO, 259 CR 15.

401 Will of Francis Ram, (d. 1750), ERO, T/G 23/ 1-37.

402 Although one source says Thomas died in infancy geneological and circumstantial evidence suggests he was born about 1698, went to Colchester Grammar School in 1709 (see Round, Register of scholars admitted to Colchester School), became a surgeon, and died in Layer de la Haye in 1776.

403 ERO, 123 BR 21.

404 See the wills of Sarah Pearson (d. 1763) ERO 359 CR 16, and William Pearson (d. 1740), ERO, 61 CR 15.

405 Ordnance Survey One Inch Series, Reprint of the first edition, sheet 64.

406 ERO, D/DSr F6/2.

407 Ibid.

408 Ibid.

409 ERO, D/DSrT2.

Notes to pp. 224-232

410 ERO, D/DSrB2.

411 ERO, D/DHt/t 72/111, *Colchester Trade Directory 1793.*

412 ERO, D/DSrB2.

413 ERO, D/DHt/t 72/111, *Colchester Trade Directory 1793.*

414 ERO, D/DU 507/31, A *Plan of Monkwick and other Lands the Property of Ralph Ward, Esq.,* 1806.

415 Leonard H Gant, *History of Berechurch in the County of Essex,* n.d., pp. 5-6.

416 VCH History of Essex, vol 9, p. 412.

417 Shani D'Cruze, *The Middling Sort in Provincial England – Politics and Social Relations in Colchester 1730-1800,* University of Essex Ph D thesis, 1990, p. 67.

418 Butt, *Biographical Dictionary* p. 151.

419 ERO, D/DB T1593, copy of the will of John Bawtree 2 (d. 1824).

420 R W Ram, *The Social Evolution of Five dissenting Congregations in Birmingham, 1750-1870,* University of Birmingham Ph D thesis, 1972. Chapter 4, *Social Mobility,* pp. 97-137, indirectly reveals the extent of intermarriage.

421 Ibid., Chapter 4.

422 Leonora Davidoff and Catherine Hall, *Family Fortunes, Men and women of the English middle class 1780-1850,* 1987, especially pp. 211-222.

423 Major R W Adye, *The Pocket Gunner,* 1798.

424 Essex Society for Family History, *Monumental Inscriptions at St Andrews Church Abberton.*

425 J B Butt, *The Drinks Trade,* unpublished essay in the Biographical Dictionary papers.

426 ERO, 61 CR 15.

427 ERO, D/P 255/1/1.

428 See internal reference, pp. 218-20.

179 Will of John Bawtree 1, (d. 1782), ERO, D/ACW 33/3/10.

430 ERO, D/DEl/T16.

431 Stephen Twining, *The House of Twining, 1706-1956,* 1956, p. 59.

432 ERO, D/Del F47.

433 Will of John Mills, (d. 1822), ERO, D/Del F48.

434 He was shot by Anne Broderick. See entry for Batter and Haddock in the bibliography section of VCH of Essex, vol. 9.(There is also a reference to a Haddock family of Leigh in this section).

435 See ERO, T/A 535/1, *List of Records of Mills, Batter and Co Bank 1884-91* and an essay by G E Ascinder for references to Mills, Batter and Co, Colchester and Essex Bank in the Gurney papers (A18A) now part of the historical records of Barclays Bank.

436 Will of John Bawtree 2, ERO, D/DEl/T16.

437 Will and papers relating to G H Errington. ERO, D/Del F49.

438 Geoffrey Martin, *Story of Colchester from Roman Times to the Present Day,* 1959. See also ERO, Acc.C104 (estate and family papers, box 2), and VCH for Essex vol. 9, p. 139.

439 VCH of Essex vol. 9, p. 262.

440 J B Penfold, *The History of the Esex County Hospital, Colchester, 1820-1948,* 1984, p.3.

441 The will of John Bawtry 2 (d. 1824), makes this clear. John Ram had an interest in Badcocks in 1784 and it is possible that John Bawtree 2 obtained his interest in it as a by product of John Ram's bankruptcy.

442 The Essex Society for family History, *Monumental Inscriptions at St Andrew's Church, Abberton,* 1997.

443 VCH of Essex, vol. 9, pp. 211-212.

444 ERO, D/DEl F37.

[445] ERO, D/DelF39.

[446] See internal reference, p. 253.

Notes to pp. 233-252

[447] SRO, HA 108/1/14/24. Manorial records for the Manor of Stoke next Nayland with Shardlowes and Withermarsh. Steward's papers – a bundle with correspondence concerning the Ram family.

[448] ERO, no reference available. Letter of Elizabeth Jane Ram, May 16 1871.

[449] Davidoff and Hall, p. 210.

[450] See internal reference, chapter XVII, the paragraphs on *The descendants of John Ram,* pp. 246-48.

[451] This is known from a biographical note in Joseph Ram's claim of 1819 to become a poor rate charge on Layer de la Haye. See ERO, P/LwR 20

[452] See internal reference, chapter XVII, the paragraphs on *The descendants of John Ram* 5C, p. 247.

[453] ERO, D/ACR 19/689.

[454] Bensusan Butt, *Biographical Dictionary,* Box 13, vol. 1, p. 11. The comments are based on advertisements in the *Ipswich Journal* on 19 October 1782, 22 February 1783, and 12 April, 1783.

[455] *The King's Own Regimental Calendar,* 1897, p. 7 onwards.

[456] *The Guardian,* 4 May 2004. See an article about the history of The Queen's Lancashire Regiment on p. 5.

[457] This book is in the possession of Dr R W Ram.

[458] These photographs are in the possession of Dr R W Ram.

[459] There are several letters in the possession of Dr R W Ram.

[460] See internal reference chapter XIII, especially the paragraphs on *The end of a long tradition,* pp. 166-67.

[461] Suffolk Family History Society, Suffolk burial index CD.

[462] D R Grace and D C Phillips, *Ransomes of Ipswich – A History of the Firm and a Guide to its records,* 1975, p. 5.

[463] See internal reference, p. 152.

[464] See 1881 census.

[465] Thanks are due to John Matthews for the information about the training ship Cornwall which will appear on the web site of Thurrock Local History Society in due course (as at Summer 2006) – www.thurrock-community.org.uk/historysoc.

[466] These letters are in the possession of Dr R W Ram.

[467] 1881 Census.

[468] See internal reference, chapter XV, the paragraphs on *The will and bankruptcy of John Ram (1739-1810),* pp. 196-202.

[469] Photograph of Stephen Adye Ram, in Mr Malden, *The Ram family in Colchester,* B L, Add. 38617.

[470] JA Venn, *Alumni Cantabrigienses,* 1953, pt II 1752-1900, vol V.

[471] DNB article on Richard Preston, (1768-1850). In this he is called a legal author who originated in Devon. He began his career as an attorney, but wrote an early book on conveyancing which led to him going to the Inner Temple. After practising there for several years as a certified conveyancer he was called to the bar in 1807. He became a bencher in 1834, when he also took silk. He was reader in 1844. He represented Ashburton in Parliament 1812-18 and was a robust advocate of the imposition of the corn duties. He made big land investments in Devon through his conveyancing work. He was intensely conservative. He had a deep knowledge of real-property law, and his works on conveyancing are masterpieces of patient research and lucid exposition. He was for some time Professor of Law at Kings College, London. He died at Lee House, Chulmleigh, in north Devon.

[472] Sir William Holdsworth, *A History of the English Law,* 1938, Vol. VII, p. 384-400.

[473] This is evident from the number of references to it in Amazon Books in 2009.

474 Holdsworth, vol. XII, pp. 102-46.
475 Holdsworth, vol. XV, pp. 266-67.
Notes to pp. 249-263

476 James Ram, *A Treatise on Facts as Subjects of Enquiry by a Jury*, etc', 1851.
477 *Solicitor's Journal*, B L, 7611aaa.
478 *London Athenaeum*, 1861, vol. ii, p. 277.
479 A W B Simpson, Biographical Dictionary of the Common Law, 1984, p. 441-2.
480 Holdsworth, vol. XII, p.146.
481 See DNB article on James Ram.
482 Ibid.
483 Records of the Inner Temple. All this information has been accessed and provided by Dr Clare Rider, the Archivist.
484 Hamilton Ellis, *British Railway History, 1830-1876*, 1960, pp. 89-90.
485 For the way in which this property came into James Ram's possion and its history internal reference, p. 218.
486 See internal reference chapter XV, the paragraphs on *Renewed prosperity*, especially pp. 218-20.
487 All this information about the titles to the two farms comes from SRO-Ipswich branch, HA 108/2/89.
488 Ibid.
489 See internal reference, pp. 32 and 71.
490 Major S P Adye, *Punishments and Rewards*, 1778, 1797 and 1800.
491 James Ram, jun., *Notes upon The General Examination at the Royal Military College of Sandhurst, of Candidates for Direct Commissions in the Army*, 1855.
492 Ibid., p.2.
493 James Ram, *The Philosophy of War*, 1878.
494 SRO- Ipswich branch, HA 108/2/89.
495 This information has kindly been extracted from the Suffolk County and Halesworth directories by Ivan Sparkes.
496 J W Newby, *The Patrick Stead Hospital*, 1964, pp. 16-17.
497 Newby, p.31.
498 See internal reference, p. 168.
499 The information given here about the Willett Rams is taken from Newby, p. 31.
500 Michael McLean and Sheila Upjohn, *St John Timberhill Norwich*, 1982, with revisions by John Mountney in 1989, pp. 2-3.
501 Ibid., pp. 2-5.
502 GT Rimmington, *Edwardian Clerical Incumbents in Leicestershire*, The Local Historian, vol. 35, no.1, Febuary, 2005, pp. 52-53.
503 NRO, Additional parish records of Norwich, St John Timberhill, *Papers of Father Edward Ram, 1879-1917*, PD74/.
504 Ibid., item called, *Personal reflection*, 153, p. 29.
505 Ibid., p. 31.
506 Ibid., p. 38.
507 Ibid., p. 53.
508 Edward Ram, *Leading Events in the History of the Church of England*, 1888.
509 Ibid., pp. 100-102.
510 W N Yates, *Anglican Ritualism in Victorian Britain*, 2000, p. 379. The conclusions on pages 375-385 are a useful summary of the contribution made by the Ritualist Movement.
511 NRO, *Papers of Father Edward Ram*, PD74/142 and 151.
512 Yates, p. 162.

Part 4. History and *The Thread*

[1] Peter Earle, *The Making of the English Middle Class – Business Society and Family Life in London, 1660-1730*, 1989, pp. 137-143.

Notes to pp. 272-302

[2] Ibid., pp. 146-154.

[3] Wrigley and Schofield, *The Population History of England*, p. 466.

[4] Ed. M Anderson, *British Population History, from the Black Death to the present day*, 1996, pp. 158-181.

[5] Wrigley and Schofield, Table 8.12 on p. 334.

[6] Ibid., Table 8.12 on p. 332.

[7] Ibid., pp. 333, 335 and appendix 3.

[8] See Part B of Appendix 2.

[9] M McIntosh, *A Community Transformed*, note on p. 117.

[10] Ed. Phillipe Ariès and Georges Duby, *A History of Private Life, vol. 2, Revelations of the Medieval World*, 1999, pp. 212-226.

[11] Ibid., p. 18.

[12] Ibid., pp. 17-23.

[13] Ibid., p. 5.

[14] David Eastwood, *Governing Rural England, Tradition and Transformation in Local Government 1780-1840*, 1994, pp. 241 -43.

[15] A W B Simpson, *An Introduction to the History of Land Law*, 1961, p.162.

[16] The Office for National Statistics, see especially Labour Force Survey – employment status by occupation.

[17] See p.397.

[18] Campbell 'The English Yeoman Under Elizabeth and the Early Stuarts', p. 264.

[19] Ibid., p. 268.

[20] Ibid., p. 269.

[21] Earle, *The Making of the English Middle class*, p. 13.

[22] See internal reference chapter VI, the paragraphs on *Class, the Ram family, and identity*, pp. 60-62.

[23] Jenny Uglow, *The Lunar Men, the friends who made the future, 1730-1810*, 2002.

[24] See internal reference, pp. 226-30.

[25] French, pp.104-10.

[26] See internal reference, chapter XIII, especially *Power and status in the community III*, pp. 152-53.

[27] Campbell, p. 376.

[28] Ibid., p. 364-65.

[29] Ibid., p. 372-73.

[30] Ibid., p. 104.

[31] See internal reference, p. 134.

[32] See internal reference, p. 146.

[33] See internal reference, pp. 170-71.

[34] R D Smith, p. 99 and p. 236.

[35] Harold Smith, *The Ecclesiatical History of Essex under the Long Parliament and the Commonwealth*, n.d., (about 1931), p. 48.

[36] R D Smith, p. 158.

[37] Ibid., p. 361.

[38] O'Day, p. xviii.

[39] Ibid., p. 34-35.

[40] Ibid., pp. 4-5.

[41] Ibid., p. 127.

[42] See internal reference, pp. 126-27.

[43] See internal reference, pp. 125-26.

[44] O'Day, p. 118.

[45] Ibid., p. 182.

⁴⁶ Ibid., p. 169-70.
⁴⁷ Ibid., p. 168.
Notes to pp. 302-339

⁴⁸ O'Day, p.175.
⁴⁹ For related discussion see internal reference, p. 226-32.
⁵⁰ See internal reference, pp. 310-11.
⁵¹ See internal reference, p. 220.
⁵² Campbell, pp. 382-83
⁵³ Ibid., p. 386.
⁵⁴ Ibid., p. 387.
⁵⁵ R D Smith, pp. 77-86. Payment of poor rates, wealth, and occupations.
⁵⁶ Earle, *The Making of the English Middle Class*, pp. 244-45.
⁵⁷ French, especially chapter 2, Parish Office and the Formation of Social Identity, pp. 90-140.
⁵⁸ French, p.120.
⁵⁹ See internal reference, pp. 221-23.
⁶⁰ Earle, p.195.
⁶¹ ERO, D/DHh/M174.
⁶² See Part 2, especially chapter VI.
⁶³ Ariès and Duby, especially chapter 5.
⁶⁴ Jose Harris, *The Penguin Social History of Britain, Private Lives, Public Spirit: Britain 1870-1914*, 1994.
⁶⁵ Ibid., chapter VIII.
⁶⁶ Ibid., chapter III.
⁶⁷ Barry and Brooks, *The Middling Sort of People*, p. 4.
⁶⁸ G E Evans, p. 241.

Part 5. The modern world and *The Thread*

¹ Wrightson, English Society, 1580-1680, pp. 25-45.
² See *Unleashing Aspirations. The Final Report of the Panel on Fair Access to the Professions*, July 2009.
³ Shani d'Cruze, Ph D thesis, p. 459.
⁴ Earle, pp. 4-5.
⁵ Barry and Brooks, pp. 2-3.
⁶ Earle, pp. 6-7.
⁷ Ibid., pp.8-9.
⁸ Ibid., pp.13-14.
⁹ Ibid., p. 34.
¹⁰ Barry and Brooks, p. 4.
¹¹ Ibid., p. 10.
¹² Ibid., p.10.
¹³ Ibid., p. 11.
¹⁴ Ibid., p. 11.
¹⁵ Churches Together in Britain and Ireland, Churches Commission on Mission, *Findings on Local Churches Initial Report*, 2000, and Values Sharing Central Working Group, *A Summary of our Discoveries and Findings*, 1998, These two reports were part of a research programme called Building Bridges of Hope – Learning together to be mission churches for England Ireland Scotland and Wales organised by The Churches Commission on Mission, part of Churches Together in Britain and Ireland.
¹⁶ I revisited the project in 2008 to find that relationships between the nightshelter and the official world had improved considerably, largely because a more sharing relationship had been established. See unpublished text by Jeanne Hinton and R W Ram on *The Community Building Journey*.

[17] See internal reference, p. 315.

[18] R B Shoemaker, *Gender in English Society, 1650-1850*, 1998.
Notes to pp. 339-359

[19] Ibid., pp. 115 and 117.

[20] Arnold Toynbee, *A Study of History*, 1961.

[21] Lawrence Stone, *The Crisis of the Aristocracy*, p. 29.

[22] Aries and Duby, pp. 104-05.

[23] Campbell, p. 386.

[24] Ibid., p. 387.

[25] See internal reference, pp. 292-93.

[26] Wrightson and Levine, *Poverty and Piety in an English Village*, especially chapter 5. *Conflict and Control: The Villagers and the Courts*, p. 110 following.

[27] See internal reference, p. 331.

[28] Robin Dunbar, *Gossip and the Evolution of Human Language*, 2004.

[29] N J G Pounds, *A History of the English Parish*, 2000, pp. 250-290.

[30] Ibid., p. 254.

[31] Ibid., p. 278, quoted from F M Stenton, *Documents Illustrative of the Social and Economic History of the Danelaw*, Rec Soc Ec Hist, 5 (1920), lxi-lxii.

[32] Ibid., p. 279, quoted from M K McIntosh, *Autonomy and Community: The Royal Manor of Havering, 1200-1500*, 1986, pp. 1-6 and 182-85.

[33] Eamon Duffey, The Voices of Morbath, Reformation and Rebellion in an English Village, 2003.

[34] Alan Macfarlane, *The Origins of English Individualism*, 1978.

[35] Evans, p. 242.

[36] See internal reference, p. 81.

[37] Dunbar, p. 77. The points made about social groups in these paragraphs are based on Dunbar, pp. 69-77.

[38] See internal reference, pp. 106-07.

[39] See Ed. E A Wrigley, *An Introduction to English Historical Demography*, 1966, pp. 177-78.

[40] Dunbar, p. 203.

[41] Eileen Spring, Land Law and Family, p. 179.

[42] *The Times*, 6 December, 2005, p. 26.

[43] *The Guardian*, May 19, 2005, p. 26.

[44] Roland Allen, *Missionary Methods, St Paul's or Ours?*, 1993.

[45] See report *On the State of the Countryside*.

[46] *25th British Social Attitudes Report*, as reported in *The Times*, 28 January, 2009, p. 12.

INDEX

There are two indexes, one covering subjects and the other names, using page numbers as locators. The indexes do not cover the introductory pages, bibliographical notes or the appendices. The subject index includes places discussed (but not passing mentions), and all are in Essex unless otherwise indicated. In the names index entries are recorded in the following way. Where known, the name is followed by the birth and death dates in brackets (1801-1881), or if not, the birth date (b. 1901) or the death date (d. 1822), or the century (16C). abt. indicates an approximate date, and bef. or aft. indicates before or after the year given. Women appear under their married names with their maiden names shown in brackets. With the exception of the Ram family, individuals are generally grouped together under their family names. Where names appear in Appendix 1 Family Timeline, locators are in italics and show the section number/reference number thus: Ram, Daniel 2/51 is in Section 2, number 51.

Names

Adye family 33, 227-28, 229, 255; Elizabeth Jane *see* Ram, Elizabeth Jane; Elizabeth Sarah (1771-1857) (Bawtree) 227-28, 233-34; John (b. 1857) (Major General Sir) 255; John Millar (General Sir, Governor of Gibralter) 255; Ralph Willett (d. 1804) (Major) 227-28, 232-33, 255; Stephen (1772-1838) (Major General) 255; Stephen (d. 1794) 227

Algar, John 229

Allan, Roland (author) 357

Allport, Gordon (psychologist) 51-52

Argor family: John 296; Sara (b. 1610) (Ram) 4c/41, 296

Arwaker family: Joan (d. 1576/77) 137; John (d 1572) 137

Atkinson, Katherine 176

Atwood family 172, 178-80, 188, 288, 308; John (b. 1599) 180, 193; Katherine *see* Ram, Katherine; William (b. 1596) 180

Aylett, Richard (d. 1599) 145, 293

Ayloffe family 183; William (early 17C) (Sir) 183

Bacon family 192

Barnard/Barnarde family 106-7, 109, 135-36, 137; Henry (late 16C) 137; Richard 109

Barry, Jonathan (editor) 325, 331, 333

Bawtree family 226-33, 235, 291; Elizabeth Sarah *see* Adye, Elizabeth Sarah; George 230-31; Jane (1762-1812) (Ram) 4c/79, 223, 227, 229, 232, 233, 253; John 1 229; John 2 (1762-1824) 226, 227-33; John 3 4c/93, 230, 231-33; Samuel 229, 230, 233; Sarah (d. 1782) (Pearson) 228-29; Stephen (d, 1832) 233; William 229, 230

Bayles family 216-17; Thomas 216-17; Thomas (d. 1775) (mayor) 217

Beale, William (Master of Jesus College, Oxford) 213

Bearblock family 191-92; James 192; Joan *see* Ram, Joan; Susan *see* Ram, Susan; William (d. 1620) 191, 192

Benham, John (Sir) 192

Berblock, Sarah 188

Billyreca (or Billyrica), John (16C) 137

Bohun family, de 96, 102, 133; John, Count of Hereford 96

Boltwood family 166; Abigail *see* Ram, Abigail; Edward (early 19C) 166; Thomas (d. 1822) 165, 311

Bouchard, Thomas (psychologist) 47-49

Boutflower, D. S. (author) 29

Bright family: Elizabeth (d. 1595) 187; John (d. 1578) 187

Brooks, Christopher (editor) 325, 331, 333

Brown, Martha *see* Ram, Martha (Brown)

Browne, Jacob 216

Bush, Thomas 162

Bushe, John 187

Butler-Sloss, Dame Elizabeth (former President of High Court Family DIvision) 353-54

Butt, John Bensusan (author) 198, 200, 201, 228

Buxton, Thomas (apothecary) 209, 210

Cade, Jack 112-13

Campbell, Mildred (author) 61, 108, 111-12, 118, 139, 142, 292-93, 305, 345

Carr family: Fanny Elizabeth (b. 1824) (Ram) 3/93, 166; Mary (b. 1597) (Ram) 4c/34, 210, 296; Nathaniel 296

Subjects